LEVEL Z

SCOPE ENGLISH ANTHOLOGY

Literature and Reading Program

The Scope English Story

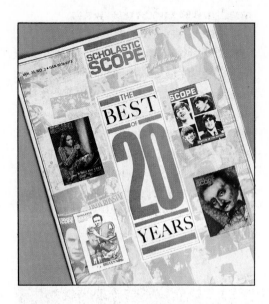

In 1964, when Scholastic first published it, SCOPE Magazine was a near-revolutionary publication: a magazine designed to bring good literature and reading, and useful skills, to young people. Now, after more than twenty years, SCOPE is the most widely used magazine in junior and senior high school Reading and English programs—reaching nearly 40 percent of all secondary schools in the United States.

Teachers have found SCOPE Magazine so useful in motivating readers that they have asked for a more permanent resource containing the high quality reading selections and activities found in every issue of SCOPE. So we developed SCOPE ENGLISH—a complete English program including both reading and literature as well as a comprehensive writing and language program. Teachers all over America are finding in SCOPE ENGLISH precisely those qualities that made SCOPE Magazine so popular: It makes English easier to learn, more motivating, more teachable. We've included selections from the magazine that are of high interest to students—stories, poems, plays, TV scripts, articles and more—as well as tried-and-true teacher favorites that create a basic curriculum framework. The reading levels of these selections are accessible to all junior and senior high school students, grades 6–12, yet the ideas are challenging and provocative. SCOPE ENGLISH includes an *Anthology* at each grade level, organized by themes, authors, or genres, and a *Writing and Language* text, written in clear, conversational style.

SCOPE ENGLISH contains eye-catching photos and illustrations that actually aid in students' understanding of the important events in a selection. An illustration is provided every three to five pages of text, to make the reading experience less threatening for the students. All the materials motivate secondary students to read more and write better.

More than twenty years after SCOPE Magazine first brought the SCOPE philosophy to the English classroom, we're proud to be able to reach you with the SCOPE ENGLISH program. We hope you will find these materials just as useful and helpful as you've found SCOPE Magazine to be in making English learning easier and more satisfying.

LEVEL Z

SCOPE ENGLISH ANTHOLOGY

Literature and Reading Program

Edited by
Scholastic Scope Editors

SCHOLASTIC INC.

LITERATURE CONSULTANT

Jane Yolen
Author

READING CONSULTANT

Paul W. Warshauer
English Teacher
Las Virgenes Unified School District
Calabasas, California

CURRICULUM CONSULTANTS

Julie Collins
English Department Chairperson
Griffith Junior High School
Los Angeles, California

Mary Ellen Vogt
Coordinator of Curriculum
   and Staff Development
Central Catholic High School
Modesto, California

Barbara Allison
Miller Elementary School
San Diego, California

Mary Ruth Carter
Coordinator, Secondary English
Amarillo, Texas

Dr. H. Kaye Griffin
Klein Independent School District
Klein, Texas

Adrian W. McClaren
Supervisor of English
Memphis City Schools
Memphis, Tennessee

Ellen Sherman
Head of Reading Department
Lauderdale Lake Middle School
Lauderdale Lake, Florida

ACKNOWLEDGMENTS

Grateful acknowledgment is made to the following authors and publishers for the use of copyrighted materials. Every effort has been made to obtain permission to use previously published material. Any errors or omissions are unintentional.

Harcourt Brace Jovanovich, Inc. for adaptation of ALL THE CATS IN THE WORLD by Sonia Levitin. Copyright © 1982 by Sonia Levitin.

William Morrow & Company for "Paula the Cat" from VACATION TIME by Nikki Giovanni. Copyright © 1980 by Nikki Giovanni.

(Acknowledgments continue on page 445)

ISBN 0-590-34615-6

12 11 10 9 8 7 6 5 4 3 2 1   7   7890/98

LEVEL Z
Contents

SECTION 10 The Miracle Worker

LEVEL Z
Skills Lessons

UNDERSTANDING LITERATURE

Reading Various Types of Literature

Plot

Characterization

Conflict

Note: Each page indicates the first time a skill is taught or practiced. In most cases, each skill is tapped several times in this book.

Setting

Point of View

Theme

Mood and Imagery

READING COMPREHENSION

VOCABULARY / WORD ATTACK

ORAL LANGUAGE DEVELOPMENT

PROCESS WRITING

WRITING ABOUT THE SELECTION

Note: Each page indicates the first time a skill is taught or practiced. In most cases, each skill is tapped several times in this book.

RESEARCH AND STUDY SKILLS

CAT TALES

*I can rarely remember
having passed a cat in the street
without stopping to speak to it.*

—Bruce Marshall

A harmless necessary cat.

—Shakespeare

Introduction

Why do you think people have cats for pets? They don't fetch the paper or come to you when you call them like dogs do. They don't talk like parrots. Is it because cats are playful and fun? Is it because they are good companions? Or is it because there is some kind of mystery in a cat's eyes?

As one 11-year-old cat owner said about her Minsky:

"At first, we all wanted the chocolate brown poodle, but he was too expensive. We got Minsky the kitten for free. I was afraid he would scratch me. Then I found out that he scratches people that try to harm me but he won't scratch me unless I pick him up the wrong way or tickle him on the belly. He likes it when I scratch him; then he's happy and purrs. I like my cat because he has a cute face, just like a kitten, even though he is now three years old. Cats are good pets because they don't bark, they are small, they walk around the house, you don't have to buy steak for them, they are easy to play with, you don't have to train them, they are soft and sleep with you."

Usually, people think about having cats as pets and taking care of them. But maybe it is just the opposite. Maybe cats really take care of people and what happens to people is because of the cats they know. Or maybe cats and people take care of each other. In this section you will read about some cats that live in both strange and ordinary places.

In "All the Cats in the World," an old woman visits some hungry cats on a beach every day to feed them. But an old man who screams at her doesn't seem to like her, or the cats, or does he?

Cats cause a young boy to leave his home town in "The Boy Who Drew Cats," but later, cats save him from a dangerous creature.

In "Stuart and Snowbell," the Little's son Stuart has disappeared, and it seems the cat Snowbell knows some answers.

Three poems: "Paula the Cat," "The Naming of Cats," and "The Stray Cat," introduce cats with opposite goals. While Paula wants to leave home for travel and adventure, the stray cat wants to find a home. Then, there are cats with secret names nobody knows.

Through meeting all the cats in this section, you may learn some surprising things about what cats think about this life, and what they see before their third eyelid closes and they sleep. You might discover that cats and people aren't as different as they seem to be.

All the Cats in the World

by Sonia Levitin

Every day a lonely old woman named Mikila climbs the rocks at the seashore to feed the cats. She finds comfort in taking care of them, until the day the lighthouse keeper begins to make fun of her. Read the story to find out what Mikila unexpectedly learns from this gruff old man.

Down by the seaside, among the rugged rocks and cliffs and in the shadow of an old lighthouse, lived many, many cats of different kinds and different colors. All were wild. They howled in the night.

Some had been left by thoughtless people. Others had strayed from their homes. Many had been born right at the water's edge, so this was the only home they had ever known.

Now, it happened that two old women, noticing the cats, began to feed them. Soon they came every morning, just after dawn, with sacks full of food — liver scraps, fish heads, and bread crusts. The two women, Nella and Mikila, were good friends. They were still quite nimble and strong. They would clamber down among the rocks, calling, making certain that every cat got its share.

"Ah, Mittens," Nella or Mikila would say, "here is your breakfast. Good morning, little Tabby, Tiger, and Freckles."

After each cat had eaten and licked its whiskers and paws, up the rocky path the women climbed, slower now and hot from the morning sun, talking as good friends do.

One day poor Nella died, and Mikila was left all alone. She wept bitterly. She went to the church to pray.

Late in the afternoon she remembered the cats. She had not fed the cats!

Weary and sad as she was, Mikila hurried to the fishmonger, the butcher, and the grocer, and for a few pennies she gathered the scraps for her cats.

She arrived at the cliffs, hot and out of breath. When the cats saw Mikila, they emerged from behind the rocks meowing, their tails held high. "Where were you?" they seemed to say reproachfully. "We were hungry. Why did you fail us?"

"I did not fail you, my little ones," Mikila said, as though they had really spoken. "Our friend, Nella, is no more on this Earth. But you will not go hungry, as long as there is a breath in Mikila's body."

Suddenly Mikila heard gruff laughter. She looked about, startled. Partway up the slope, on a long, flat rock, a bearded old man sat looking down at her.

"Woman!" he called. "What are you doing with that sack of food?"

"I'm feeding the cats!" shouted Mikila. "What does it look like to you?"

"It looks like a foolish woman," replied the man rudely, "meddling where she doesn't belong."

"I belong here as well as you!" retorted Mikila.

"I belong here well enough," called the man, "for I am keeper of the lighthouse."

"Then keep your lighthouse," shouted Mikila, "and leave me alone!"

Still the old man watched. By and by he called down, more curious than rude, "Woman, pray tell me, are you so rich that you can afford to feed these filthy creatures?"

Mikila retorted, "I manage with a few pennies a day, buying leftovers from the shops. Is it any business of yours?"

Angrily she left, determined to bring even more scraps tomorrow. She would show that old man — what did she care that he thought her foolish?

The next day Mikila's sack was heavy as she went down to the sea, calling, "Tina, Bennie, and Spots! Here Tabby, Minnie, and Puff."

Again she heard harsh laughter from up on the ledge.

"Old woman!" the man called down. "Aren't you afraid, at your age, to climb those rocks? You could fall and break your legs!"

"I'm not afraid!" She laughed and thumbed her nose at him.

It rained the next day, and Mikila yearned to stay home. But the old man might think she was afraid, so she covered her head with a kerchief and went as usual to feed the cats.

This time the man was not there. But Mikila heard the deep bellow of the foghorn, and she saw the broad beam of light coming from the lighthouse. She knew he was tending to his job.

Just as Mikila finished, the old man appeared at the top of the ridge, followed by a pet goat. He did not come down, for the rocks were wet and slippery, but called out, "Old woman! How stubborn you are to come out even in this bitter weather! I have never seen such a one as you!"

"I am not stubborn, I am faithful!" Mikila shouted.

The old man shook his head, laughing, and disappeared inside the lighthouse.

Mikila walked away slowly, her feet sinking into the wet sand. Her clothes clung to her body, and she shivered. At home, a hot bath and a cup of tea did much to restore her spirits, but she felt very tired and soon began to sneeze.

The next morning Mikila's throat was sore. Her head hurt. Surely the cats could manage without her for just one day, she thought.

Then she remembered the old man's rude laughter and her talk about being faithful.

"One who is faithful does not give up so easily." She grunted and groaned all the way down to the shore.

As before, the old man sat upon the

rock shelf, and when he saw Mikila, he called down, "Old woman, tell me one thing. *Why* do you feed these cats?"

"BECAUSE THEY ARE HUNGRY!" Mikila shouted.

"Hungry!" The man held his sides with laughter. "Hungry! Ha-ha-ha! That's a good one! Don't you know there are millions of hungry cats in the world? Can you feed all the cats in the world?"

Mikila did not answer. Wearily she gathered up her empty sack and went home, weeping.

That night Mikila's bones ached. Even hot tea did not help. For three days and nights she lay sick with fever. The old man's words echoed in her head: "Woman, you are wasteful and stubborn and foolish." She thought, "It is true. I can never feed all the hungry cats in the world. I am tired and sick. Most of all, I am sick and tired of being taunted by that terrible old man. I will go no more to feed the cats." She lay in her bed grieving.

At last she slept deeply, and on the fourth morning she woke up feeling strong — not only strong but determined; not only determined but angry!

She got up in haste, pulled on her clothes, snatched up her sack, and hurried to gather food for the cats.

As she hustled, Mikila planned what she would tell that rude old man. *He* was the foolish one, the stubborn one, the stupid one. Couldn't he see that what *he* did every day in his lighthouse was exactly the same as feeding the cats?

She could hardly wait to catch him on the ledge and shout up, "Why do you bother to send a beam from your lighthouse? You can't save every ship in the ocean. You can't guide them all safely to shore. Why do you even try?"

As Mikila picked her way down the rocky path, she called, "Come, Tiger, Mittens, Freckles, Puff. Oh, my poor little ones. Mikila is here."

She expected to see the cats shivering, half dead from hunger. But instead they leaped nimbly out, playfully rubbing against her legs.

"Ah, my dear ones," Mikila exclaimed, "how I have missed you! But — you look well fed. How can it be?"

Now Mikila saw the old man's goat licking salt from the rocks, and in the next moment there was the old man himself. He stood bent toward the shyest of the cats, feeding it from a sack of scraps.

"What are you doing?" cried Mikila in surprise.

He turned and stammered, "I — why — I — what does it look like to you, old woman?"

Mikila stared at him until his face grew very red and he looked away out to sea.

"Are you so rich," she taunted, "that you have money to waste on these filthy creatures?

The old man shuffled his feet.

Mikila folded her arms and asked, "Why do you come out in this bitter weather? What a foolish man you are!"

The old man smiled slyly while the cats milled about his feet. "Actually," he said, "it was not my idea."

"Then whose?" asked Mikila, tapping her foot.

My goat's. Ulysses. He dragged me down here. What else could I do?"

"You could have stayed in your lighthouse," said Mikila.

"But Ulysses is very stubborn," replied the man. "He is also strong and clever. In fact," said the man with a grin, "he is in many ways like you."

"Like me?" Mikila tossed her head. "Many thanks for comparing me to a goat!"

"But this goat," said the man earnestly, "is my good friend." He patted the goat's head, with its stubby horns and stiff hair. "We have many conversations."

"Then Ulysses must have told you," said Mikila dryly, "that you cannot possibly feed all the cats in the world."

The old man grinned broadly, and his face creased into a thousand wrinkles. "Of course," he replied. "We all know that. But I can at least feed these close at hand. It is much the same," he added, "as tending the lighthouse."

Mikila was silent for a long moment. Then she smiled. "Since Ulysses cares so much about the cats," she said, "send him to me tomorrow. I will show him which shops sell the very best scraps."

"A fine idea," exclaimed the old man. "But Ulysses goes nowhere without me. We shall come together." He turned and, imitating Mikila's own high voice, said, "Good-bye now, Roscoe, Tiger, and Puff. See you tomorrow!"

And so, each day after that, the man and the woman and the goat went together to buy the scraps and feed the cats — not all the cats in the world, but the ones that lived among the rocks in the shadow of the old lighthouse. You can see the three of them walking up the rocky path together, talking and laughing as good friends do.

READING COMPREHENSION

Summarizing. Choose the best phrase to complete each sentence. Then write the complete statements on your paper.

1. Two old women, noticing many wild cats by the seaside began to _____ (feed them, drive them away, hide their food).

2. At first, the old man at the lighthouse thought that Mikila _____ (seemed wise, was foolish, was very sweet) to feed the cats.

3. After an illness, Mikila went back to find the cats _____ (shot to death, well fed, driven away) by the old man.

4. Mikila and the old man finally _____ (go away together, become friends, leave the cats).

Interpreting. Write the answer to each question on your paper.

1. Why did the old man think that feeding the cats was a foolish thing to do?

2. Why did Mikila think that what the old man did for the ships was the same as what she did by feeding the cats?

3. In the end, what conclusion did the old man reach about feeding the cats?

For Thinking and Discussing. This story is about feeding hungry cats. But it is also a story about friendship. What do you think the author is saying about friendship? Do you agree with her? Explain why or why not.

UNDERSTANDING LITERATURE

Plot. Every story has a *plot*. The plot is the order of important events in a story. The order of events, the *sequence*, keeps the reader interested in the story. The plot has a beginning, a middle, and an end.

Below are some important events from "All the Cats in the World." Write the events on your paper in the order in which they occur in the story. Look over what you have written. Is there a beginning, a middle, and an end? Check your plot with the story.

1. The old man at the lighthouse makes fun of Mikila for feeding the cats.

2. Nella and Mikila feed the cats at the seashore.

3. Mikila gets sick and stays in bed for three days and three nights.

4. Mikila feeds the cats by herself after Nella dies.

5. Mikila and the old man feed the cats together.

6. Mikila finds the old man feeding the cats.

WRITING

Write a paragraph about Mikila. Begin by stating whether you think she was stubborn (unreasonable), as the old man said, or faithful (loyal). Then use events from the plot of the story as examples to support your ideas. Present these events in the order in which they occur.

Paula the Cat

by Nikki Giovanni

Paula the cat
not thin nor fat
is as happy as house cats can be

She reads and she writes
with all the delights
of intelligent cats up a tree

Tired of the view
she chose to pursue
a fate unbeknownst to the crowd

Finding a boat
locked up in a moat
she boarded and shouted out loud

I'm Paula the cat
not thin nor fat
as happy as house cats can be

But now I've the urge
for my spirit to surge
and I shall go off
to sea

---

1. Do you think Paula was really happy as a house cat? Why?
2. Why did Paula go off to sea?
3. Does the poet want you to think of all the events in the poem as things that really happened? Explain why or why not.

The Boy Who Drew Cats

by Lafcadio Hearn

*This story is based on an old Japanese legend. In it, there's a boy
with a special interest in cats, a priest who gives a mysterious
warning, a haunted temple — and cats that suddenly come alive,
leaping out from pictures on the wall.*

Along, long time ago, in a small country village in Japan, there lived a poor farmer and his wife, who were very good people. They had a number of children and found it hard to feed them all. The eldest child, a son, was strong enough when only 14 years old to help his father, and the little girls learned to help their mother almost as soon as they could walk.

But the youngest child, a little boy, did not seem to be fit for hard work. He was very clever — cleverer than all his brothers and sisters — but he was quite weak and small, and people said he could never grow very big. So his parents thought it would be better for him to become a priest than to become a farmer. They took him with them to the village temple one day and asked the good old priest who lived there if he would have their little boy for his pupil, and teach him all that a priest ought to know.

The old man spoke kindly to the lad and asked him some hard questions. So clever were the answers that the priest agreed to take the little fellow into the temple and to educate him for the priesthood as an altar boy.

The boy learned quickly what the old priest taught him and was very obedient in most things. But he had one fault. He liked to draw cats during the study hours, and to draw cats where cats ought not to be drawn at all.

Whenever he found himself alone, he drew cats. He drew them on the margins of the priest's books, and on all the screens and walls and pillars of the temple. Several times the priest told him this was not right, but the boy did not stop drawing cats. He drew them because he could not really help it. He had what is called "the genius of an artist," and just for that reason he was not quite fit to be an altar boy. A good altar boy should study books.

One day, after he had drawn some very clever pictures of cats upon a paper screen, the old priest said to him severely, "My boy, you must go away from this temple at once. You will never make a good priest, but perhaps you will become

27

a great artist. Now let me give you a last piece of advice, and be sure you never forget it. *Avoid large places at night; keep to small!*"

The boy did not know what the priest meant by saying, *"Avoid large places at night; keep to small!"* He thought and thought while he was tying up his bundle of clothes to go away, but he could not understand those words, and he was afraid to speak to the priest anymore, except to say good-bye.

He left the temple very sorrowfully and began to wonder what he should do. If he went straight home, he felt, his father would punish him for having been disobedient to the priest. Then he remembered that in the next village, 12 miles away, there was a very big temple. He had heard there were several priests there, and he made up his mind to go and ask them to take him for their altar boy.

Now, that big temple was closed up, but the boy did not know this fact. The reason it had been closed up was that a goblin had frightened the priests away and then had taken possession of the place. Some brave warriors had afterward gone to the temple at night to kill the goblin, but they had never been seen alive again. Nobody had ever told these things to the boy, so he walked all the way to the village, hoping to be kindly treated by the priests.

When he got to the village it was already dark, and all the people were in bed. He saw the big temple on the hill on the other end of the principal street, and he saw there was a light inside. People who tell the story say the goblins used to make that light to tempt lonely travelers to ask for shelter. The boy went at once to the temple and knocked. There was no sound inside. He knocked and knocked again, but still nobody came. At last he pushed gently at the door and found that it had not been fastened. He went in and saw a lamp burning — but no priest.

He thought that some priest would be sure to come very soon, so he sat down and waited. Then he noticed that everything in the temple was gray with dust and thickly spun over with cobwebs. He thought to himself that the priests would certainly like to have an altar boy to keep the place clean, and wondered why they had allowed the place to get so dusty. What most pleased him, however, was some big white screens, good to paint cats upon. Though he was tired, he looked at once for a writing box. When he found one, he ground some ink and began to paint cats.

He painted a great many cats upon the screens, and then he began to feel very, very sleepy. He was just on the point of lying down to sleep beside one of the screens when he suddenly remembered the words *"Avoid large places at night; keep to small!"*

The temple was very large and he was alone, and as he thought of these words — though he could not quite understand them — he began to feel for the first time a little afraid. He resolved to look for a small place in which to sleep. He found a little cabinet, with a sliding door, and shut himself up in it. Then he lay down and fell fast asleep.

Very late in the night he was awakened

by a most terrible noise — a noise of fighting and screaming. It was so dreadful that he was afraid even to look through a chink of the little cabinet. He lay very still, holding his breath fearfully.

The light that had been in the temple went out, but the awful sounds continued and became more awful, and all the temple shook. After a long time silence came, but the boy was still afraid. He did not move until the light of the morning sun shone into the cabinet through the chinks of the little door.

Then he got out of his hiding place very cautiously and looked about. The first thing he saw was that the floor of the temple was covered with blood. And then he saw, lying dead in the middle of it, an enormous, monstrous rat — a goblin-rat bigger than a cow!

But who or what could have killed it? There was no man or other creature to be seen. Suddenly the boy observed that the mouths of all the cats he had drawn the night before were red and wet with blood. Then he knew that the goblin had been killed by the cats he had drawn. And then also, for the first time, he understood why the wise old priest had said to him, *"Avoid large places at night; keep to small!"*

Afterward that boy became a very famous artist. Some of the cats that he drew are still shown to travelers in Japan.

READING COMPREHENSION

Summarizing. Choose the best phrase to complete each sentence. Then write the complete statements on your paper.

1. When the boy who drew cats was told that he could not be a good priest, he _____ (returned to the farm, went to another temple, became a lawyer).

2. The big temple was _____ (closed up and empty, looking for new priests, full of white screens) because a goblin had frightened the priests away.

3. While the boy was sleeping in a small cabinet, the _____ (village people, cats he drew on the screens, priests who had left the temple) killed the goblin-rat.

4. The cats that the boy drew became _____ (lost, killed, famous).

Interpreting. Write the answer to each question on your paper.

1. Why did the boy's parents think that it would be better for the boy to become a priest than a farmer?

2. What did the boy do during study hours?

3. How did the priest's advice about avoiding large places help the boy?

For Thinking and Discussing. What does the author mean when he says the boy had "the genius of an artist"? How did this genius cause trouble for the boy? How did it help him?

UNDERSTANDING LITERATURE

Setting. Every story has a setting. The setting is the time when and the place where the events of the story happen.

Look back at the first paragraph of "The Boy Who Drew Cats."

1. Where does the story take place?

2. When does the story take place?

As a story continues the setting may change. Events may happen at different places and times.

Each statement below is about the setting of "The Boy Who Drew Cats." On your paper, write *where, when,* or *where and when* to show if the statement tells about a place or a time.

3. "They took him with them to the village temple . . . ."

4. "When he got to the village it was already dark, and everyone was in bed."

5. "He found a little cabinet, with a sliding door, and shut himself up in it."

6. "Very late in the night he was awakened by a most terrible noise . . . ."

7. "He did not move until the light of the morning sun shone into the cabinet through the chinks. . . ."

WRITING

Imagine that you are the boy in "The Boy Who Drew Cats." Write a letter to your parents. Make up things that have happened to you since you left home. Describe them telling *when* and *where* they occurred.

The Naming of Cats

by T.S. Eliot

The Naming of Cats is a difficult matter,
   It isn't just one of your holiday games;
You may think at first I'm as mad as a hatter
When I tell you, a cat must have THREE DIFFERENT NAMES.
First of all, there's the name that the family use daily,
   Such as Peter, Augustus, Alonzo or James,
Such as Victor or Jonathan, George or Bill Bailey —
   All of them sensible everyday names.
There are fancier names if you think they sound sweeter,
   Some for the gentlemen, some for the dames:
Such as Plato, Admetus, Electra, Demeter —
   But all of them sensible everyday names.
But I tell you, a cat needs a name that's particular,
   A name that's peculiar, and more dignified,
Else how can he keep up his tail perpendicular,
   Or spread out his whiskers, or cherish his pride?
Of names of this kind, I can give you a quorum,
   Such as Munkustrap, Quaxo, or Coricopat,
Such as Bombalurina, or else Jellylorum —
   Names that never belong to more than one cat.
But above and beyond there's still one name left over,
And that is the name that you never will guess;

The name that no human research can discover —
　But THE CAT HIMSELF KNOWS, and will never confess.
When you notice a cat in profound meditation
　The reason, I tell you, is always the same:
His mind is engaged in a rapt contemplation
　Of the thought, of the thought, of the thought of his name:
　　His ineffable effable
　　Effanineffable
Deep and inscrutable singular Name.

---

1. According to the poet, how many names must a cat have? Describe each type of name.

2. How is a cat's singular name different from its sensible everyday name?

3. According to the poet, why is a cat's "deep and inscrutable singular name" its most important name?

Stuart and Snowbell

by E.B. White

Mr. and Mrs. Little of New York City are surprised and delighted when their son Stuart turns out to be a mouse. But Snowbell the cat is not pleased at all — and Stuart finds this out the hard way.

When Mrs. Frederick C. Little's second son arrived, everybody noticed that he was not much bigger than a mouse. The truth of the matter was, the baby looked very much like a mouse in every way. He was only about two inches high; and he had a mouse's sharp nose, a mouse's tail, a mouse's whiskers, and the pleasant, shy manner of a mouse. Before he was many days old he was not only looking like a mouse but acting like one, too — wearing a gray hat and carrying a small cane. Mr. and Mrs. Little named him Stuart, and Mr. Little made him a tiny bed out of four clothespins and a cigarette box.

Unlike most babies, Stuart could walk as soon as he was born. When he was a week old he could climb lamps by shinnying up the cord. Mrs. Little saw right away that the infant clothes she had provided were unsuitable, and she set to work and made him a fine little blue worsted suit with patch pockets in which he could keep his handkerchief, his money, and his keys. Every morning, before Stuart dressed, Mrs. Little went into his room and weighed him on a scale which was really meant for weighing letters. At birth Stuart could have been sent by first class mail for three cents, but his parents preferred to keep him rather than send him away; and when, at the age of a month, he had gained only a third of an ounce, his mother was so worried she sent for the doctor.

The doctor was delighted with Stuart and said that it was very unusual for an American family to have a mouse. He took Stuart's temperature and found that it was 98.6, which is normal for a mouse. He also examined Stuart's chest and heart and looked into his ears solemnly with a flashlight. (Not every doctor can look into a mouse's ear without laughing.) Everything seemed to be all right, and Mrs. Little was pleased to get such a good report.

"Feed him up!" said the doctor cheerfully, as he left.

The home of the Little family was a pleasant place near a park in New York City. In the mornings the sun streamed in through the east windows, and all the Littles were up early as a general rule. Stuart was a great help to his parents, and to his older brother George, because of his small size and because he could do things that a mouse could do and was agreeable about doing them. One day when Mrs. Little was washing out the bathtub after Mr. Little had taken a bath, she lost a ring off her finger and was horrified to discover that it had fallen down the drain.

"What had I better do?" she cried, trying to keep the tears back.

"If I were you," said George, "I should bend a hairpin in the shape of a fishhook and tie it onto a piece of string and try to fish the ring out with it." So Mrs. Little found a piece of string and a hairpin, and for about a half-hour she fished for the ring; but it was dark down the drain and the hook always seemed to catch on something before she could get it down to where the ring was.

"What luck?" inquired Mr. Little, coming into the bathroom.

"No luck at all," said Mrs. Little. "The ring is so far down I can't fish it up."

"Why don't we send Stuart down after it?" suggested Mr. Little. "How about it, Stuart, would you like to try?"

"Yes, I would," Stuart replied, "but I think I'd better get into my old pants. I imagine it's wet down there."

"It's all of that," said George, who was a trifle annoyed that his hook idea hadn't worked. So Stuart slipped into his old pants and prepared to go down the drain after the ring. He decided to carry the string along with him, leaving one end in charge of his father. "When I jerk three times on the string, pull me up," he said. And while Mr. Little knelt in the tub, Stuart slid easily down the drain and was lost to view. In a minute or so, there came three quick jerks on the string, and Mr. Little carefully hauled it up. There, at the end, was Stuart, with the ring safely around his neck.

"Oh, my brave little son," said Mrs. Little proudly, as she kissed Stuart and thanked him.

"How was it down there?" asked Mr. Little, who was always curious to know about places he had never been to.

"It was all right," said Stuart.

But the truth was the drain had made him very slimy, and it was necessary for him to take a bath and sprinkle himself with a bit of his mother's violet water before he felt himself again. Everybody in the family thought he had been awfully good about the whole thing.

Home Problems

Stuart was so helpful when it came to Ping-pong. The Littles liked Ping-pong, but the balls had a way of rolling under chairs, sofas, and radiators, and this meant that the players were forever stooping down and reaching under things. Stuart soon learned to chase balls, and it was a great sight to see him come out from under a hot radiator, pushing a Ping-pong ball with all his might, the perspiration running down his cheeks. The ball, of course, was almost as high as he was, and he had to throw his whole weight against it in order to keep it rolling.

The Littles had a grand piano in their living room, which was all right except that one of its keys was a sticky key and didn't work properly. Mrs. Little said she thought it must be the damp weather, but

I don't see how it could be the damp weather, for the key had been sticking for about four years, during which time there had been many bright clear days. But anyway, the key stuck, and was a great inconvenience to anyone trying to play the piano. It bothered George particularly when he was playing the "Scarf Dance," which was rather lively. It was George who had the idea of stationing Stuart inside the piano to push the key up the second it was played. This was no easy job for Stuart, as he had to crouch down between the felt hammers so that he wouldn't get hit on the head. But Stuart liked it just the same: it was exciting inside the piano, dodging about, and the noise was quite terrific. Sometimes after a long session he would emerge quite deaf, as though he had just stepped out of an airplane after a long journey; and it would be some time before he really felt normal again.

Mr. and Mrs. Little often discussed Stuart quietly between themselves when he wasn't around, for they had never quite recovered from the shock and surprise of having a mouse in the family. He was so very tiny and he presented so many problems to his parents. Mr. Little said that, for one thing, there must be no references to "mice" in their conversation. He made Mrs. Little tear from the nursery songbook the page about the "Three Blind Mice, See How They Run."

"I don't want Stuart to get a lot of notions in his head," said Mr. Little. "I should feel badly to have my son grow up fearing that the farmer's wife was going to cut off his tail with a carving knife. It is such things that make children dream bad dreams when they go to bed at night."

"Yes," replied Mrs. Little, "and I think we had better start thinking about the poem ' 'Twas the night before Christmas when all through the house not a creature was stirring, not even a mouse.' I think it might embarrass Stuart to hear mice mentioned in such a belittling manner."

"That's right," said her husband, "but what shall we say when we come to that line in the poem? We'll have to say something. We can't just say ' 'Twas the night before Christmas when all through the house not a creature was stirring.' That doesn't sound complete; it needs a word to rhyme with house."

"What about louse?" asked Mrs. Little.

"Or grouse," said Mr. Little.

"I suggest souse," remarked George, who had been listening to the conversation from across the room.

It was decided that louse was the best substitute for mouse, and so when Christmas came around, Mrs. Little carefully rubbed the word mouse from the poem and wrote in the word louse, and Stuart always thought the poem went this way:

'Twas the night before Christmas
when all through the house
Not a creature was stirring,
not even a louse.

The thing that worried Mr. Little most was the mousehole in the pantry. This hole had been made by some mice in the days before the Littles came to live in the house, and nothing had been done about stopping it up. Mr. Little was not at all

sure that he understood Stuart's real feeling about a mousehole. He didn't know where the hole led to, and it made him uneasy to think that Stuart might some day feel the desire to venture into it.

"After all, he does look a great deal like a mouse," said Mr. Little to his wife. "And I've never seen a mouse yet that didn't like to go into a hole."

Washing Up

Stuart was an early riser: he was almost always the first person up in the morning. He liked the feeling of being the first one stirring; he enjoyed the quiet rooms with the books standing still on the shelves, the pale light coming in through the windows, and the fresh smell of day. In wintertime it would be quite dark when he climbed from his bed made out of the cigarette box, and he sometimes shivered with cold as he stood in his nightgown doing his exercises. (Stuart touched his toes ten times every morning to keep himself in good condition. He had seen his brother George do it, and George had explained that it kept the stomach muscles firm and was a fine abdominal thing to do.)

After exercising, Stuart would slip on his handsome wool wrapper, tie the cord tightly around his waist, and start for the bathroom, creeping silently through the long dark hall past his mother's and father's room, past the hall closet where the carpet sweeper was kept, past George's room, and along by the head of the stairs till he got to the bathroom.

Of course, the bathroom would be dark, too, but Stuart's father had

thoughtfully tied a long strip to the pull-chain of the light. The string reached clear to the floor. By grasping it as high up as he could and throwing his whole weight on it, Stuart was able to turn on the light. Swinging on the string this way, with his long bathrobe trailing around his ankles, he looked like a little old friar pulling the bellrope in an abbey.

To get to the washbasin, Stuart had to climb a tiny rope ladder which his father had fixed for him. George had promised to build Stuart a small special washbasin only one inch high and with a little rubber tube through which water would flow; but George was always saying that he was going to build something and then forgetting about it. Stuart just went ahead and climbed the rope ladder to the family washbasin every morning to wash his face and hands and brush his teeth. Mrs. Little had provided him with a doll's size toothbrush, a doll's size cake of soap, and a doll's comb — which he used for combing his whiskers. He carried these things in his bathrobe pocket, and when he reached the top of the rope ladder he took them out, laid them neatly in a row, and set about the task of turning the water on. For such a small fellow, turning the water on was quite a problem. He had discussed it with his father one day after making several unsuccessful attempts.

"I can get up onto the faucet all right," he explained, "but I can't seem to turn it on, because I have nothing to brace my feet against."

"Yes, I know," his father replied, "that's the whole trouble."

George, who always listened to conversations whenever he could, said that in his opinion they ought to construct a brace for Stuart; and with that he got out some boards, a saw, a hammer, a screwdriver, a brad-awl, and some nails, and started to make a terrific fuss in the bathroom, building what he said was going to be a brace for Stuart. But he soon became interested in something else and disappeared, leaving the tools lying all over the bathroom floor.

Stuart, after examining the mess, turned to his father again. "Maybe I could pound the faucet with something and turn it on that way," he said.

So Stuart's father provided him with a very small hammer made of wood; and Stuart found that by swinging it three times around his head and letting it come down with a crash against the handle of the faucet, he could start a thin stream of water flowing — enough to brush his teeth in, anyway, and moisten his washcloth. So every morning, after climbing to the basin, he would seize his hammer and pound the faucet, and the other members of the household, dozing in their beds, would hear the sharp plink plink plink of Stuart's hammer, like a faraway blacksmith, telling them that day had come and that Stuart was trying to brush his teeth.

Exercise

One fine morning in the month of May when Stuart was three years old, he arose early as was his custom, washed and dressed himself, took his hat and cane, and went downstairs into the living room to see what was doing. Nobody was around but Snowbell, the white cat belonging to Mrs. Little. Snowbell was another early riser, and this morning he was lying on the rug in the middle of the room, thinking about the days when he was just a kitten.

"Good morning," said Stuart.

"Hello," replied Snowbell, sharply. "You're up early, aren't you?"

Stuart looked at his watch. "Yes," he said, "it's only five minutes past six, but I felt good and I thought I'd come down and get a little exercise."

"I should think you'd get all the exercise you want up there in the bathroom, banging around, waking all the rest of us up trying to get that water started so you can brush your teeth. Your teeth aren't really big enough to brush anyway. Want to see a good set? Look at mine!" Snowbell opened his mouth and showed two rows of gleaming white teeth, sharp as needles.

"Very nice," said Stuart. "But mine are all right, too, even though they're small. As for exercise, I take all I can get. I bet my stomach muscles are firmer than yours."

"I bet they're not," said the cat.

Stuart glanced around the room to see what he could do to prove to Snowbell what good stomach muscles he had. He spied the drawn window shade on the east window, with its shade cord and ring, like a trapeze, and it gave him an idea. Climbing to the windowsill he took off his hat and laid down his cane.

"You can't do this," he said to the cat. And he ran and jumped on the ring, the way acrobats do in a circus, meaning to pull himself up.

A surprising thing happened. Stuart had taken such a hard jump that it started the shade: with a loud snap the shade flew up clear to the top of the window, dragging Stuart along with it and rolling him up inside, so that he couldn't budge.

"Holy mackerel!" said Snowbell, who was almost as surprised as Stuart Little. "I guess that will teach him to show off his muscles."

"Help! Let me out!" cried Stuart, who was frightened and bruised inside the rolled-up shade, and who could barely breathe. But his voice was so weak that nobody heard. Snowbell just chuckled. He

was not fond of Stuart and it didn't bother him at all that Stuart was all wrapped up in a window shade, crying and hurt and unable to get out. Instead of running upstairs and telling Mr. and Mrs. Little about the accident, Snowbell did a very curious thing. He glanced around to see if anybody was looking, then he leapt softly to the windowsill, picked up Stuart's hat and cane in his mouth, carried them to the pantry, and laid them down at the entrance of the mousehole.

When Mrs. Little came down later and found them there, she gave a shrill scream which brought everybody on the run.

"It's happened," she cried.

"What has?" asked her husband.

"Stuart's down the mousehole."

Rescued

George was in favor of ripping up the pantry floor. He ran and got his hammer, his screwdriver, and an ice pick.

"I'll have this old floor up in double-quick time," he said, inserting his screwdriver under the edge of the first board and giving a good vigorous pry.

"We will not rip up this floor till we have had a good search," announced Mr. Little. "That's final, George! You can put that hammer away where you got it."

"Oh, all right," said George. "I see that nobody in this house cares anything about Stuart but me."

Mrs. Little began to cry. "My poor dear little son!" she said. "I know he'll get wedged somewhere."

"Just because you can't travel comfortably in a mousehole doesn't mean that it isn't a perfectly suitable place for Stuart," said Mr. Little. "Just don't get yourself all worked up."

"Maybe we ought to lower some food to him," suggested George. "That's what the State Police did when a man got stuck in a cave." George darted into the kitchen and came rushing back with a dish of applesauce. "We can pour some of this in, and it will run down to where he is." George spooned out a bit of the applesauce and started to poke it into the hole.

"Stop that!" bellowed Mr. Little. "George, will you kindly let *me* handle this situation? Put that applesauce away immediately!"

Mr. Little glared fiercely at George.

"I was just trying to help my own brother," said George, shaking his head as he carried the sauce back to the kitchen.

"Let's call to Stuart," suggested Mrs. Little. "It's quite possible that the mousehole branches and twists about, and that he has lost his way."

"Very well," said Mr. Little. "I will count three, then we will all call, then we will all keep perfectly quiet for three sec-

onds, listening for the answer." He took out his watch.

Mr. and Mrs. Little and George got down on their hands and knees and put their mouths as close as possible to the mousehole. Then they all called: "Stooooo-art!" And then they all kept perfectly still for three seconds.

Stuart, from his cramped position inside the rolled-up shade, heard them yelling in the pantry and called back, "Here I am!" But he had such a weak voice and was so far inside the shade that the other members of the family did not hear his answering cry.

"Again!" said Mr. Little. "One, two, three — Stooooo-art!"

It was no use. No answer was heard. Mrs. Little went up to her bedroom, lay down, and sobbed. Mr. Little went to the telephone and called up the Bureau of Missing Persons, but when the man asked for a description of Stuart and was told that he was only two inches high, he hung up in disgust. George meantime went down cellar and hunted around to see if he could find the other entrance to the mousehole. He moved a great many

trunks, suitcases, flower pots, baskets, boxes, and broken chairs from one end of the cellar to the other in order to get at the section of the wall which he thought was likeliest, but found no hole. He did, however, come across an old discarded rowing machine of Mr. Little's, and, becoming interested in this, carried it upstairs with some difficulty and spent the rest of the morning rowing.

When lunchtime came (everybody had forgotten about breakfast) all three sat down to a lamb stew which Mrs. Little had prepared, but it was a sad meal, each one trying not to stare at the small empty chair which Stuart always occupied, right next to Mrs. Little's glass of water. No one could eat, so great was the sorrow. George ate a bit of dessert but nothing else. When lunch was over Mrs. Little broke out crying again, and said she thought Stuart must be dead. "Nonsense, nonsense!" growled Mr. Little.

"If he *is* dead," said George, "we ought to pull down the shades all through the house." And he raced to the windows and began pulling down the shades.

"George!" shouted Mr. Little in an exasperated tone, "if you don't stop acting in an idiotic fashion, I will punish you. We are having enough trouble today without having to cope with your foolishness."

But George had already run into the living room and had begun to darken it, to show his respect for the dead. He pulled a cord and out dropped Stuart onto the windowsill.

"Well, for the love of Pete," said George. "Look who's here, Mom!"

"It's about time somebody pulled down that shade," remarked Stuart. "That's all I can say." He was quite weak and hungry.

Mrs. Little was so overjoyed to see him that she kept right on crying. Of course everybody wanted to know how it happened.

"It was simply an accident that might happen to anybody," said Stuart. "As for my hat and cane being found at the entrance of the mousehole, you can draw your own conclusions."

READING COMPREHENSION

Summarizing. Choose the best phrase to complete each sentence. Then write the complete statements on your paper.

1. Stuart was sometimes helpful and sometimes a problem because he _____ (was tiny and looked like a mouse, didn't get along with Snowbell, was always the first person up).

2. When Stuart was caught inside a shade, Snowbell _____ (told Mrs. Little, put Stuart's hat and cane near the mousehole, showed off his teeth).

3. George pulled down the shades because _____ (he heard Stuart's voice, Mrs. Little could not stop crying, he wanted to show his respect for the dead).

4. Why did Snowbell not help Stuart out of the shade?

Interpreting. Write the answer to each question on your paper.

1. What helpful things could Stuart do because of his size?

2. Why did Stuart's parents avoid mentioning the word *mouse* in front of him?

3. What did his family think when they saw Stuart's hat and cane near the mousehole?

For Thinking and Discussing. What are the advantages of being small? What are the disadvantages? If you had a choice, would you prefer to be tiny, medium, or large? Why?

UNDERSTANDING LITERATURE

Characters. Characters are the people and animals in the story. The reader learns about the characters through their speech (the things they say); their actions (the things they do); and their thoughts.

On your paper, write *speech*, *action*, or *thoughts* to show how each quotation below from "Stuart and Snowbell" gives information about a character.

1. "Mrs. Little carefully rubbed the word mouse from the poem and wrote in the word louse . . . ."

2. "He didn't know where the hole led to, and it made him uneasy to think that Stuart might someday feel the desire to venture into it."

3. "Snowbell just chuckled. He was not fond of Stuart and it didn't bother him at all that Stuart was all wrapped up in a window shade . . . ."

4. "He leapt softly to the windowsill, picked up Stuart's hat and cane in his mouth, carried them to the pantry and laid them down at the entrance of the mousehole."

5. "It's about time somebody pulled down that shade, that's all I can say."

WRITING

Write a paragraph describing the character George. Tell whether George was the kind of person you would want for a brother or a friend. Support your description with things George said, thought, and did.

The Stray Cat

by Eve Merriam

It's just an old alley cat
that has followed us all the way home.

It hasn't a star on its forehead,
or a silky satiny coat.

No proud tiger stripes, no dainty tread,
no elegant velvet throat.

It's a splotchy, blotchy
city cat, not pretty cat,
a rough little tough little bag of old bones.

"Beauty," we shall call you.
"Beauty, come in."

---

1. According to the speaker in the poem, what image or picture do people have of a pretty cat?

2. Why do you think the speaker in the poem named the cat Beauty?

VOCABULARY

Synonyms. Words that have the same meaning, or almost the same meaning are called *synonyms*. For example, when the priest discovered that the boy had drawn cats on the temple walls, he said, "This was not right." *Correct, proper, acceptable,* and *good* are all synonyms for right in this statement.

The sentences below are from the selections you have just read. Write each italicized word on your paper. Then write its synonym from the following list.

talks   laughed   spotty   odd

special   jumped   follow

upright   clever   tell

1. It's a *splotchy*, blotchy city cat, not pretty cat, ...

2. But THE CAT HIMSELF KNOWS, and will never *confess*.

3. But I tell you a cat needs a name that's *particular*.

4. We have many *conversations*, Ulysses and I.

5. She reads and she writes with all the delights of *intelligent* cats up a tree.

6. Else how can he keep up his tail *perpendicular*, ...

7. Tired of the view she chose to *pursue* a fate unbeknownst to the crowd.

8. But instead they *leaped* nimbly out, playfully rubbing against Mikila's legs.

9. Instead of running upstairs, Snowbell did a very *curious* thing.

10. Snowbell just *chuckled*.

READING

Author's Purpose. Most stories are written to entertain readers. Different stories entertain in different ways. Amusing stories make readers laugh. Scary stories entertain by sending shivers up a reader's spine. The *author's purpose* for writing the story helps him or her decide what kind of details to include.

The questions below are about each author's purpose in the stories from this section. Write the answer to each question in a complete sentence.

1. Which of the following details from "The Boy Who Drew Cats" best shows that the author's purpose is to entertain the reader with a scary story?

   ☐ The boy painted a great many cats upon the screens.

   ☐ A goblin had frightened the priests away and now lived at the temple.

   ☐ Although the boy was tired, he looked for a writing box.

2. Which of the following details from "Stuart and Snowbell" best shows that the author's purpose is to make the reader laugh?

☐ George did exercises to keep his muscles firm.

☐ The Littles' second son looked and acted very much like a mouse.

☐ Snowbell the cat was not very fond of Stuart.

Sometimes an author may want to do more than entertain. He or she may want to get a serious message across to the readers.

3. Which of the following quotations do you think best expresses the author's message in "All the Cats in the World"?

☐ "One person may not be able to feed all the cats in the world, but I can at least feed these close at hand."

☐ "Woman, are you so rich that you can feed all these filthy creatures?"

☐ "I am sick of being taunted by that terrible old man."

QUIZ

The following is a quiz for Section 1. Write the answers in complete sentences on your paper.

Reading Comprehension

1. In "All the Cats in the World," why didn't Mikila feed the cats for three days?

2. In "The Boy who Drew Cats," how did the boy know that the goblin had been killed by the cats he had drawn?

3. In "Stuart and Snowbell," why did Mrs. Little tear "Three Blind Mice" out of the nursery songbook?

4. In the poem "Paula the Cat," what does Paula have an urge to do?

5. In "The Naming of Cats," what is special about the second name a cat has?

Understanding Literature

6. In "All the Cats in the World," the reader learns about the old man through his speech and his actions. What did the old man say that might make you think he was unkind? What did he do that might make you think he was kind?

7. What are the three most important events from the plot of "The Boy Who Drew Cats"? Write them in the order in which they occur.

8. The story "Stuart and Snowbell" takes place after the Little's second son, Stuart, is born. Where does the story take place?

9. Although Stuart in "Stuart and Snowbell" is a mouse, he is very human. How does the author make this character seem human? Support your answer with examples from the story.

10. How do the poems in this section, "Paula the Cat" and "The Naming of Cats" differ? Which do you like better?

WRITING

Description. Description helps a reader understand a character. It also allows a reader to form a mental image or picture of how a character looks. In this section of the book, you have read descriptions of some unusual characters. Several of them, including Snowbell and Paula, have been cats. Others have been different kinds of animals—Ulysses the Goat, the Goblin Rat, and that most unusual mouse, Stuart Little.

Now you can write your own description. Read each step to help guide you in your writing.

Step 1: Set Your Goal

Choose one of the following topics for a description.

☐ Describe a cat that you have read about in this section.

☐ Describe a real cat or another animal that you know.

Step 2: Make a Plan.

Plan what you are going to say. Start by making a list of details that describe the animal.

For example, imagine that you want to describe a pet dog named Samantha. Here is a list of details you might use:

☐ Name: Samantha (Sam)

☐ Size: big enough to stand up and lick people's faces

☐ Eyes: big, round, brown

☐ Ears: short, pointed

☐ Tail: long, thin

☐ Fur: short, tan fur that feels like brush bristles

☐ Voice: loud, deep bark

☐ Personality: friendly

☐ Other details: shakes hands with her left paw, plays catch with her tennis ball

Step 3: Write the First Draft

Write your description in one paragraph. Begin by stating what animal you are describing. Then use your details to describe the animal. End the paragraph with a sentence that sums up the description.

1. Begin your paragraph by stating what you are describing. For example, you might begin this way:

   My favorite dog is named Samantha.

2. Use your details to describe the animal. Here is an example:

   Although Samantha is a female, I call

47

her Sam. Sam is a very big dog. She is so big, she can put her paws on most people's shoulders and lick their faces. She has big, round, brown eyes, short pointed ears, and a long, thin tail. Her short, tan fur feels like the bristles of a brush. Sam has such a loud, deep bark that many people think she is unfriendly, but she is very friendly. Once she gets to know you, Sam will shake your hand with her left paw. Sam's favorite activity is playing catch with her tennis ball.

3. End your paragraph with a sentence that sums up the description, for example:

I know that you would like Sam if you met her.

Step 4: Revise

Read your description. Will a reader be able to form a good mental picture from it? Add any important details you have left out. Correct any errors in spelling and punctuation. Make a final, neat copy of your description.

ACTIVITIES

Word Attack. When the letter *a* is followed by two consonants or by one consonant and no vowel, it usually stands for the short *a* sound:

alley   cat

When *a* is followed by *i*, *y*, or a consonant and then a vowel, it usually stands for the long *a* sound:

tail   say   name

Pronounce the following words from the poem "The Naming of Cats." Then copy them on your paper and write *short a* or *long a* for each.

Plato   hatter   Quaxo

fancier   holiday   rapt

Speaking and Listening. Practice reading the first four lines of "The Naming of Cats" out loud. Use the punctuation and the capitalization in the poem to help you decide when to pause and what to stress in your reading. As you read, listen to rhymes that you hear and the rhythm of the lines.

Researching. There are many different members of the cat family, including lions, tigers, and leopards. Choose one kind of big cat. Go to the library. Look in the card catalog for the cat you have chosen. For example, if you have chosen a lion, look in the drawer containing the letters *li* for subject cards about lions. The cards will list the books the library has on that subject. They will also tell you something about each book, and they will show what shelves the books are on.

Use the library books to find out the facts asked for in the chart shown. Make a copy of the chart on your paper and

CAT FACTS

	Lion	Tiger
SIZE	length-8 feet or more weight-250 pounds or more	
APPEAR-ANCE	mane-brown, black or blond coat-brownish yellow	
HABITS	stays in specific area does not allow strange animals to hunt in its area stays together as a family for years.	
WHERE IT IS FOUND	both cool climates and semi-desert areas chooses area with some vegetation and a ready supply of food and water.	

fill in the facts about the cat you have chosen. Facts about lions have been filled in as an example.

Creating. Snowbell is the name of a white flower. It is also the name Mr. and Mrs. Little gave to their pet in "Stuart and Snowbell." Write a name that you think would be more fitting for the Little's pet. You can pick an ordinary name like James or make up a special name. Then make two lists. On the first list, write the reasons why the Littles might have picked the name they did. On the second list, write the reasons why you feel the name you picked is better.

SOMEBODY SPECIAL

*I announce the great
individual, fluid as Nature, chaste,
affectionate, compassionate,
fully arm'd.*

—Walt Whitman

Introduction

Nothing special about you? You think you're just like anybody else? Well, think again.

It may sound too simple, but being special is being yourself. There is no one in the world exactly like you. By trying to be the best person you possibly can, you are being special.

Many people have things in common with other people. They like to do similar things, and can do them well. But each person is an individual. Each person has his or her own personality that is special. For example, in an exercise class, everyone may be doing the same movement, but each person has his or her own style that is special. Or in school, everyone may read the same book, but each student will think about it in his or her own special way.

Think about what things make you feel good, or what things make you laugh, or what foods you like to eat. If you made a list of everything in the world that you like, your list would be your own and different from anyone else's list.

Special people can be anybody and everybody. Imagine how boring life would be if everybody was the same. But fortunately, each person is unique. Each person has his or her own special interest, friends, dreams. Here is what some 11-year-olds said about who they thought was special and why:

"My best friend, because I can do a lot of things with her like go shopping at the mall, and tell her secrets."

"My mother, because she pays the rent, buys the food, and drives the car."

"My science teacher because he does fun experiments like heating a mixture of baking soda and vinegar to cause an explosion."

"My gym teacher, because he makes me feel special."

"My uncle, because he listens to my problems and gives me good advice."

In this section you will read about people who became famous special people. You will see they did not think about becoming famous. They did not worry about being special. Like you, they were special just by being themselves. They simply followed their interests, or did the best they could do to survive.

In "You Are Somebody Special," Bill Cosby wanted to be a great jumper and a great football player on the first try, but it didn't happen that way. It took a lot of talking to himself to get where he wanted to go.

In "Janette's Winter," a young girl was faced with a life and death situation. If she wanted to see people again, she would have to figure out how to live through a winter alone in her wagon in the mountains.

In "Peculiarsome Abe," friends and

family thought Abe was strange because he read so much. But he kept reading. He found something special in books, and he tried to tell people what that was.

In "The Poets' Portrait Gallery," three poems describe people who had unusual interests. Anton Van Leeuwenhoek liked to see what the normal eye could not see. Harriet Tubman traveled from south to north many times to save people's lives.

Louise Nevelson found an important way to use old junk.

The people in these stories were both famous and special. But you don't have to be a famous person to be a special one. All you have to do is be true to yourself and work hard, and your special qualities will develop. So, next time you look in a mirror, think again about how the person you see is special.

You Are Somebody Special

by Bill Cosby

It may be hard to believe, but many very famous people had trouble keeping up their self-confidence when they were younger and in school. Read the story to see how a junior-high-school student named Bill Cosby overcame his fears and learned he was somebody special.

In 1951, I started junior high school. I wasn't really interested in school until I saw this fellow named Sporty high-jumping.

It was after school, and he was practicing alone in the gym. He was jumping at four feet six inches. At that time, I was five feet three inches tall, and very thin. But Sporty made high-jumping look simple.

I watched him make his approach, jump over the bamboo bar, and land on the mats. He had on his gym clothes and a classy-looking pair of track shoes. I wanted to high-jump, too.

Now, Sporty and I jumped in different styles. Mine was a sort of "running from the scene of the crime" jump. Sporty's was the classic Eastern Roll. He approached the bar with a certain number of steps. Then he planted his right foot on the ground (because he was left-footed) and threw his left leg up. As he began to clear the bar, he flattened out his body.

He kicked his back leg up so it wouldn't hit the bar. Then he landed smoothly on his back.

Then I tried it my way. I ran toward the bar from an angle. Then I stopped, planted both feet, and jumped straight up, bringing my knees up to my chin. When I came down, I broke the bamboo bar.

This upset Sporty very much. He told me he had worked by himself in the gym for three weeks. He said I was the first fool to come in and break the bar. So I apologized and asked him if he would show me how to do it right.

Mr. Lister

Just then, Mr. Richard Lister appeared. He was our gym teacher, and a very kind gentleman who had high-jumped in college. I think his record was six feet nine inches. To Sporty and me, that was out of this world. So when he offered to work with us, we couldn't wait.

I told my mother I would be home late

from then on, because Sporty and I would be high-jumping after school. My mother wanted to know if there was a high-jumping team. I said, "No, but Sporty and I have a great time just jumping over this bamboo bar." Then she asked me if I had done my homework.

The next day, I went to the gym after school to practice. The first thing Mr. Lister told us to do was warm up. He showed us how to do a set of exercises. These were exercises we had done earlier, in gym class. I notified Mr. Lister that I had already done them.

"You're going to have to do them again," he told me. "You have to get your blood flowing. You have to warn your body that it's going to jump higher than it's ever jumped before."

So Sporty and I ran around the gym. I thought it was kind of silly. I thought we'd make ourselves too tired for high-jumping.

I found out this was not true. Somehow we had enough energy to jump for the next three hours.

By the time I had broken three bars, Mr. Lister decided to work on my style. I had a lot of energy, but I wasn't smooth like Sporty.

Somehow, when I watched Sporty jump, I thought I could be a jumper. I had proved I could jump well in basketball by getting a lot of rebounds. I knew I had coordination, because I was one of the top athletes in my gym class. What was the problem?

Lesson One

Mr. Lister said, "Son, in order to do anything well, you must start from lesson

one. Then we go to lessons two, three, four, and five. These lessons have been drawn up by people who have tried them and found that they work.

"After you have learned them, you might decide this is not the right way for you. At that point, you might make some changes. But meanwhile you are fighting yourself."

So Mr. Lister and I worked on a smooth approach to the bar. At first it was set at the embarrassing height of two feet. I made my five-step approach, lifted my left leg, and threw my arms up. I cleared the bar and landed on my back. I did this 20 times. Each time, Mr. Lister said, "Good."

Finally, I said, "Yes, but the bar is only two feet high!"

He said, "It is better to make it at two feet than to break another bar at four feet. Think how many bars we've saved. You've jumped 20 times. You've saved 20 bars."

After a while, I was jumping with Sporty at four and a half feet. Then Sporty moved the bar to four feet nine inches. This was a real challenge. The bar was now about as high as my eyes.

As I made the approach, I became frightened. I wasn't afraid of hurting myself or breaking the bar. I was frightened because this looked like something I couldn't do.

The closer I got to the bar, the more I was sure I couldn't do it. The more I accepted the fact that I couldn't do it, the more I didn't prepare myself to jump. In other words, my mind said no, so my body didn't really try.

I did exactly what I thought I was going to do. I knocked the bar off. As a matter of fact, I grabbed the bar with my left hand, never leaving the ground.

I put the bar back up. Sporty ran at it and jumped. His leg touched the bar, but the bar stayed up. He had made a jump of four feet nine inches.

Of course, Sporty and I were now competing against each other. I thought, "If Sporty can do it, I'd better do it."

I stood on my mark. I started with the right foot and took three steps. Then I thought, "You can't make it." Again, as I finished the last two steps, I grabbed the bar.

Now Sporty approached the bar again. He made his jump. This time he knocked the bar off, and I felt better.

After talking to myself, I realized something. By being afraid to fail, I was only making a halfhearted try.

So I stood at the mark and tried to block out negative thoughts. I thought of all the good things about myself.

Six Inches Over

I approached the bar. No negative thoughts came into my mind. I jumped, and I found myself looking down on the bar. I was at least six inches over it, and I was happy.

(Now I am going to freeze that moment, so you can get the feeling of what happened. As I go over the bar, I see that I am six inches over. I say to myself, "I've done it!" I hear cheers from all the little people in my brain: "Yeah, we've done it!")

However, I had forgotten to complete the jump. So as I sailed over the bar, my second leg knocked it off. Still, I had cleared it by a good six inches.

As I put the bar up quickly and walked back, Sporty said, "You know, you really made that." We were both excited and talking fast. For some reason, Sporty felt very good about what I had done.

The next time, I remembered to kick and clear my second leg. So it was no longer a problem to jump four feet nine inches. I felt sure of myself.

Now I began to wonder how high I could go. Could I jump five feet two? Impossible! I was only five feet three. How could I jump my height? But wouldn't it be wonderful if I could!

That day was a great day for me. I had learned to talk to myself. I had learned to reason with myself and to believe in

myself. As long as I could think good things about myself, I could achieve.

Football

I went on to high school, where I went out for football. I made the junior varsity, even though I knew nothing about organized football. I made the team because I was the fastest person there. I knew that because I had won the sprint.

On the bulletin board, a sign said you should weigh 135 pounds to play football. I weighed 125.

The coach put me on the fifteenth team. This was the first time I had ever worn a real football uniform. It was also the time I learned that football plays were worked out in advance. Until then, I had thought the captain told the guys where to run. I thought he said, "I want you to run over there." I didn't know the plays were called by numbers.

So I didn't feel secure. I was happy to have on the uniform. It made me feel like a real football player. But I was really frightened. The fifteenth team was made up of skinny guys. We were the team everybody was supposed to run over.

I'll never forget that day. Our team learned three or four plays. Then the coach decided we would practice with another team.

I was left halfback. On play 44, I was handed the ball. I was supposed to run between the guard and the tackle.

I ran that play with my eyes closed, because I was afraid. Then I felt as though walls had fallen on me. I also felt a great deal of pain in my front teeth. I had fallen, and my face had hit the heel of someone's shoe.

I remember thinking, "Oh, no! My teeth have been knocked out!" I reached up and touched my two front teeth. (I was very proud of them.)

As I walked back to the huddle, I wondered if I really wanted to play this game. This was different from the football I had played on the street. It was a lot more fun on the street.

The next play was 22. Now the right halfback was supposed to do what I had just tried to do. He got creamed, as I knew he would.

This didn't make any sense to me. I decided I'd turn in my uniform after practice. I'd try out for another sport instead.

Touchdown

The next play was 44 again. I thought, "This time, they are not going to hit my face." (There were no face guards in those days.)

The quarterback handed me the ball, and I kept my eyes open. For some weird reason, there was space to run through. I hit the space fast, and no one touched me. Since there were no goalposts, I decided to run as fast as I could. Then it would have to be a touchdown.

After I ran maybe 99 yards, I heard the coach's whistle. Then he yelled, "Someone catch him before he runs into the locker room."

I ran back with the ball under my arm, feeling great. I had scored a touchdown. There was a big smile on my face. I took it off before I got back to the coach. You

have to act cool, you know, after you've done something great.

The next play was 22 again. Once more, the other halfback got smeared. Then there was another 44, and I got smeared. I wondered again if I should go out for another sport. But I had already scored a touchdown, so I felt I could do it again and again.

When we finished practice, I knew the other players were looking at me. I had done something no one else had done that day. I had scored a touchdown. Not even the guys on the first team had done that.

The next day, I went to practice already warmed up. I was a different person mentally. I was somebody special.

Sure enough, we ran old 44, and I made another touchdown. Well, now I knew I

was good. When I ran back, the guys on the fifteenth team were all clapping for me. I still didn't let the coach see me smile, but inside I felt great.

The next day, the coach said, "Cosby, you're now on the second team." I smiled. That day, I made another touchdown — the same old 44.

First Team

I soon became the first-string left halfback. My reputation reached the varsity: Some kid on the junior varsity was running touchdowns left and right!

In the locker room, I noticed that some of the varsity players were looking at me. So I puffed up my little 125-pound self to look 135 pounds. I felt good.

You Are Special

Self-confidence has a lot to do with how well you perform. Even if you do not succeed completely, it has a lot to do with how much progress you make.

When you choose to do something, you can learn things you've never tried before. You can become successful. But first you must have a feeling for success.

How do you get this feeling? Try. If you don't try, you'll never know if you could have succeeded.

Here are some questions for you:

What is success?

What have you accepted about yourself?

Who is it you want to be? If you can't be that person, then who will you be?

The outcome is up to you. The possibilities are wide open.

READING COMPREHENSION

Summarizing. Choose the best phrase to complete each sentence. Then write the complete statement on your paper.

1. Bill learned to jump by starting _____ (to copy Sporty, at the five foot bar, at lesson one).

2. To be able to jump higher, Bill needed not only to learn the skills, but also to _____ (beat Sporty, grow much taller, believe in himself).

3. When he played football, Bill learned that to succeed he must _____ (score a touchdown, overcome fear, run faster).

Interpreting. Write the answer to each question on your paper.

1. What did Bill think about himself after failing to jump four feet nine inches a few times?

2. How was Mr. Lister helpful to Bill in his learning to jump?

3. Why did Bill write about all the times he failed?

4. Why does Bill think it is important to keep trying?

For Thinking and Discussing. Think about a time you kept on trying until you succeeded. How did this experience make you feel? Is there a time when trying over and over would not be helpful? How can you know if you should keep on trying?

UNDERSTANDING LITERATURE

Autobiography and First Person Point of View. "You Are Somebody Special" is an *autobiography*. Autobiography is the true story a person writes about his or her life. Bill Cosby, the author, uses the words *I* and *me* to tell about his life. When a story uses the words I and me it is told from the *first person point of view*.

Each description below is from Bill's autobiography. Match each description with the thought that tells Bill's point of view. Does the description or the thought tell you more? Why?

Descriptions

1. "I approached the bar. No negative thoughts came into my mind. I jumped, and I found myself looking down on the bar."

2. "The closer I got to the bar, the more I was sure I couldn't do it. The more I accepted the fact that I couldn't do it, the more I didn't prepare myself to jump."

Thoughts

a. If you think you will fail, you will never really try to succeed.

b. Belief in yourself helps you succeed.

WRITING

Write a paragraph telling how you learned a skill like swimming or riding a bicycle. Tell how long it took, and how you felt after you learned it.

Janette's Winter

by Barbara Bloom

Imagine yourself completely alone in the wilderness — for a whole winter. What would you do? How would you survive? Those were just the questions Janette Riker asked herself when her pioneer family disappeared on their trip out West in 1849. She faced six months alone in the Rocky Mountains of Montana.

The sun was just beginning to set over the Montana mountains that September day in 1849. Its rays were still warm. Yet Janette Riker shivered and drew her homespun shawl tighter around her shoulders. Eagerly, fearfully, she looked from one snowcapped peak to another. Except for the green grasses bending gently in the breeze, there was no movement.

"Oh, where are you?" she whispered anxiously. "Papa, why don't you and the boys come back? What's happened to you?"

Janette and her father and two brothers had stopped their Conestoga wagon in this lovely mountain valley. They needed to rest the oxen and hunt fresh game. They knew they couldn't stay long. It was late in the season. And they were in a hurry to reach Oregon. So yesterday, while Janette washed their extra clothes in the small gurgling stream, her father and the boys went hunting. They promised to bring home meat in time for dinner.

Late that afternoon Janette started a campfire. Her mouth watered at the thought of fresh roasted meat. But evening came without any sign of the three men. Before long Janette was surrounded by the vast, dark silence. Fearing the wild animals she knew roamed the hills, she climbed into the wagon. Then she snatched the rifle from its rack and sat with her back pressed against the wooden backboard.

All night she crouched like that. She listened for the return of her family. But she heard only the howling of wolves and the wailing of the night winds. When the sun first showed above the jagged mountains, she jumped from the wagon.

At first it was easy to follow the tracks left by her father and brothers the day before. But after a few miles the trail disappeared in the powdery sands of a dry riverbed. Janette ran along the banks in both directions crying, "Papa! Tom! Billy!"

At the foot of the mountains she shouted. Only her own voice echoed back

from the overhanging rocks. Hour after hour she wandered among the hills around the valley, calling. But there was no answer.

In the late afternoon she returned to the camp. She had found nothing. She knew nothing.

Now, standing alone in the wilderness, she trembled with fear. The family's two oxen were grazing peacefully nearby, Janette threw her arms around one of them. "Surely they'll come back soon," she said. Then she set about preparing for another long, sleepless night in the wagon — alone.

The days that followed became a blur in Janette's memory. Every morning she set out in a new direction. She called and searched for her father and brothers. At night she returned, exhausted, to the empty meadow and the patient oxen. She grew accustomed to sleeping alone in the wagon. She got used to the howling of the wolves. But her dreams were filled with visions of her father and brothers. She dreamt they were lost and perhaps hurt somewhere in the wilderness around her. Once she thought she heard Tom's voice calling to her from the darkness. But it was only the wind sighing in the pine trees.

Finally one morning, Janette just stood and stared at the tall mountains rising all around her. She did not know where else to look for her family. Hours later, when the sun began to set, she forced herself to admit the horrible truth. Her father and brothers were not coming back. She was alone in the middle of a vast, fierce wilderness. Turning to the oxen she cried,

"What's to become of me? I can't drive the wagon through those passes!"

Her only answer was the rustle of the wind in the trees and the contented munching of the animals.

It was too much for Janette. She sank to the ground and sobbed. Her wails and moans echoed through the valley. She knew that no one could hear her. There would be no wagon along the trail until spring.

Janette cried until she could cry no more. Then at last she tried to shake off her grief. She drew a deep breath. She smelled the sweet, fresh earth. She knew that she couldn't take the wagon over the mountain by herself. She would have to stay in this valley until help came. But to survive the winter, she would need a shelter.

She got up and wiped her eyes. Then she went to the wagon, found the ax, and walked to the woods. There she began chopping down trees. She worked until her arms ached. By sundown she had felled only two birch saplings. The next day she cut down two more trees. The day after, she cut down three.

Finally, after a week's hard work, she had 15 saplings of about equal length. With the spade she dug holes side by side in the earth until they formed a circle 15 steps around. Into each hole Janette set a tree. Then she dragged the butter churn to the center of the circle and climbed up on it to lash the saplings together. When she finished, her shelter looked like a tepee. The next day she pulled up clumps of prairie grass and stuffed them between the cracks, so the wind could not get in. And

over her shelter she stretched the white canvas cover from the Conestoga wagon. That way the rain could not fall through the top. She hammered the canvas firmly into the ground with the stakes her father had brought to mark off their new land in Oregon. Janette left one flap open to use as a door.

"Look at that!" She proudly showed her oxen the odd little shelter, which had taken her more than two weeks to build. Her shoulders hurt. She had blisters on her hands. But still she laughed.

Then she blinked hard to stop her tears. No one was there to laugh with her.

After a while Janette pulled the half empty bags of coffee, rice, sugar, salt, flour, beans, and cornmeal down from the wagon. She took them into her house. She pushed the small iron stove over the side of the wagon. Then she dragged it in, too, along with all the wool blankets and buffalo robes. On top of the stack of blankets she gently laid the patchwork quilt her mother had sewn before she died. This would be her bed.

That night it rained, and the next day there was frost on the ground. Once again Janette shouldered her ax and made for the forest, this time to chop the wood she would need to keep her stove burning throughout the winter.

The nights were growing colder and the days were growing shorter. Finally the day came when she had to break through the ice of the small stream so the oxen could drink. All day she thought of the animals. They were the only companions she had. She loved their dear, familiar faces. But she would need their meat more than their company if she was to last the winter.

The next morning Janette took up the rifle. She stood before the fatter of the oxen. Trembling, she aimed at its broad forehead. Then she closed her eyes, and pulled the trigger. The gun kicked her shoulder and knocked her onto the ground, but the huge beast fell — dead.

Slowly Janette rose and brought out the butcher knife. She cut into the hind flesh and carved pieces larger than her hand. Each one she covered with salt and stacked in a barrel. Though she had never done it by herself before, she had watched her father pack away meat every fall since she was a small child.

That night Janette was awakened from an exhausted sleep by fierce, savage growls outside her hut. The noise sounded like mad dogs. But she knew it must be wolves or mountain lions. They were attracted by the smell of the freshly slaughtered meat. They paced around the shelter, sniffing and clawing and scratching at the canvas. For a moment she could hardly breathe. What if they forced their way inside? Throwing off her quilt, Janette pushed several logs in front of the door flap. Then she cocked her rifle.

"Don't come in," she whispered desperately. But the clawing and scratching became more violent. Janette feared the worst. Then suddenly she heard other noises farther away. There was a savage scream from an animal, galloping scrambles, some commotion — then silence. Had they gone?

Janette relaxed her grip on the rifle. She began trembling violently. She could not hear any more noises. Still, the night seemed endless.

The next morning she saw many animal tracks in the earth around her shelter. Her one remaining ox was gone. She never found out whether the creature had tried to hide in the woods or whether it had been killed by the hungry wolves. The next night the wild animals returned, and the next, and the next throughout the long autumn. Every night Janette sat up with her rifle. She was afraid to sleep.

Every morning she was stiff and tired.

Then, one afternoon, the snow began to fall. Janette brought in an extra supply of logs. That night she heard the wind blowing wildly outside as she snuggled under her warm quilt. In the morning she couldn't crawl out of her hut. But she did manage to cut a small hole in her canvas roof. She had to dig away the snow to make a smoke hole for her stove. Shivering, she piled on fresh wood and waited out the storm.

Janette finally tunneled her way outside two days later. Snow lay deep in the valley, almost as high as her shelter. She caught her breath at the wild beauty of it all — and tried not to think how alone she was.

Day after day Janette heard the howl of the wind as it drove the snows before it. Every morning she cleared the smoke hole in her roof. Then she cooked beans and corn cakes. On clear days she trudged to the woods. She chopped more logs for her woodpile and kept a careful lookout for wild animals. But after the first heavy snowfall she was never again bothered by them.

Often during that long, cruel winter, Janette sat inside and thought of her family. She remembered the gentle sound of her father's voice. She pictured Tom's face with its broad smile. She thought of Billy's deep laugh. More and more, she dreamed of the happy times they had spent together back home in Illinois. How she longed for the familiar white farmhouse with the blue flowers growing by the door. And how she wished that the people she loved had stayed safe inside its walls!

The slow days passed into weeks and the weeks into months. Janette grew pale and thin. Her food supply got very small. She began rationing her already skimpy meals.

Then one day the call of an eagle pierced her quiet. Janette crawled outside in time to see the huge bird flying lazily across the sky. She felt a mild wind brush her cheeks. She saw that the snow was melting from the pine branches. It must be spring! Janette's heart began to beat wildly. Perhaps now some other settlers would pass through her valley!

But the spring thaw only brought new troubles for Janette. Within a week the warm sun had turned the snowdrifts into small, muddy rivers. Water covered the floor of her shelter. It soaked her bed and flooded her stove.

Janette knew that she must leave her winter home. The wagon stood above the wet ground, its frame bare as a skeleton. Gathering the last of her strength, she pulled the shabby canvas from her shelter. Then she draped it back over the wagon frame. She carried her mother's quilt, the rifle, the almost empty bag of cornmeal, and the last few pieces of salted meat back to the wagon bed.

All the rest of that day, Janette huddled in the wagon. With no way to build a fire, she ate her meat raw and her cornmeal uncooked. At night she fell into an uneasy sleep. Her dreams were punctuated by the steady drip, drip of the melting snow. For weeks Janette, exhausted, kept her eyes on the distant mountain passes. She still hoped to see a wagon. She had done all she could to save herself. Now, with no fire and precious little food left, she simply waited — and hoped.

Patches of grass had begun appearing in the flooded valley. At last, one morning Janette heard hoofbeats. She shook with excitement. But she was too weak to climb out of the wagon. The sound of horses came nearer, and her trembling grew worse. At last she stuggled to the end of the wagon and threw open the flap.

There, arranged in a semicircle around her, was a small band of Indian braves mounted on pinto ponies. Janette knew the Indians in these parts did not take kindly to white settlers invading their land. But her relief at seeing other human faces overcame whatever fear she might have felt.

"Please," she said, "help me. Papa — Tom — Billy — they've all gone."

The hunting party stared at her, as their ponies snorted and pawed the ground.

Then Janette lost all the self-control that had kept her alive through her ordeal. She didn't know if the Indians could understand her language. But the words burst from her like the rushing waters of a spring stream. She told them about arriving in the valley and losing her family. She told them about searching the surrounding mountains. She told them about building her shelter and gathering fuel. She told them about killing her ox, about hearing the wolves. She told them about eating raw meat and cornmeal. But

mostly she told them about living alone through the long, dark winter months.

As she spoke, the braves looked from Janette to her shelter. Then they looked to the wagon, and back at Janette again. She couldn't seem to stop talking. They must understand — they must!

Slowly, the Indian who appeared to be their leader nodded his head. "Brave," he said, pointing to her makeshift camp. "Very brave."

Janette drew a deep breath. Maybe he had understood her words. Maybe he had just seen for himself what she had gone through. Anyway, he had understood! She brushed away tears as the Indian slid off his pony.

"Come," he commanded. He held out a hand to help her from the wagon. "We will go to your people."

"People," Janette whispered. This time she didn't try to stop the flow of tears.

In that spring, more than a hundred years ago, the Indians took Janette Riker across the mountains to the settlement that is now Walla Walla, Washington. There she stayed for quite a time. She questioned all the travelers who stopped by on their way west. But no one ever found any sign of her father and brothers.

Janette later married another pioneer and lived to a very old age. Her daughters and granddaughters, and even their daughters, never tired of telling the story of how she survived the winter of 1849 — alone.

READING COMPREHENSION

Summarizing. Choose the best phrase to complete each sentence. Then write the complete statement on your paper.

1. Janette was left alone because her father and brothers _____ (went to Oregon, hunted for food, sold the oxen in town).

2. By building a shelter, killing one ox for food, and protecting herself from wild animals, Janette was able to _____ (survive the long winter alone, find her family, settle in Walla Walla.

3. The Indians who found Janette in the spring thought she was _____ (not worth listening to, very brave, afraid of strangers).

Interpreting. Write the answer to each question on your paper.

1. What things did Janette have to take care of to survive?

2. What caused the wild animals to leave her alone?

3. How did Janette know what to do with the ox meat?

4. How did Janette keep busy during her first months alone?

5. How was Janette very brave during the winter of 1849?

For Thinking and Discussing. If Janette were left alone by her family today rather than over a hundred years ago, would her experiences have been different?

UNDERSTANDING LITERATURE

Biography and Third Person Point of View. "Janette's Winter" is a *biography.* A biography is a true story about a person's life written by another person. It is usually written from the *third person point of view.* The author uses the words *he, she,* and *they* to talk about the people in the story. In the third person point of view the author is not a character in the story. Read these two examples:

First person point of view: "At the foot of the mountains I shouted, but only my voice echoed back . . ."

Third person point of view: "At the foot of the mountains she shouted, but only her voice echoed back . . ."

Rewrite the following passage so that it is the third person. Then find the passage in "Jeanette's Winter." Underline any words that are different in the passage you have written.

All night I crouched like that. I listened for the return of my family. But I heard only the howling of wolves and the wailing of the night winds. When the sun first showed above the jagged mountains, I jumped from the wagon.

WRITING

Imagine you are a newspaper reporter. Write a one-paragraph article about Janette's experiences. Write in the third person. Your article should answer these questions about what happened: *Who? What? When? Where? Why? How?*

Peculiarsome Abe

by Carl Sandburg

A poor, plainspoken farm boy like Abe Lincoln was the last person you'd expect to find hunched over a book — or so his friends and family thought. They didn't know quite what to make of Abe's fixation with learning. They would have been shocked to know that he would one day be President of the United States.

The farm boys in their evenings at Jones's store in Gentryville talked about how Abe Lincoln was always reading, digging into books, stretching out flat on his stomach in front of the fireplace, studying till midnight and past midnight, picking a piece of charcoal to write on the fire shovel, shaving off what he wrote, and then writing more — till midnight and past midnight. The next thing Abe would be reading books between the plow handles, it seemed to them. And once, trying to speak a last word, Dennis Hanks said, "There's suthin' peculiarsome about Abe."

He wanted to learn, to know, to live, to reach out; he wanted to satisfy hungers and thirsts he couldn't tell about, this big boy of the backwoods. And some of what he wanted so much, so deep down, seemed to be in the books. Maybe in books he would find the answers to dark questions pushing around in the pools of his thoughts and the drifts of his mind.

He told Dennis and other people, "The things I want to know are in books; my best friend is the man who'll git me a book I ain't read." And sometimes friends answered, "Well, books ain't as plenty as wildcats in these parts o' Indianny."

This was one thing meant by Dennis when he said there was "suthin' peculiarsome" about Abe. It seemed that Abe made the books tell him more than they told other people. All the other farm boys had gone to school and read *The Kentucky Preceptor,* but Abe picked out questions from it, such as, "Who has the most right to complain, the Indian or the Negro?" and Abe would talk about it, up one way and down the other, while they were in the cornfield pulling fodder for the winter. When Abe got hold of a storybook and read about a boat that came near a magnetic rock, and how the magnets in the rock pulled all the nails out of the boat so it went to pieces and the people in the boat found themselves floundering in

71

water, Abe thought it was funny and told it to other people. After Abe read poetry, especially Bobby Burns's poems, Abe began writing rhymes himself. When Abe sat with a girl, with their bare feet in the creek water, and she spoke of the moon rising, he explained to her it was the earth moving and not the moon — the moon only seemed to rise.

John Hanks, who worked in the fields barefooted with Abe, grubbing stumps, plowing, mowing, said: "When Abe and I

stop and read." He liked to explain to other people what he was getting from books; explaining an idea to someone else made it clearer to him.

The habit was growing on him of reading out loud; words came more real if picked from the silent page of the book and pronounced on the tongue; new balances and values of words stood out if spoken aloud. When writing letters for his father or the neighbors, he read the words out loud as they got written. Before writing a letter he asked questions such as: "What do you want to say in the letter? How do you want to say it? Are you sure that's the best way to say it? Or do you think we can fix up a better way to say it?"

As he studied his books his lower lip stuck out; Josiah Crawford noticed it was a habit and joked Abe about the "stuck-out lip." This habit too stayed with him.

He wrote in his sum book, or arithmetic, that compound division was "when several numbers of Divers Denominations are given to be divided by 1 common divisor," and worked on the exercise in multiplication: "If 1 foot contains 12 inches I demand how many there are in 126 feet." Thus the schoolboy.

What he got in the schools didn't satisfy him. He went to three different schools in Indiana, besides two in Kentucky — all together about four months of school. He learned his A B C, how to spell, read, write. And he had been with the other barefoot boys in butternut jeans learning "manners" under the schoolteacher Andrew Crawford, who had them open a door, walk in, and say, "Howdy

came back to the house from work, he used to go to the cupboard, snatch a piece of corn bread, sit down, take a book, cock his legs up high as his head, and read. Whenever Abe had a chance in the field while at work, or at the house, he would

do?" Yet what he tasted of books in school was only a beginning, only made him hungry and thirsty, shook him with a wanting and a wanting of more and more of what was hidden between the covers of books.

He kept on saying, "The things I want to know are in books; my best friend is the man who'll git me a book I ain't read." He said that to Pitcher, the lawyer over at Rockport, nearly 20 miles away, one fall afternoon, when he walked from Pigeon Creek to Rockport and borrowed a book from Pitcher. Then when fodder-pulling time came a few days later, he shucked corn from early daylight till sundown along with his father and Dennis Hanks and John Hanks, but after supper he read the book till midnight, and at noon he hardly knew the taste of his corn bread because he had the book in front of him. It was a hundred little things like these which made Dennis Hanks say there was "suthin' peculiarsome" about Abe.

READING COMPREHENSION

Summarizing. Choose the best phrase to complete each sentence. Then write the complete statement on your paper.

1. Some people thought Abe was peculiar because of his _____ (love of books, love of farming, strange ways of eating).

2. Abe _____ (hated books, wanted to read more books, dreamed of becoming a writer) because he had a lot of questions in his mind.

3. In order to find answers to his questions, Abe would _____ (walk miles for a book, plow his neighbors' field, write letters to boat builders).

Interpreting. Write an answer to each question on your paper.

1. Why wasn't Abe satisfied with what he learned in school?

2. Why did Abe write with charcoal on the fire shovel?

3. What did Dennis Hanks mean when he said, "There's sunthin' peculiarsome about Abe"?

4. How did Abe show he wanted to share what he learned with others?

For Thinking and Discussing. Abe Lincoln had little education in school, yet he became President of the United States. Do you think that someone with the same education as Abe could become President today? Why or why not?

UNDERSTANDING LITERATURE

Identifying Point of View. The story "Peculiarsome Abe" is told from two different points of view. The author, Carl Sandburg makes statements from a third person point of view. Abe and the people who knew him makes statements from a first person point of view.

On your paper, write whose point of view is given in each statement below: Carl Sandburg's, Abe's, or John Hank's.

1. "He wanted to learn, to know, to live, to reach out; he wanted to satisfy hungers and thirsts he couldn't tell about, this big boy of the backwoods."

2. "When Abe and I came back to the house from work, he used to go to the cupboard, snatch a piece of corn bread, sit down, take a book . . . and read."

3. "Maybe in books he would find the answers to dark questions pushing around in the pools of his thoughts and the drifts of his mind."

4. "The things I want to know are in books; my best friend is the man who'll get me a book I ain't read."

WRITING

Imagine that you are Abe Lincoln. As you walk home from school, you come across two schoolmates talking about the full moon rising, and you join in. Write the conversation. Quote what you say and what your friends say.

The Poets' Portrait Gallery

Here are three poems, each about a famous person who was an independent thinker. The poets have used words, not paint or a camera, to create these portraits.

Harriet Tubman was famous for her daring rescues of slaves in the 1800s. Anton Van Leeuwenhoek lived in the 1700s and was famous for inventing the microscope. Louise Nevelson is an American artist who creates unusual sculptures. Any encyclopedia can tell you these facts and more. As you read the poems below, you will discover things about these famous people that only a poet could show you.

Harriet Tubman

by Eloise Greenfield

Harriet Tubman didn't take no stuff
Wasn't scared of nothing neither
Didn't come in this world to be no slave
And wasn't going to stay one either

"Farewell!" she sang to her friends one
night
She was mighty sad to leave 'em
But she ran away that dark, hot night
Ran looking for her freedom

She ran to the woods and she ran
through the
          woods
With the slave catchers right behind her
And she kept on going till she got to the
          North
Where those mean men couldn't find her

Nineteen times she went back South
To get three hundred others
She ran for her freedom nineteen times
To save Black sisters and brothers

Harriet Tubman didn't take no stuff
Wasn't scared of nothing neither
Didn't come in this world to be no slave
And didn't stay one either

          And didn't stay one either

The Microscope

by Maxine Kumin

Anton Leeuwenhoek was Dutch.
He sold pincushions, cloth, and such.
The waiting townsfolk fumed and fussed
As Anton's dry goods gathered dust.

He worked instead of tending store,
At grinding special lenses for
A microscope. Some of the things
He looked at were:

                mosquitoes' wings,
the hairs of sheep, the legs of lice,
the skin of people, dogs, and mice;
ox eyes, spiders' spinning gear,
fishes' scales, a little smear
of his own blood,

                and best of all
the unknown, busy, very small
bugs that swim and bump and hop
inside a simple water drop.

Impossible! Most Dutchmen said.
This Anton's crazy in the head,
We ought to ship him off to Spain.
He says he's seen a housefly's brain.
He says the water that we drink
Is full of bugs. He's mad, we think!

They called him dumkopf which means
dope.

Louise Nevelson

by M. B. Goffstein

Louise Nevelson
took a shipbuilder's name,
and the things she makes
are seaworthy.
The wooden refuse
of New York City's streets,
of the sea,
lumberyard scraps,
and lathe-turned products
are gathered up by her
and taken home
and painted black as tar.

Louise Nevelson
wears beautiful clothes:
an early American quilt
made into a skirt,
a denim shirt,
and an emperor's robe
for work or sleeping.
Box upon box
she stacks into walls —
not only black,
but white or gold,
or clear or steel!

Years or days later,
or right away,
with a practical hand
and eye,
they're placed
inside black boxes.
The quiet talk
among the black forms
in each black box
is never-ending.
They are radio receivers
of silence.

Why are the black boxes
whispering?
Of what do the white boxes
sing?
And the golden boxes
proclaim what?
Freedom, equality,
wastefulness, beauty.
Something American!
Louise Berliawsky
sailed to America,
and created American art.

READING COMPREHENSION

Summarizing. Choose the best phrase to complete each sentence. Then write the complete statement on your paper.

1. In "Harriet Tubman," Harriet ran away to the North in order to _____ (be free, find her relatives, get a job).

2. In "The Microscope," instead of taking care of his dry goods store, Anton Van Leeuwenhoek spent his time _____ (catching insects, grinding lenses, cleaning fish).

3. In "Louise Nevelson" Louise has become _____ (a great shipbuilder, an American artist, a Russian author).

Interpreting. Write the answer to each question on your paper.

1. In "Harriet Tubman," how often did Harriet run for freedom? Why did she keep going back?

2. Harriet Tubman, Louise Nevelson, and Anton Van Leeuwenhoek each did something special for people. How did each one contribute to the world?

3. How were the lives of Harriet, Anton, and Louise unusual?

For Thinking and Discussing. The poets in this section use words to paint a picture. How are the poems the same as and different from paintings? Which tells you more about a person?

UNDERSTANDING LITERATURE

Poetry. You have probably noticed that poems look and sound different from other forms of writing. Poets write their words into lines instead of sentences. They group these lines into *stanzas* instead of paragraphs. For example, the poem "The Microscope" contains four stanzas. The first stanza has four lines. The second stanza has twelve lines (or fourteen, if you count "mosquito's wings" and "and best of all" as separate lines). Answer the following questions about stanzas. Look back to the poems to help you.

1. How many lines are in the first stanza of "Harriet Tubman"?

2. What stanza from "Louise Nevelson" describes her clothes?

Many poems rhyme. Two words *rhyme* when they end with the same sound. Two lines rhyme when they end with rhyming words. The pattern of a poem's rhyme is called the *rhyme scheme*. Look back to "The Microscope." Notice the rhyming words that end each line. Every two lines rhyme.

3. Look at the poem "Harriet Tubman." Which lines rhyme? Write a sentence to describe the rhyme scheme.

WRITING

All the poems in this section describe people. Write a two-stanza poem about yourself or a person you know well. Your poem does not need a rhyme scheme but the words should be carefully chosen.

VOCABULARY

Expressions. An *expression* or *idiom* is a word or group of words with special meaning. For example: When the carpenter realized he could not finish building the house by the end of the week, he decided to *throw in the towel*. The expression *throw in the towel* means "to give up."

The quotations below are from the selections you have just read. Choose the correct meaning of each italicized expression. Write the answer on your paper.

1. "Then I stopped, *planted both feet*, and jumped straight up, bringing my knees up to my chin." (put both feet into the soil, put both feet firmly on the ground)

2. "I had a lot of energy, but I wasn't *smooth* like Sporty." (graceful, without lumps)

3. "I think his record was six feet nine inches. To Sporty and me, that was *out of this world*." (wonderful, from another planet)

4. "Then at last she tried to *shake off* her grief." (forget her grief, dance away her grief)

5. "Abe Lincoln was always reading, *digging into books.* . . ." (very involved in reading books, using books as shovels)

6. "Yet what he *tasted of books* in school was only a beginning. . . ." (ate of books, sampled of books)

READING

Main Idea and Detail. The main idea of a paragraph tells what the paragraph is about. The main idea may be at the beginning, the middle, or at the end of a paragraph. Read the following paragraph from "You Are Somebody Special."

"Somehow, when I watched Sporty jump, *I though I could be a jumper*. I had proved I could jump well in basketball by getting a lot of rebounds. I knew I had coordination, because I was one of the top athletes in my gym class."

The main idea of the above paragraph is in italics. The main idea is that Bill thought he could be a jumper. He supports or explains his main idea when he says, *I could jump well in basketball* and *I knew I had coordination*.

Read the following paragraphs from the stories in this section. Write the main idea of each paragraph. Then list one or two details that support the main idea.

1. "That day was a great day for me. I had learned to talk to myself. I had learned to reason with myself and to believe in myself. As long as I could think good things about myself, I could achieve."

2. "Often during that long, cruel winter, Janette sat inside and thought of her family. She remembered the gentle sound of her father's voice. She pictured Tom's face with its broad smile. She thought of Billy's deep laugh. More and more, she dreamed of the happy times they had spent together back home in Illinois. How she longed for the familiar white farmhouse with the blue flowers growing by the door. And how she wished that the people she loved had stayed safe inside its wall!"

3. "The farm boys in their evenings at Jones's store in Gentryville talked about how Abe Lincoln was always reading, digging into books, stretching out flat on his stomach in front of the fireplace, studying till midnight and past midnight, picking a piece of charcoal to write on the fire shovel, shaving off what he wrote, and then writing more—till midnight and past midnight. The next thing Abe would be reading books between the plow handles, it seemed to them."

QUIZ

The following is a quiz for Section 2. Write the answers in complete sentences on your paper.

Reading Comprehension

1. Why did Bill Cosby from "You Are Somebody Special" make the junior varsity football team even though he did not weigh 135 pounds?

2. How did Janette from "Janette's Winter" decide what to do when she found herself alone?

3. Why did Abe from "Peculiarsome Abe" like to explain his ideas to other people?

4. In the poem "Harriet Tubman," Harriet returned to the South many times. How many people did Harriet save from slavery in those trips?

5. In the poem "The Microscope," Why did people think Anton Leeuwenhoek was mad?

Understanding Literature

6. All the selections in this section are biographies. How is "You Are Somebody Special" different from the other biographies in this part of the book?

7. How do you think the author of "Janette's Winter" found out about Janette Riker's life? Why did she write about Janette from a third person point of view?

8. What important fact about Abe Lin-

coln as a child is emphasized in "Pe-culiarsome Abe"?

9. In the poem, "Harriet Tubman," the lines "Harriet Tubman didn't take no stuff/ Wasn't scared of nothing neither/ Didn't come in this world to be no slave/ And wasn't going to stay one either," are found at the beginning of the poem and at the end. Why did the author repeat these lines?

10. From what point of view is the poem "Louise Nevelson" written? Why did the poet choose that point of view?

WRITING

A First Person Account. In a first person account, an author uses the words *I* and *me* when telling of events that take place. The author may be a main character or a minor character in the story.

You are going to write a first person account in which you are the main character. Read each step to help guide you in writing.

Step 1: Set Your Goal

Choose one of the following topics for a first person account.

☐ Choose an exciting event in your own life that you would like to write about.

☐ Imagine that you are Janette Riker. Write about the time you heard the wild animals outside your hut.

☐ Imagine that you are Abraham Lincoln. Write about the time you walked twenty miles to borrow a book.

Step 2: Make a Plan

Make a list of the actions that took place and how you felt about them.

For example, imagine that Bill Cosby is planning his account of football practice. He might list his actions and feelings this way:

☐ I ran with my eyes closed. I felt afraid.

☐ I fell down. I felt as though walls had fallen on me.

☐ I hit the heel of someone's shoe. I felt pain in my front teeth.

☐ I walked back to the huddle. I wondered if I really wanted to play football.

Now list your actions and your feelings in the topic you chose.

Step 3: Write the First Draft

Your first person account should be four or five paragraphs. The first should state where you were and what you were doing. The next two or three should be your actions and feelings. The last paragraph should tell what happened at the end and your ideas.

1. Begin by stating where you were and what you were doing. For example,

Bill Cosby starts his account of football this way:

"I went on to high school, where I went out for football."

2. Next write two or three paragraphs using your list of actions and feelings.

3. End your account by telling what happened at the end and your idea about it. Bill Cosby ends his football story this way:

"I had scored a touchdown. Not even the guys on the first team had done that."

Step 4. Revise

Check your account one more time. Have you told an interesting story? Make sure that readers can tell what happened and how you felt about it. Have you written in the first person, using *I* and *me*? Correct mistakes in spelling, grammar, and punctuation. Make a final neat copy.

ACTIVITIES

Word Attack. When the letter *ch* come together in a word, sometimes they stand for the sound you hear at the beginning of the word *chopped*: She *chopped* more logs.

When a *t* comes before the *ch*, the letters always have the sound you hear in the word *catchers*:

With the slave *catchers* right behind her, she escaped to the North.

At other times when the letters *ch* come together in a word, they stand for the sound you hear at the beginning of *school*: It was after school.

If you are not sure which sound *ch* sounds for, try saying the word both ways. See which sounds like a word you know.

Pronounce the word with a *ch* in each sentence below. Then copy them on your paper. Write *chopped,* or *school* next to each to show which *ch* sound it has.

1. He lay on his stomach in front of the fireplace.
2. He was picking up a piece of charcoal for writing.
3. She had felled only two birch saplings.
4. He approached the bar.
5. I had scored a touchdown.
6. Only her own voice echoed back.
7. Then she snatched the rifle.
8. All night she crouched.
9. She called and searched for her father and brothers.
10. The coach put me on the fifteenth team.

Speaking and Listening. Carl Sandburg was famous for his work as a poet as well as for his writing about Abraham Lincoln. Practice reading the first paragraph of "Peculiarsome Abe" out loud. Notice that his paragraph has many long sentences. Use the punctuation marks in the paragraph to help you in your reading.

Pause when you come to a comma or a dash. Pause even longer when you come to a period. As you read, listen to the flow of the words. Does it remind you of reading a poem? Why or why not?

Researching. Susan B. Anthony, Jackie Robinson, Walt Disney, Pablo Picasso, Louis Pasteur, and Sally Ride are just a few of the people who have made a special contribution to our world. Choose one of these people.

Find out what special contribution the person has made by using a biographical dictionary.

A *biographical dictionary* gives information about famous people. The people are usually listed in alphabetical order by their last names. For example, if you wanted information about Louis Pasteur, you would look for the letter *P*. He would be listed as *Pasteur, Louis.*

Biographical dictionaries cannot list every famous person. If the person you choose is not in the first biographical dictionary you look at, try another biographical dictionary or an encyclopedia.

Use the facts you find out to write a paragraph explaining who the person was and why he or she was special.

Creating. Write a biographical page about yourself. Include the information listed here in your page.

An American Biography of: _____

☐ Date and place you were born:

☐ Where you have lived:

☐ Where you attended school and the dates of your attendence:

☐ What school activities and subjects you enjoyed:

☐ What out-of-school activities do you enjoy:

☐ Something you did that pleased you:

☐ Your favorite book:

☐ Your favorite song:

☐ Your favorite movie:

☐ Your favorite cartoon character:

☐ Two people you admire or respect and why:

CLYDE ROBERT BULLA

*Experience is forever
sowing the seed of one thing
after another.*

—Manilius

Introduction

An Autobiography, by Clyde Robert Bulla

I was born on January 9, 1914, near the little town of King City, Missouri. My brother, two sisters, and I all went to school in a one-room schoolhouse in the country, not far from the farm where we lived.

A Farm Boy Becomes a Writer

I always liked words and putting them together. It seemed natural to me that I should want to be a writer. It didn't seem natural to anyone else in my family or in the community where I lived. A farm boy was supposed to be a farmer.

Still, I began writing when I was very young. *A Grain of Wheat* (p.92) is an autobiographical essay about my beginnings as a writer. All through school I wrote and sent my stories out to magazines, but I was 20 before the first one was published. After that, more of my stories were sold to magazines, but not many more. I was not making a living. I left the farm and went to work on a weekly newspaper in my hometown.

After years of setting type, helping the printer, keeping books, and collecting bills, I was given some writing to do on the newspaper. It was a weekly column called "People & Places," which meant that I could write about almost anything that interested me.

A Writer Finds His Readers

A woman in another state saw some of the columns. She was an elementary-school teacher, and she wrote children's stories for Sunday-school magazines. She suggested that I try writing for young people.

All my writing had been for adults. I wasn't at all sure I could write for boys and girls, but I tried. I wrote a book, *The*

Donkey Cart, which was published in 1946. Later I tried again, this time with a book called *Riding the Pony Express.* By this time I was sure I liked writing for young people. I wanted to keep on.

I moved to Los Angeles, California, and continued to write books for boys and girls. More than 60 have been published.

Between books, I began to travel — first in the United States, Mexico, and Canada, then to places farther away. I have been to most of the countries of Europe, to some of the Pacific Islands, Australia, and Eastern Asia. One of my favorite ways to travel is by freight boat, especially boats that stop in strange and out-of-the-way ports.

The novel *Take Care of Dexter* (p.97) is also based on my own life, when I was a boy on the farm. The crippled horse lived near me, and I saw him often, but it was many years before I thought of writing about him. Sometimes a writer has to look back on a story to see it clearly.

A Grain of Wheat
A Writer Begins

by Clyde Robert Bulla

In this brief story from his childhood, the author tells of his longing to become a writer. He shows how a lasting belief in himself helped his dream grow into a reality.

There was always work to be done on a farm. Boys and girls had their special chores. My first ones were filling the woodbox and feeding the animals.

The woodpile was in the barn lot. There were big pieces of wood to be burned in the heating stove. Smaller pieces were for the cook stove.

Sometimes I carried the wood in my arms. Sometimes I hauled it in a little wagon or the two-wheeled cart. I brought it to the back door and piled it in the woodbox in the kitchen.

I took corn to the pigs and chickens. I fed skim milk to the calves.

In summer I hoed weeds out of the vegetable garden and sometimes out of the cornfield.

But there was time to play, time for long walks in the woods. I looked for rocks along the creek. I knew where to find May apples. They grew on plants that looked like little green umbrellas. The apples were yellow and squashy. They smelled better than they tasted. Ripe gooseberries were good. (Not green ones; they were so sour I could never eat one without making a face.) Wild blackberries were even better. Wild raspberries were best of all.

Always my dog was with me in the woods, until one day. He wasn't waiting when I went out in the morning. He wasn't there when I came back.

Days and weeks went by. I looked for him. I called him. Every evening I went out to the front gate and called, "Here, Carlo — Here, Carlo!" He didn't come home.

School started. I was in the third grade. Wayne King was in the fifth. He came up to me in the schoolyard. "I know what happened to your dog," he said.

"What?" I asked.

"He's dead," said Wayne. He was looking at me, as if he wanted to see how I was taking it.

"He's not dead," I said.

"Yes, he is," said Wayne. "He got poisoned."

I went home. "Wayne says Carlo is dead," I said.

My father and mother looked at each other.

My mother said, "Yes, he is dead. We didn't want to tell you." Dogs had been killing George Hayne's sheep, she said. He had put out poison for the dogs, and Carlo had eaten some of it.

"George was sorry," my mother said. "He knew how much you liked Carlo."

"Carlo didn't run with other dogs," I said. "Carlo didn't kill his sheep."

"George never thought he did," said my mother. "Carlo just happened to be at his place and ate some of the poison."

She was looking at me, a little the way Wayne had. She must have thought I was going to cry.

I didn't cry. But I missed Carlo. Sometimes I still miss him.

As I grew older, I began to see that my mother and father were not happy. It was partly because we were poor, but there were other reasons.

My mother had been a town girl. She had gone through high school. That was more education than most people had in those days. She had never wanted to live on a farm. She thought she belonged in town or in a city.

She wanted to do her work in the morning, then put on a pretty dress, sit on the porch, and watch the people go by.

Our house was far back off the road, behind a row of hedge trees. She wanted the trees cut so she could see the road. My father and brother cut the hedge, but it didn't seem to help. Not many people went by.

My father had more education than my mother. He had gone to college to study science and engineering. He wanted to be the first man to fly. In his father's barn he had started to build an airplane.

His father always laughed at him. "Nobody ever made a plane that would fly,"

he said. "What makes you think *you* can?"

My Grandfather Bulla had two farms. My father went to work on one of them. That was where he took my mother when they were married.

"We won't stay here long," he said. "This is just till I get into something else."

Years later they were still there.

The Wright brothers were about my father's age. They made an airplane that would fly.

My father was never the same after he heard about it.

It seemed he and my mother had taken a wrong turn. That turn had led them to the farm. Neither of them wanted to be there, but somehow they couldn't get away. I hoped this would never happen to me.

I wanted to be a writer. I was sure of that.

"I'm going to write books," I said.

My mother said, "Castles in the air."

"What does that mean?" I asked.

"It means you're having daydreams," she said. "You'll dream of doing a lot of different things, but you probably won't do any of them. As you get older, you'll change."

I went from the second grade to the third to the fourth, and I hadn't changed. I still knew what I wanted to be.

I thought about writing and talked about it. I talked too much.

My father told me he was tired of listening to me.

"You can't be a writer," he said. "What do you know about people? What do you know about the world? Where have you ever been? What have you ever done? You don't have anything to write about."

When I thought over what he had said, it seemed to me he was right. I stopped writing. But not for long.

The nearest city was St. Joseph, Missouri. Our newspaper came from there. In the paper I read about a contest for boys and girls — "Write 'The Story of a Grain of Wheat' in 500 words or less." First prize was $100. There were five second prizes of $20 each. After that there were 100 prizes of $1 each.

I began to write my story. It started something like this: "I am a grain of wheat. I grew in a field where the sun shone and the rain fell."

I didn't tell anyone what I was doing. When my story was finished, I made a

neat copy. I mailed it in our mailbox down the road.

Time went by. I began to look for the paper that would tell who had won the contest. At last it came.

There was a whole page about the contest. I saw I hadn't won the first prize. I hadn't won a second prize either. That was a disappointment. I had thought I might win one of the second prizes.

I read down the long list at the bottom of the page — the names and addresses of the boys and girls who had won the $1 prizes. Surely my name would be there. It *had* to be!

I read more and more slowly. Only a few names were left.

And one of them was mine! "Clyde Bulla, King City, Missouri."

"I won!" I shouted.

My mother looked at my name. "That's nice," she said.

Nice? Was that all she could say?

I started to show the paper to my father. There was something in his face that stopped me. I could see he wasn't happy that I had won a prize.

My sister Corrine was there. I could see she wasn't happy either. She was sorry for me because all I had won was a dollar.

Didn't they know it wasn't the dollar that mattered?

I had written a story that was all mine. No one had helped me. I had sent it off. How many other boys and girls had sent their stories? Maybe a thousand or more. But my story had won a prize, and my name was here in the paper. I was a writer. No matter what anyone else might say, I was a writer.

READING COMPREHENSION

Summarizing. Choose the best phrase to complete each sentence. Then write the complete statement on your paper.

1. There was always work to be done on the farm, but there was also time for _____ (long walks in the woods, feeding pigs, carrying pieces of wood).

2. The author found out that his parents were not happy because _____ (there was too much work, they did not follow their dreams, the Wright brothers invented the airplane).

3. When the author won $1 for his story, his family _____ (shared his joy at becoming a writer, thought he should have won more, let him work on a newspaper).

Interpreting. Write the answer to each question on your paper.

1. How did the author feel when he found out that his dog, Carlo, was dead?

2. When he realized that his parents were unhappy, what conclusion did the author reach about himself?

3. Why was the dollar prize important to the author?

For Thinking and Discussing. Why do you think his family did not help Clyde Robert Bulla to become a writer? Do you think life as a writer is harder than life as a farmer? Why or why not?

UNDERSTANDING LITERATURE

Autobiography and Inferring Feelings. "A Grain of Wheat" is an example of autobiography. In it, the author tells the story of his own life. An autobiography usually describes two kinds of things: (1) important events from the author's life; (2) the author's feelings about these events. Although Clyde does not always say exactly how he feels, his writing makes it easy for a reader to guess or *infer* his feelings.

Write the following events in the correct order. Then for each event, describe Clyde's feelings using the words below.

lonely excited sad disappointed

angry proud hopeful

1. Wayne King tells Clyde about Carlo.

2. Clyde wins a dollar for his story.

3. Clyde stops writing when his father tells him to.

4. Clyde mails his story.

5. Clyde realizes that his parents are not happy.

WRITING

Clyde Bulla pretended he was a grain of wheat in his story. Pretend you are a postcard. Your postcard tells about important events in your own life. Tell where you are. Tell where you lived, who bought you, where you were sent, and what your trip was like. Tell about your feelings.

"Take Care of Dexter,"
Part One

by Clyde Robert Bulla

This is the story of a boy named Dave, who meets a mysterious new neighbor from a nearby farm — someone with an unusual talent, an exciting past, and a special pony called Dexter.

In all his life, Dave Weber had never had new neighbors. But now there were rumors that new people would be moving into the old, run-down Temple place down the road.

Everyone at school was talking about the new people. They knew that the family's name was Arvin and that there was a 15-year-old boy named Alex. His parents' names were Yetty and Paul. There was an uncle named Jon. They had two cows, a team of horses, three pigs, and the boy had a pony.

As the days went by, Dave saw the people working. They worked hard, but they didn't seem to know much about farming. They were putting a fence around the land when they should have been plowing and planting. Wayne Ogle, who was Dave's age and lived near the Temple place, told everyone that the new people were not friendly.

One Sunday afternoon, Dave walked past the Arvins'. Suddenly, he heard the pounding of hooves. Over the hill came Alex Arvin on his pony. The pony's mane and tail were flying. Alex was leaning forward in the saddle like a trick rider. They came up so suddenly that Dave had to jump to get out of the way. He fell backward into the ditch.

Alex had stopped and was riding back. Dave felt foolish, but Alex was not laughing.

"Are you all right?" he asked.

"I think so," said Dave.

"You're bleeding," said Alex.

Dave looked at his hand. "I must have scratched it."

"We'd better take care of it. Come on up to the house." Alex jumped down. He led the pony and walked beside Dave.

"I guess you know I'm Alex Arvin."

"I'm Dave Weber," said Dave.

"And this is Dexter." Alex patted the pony's neck. The pony was dancing along as if he would rather run than walk. Once he put his head down and took a nip at Alex's arm.

"He bit you!" said Dave.

Alex laughed. "He was pretending. He likes to pretend he's a wild horse."

Dave looked at Dexter. "I never saw a horse like him before," he said.

"He's part Indian pony," said Alex. "We've been together a long time now. My father and I went to this place where the horses were, and Dexter and I chose each other."

"How do you mean?" asked Dave.

"I went straight to him, and he came straight to me. People said his legs were too short and he was too thick through the chest. It didn't matter to me. Dexter was my horse, and that was all I cared about. I talk to him all the time, and he listens."

They went up to the house. Alex's mother was in the doorway.

"This is Dave," said Alex. "He hurt his hand."

"It isn't anything," said Dave, but she led him inside and washed his hand.

"It's not a deep scratch," she said. "We don't need to wrap it up."

A moment later, two men came in. The younger man said, "I'm Paul Arvin, Alex's father," and he shook Dave's hand. The other man made a little bow. There was something mocking about it.

"Sit down, everyone," said Mrs. Arvin. "It's teatime."

They sat on the floor at a low table. The table was a board with bricks for legs. In the middle was a jar with yellow weed-flowers in it.

Mrs. Arvin brought tea, milk, and cakes. The cakes had an odd taste, but Dave liked them. They were made with spices that he had never tasted before. Mrs. Arvin kept passing them to him, but he ate only two. Then he said he had to go.

"I'll give you a ride," said Alex.

"Oh, I can walk," said Dave.

"Dexter needs exercise," said Alex.

Dave saw that Alex wanted to ride him home. "All right," he said.

As they all got up, Alex's uncle asked Dave, "What brought you here?"

Dave didn't understand.

"No other neighbor has set foot in this house since we've been here," said Alex's uncle. "They've come to the fence to ask questions, but they've never been to the house. What brought you here?"

Alex spoke. "I asked him."

"I see," said his uncle. He looked down at Dave, and again made his mocking little bow.

The next day, Dave went to visit Alex again. Mrs. Arvin came to the door. "I don't know where Alex is," she said. "He may be in the barn."

Dave went to the barn. As he stepped inside, the rain began to pour, but the barn felt dry. There was hay in the loft. He could see bunches of it hanging through the square opening over his head. The cows and horses were in the stalls. Dexter was in a stall on the side. The pony watched him, rolling his eyes a little.

Dave laughed at him. "Wild horse!" he said.

"Hello!" he called. The sound of the rain drowned out his voice.

A ladder led to the loft. He climbed it. He stopped with his head through the opening, not quite believing what he saw. Three trapezes hung in a row from the roof. On the first one stood Alex — Alex in black tights with silver spangles! He was standing with one knee bent and one arm out.

Suddenly, he dropped off the trapeze and caught the next one. He swung to the third trapeze and caught it.

For a minute he seemed to be flying back and forth across the barn. Again he stood up on the first trapeze. He leaped for the next one. He saw Dave's face below. He lost his hold and fell.

Dave came up the ladder. "Alex!" he said. "Are you hurt?"

Alex was lying on the hay. He didn't look at Dave. "No," he said. "It didn't hurt me."

"Did I make you fall?" asked Dave.

Alex got up and disappeared behind a pile of hay. When he came out, he had on a shirt and overalls.

Dave said, "What you were doing up there — that was good!"

Alex climbed down the ladder. Dave followed him to the stall where Dexter was. The pony snorted.

"Is he afraid of me?" asked Dave.

"No," said Alex. He took a brush and began to brush the pony.

Dave wanted to ask about the trapezes, but there was something in Alex's face that stopped him. Alex looked almost

angry as he brushed at Dexter's coat.

Finally, Alex spoke. "I don't care myself," he told Dave. "There's nothing wrong with being in the circus. But my Uncle Jon thinks it is best to keep it secret."

"The circus!" said Dave. "You were in the circus?"

Alex gave him a long look. "You mean you didn't guess?"

Dave shook his head.

you why we came here?"

"Not if you don't want to."

"I want to. I think we're going to be friends, and if we're friends then we have to trust each other." They were all circus people, Alex said — he and his mother and father and Uncle Jon. Even Dexter was a circus horse. "My father and Uncle Jon had a trapeze act, and they were teaching me. My mother rode horses in the ring, but she never liked the circus much.

"About two years ago Uncle Jon fell off a high trapeze. The net caught him, but he wasn't the same after that. He had dizzy spells. My father didn't feel safe working with him anymore.

"Last summer we were on our way from Texas to Chicago. We were driving our own truck and seeing the country. We came past this place. My mother saw the house, and said it was what she'd wanted all her life. We talked about coming here and being farmers. It was just in fun at first. Then my mother said she really meant it. My father wanted to make her happy. Uncle Jon said he'd always wanted to be a farmer."

"What about you?" asked Dave.

"I like the circus," said Alex, "but I thought I might like the country, too. We put in all the money we had. So did Uncle Jon. When we moved in, we wanted to be like everybody else here. We were afraid the neighbors would think we were odd if they knew we were circus people, so we didn't tell anybody. It wouldn't have mattered anyway. They think we were crazy to buy this place. They laugh at the way we run the farm."

"Where did you think I learned the trapezes?" asked Alex. "Where did you think I got the tights I was wearing?"

"I didn't think about that," said Dave.

"You would have thought about it after a while," said Alex. "And the people you tell — they'd think about it."

"I won't tell anyone," said Dave. "Not if you don't want me to."

They were quiet for a while.

Alex asked, "Do you want me to tell

"You've done a lot of work here," said Dave.

"Yes, but we don't seem to grow anything." Alex picked up a handful of hay. "We had to buy this. It's mostly for Dexter. Uncle Jon said the pony could eat grass, but Dexter likes hay, too, and he's used to it."

"Besides, it makes a good landing place under the trapezes," said Dave.

"Yes, it does. Do you want to try them?" asked Alex.

"I couldn't even get up there," said Dave, as the two climbed back up to the loft.

"It's easy. See? I nailed pieces of wood up the wall. You can climb them like a ladder. Then you reach out and catch the first trapeze. Try it."

Dave tried it. He caught the trapeze. His hands slipped and he fell.

"That wasn't bad. You made a good fall," said Alex. "Maybe we can work up an act together — after you've practiced a few weeks."

"A few years, you mean." But Dave was excited, thinking how it might be — him and Alex on trapezes, with a thousand faces looking up from below.

When Dave went home, he found a place to practice. It was in a cherry tree behind the house. Some of the branches grew out straight from the trunk. He practiced swinging on them.

The next Sunday he went to the Arvins'. Alex met him at the gate.

"I've been practicing," said Dave.

"Practicing?" said Alex.

"You know — for our great circus act." Dave made a joke of it, but Alex

didn't smile. They went to the barn. Silently, Alex led the way up.

Dave looked into the loft. The trapezes were gone.

"What — ?" he began.

"Uncle Jon did it," said Alex. "I came out yesterday, and he was sawing away with his knife."

"Why?" asked Dave.

"He said I spent too much time out here. He said we should all work harder. Then we'd be better farmers, and everyone wouldn't be laughing at us."

Alex's face was bitter. "If he didn't want me to have the trapezes, why didn't he say so? I'd have taken them down. He didn't have to . . . well, it's done, and that's the end of it. Come on. Let's get out of here."

They went outside.

"After Uncle Jon cut the ropes, I went to the woods," said Alex. "I stayed all day, and I found something. I'll show you."

They walked across the pasture and into the woods. The trees grew close together. Only a little sunlight came through. They came to the creek. The water was dark and deep. They walked across on a fallen tree.

"There's what I found," said Alex, "between those two pine trees."

It was the four walls of an old log cabin almost covered by a mat of vines. "There's a door somewhere," said Alex.

"We could make a roof easily," said Dave. "We could lay poles across the top and cover them with sod."

"Maybe I'll put in a floor, too," said Alex, "and put up a sign that says, 'Alex's

Hideaway.' Maybe I'll live here and be a hermit."

Dave laughed, but he had a feeling that Alex was half serious.

Autumn came and then winter, and Dave saw Alex less and less. One day, when they met at Alex's gate, Alex said, "Things are getting worse."

"What things?" asked Dave.

"Things at home. It's Uncle Jon. He's been saying we're all against him. Now he says we have to go."

"Go where?" asked Dave.

"He doesn't care, as long as we're out of his way."

"He couldn't make you go," said Dave. "It's three against one."

"He says the farm is in his name. He can put us out anytime he wants to."

"Do you think he can?" asked Dave.

"Maybe. I don't know. My father says he won't go. He says he's put too much time and money into this place to walk out and leave it."

"Your uncle couldn't farm it by himself," said Dave.

"He doesn't think about that." The wind blew into Alex's face and he shivered. "Well — sometimes there's nothing you can do but wait."

One morning, after a bad storm, there were footsteps on Dave's porch. His father went to the door. Neighbors, Mr. Ogle and his son Wayne, were outside.

They clumped into the kitchen in their rubber boots. Their eyes were bright and their faces were red. They began to talk at once in loud voices.

"Slow down," said Dave's father. "I can't hear what you're saying."

"I said, I couldn't call you on the phone," said Mr. Ogle. "The phone line's not working. The wind blew down a pole. Boy, it was quite a night."

"It was a bad storm," said Mr. Ogle. "You don't know the things that happened last night."

"Jon Arvin —" began Wayne.

His father gave him a shake. "You just keep quiet. I'm telling this."

He told his story slowly, as if he enjoyed it and wanted to make it last.

Yesterday afternoon, he said, the sheriff and his son had come out to the Arvins'. They were on horseback, as the roads were too muddy for a car. Mr Ogle went over to see what was happening. He found out that Jon Arvin wanted to put the rest of the Arvins off the place. Jon had seen a lawyer, and the lawyer had gone to the sheriff. Jon was waiting in town till the sheriff had put the others off the farm.

But Paul Arvin wouldn't go. He had locked himself in the house with his wife and his son. It got dark, and the storm got worse. The sheriff and his son took their horses to the barn and put them in the stall with Dexter.

The sheriff hadn't brought a flashlight, so Mr. Ogle went home and got one. The sheriff flashed the light on the house and said, "I didn't come here to make trouble, but if you don't come out, there will be trouble."

No one answered. The sheriff and his son fired their guns over the roof.

"Open the door," said the sheriff, "unless you want me to shoot the lock. If I do that, somebody might get hurt."

Paul Arvin called out, "Don't shoot anymore. I have my wife and son here." He opened the door. "Here I am," he said. "Come and arrest me."

The sheriff said, "I don't want trouble. I'm just supposed to see that you get off this farm."

"Now?" asked Paul Arvin. "In the middle of the night?"

"It wasn't the middle of the night when I first told you to come out," said the sheriff. Still, he seemed to feel sorry for them.

He asked Mr. Ogle if he would hitch up a team of horses and take the Arvins to town. "I'll see that they find a place to stay," the sheriff said, "and you'll be paid for your trouble."

Mr. Ogle brought over a team and wagon. The Arvins were waiting. "I'll ride Dexter," said Alex.

They went to the barn. They flashed the light into the box stall, and saw the terrible thing that had happened. Crowded together in the dark, the sheriff's horses and Dexter had fought. Dexter was lying on the floor of the stall. He was lying very still, with his head twisted to one side.

"Keep the boy away," said the sheriff. "Don't let him see."

Alex was already in the stall. He was holding Dexter's head. "Get a doctor," he said. "We've got to get a doctor."

His father ran his hands over Dexter's chest and neck. "It's too late," he said. "Can't you see?"

He dragged Alex away.

The flashlight flickered and burned out. The sheriff tried to tell the Arvins he was sorry. Paul Arvin wouldn't talk to him. Mrs. Arvin was crying. Alex was saying, "I won't go!" But when the others got into the wagon, he got in too.

Mr. Ogle drove them to town. The sheriff found them a place to stay, but they wouldn't take it.

"Where did they go?" Dave asked. "Where are they?"

"They went to the railroad station," said Mr. Ogle. "They left on the next train. The boy wanted me to tell you something. He said, 'Tell Dave to take care of Dexter.'"

READING COMPREHENSION

Summarizing. Choose the best phrase to complete each sentence. Then write the complete statement on your paper.

1. The first time Dave saw Dexter, Alex Arvin was riding the horse so fast that Dave had to _____ (jump to get out of the way, run to keep up, lean forward in the saddle).

2. When Dave saw Alex swinging on trapezes, Alex explained that his family, including Dexter, were _____ (experienced farmers, not friendly, circus performers).

3. When Alex and his parents had to leave the farm, Alex wanted Dave to _____ (take care of Dexter, keep his trapezes, join their circus).

Interpreting. Write the answer to each question on your paper.

1. Why didn't the Arvins tell their new neighbors about the circus?

2. Why did the sheriff make the Arvins leave their own farm?

3. What happened to Dexter when the sheriff was at the farm?

For Thinking and Discussing. Why were the Arvins not well liked in their new neighborhood? Do you think it's right to dislike people who do things differently? Give reasons for your answer.

UNDERSTANDING LITERATURE

Realistic Fiction. When an author writes *fiction* he or she makes up the people and the events in a story. They are not real people or real events. In some fiction, the made-up characters and events remind us of people and things in real life. This kind of fiction is called *realistic fiction*.

"Take Care of Dexter" is realistic fiction. The author made up the events and characters in this story. But he based many characters and events on real people he knew and real experiences he had. For example, Wayne Ogle is like Wayne King, a neighbor in "A Grain of Wheat."

Write the events from the list below that could happen in real life.

1. Dave decides to bury Dexter.

2. Dexter turns out to be a talking horse.

3. A magician waves his magic wand, and Dexter jumps to his feet.

4. Dexter turns out to be badly wounded.

5. The neighbors feel so sorry that they buy Alex a new pony.

WRITING

Make up an adventure for a dog, a cat, or another animal of your choice. Think of events that could happen in real life. Write a paragraph about the adventure. Then, for fun, write another paragraph in which the animal has adventures that could not really happen.

"Take Care of Dexter,"
Part Two

Read on to find out what Dave does for his friend Alex, and for Dexter — how he makes the hard decision to go against his parents and other grown-ups, to do what he feels is right.

When Mr. Ogle and Wayne were gone, Dave put on his boots.

"Where are you going?" asked his mother.

"To take care of Dexter," he said.

"But the pony is —" She stopped. "Didn't you hear what Mr. Ogle said?"

"I heard him," said Dave. "Alex wanted me to bury his pony."

"How do you know?" asked his father.

"He asked me to take care of Dexter," said Dave. "What else could he have meant?"

"I'll go with you," his father said. "You'll need help."

They took two shovels out of the woodshed. They walked to the Arvin place. The gate was wired shut.

"There's someone here," said Dave.

Jon Arvin stood in the doorway of the house. He came out, walking slowly. Once he stumbled and almost fell. A little way from the gate he stopped and looked at them. His face was gray.

"Ah, the young man, and his father," he said. "You want to see me?"

"There's something my boy and I wanted to take care of," said Mr. Weber.

"All has been taken care of," said Jon Arvin. "I have no need of you now." He shouted, "Get out!" and began to cough.

Dave and his father drew back. His father said, as they turned toward home, "Jon Arvin is a sick man."

Two days later, Jon Arvin's lawyer went to the house with papers to be signed. No one answered his knock. The lawyer found Jon Arvin lying on the floor. He had had a stroke. He could no longer talk or recognize anybody. He was brought to a hospital.

The lawyer had the horses and cows hauled away and nailed up a "Keep Out" sign on the gate.

One day soon after this, Wayne Ogle stopped by to see Dave. He came into the barnyard, where Dave was pumping water for the cows.

"Did you ever hear from your friend?" he asked.

"What friend?" asked Dave.

"You know. Alex Arvin."

"No," said Dave.

"It's been a week. I guess you're not going to hear."

Dave waited for him to go, but Wayne sat down on the edge of the water tank.

"I know something I'm not supposed to tell," said Wayne.

"Then don't tell," said Dave.

"I'll just tell you," said Wayne. "Who do you think was at the Arvin place yesterday?"

"The lawyer," said Dave.

"Somebody else. You'd never guess who. It was Mary."

"Mary Haines?"

"Yes, Mary Haines. She was hunting mushrooms — she and her cousin. They came running out of the timber like scared rabbits. Mary tore her dress getting over the fence."

"What were they running for?"

"They were close to that old cabin and they thought they saw a ghost or something," said Wayne. "Mary said it looked like a bear, and her cousin thought it was a man. I was across the road when they came out of the timber. They didn't want me to tell. They weren't supposed to be there, you know."

"What do you think it was they saw?" asked Dave.

"I don't think they saw anything," Wayne answered. "Maybe they heard some little sound and they both ran. Mary always was scared of her shadow."

It wasn't true, Dave thought afterward. Mary wasn't scared of her shadow. In all the years they had gone to school together, he couldn't remember anything she had been scared of.

She saw something in the timber, he told himself. Mary saw something . . . .

That night Dave dreamed about Alex. Alex was talking. Dave tried to hear, but

there was a wind that blew the words away. He woke up. The dream seemed real. For a few moments, he thought Alex was in the room. He lay there thinking. What if Alex had come back? Once he had told Dave that he would live in the cabin and be a hermit.

When it was daylight, Dave put on his clothes and went outside. The air was cool. The morning was still.

He cut across the fields to the cabin. Weeds and brush had been cleared from the doorway. Poles had been cut and laid across the top. Alex had done the work! Dave knew it had been Alex. He went into the cabin.

But it was an empty shell. Now he recalled what Alex had said the last time they talked together — that he had worked on the cabin and cleared away some of the brush a long time ago. Dave began to feel foolish. Why had he thought Alex would be here? Why would Alex come back? What was there to bring him back?

Dave sat down on the leaves that covered the cabin floor. The sun was up. He knew he should be getting home, but he felt tired, and the leaves were like a bed. He leaned back. His eyes closed. Then, suddenly, he sat up. He heard slow and heavy footsteps.

Through the doorway he saw the bushes moving. They parted and a face looked out. It looked toward the cabin and disappeared. Dave got to his feet and went outside. He could still hear the footsteps. He began to run, following them. He fought his way through the bushes until he could see the moving figure ahead.

"Dexter!" he shouted. "Dexter!"

The horse stopped and looked back. Then he went plunging on, his hind legs dragging stiffly.

Dave ran home. He said, "I saw Dexter! He's alive!"

His mother and father were at the breakfast table. "Tell us what this is about," said his father.

"I went to the old cabin. I had a feeling Alex would be there. But it was Dexter. He was all scratched and crippled. He tried to run away from me. I was afraid he might hurt himself, so I didn't go too close —"

His mother said, "I don't see how it could have happened."

"I see how it might have happened," said his father. "Everybody thought the pony was dead, but no one made sure."

"And after everyone was gone, Dexter dragged himself into the woods," said Dave. "That's how it happened."

Dave and his father went to look for Dexter. They found him by the creek. "It looks like his hind legs are badly hurt," said his father.

"Can that be fixed?" asked Dave.

Mr. Weber shook his head. "It surprises me that the pony could get out of the barn and into the woods. It surprises me that he can walk at all."

"He was always strong," said Dave, "and his legs aren't broken. I think he's going to get better."

"No," said his father. "I don't think so. And if he was mine, I wouldn't want him to go on living that way."

"He doesn't belong to us," said Dave. "He belongs to Alex."

His father shrugged sadly.

The next day there was a letter from Alex:

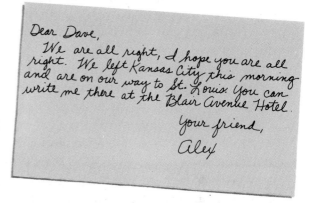

Dear Dave,
We are all right, I hope you are all right. We left Kansas City this morning and are on our way to St. Louis. You can write me there at the Blair Avenue Hotel.
Your friend,
Alex

Dave tried to call Alex on the phone. A woman at the hotel told him, "There's no one here named Arvin."

"He must not be there yet," said Dave's mother. "Why don't you write him a letter?"

Dave wrote to Alex:

Dear Alex,
It will be hard for you to believe this, but Dexter is alive. He was badly hurt, but he can now walk. Your Uncle Jon had a stroke and is in the hospital, so no one is left on the farm. I will look after Dexter until you come back. Let me know when you are coming. You can stay with me.
Your friend,
Dave

But a week later, Dave's letter came back. Beside Alex's name someone had written, "Not here."

"What shall I do now?" Dave asked.

"Wait for him to write again," his mother said.

A month went by, with no letter from

Alex. Dave went to the Arvin place every day. He made a feed box near the cabin. Sometimes he left salt in the box, or a few ears of corn. Almost always, when he went back, the salt had been licked up or the corn was gone.

Sometimes Dave found Dexter in the deepest, darkest part of the woods. He would talk to the pony as he knew Alex did. "Your mane and your tail are full of burrs. Why don't you let me comb them out? You don't trust me, do you?"

Whenever he tried to go near Dexter, the pony shied away. He could not run well but he moved quickly.

"Somebody should shoot that old horse," said Wayne one day.

"You'd better not say that again," said Dave.

"Don't jump on me. I'm not the only one who says it."

"Who else says it?"

"My father, for one. And if you want to know the truth," said Wayne, "your father says it, too."

"I don't believe it," said Dave.

"Go ask him."

"I will."

Dave went home and told his father what Wayne had said. "Did you say it?" he asked.

"All the neighbors have been talking about that pony," said father. "No one thinks it's right for him to continue suffering."

"But he's getting better. He can move faster than he could at first."

"He'll always be crippled."

"Does that mean he can't go on living?"

"He's all alone," said his father. "Nobody wants him. How long can he go on taking care of himself?"

"I'll take care of him," said Dave. "I'll bring him over here."

"You'll not bring him over here. I wouldn't have such an animal on my farm." His father sounded angry. "It's no kindness to the horse to let him go on like this. Can't you see that?"

"He's Alex's horse," said Dave. "We haven't any right to decide what to do with him."

"Alex is gone, and we may never see him again," said his father. "Somebody else may have to decide."

Summer ended and school began. One November morning, Wayne Ogle caught up with Dave on the way to school. Wayne looked excited.

"I know something I'm not supposed to tell," he said.

Dave kept walking.

"Don't you want to know what it is?" asked Wayne.

"No," said Dave.

"I wasn't going to tell you anyway," said Wayne. But in the schoolyard, while they were waiting for the bell to ring, Wayne said, "You won't be seeing that old pony anymore."

"What?!" Dave said.

"I said, you won't be seeing that old pony anymore."

"Dexter? You mean Dexter? What are you talking about?"

Wayne laughed. "You're not going to find out any more from me."

The bell rang. Wayne started toward the schoolhouse. Dave caught him by the

110

arm. "What about Dexter? Why won't I see him anymore?"

"That's for me to know and you to find out."

"*Tell* me!" Dave gave him a shove, and Wayne fell.

"Let me go." Wayne tried to get up. "The bell's ringing."

Dave sat on him, holding him down. "What about Dexter?"

"My father's going to shoot him, that's what."

"You're lying," said Dave.

"I'm not."

"You *are* lying!"

"No, I'm not. There was a meeting last night, and the men said — they said the pony couldn't live through the winter, and the thing to do was to shoot him — and my father is going to do it."

"When?" asked Dave.

"Now. This morning."

Dave jumped up. He began to run. Wayne shouted after him. "You'd better come back here. Didn't you hear the bell?"

Dave was already out of the schoolyard. He was running down the road toward the Arvins' woods.

He climbed over the fence. He tried to think where Dexter might be. In the oak grove? By the creek? If he could drive him deeper into the woods, where Mr. Ogle couldn't find him . . . .

He came to the creek. Wayne's father was there in a red hunting jacket. He had a rifle in his hands. On the other side of the creek was Dexter, his head up, his eyes watching.

"Don't!" cried Dave.

Mr. Ogle almost dropped his rifle. "What are *you* doing here?"

"Don't do it!" said Dave. "You *can't* do it!"

"Don't tell me what I can't do." Mr. Ogle lifted the rifle. Dexter was still watching. He seemed to be waiting. Mr. Ogle took aim. He stopped and rubbed his eyes. He said to Dave, "Go somewhere else. Go on — get out!"

He aimed again. He took a step forward, almost as if he wanted to frighten the pony away. But Dexter stood quietly. Mr. Ogle was shaking. He said, "Why does he keep looking at me? I can't do it when he looks at me — when you both look at me!"

He put the rifle over his shoulder and went stamping away. Dave heard his steps in the dry leaves. Then the woods were still. Dave felt weak. There was a blur in front of his eyes. When he could see again, he looked across the creek. Dexter was gone.

Afterward Dave heard his father and mother talking. "He said he could do it," his father said. "He wasn't as brave as he thought he was."

"It looks as if no one is going to be so brave," said his mother.

Dave's father shook his head. "That old horse won't get through the winter."

Before the start of cold weather, Dave went to the woods and built a shed against the cabin. He made it of poles and covered the roof with dry grass so the pony would have shelter. Dave took corn to the woods, and when the creek froze he chopped holes in the ice so Dexter could have water.

One day in January, Dave found Dexter standing in a hollow near the creek. The pony's feet were trapped in the mud.

With a lot of hard work, Dave dug him out and freed him. But Dexter was never quite the same after that. He was more shy than ever. He moved more slowly.

Night after night, Dave thought of Dexter alone in the woods. He thought of what his father had said — "That old horse won't get through the winter."

But on the first warm day of spring, Dexter came hobbling out into the pasture. He was so thin that every rib showed. His eyes were tired. And Dave saw that the pony had grown old.

Spring passed, and most of the summer. One afternoon, while Dave was trimming the hedge along the road, a car came by. A young man jumped out. The car went on.

The young man was tall and brown. He wore a hat that shaded his face. "Dave?" he said.

"Yes." Dave put down his ax.

"You don't know me." The young man came closer.

Dave stood still. "Alex!" he said.

They shook hands.

"Are you all right?" asked Alex.

"Yes," said Dave. "Are you?"

"Yes." Alex began rather quickly. "I've been all over since I saw you last. We went back to the circus. Then we had a chance to work on this ranch in Texas, and that's where we are now. I didn't know if you'd remember me."

"I remember you," said Dave.

"You didn't answer my letter," said Alex, "but I know how it is. You get busy with things —"

"I answered it," said Dave.

"You did?"

"My letter came back. It's funny, I still remember the name of that hotel in St. Louis. The Blair Avenue Hotel."

"We were there," said Alex. "But maybe when your letter came, we hadn't gotten there yet. It took us a while to get from Kansas City to St. Louis."

"In that letter I wrote to you about your Uncle Jon —"

"I know about him," said Alex.

"You do?"

"Yes. We thought we never wanted to see him again. But then my father said we shouldn't blame him too much, because he was sick. He wrote to him last week. The letter went to his lawyer, and the lawyer wrote to us. My father and I came up. He's at the hospital now. I hitchhiked out here, and my father is going to pick me up. But don't let me keep you from your work. I'll just wait around —"

"Do you know about — about Dexter?" asked Dave.

"If you don't mind," said Alex, "I'd rather not talk about it."

"All right. I just wanted to know if you'd seen him."

"*Seen* him?"

"Dexter is alive," said Dave.

Alex turned pale.

Dave told him what had happened.

Alex asked, almost in a whisper, "Where is he?"

"On your old place," said Dave. "Do you want to go over there?"

They walked to the Arvin place and into the woods. They passed the cabin with the shed on one side of it.

"You made that for him, didn't you?" asked Alex. "And that feed box."

They went on.

"Are you sure he's here?" asked Alex.

"I saw him two days ago," said Dave, and he began to feel afraid.

They came to the far side of the woods. Alex had been walking ahead. He stopped. There among the trees was Dexter. He started away, his hind legs dragging through the grass. He looked back at them through the matted hair that hung over his eyes.

"He knows me," said Alex. "Dexter —"

He began to cry.

In the morning, Alex and his father were back in a pickup truck. Hitched to the truck was a horse trailer.

Dave rode with them to the old Arvin place. They found the pony where he had been the day before.

Alex had brought a halter. He slipped it over Dexter's head.

"Come on," he said. "I'm taking you home. You and I are going to Texas. Now what do you think of that?" And Dexter let himself be led through the woods and across the pasture.

Dave opened the gate. The three of them half lifted, half pushed the pony into the trailer.

Alex's father said to Dave, "Get in. We'll take you back to your house."

"No, thank you," said Dave. "It's hard to turn around with the trailer. I'll walk."

"Good-bye," said Alex. "I'll see you."

"I'll see you," said Dave.

The truck and the trailer drove out of sight.

Dave looked down the empty road. Alex was gone again. Now Dexter was gone, too. Yet they would never really be gone, because of the way he remembered them.

Alex on the trapezes.

Alex racing along on the pony.

Dexter coming out of the woods in the spring.

Now he could imagine a new picture: Dexter in a green pasture with a barn nearby, and the house where Alex lived. Alex talking to the pony, and the pony listening.

READING COMPREHENSION

Summarizing. Choose the best phrase to complete each sentence. Then write the complete statement on your paper.

1. Dave and his father _____ (took care of Dexter, could not bury Dexter, closed up the farm) because Jon Arvin told them to get out.

2. When Dave learned that Mary Haines had heard something in the woods, he went there and found _____ (Alex came back, Jon Arvin's ghost, a scratched and crippled Dexter).

3. After Dave helped the pony get through the winter, Alex _____ (returned and took Dexter with him to Texas, had to shoot Dexter, never saw Dexter again).

Interpreting. Write the answer to each question on your paper.

1. What did taking care of Dexter mean to Alex and to his father?

2. Why did Mr. Ogle want to shoot Dexter, and why didn't he do it?

3. How did Dave help Dexter get through the winter?

For Thinking and Discussing. Why do you think Dave took care of Dexter even though everyone else said the pony wouldn't make it through the winter? Do you think Dave did the right thing, or would it have been better to let Mr. Ogle end the animal's life? Give reasons.

UNDERSTANDING LITERATURE

Theme. The *theme* of a story is the author's message. One important theme in "Take Care of Dexter," Part Two is, "friends should be loyal."

On your paper, list the actions below that support the theme of friendship and loyalty.

1. Dave and his father go to bury Dexter.

2. Jon Arvin tells the Webers to get off his farm.

3. Wayne tells Dave that Dave's father thinks Dexter should be shot.

4. Alex sends Dave a letter.

5. Dave sits on Wayne and holds him to the ground.

6. Mr. Ogle tries to shoot Dexter.

7. Dave leaves salt and corn for Dexter.

8. Alex hitchhikes to Dave's house to see him.

9. Dave's father does not allow Dave to take care of Dexter on their farm.

10. Wayne Ogle tells Dave he probably won't hear from Alex.

WRITING

Suppose your best friend moved away. Write a letter to him or her describing what your life is like. What would you do to remain a loyal friend? Describe it in your letter.

VOCABULARY

Multiple Meanings of Words. Some words have more than one meaning. The way a word is used in a sentence helps you know what the meaning is. For example, in the sentence "Jon Arvin took a *gander* at Dave out of the corner of his eye," the word *gander* can mean "goose" or "look." It is impossible for Jon to take a goose out of the corner of his eye. By reading the whole sentence, you can tell that "goose" is not the meaning of the italicized word. *Gander* is used here to mean "look."

Find the meaning of each italicized word below as it is used in the sentence. Write the word and the definition on your paper. Then choose a different definition for the same word. Write a sentence using that word to show the meaning you selected.

1. He had worked in the cabin and cleared away some *brush*. (small plants and trees, quick touch, tool with bristles)

2. He *slipped* it over Dexter's head. (put on quickly, fall down, move quickly)

3. Mr. Ogle brought over a *team* and wagon. (group of animals, gang of people, group in football)

4. I went *straight* to him, and he came straight to me. (honest, correct, move in a line)

5. Sometimes a writer has to look *back* on a story to see it clearly. (body part, into the past, position in football)

6. David had a *row* with his father. (line, move by the use of oars, quarrel)

7. David would not be able to *face* Alex if anything happened to Dexter. (outward appearance, meet bravely, the front part of the head)

8. The sheriff was keeping to the *letter* of the law when he forced the Arvins to leave the farm. (a written message, exact terms, a mark standing for sounds)

READING

Fact and Opinion. It is important to be able to tell the difference between fact and opinion. A *fact* is something that is true. A fact can be proven or can be seen. For example:

A carton that has a dozen eggs has twelve eggs in it. This is a fact. You can count the eggs to prove that the carton has twelve.

The lightning struck the tree in the front yard and split it in half. This is a fact. You can see lightning striking a tree, and you can see the damage the lightning caused.

An *opinion* is a statement that a person makes about his or her ideas, beliefs, or feelings. Opinions cannot be proved true or false. For example:

Scrambled eggs taste better than poached eggs.

Friday is the best day of the week.

Although you may not agree with someone else's opinion, you cannot prove it to be true or false.

The following statements are from the stories in this section. On your paper, write whether each is a fact or an opinion.

1. "A farm boy was supposed to be a farmer."

2. "There was always work to be done on a farm."

3. "You'll dream of doing a lot of different things, but you probably won't do any of them."

4. "My story had won a prize, and my name was here in the paper."

5. "His parents' names were Yetty and Paul."

6. "He likes to pretend he's a wild horse."

7. ". . . the neighbors would think we were odd if they knew we were circus people. . . ."

8. "Jon Arvin is a sick man."

9. "Mary always was scared of her shadow."

10. "That old horse won't get through the winter."

QUIZ

The following is a quiz for Section 3. Write the answers in complete sentences on your paper.

Reading Comprehension

1. In "A Grain of Wheat," why did the author want to be a writer?

2. In "A Grain of Wheat," what was Clyde's father's dream?

3. In "Take Care of Dexter," Part One, why did Alex's father and Uncle Jon break up their trapeze act?

4. In "Take Care of Dexter," Part One, why could Jon Arvin tell Alex and his family to leave the farm?

5. In "Take Care of Dexter," Part Two, why did Dave think Alex might have come back to live in the cabin in the woods?

Understanding Literature

6. Is "A Grain of Wheat" realistic fiction or autobiography? Explain your answer.

7. Why do you think Clyde Robert Bulla chose the title "A Grain of Wheat" for his autobiography?

8. Why is the story "Take Care of Dexter" realistic fiction?

9. One theme in the story "Take Care of Dexter" is, "friends should be loyal." Another theme in this story

is, "if you know you are right, follow your beliefs, even if those around you don't agree." List two events from "Take Care of Dexter" that show this second theme.

10. Although "A Grain of Wheat" is an autobiography and "Take Care of Dexter" is realistic fiction, they are similar, or alike. Write at least one sentence describing how these two selections are similar. Then write at least one sentence describing how they are different.

WRITING

An Opinion. An opinion is a person's belief or feeling about something. When people give you reasons for an opinion, you can understand their feelings better. They might even convince you to share their opinion.

You are going to write an opinion. You will give reasons for your opinion, and try to convince readers to share it. Read each step to help guide you in your writing.

Step 1: Set Your Goal

Choose one of the statements below to write about. Remember, you are expressing your opinion. You may agree or disagree with the statement.

☐ It is a kindness to shoot a horse like Dexter since he will always be crippled.

☐ You shouldn't try to live your dream because you will only be disappointed if it does not come true.

Step 2: Make A Plan

Plan what you are going to say. In order to convince your readers, you must support your opinions with facts and examples.

Think back to "Take Care of Dexter," Part One. Wayne Ogle says that the Arvins are not friendly people. He expresses his opinion without explaining why he feels that way. Wayne might have used the following examples to show why he had this opinion:

The Arvins are building a fence around their property.
They never invite me in.
They won't say anything about their past lives.

Now make a list of facts and examples that support your opinion about your topic.

Step 3: Write the First Draft

Your opinion should have three paragraphs. The first should state your opinion. The second should have your supporting facts and examples. The third should state your opinion and tell your reader what might be done about it.

☐ Begin by stating your opinion. For example, Wayne Ogle might have started this way:

I do not think the Arvins are friendly people.

☐ Next write a paragraph using your lists of facts and examples.

☐ End by reminding readers of your opinion and suggesting what might be done about it. Wayne Ogle might have said:

The Arvins have shown their unfriendliness by these actions. For these reasons, I think we should not try to visit the Arvins.

Step 4: Revise Your Opinion

Check your opinion one more time. Make sure you have supported your opinion with reasons. Correct any errors in spelling, grammar, and punctuation. Make a final neat copy of your letter.

ACTIVITIES

Word Attack. When the letter *y* comes at the beginning of a word, it usually stands for the sound you hear at the beginning of *young*:

I began writing when I was very *young*.

When *y* comes at the end or in the middle of a word, sometimes it stands for a vowel sound:

Dexter was *lying* on the floor.
Alex picked up a handful of *hay*.
It was a *weekly* column.

Pronounce the words in the sentence below that contain a *y* . Then copy them on your paper and write *young, lying, hay* or *weekly* according to the sound *y* makes in each.

1. Suddenly, he heard the pounding of hooves.

2. His parents' names were Yetty and Paul.

3. After years of setting type I was given some writing.

4. Dave looked down the empty road.

5. One day Wayne Ogle stopped by to see Dave.

6. I always liked words and putting them together.

Speaking and Listening. Look back to the ending of "A Grain of Wheat." Begin with the paragraph that starts, "There was a whole page about the contest." Go on to the very end of the selection. Practice reading the paragraph aloud yourself, or take turns reading it with a classmate. Read as if you were an actor playing the part of Clyde. Use punctuation marks, word clues, and what you know about Clyde to read each sentence with expression that shows Clyde's feelings.

Researching

1. Clyde Bulla grew up in farm country. He could easily write a description of a grain of wheat simply by looking out into a field. Wheat is one of the most important crops a farm can grow. We use wheat in many foods.

   Use an encyclopedia to find out more about wheat. Remember, an encyclopedia has articles about many topics. The topics are in alphabetical order.

   Use the facts you find out in the encyclopedia to write a paragraph explaining why wheat is such an important crop. Write about what climate and soil are best for growing wheat, and which insects are bad to the crop.

2. Make a "Visitor's Guide" for your town or city and state. Use encyclopedias to help you find information about your state. Your own experience of your town or city will give you a lot of information.

Creating. Imagine that ten years went by after the ending in "Take Care of Dexter." Choose either Dave or Alex and write a letter to your friend about your life. Include a drawing to show something that has changed.

Visitor's Guide

☐ Name of city or town and state

☐ Capital of state

☐ Population of state

☐ Chief products of the state

☐ State bird

☐ State flower

☐ State song

☐ State motto

☐ Drawing of state flag, if you wish

☐ Places to visit in your city or town including:

parks

historic sites

forests

notable buildings

schools

monuments

memorials

bodies of water

List where they are and what a visitor can see.

☐ Plants, trees, animals of your area

☐ Climate; temperature and weather during the year

☐ Major business in your area

☐ Special festivals celebrated in your city or town

☐ A personal reason or reasons why your city or town is special

SOMETHING OF VALUE

All human things
Of dearest value hang
on slender strings.

—Edmund Waller

Introduction

"**T**rue Value," "Save, Big Value." You see these signs in store windows, or you hear these words on the radio. Are things that are said to be "big value" really valuable, or important to you? What really is important, or of value to you? Could it be that things that are of value to one person are different from things of value for someone else?

Here is what some 11-year-olds said about what is of value to them:

"My radio, I don't let anyone touch it. I listen to it every day."

"My mother's car. Otherwise I'd have to be walking everywhere."

"My best friend. We have fun together eating ice cream."

"Having a good pillow fight with my sister."

"My friend's computer, because I learn from it."

You can see that things of value can be objects, or people, or even ideas of something that can't be put into words. Some things of value you can buy to use. Other times value is something that comes from inside a person.

The selections in this section will give you more ideas about what really is most important to you, and whether value is inside or outside a person.

In the story "The Vision of Lucila Godoy," Lucila sees something outside the window that her classmates don't see. They aren't blind, or are they? Find out how seeing with the heart can be a different value from seeing with the eyes.

In "The Wrestling Match," Salue would do anything to get a magic gris-gris to help him win the match against Jakate. Will Salue still value a gris-gris at the end of the match?

In "Precious Jade," Jade has valuable words to solve her sister-in-laws' problems. What is so special about Jade's words, and what will happen when she finds real jade in her stone wall? Read to find out whether Jade, or jade is the real value.

Three poems describe things that have such important value yet money cannot buy them at all. In "Flint" you find out that a flint is so hard it can be used to make fire. In "Birdfoot's Grampa," something important makes Grampa stop his car again and again. Read "Aunt Sue's Stories" to see why her stories are different and special.

The Vision of Lucila Godoy

by Walter Dean Myers

You may have heard the saying "Beauty is in the eye of the beholder," but have you ever seen the beauty in something that everyone else thinks is ugly? Read the story to find out how Lucila sees things differently than her friends — and what they learn from her.

CHARACTERS

Jimmy	Karen
Mrs. Liebow	Larry
Susan	Lucila
Narrator	

Scene One

Narrator: It's Monday afternoon. Mrs. Liebow has just given her students an art assignment.

Jimmy: So, first we're supposed to look at something. Then we draw something else that has the same *mood* as the thing we looked at. Right?

Mrs. Liebow: That's right.

Jimmy *(frowning):* I still don't get it.

Susan: Neither do I.

Mrs. Liebow: All right, I'll try again. *(She walks across the room.)* Would everyone please come over here and look out this window? *(They do.)* Now tell me what you see.

Karen: I see a crummy red apartment house across the street.

Larry: I see a lot of dirty old papers. And there's a broken baby carriage. It sure is ugly.

Jimmy: Man, the whole street is ugly — with a capital *U*.

Mrs. Liebow: What does all that ugliness remind you of, Jimmy?

Jimmy: A big garbage dump. *(He pauses.)* Hey, I get the assignment now! If this street reminds me of a dump, then I should draw a dump. Right?

Mrs. Liebow *(smiling):* Right! Susan, what will you draw?

Susan: A desert scene, because the whole block is so . . . so deserted. It makes me feel empty, too.

Mrs. Liebow: That's good. That feeling of emptiness is the mood you should try to give your desert.

Lucila *(quietly):* I see a warm, friendly building. It looks as if it's holding its people very close to its heart.

Karen *(staring out the window):* What building are *you* looking at?

Lucila: The same red apartment house you saw. There are beautiful curtains at the windows. They seem to be waving.

Jimmy: Waving at what?

Lucila: Us! So are the papers that are blowing around in the street.

Susan: Those torn old curtains and dirty papers are waving at us? Lucila, you must be out of your mind!

Lucila: I just say what I see.

Larry: Well, if you keep seeing stuff like that, some guys are going to come looking for you — with a straitjacket!

Scene Two

Narrator: It's later that day. All the students are standing in front of the red apartment house.

Jimmy *(putting his hand on a brick):* Ladies and gentlemen, may I call your attention to Exhibit A?

Larry: Exhibit A?

Karen: He means the brick.

Jimmy: Quiet in the jury box! '

Susan: Jury? Who's on trial?

Lucila: I am — I think.

Jimmy: You think right, Lucila. Now ladies and gentlemen, please notice that Exhibit A is faded. Notice that it is dirty. Notice the other dirty bricks.

Karen: All right, all right! We've noticed!

Jimmy: Now look closely at Exhibit B. It is a window. Notice that it is filthy. Also, it is cracked.

Lucila: So are you!

Jimmy: We will now examine Exhibit C, the papers in the street. Notice that they are *dis*gusting, *dis*tasteful, and . . . *dis*integrating before your very eyes!

Lucila: I object! Those papers don't look so bad.

Jimmy: Objection overruled! Ladies and gentlemen, I rest my case. Does the defendant wish to present hers?

Lucila: Yes. I've lived on this block all my life, and I've never thought it was ugly.

Jimmy: A very poor defense, I'm sorry to say. Case dismissed!

Lucila: Then I think . . . I think I'll go home. (*She walks slowly away.*)

Susan: Weren't you a bit rough on her, Jimmy?

Jimmy: No way, José! We had to knock her out of that dream world.

Karen: But I was just beginning to *like* her dreams — even if they *are* weird.

Scene Three

Narrator: It is now the next afternoon, and everyone is assembled in Mrs. Liebow's class.

Lucila: Mrs. Liebow, can we talk about what we saw yesterday?

Mrs. Liebow: Of course, Lucila, if you really want to.

Lucila: I do, but first I'd like to ask Jimmy a question.

Jimmy: Go ahead. But remember, I tell it like it *is*. If you want to dream, dream on your own. I deal in reality.

Lucila: Fine. What does your grandmother look like?

Jimmy: You saw the painting I did of her.

Lucila: Yes, and it's a very beautiful painting. She seems to be a very warm person.

Jimmy: She is. I told you, I deal in reality.

Lucila: Well, if you tell it like it *is*, why doesn't your painting look anything like your grandmother?

Jimmy: Hey, what are you talking about?

Lucila: I'll tell you. Go get Exhibit D from the back closet.

Jimmy (*confused*): Exhibit D?

Larry: The picture of your grandmother, you turkey.

Narrator: Jimmy gets the picture, then holds it up for the class to see.

Jimmy: Everybody here has seen my grandmother. This is exactly how she looks. Right?

Karen: Well, that's her nose, and her eyes, but . . .

Jimmy: But *what*?

Karen: I think you have to know her to *see* her like that, Jimmy.

Larry: I know what you mean, Karen. I think the picture shows what she's like to Jimmy. That she's someone very special and very beautiful.

Jimmy: She is beautiful.

Susan: But someone who didn't really know her might just see an ordinary old woman.

Lucila: That's right.

Jimmy: And when you look at these old buildings and the papers all over the street, you see *that* as beautiful?

Lucila (*shrugging*): I guess so. I see the buildings that are my neighborhood, and

the great people in them, like your grandmother.

Jimmy: Okay, okay. I guess you do make sense, after all. But how did you think of my grandmother?

Lucila: I didn't. My uncle did. He's visiting us. When I got home yesterday afternoon, I told him how bad I felt about my trial. Then he asked if you had ever painted a picture of someone you loved. So I told him about your grandmother.

Larry: Hey, Lucila, is your uncle an artist, too?

Lucila: No, but he's taught me a lot about seeing.

Susan: I'd like to know how he taught you to see this block as beautiful. I mean, with all the dirt and stuff.

Lucila: He can't see the dirt. He's blind. He taught me to see with my heart.

Narrator: They all stare at Lucila. Then they turn and stare at Jimmy, who is at the window waving.

Larry: Hey, Jimmy, what are you waving at?

Jimmy *(grinning):* Those papers in the street. They've been waving at me for years. I just thought it was about time I waved back.

READING COMPREHENSION

Summarizing. Choose the best phrase to complete each sentence. Then write the complete statement on your paper.

1. While the others in her art class saw an ugly apartment house, Lucila saw a _____ (desert scene, warm and friendly building, big garbage dump).

2. Jimmy brought the class to the front of the apartment building to _____ (make Lucila see reality, see it with his heart, prove the art teacher wrong).

3. Jimmy began to _____ (tell it like it is, wake her out of her dreams, look at things her way) when Lucila showed how he had painted someone he loved.

Interpreting. Write the answer to each question on your paper.

1. What is special about the way Lucila saw things? How did she learn to see with her heart?

2. Why does Jimmy feel the class must "knock Lucila out of her dream world."

3. How did Jimmy paint his grandmother?

4. When Jimmy waved at papers in the street, what was he really showing?

For Thinking and Discussing. If Lucila finished her drawing of the apartment house, would her picture look real? What do you think she would make sure to put in her drawing?

UNDERSTANDING LITERATURE

Theme and plot. The *theme* is the most important idea of the story. It is what the author wants to tell us. The things the author tells about in the story from the beginning to the end is the *plot*.

Sometimes the author uses the events of the story to tell about the theme. This happens in "The Vision of Lucila Godoy." The theme of "The Vision of Lucila Godoy" is that beauty can be anywhere if you care to see it. Each event in the story helps you to find out that what you see with your heart can be different from what you see with your eyes.

List the events below in the order in which they happen in the story. Then write what each event shows: seeing with your heart, or with your eyes.

1. Jimmy points out that Exhibit A is both faded and dirty.

2. Karen looks out the window and sees a crummy red apartment house.

3. Jimmy paints a picture of a very special and beautiful woman.

4. Lucila looks out the window and sees a warm friendly building.

WRITING

Think of something you love, such as a beat-up pair of sneakers or a ragged teddy bear. Write a paragraph explaining its beauty.

The Wrestling Match

A modern West African tale told by Tom Gilroy

*Winning the championship seems the most important thing to
the two wrestlers as they approach their big match. But on the
night before the contest, one of the young men learns about
something more important than victory.*

To the Serrers — the people who live in Bikole and nearby villages — nothing is more exciting than a wrestling match. All through the dry season, the large villages in the area set aside one day a week when wrestlers come from miles around to win fame and money.

All week before a big match, the villages buzz with talk of the two combatants. The men argue about who will win; the little boys wrestle in the dirt, imitating their heroes.

At the end of the dry weather, each village gives a special banner to the very best wrestler. It is a great honor, and all the wrestlers try very hard to win it.

In Bikole one year, there was great excitement as the dry season neared an end. Two wrestlers who had won all their matches would do battle on the last week of the season. The winner would be awarded the banner.

The two men were quite different from each other. Jakate was a light-skinned stranger, and people said he came from a city far to the north. He was big and strong and very handsome. He was always clowning with the young girls of the village. When Jakate wrestled, he charged his opponent immediately; all his matches were over in less than a minute.

Salue, on the other hand, was dark like a Serrer. He was tall and slender and did not look much like a wrestler. But when he fought, he crouched down, his hands in front of him, and moved like a cat. His matches lasted longer than Jakate's, and sometimes it seemed that surely he would lose. Always, though, the other wrestler fell first.

The week before their big match, neither Salue nor Jakate was seen in the village.

"They have gone to see the holy man," said the old men knowingly. "They will need special gris-gris for this fight." A gris-gris is anything blessed by a holy man, or marabout. Usually they cost a lot of money: They are said to have special powers.

Indeed the old men of Bikole were right. Jakate had gone all the way to the big city to buy a special gris-gris against Salue. The marabout lived in a big house and had many people working for him. He even had a car. The holy man smiled when he heard Jakate's request. He told the wrestler the special gris-gris would cost a lot of money, but Jakate said that did not matter. The marabout told him to come back the next day.

Early the next morning, Jakate returned. The holy man gave him a leather band and a small sack filled with leaves.

"Wear this band around your waist when you combat Salue," instructed the marabout. "And just before the match is to start, burn these leaves in the center of the ring."

Jakate paid the marabout for the gris-gris, then headed back to the village. "Now I am sure to win the banner," he thought happily.

Meanwhile, back in the country, Salue went to see his father, Latik Dione. Long ago, Latik too had been a great wrestler. But when a sickness swept through Bikole a year earlier, the old man had almost died. When Latik finally recovered, he could no longer walk. Still, he thanked

133

Yallah for letting him live, and was never bitter.

And because he had wrestled long ago, he often advised Salue on how to fight a difficult opponent. Sometimes father and son sat under the stars and talked about wrestling far into the night.

Salue found his father lying on a mat outside his hut. Already it was getting too hot to sleep inside. The rainy season was not far away.

"Good afternoon, Father," said the young man. "Are you at peace today?"

The old man smiled. He was glad his son had not forgotten the traditional greeting.

"I have only peace, my son," answered Latik. He told Salue's sister to bring another mat for her older brother.

"Father," said Salue when he was seated, "I have no money to buy a *gris-gris* for my match with Jakate."

"But, Salue," said his father, "you have not needed a *gris-gris* for any of your other fights, and you won them all."

"I know," said Salue, "but Jakate is bigger and stronger than any of the others." He hesitated, then continued, "And I am sure he has gone to see El Hadji M'Bake in the city. Surely he has a special *gris-gris* against me."

Latik looked up at the sky. He did not

think it was right that holy men sold pieces of string, telling poor people they held special powers. He did not think it was right either that the *marabouts* lived like kings, with big houses and cars. But Latik did not say this to Salue. Instead, he told his son a story.

"Many years ago," he began, "there was a young wrestler about to fight his first match in the big ring at Bikole. He borrowed as much money as he could and walked all the way to the city. The trip took two days, but the young man wanted a *gris-gris* very badly.

"When he arrived at the house of the *marabout,* the guard at the gate asked gruffly what he wanted.

" 'Have you any money?' asked the guard.

"The young wrestler reached into his pocket and pulled out all his money. The guard smiled and told the boy to enter.

"As he walked up the steps to the great house, he passed another guard pulling a blind woman toward the front gate. The woman's clothes were old and dirty, and she held a baby in her arms.

" 'Please,' she cried, 'just a little food for my baby. He is sick and will surely die.'

"But the guard would not listen. 'Come, woman,' he said, pulling her by the arm, 'the *marabout* has not time for you now.'

"The young man felt sorry for the woman, but he kept walking. He entered the magnificent house and knelt before the holy man. Old and dressed in splendid clothes, the *marabout* said the *gris-gris* would cost much money. The boy said he would pay a certain amount to win his first match. The *marabout* smiled and told him to return the following day.

"Outside the gate, the boy passed the blind woman again. She sat against the wall crying, with the baby in her arms. The wrestler said he was sorry the guard had treated her so badly. The woman stopped crying and raised her head. Her sightless eyes aimed at his, so that the boy felt for a moment she could see him.

"Without knowing why, the young man reached into his pocket and pressed all his money into the woman's hand. A smile crossed her tired and dirty face, and she said, 'Henceforth, may you and yours never have need of the *marabout* again.'

"When the boy returned to Bikole, he was sure he would lose his match. But to his surprise, he won easily. In fact, the boy wrestled for many years after that, and though he never again visited the holy man, he never lost a match."

All during his father's story, Salue listened attentively. He did not understand how it had anything to do with his match with Jakate, but he would never say that to Latik. When his father finished, Salue thanked him and went to his hut. He thought about his father's story, but could not understand what he had meant. Much later that night, he fell asleep.

On the day of the big match, Salue rode to the ring on a horsecart filled with his friends. They cheered and yelled at people around them on foot, but Salue stared straight ahead and did not say a word. He was thinking about all the people who would watch him today. What if Jakate charged, and he fell right away? He would be disgraced.

As they approached the ring, Salue pushed the idea from his head. When he entered the enclosure, the crowd roared. Jakate stopped dancing in front of a group of young girls and stared at his opponent. As the tom-toms began beating, Jakate started his dance around the ring. He stopped in front of Salue and drew a finger across his throat. The crowd roared again.

"Salue is afraid," whispered some of the old men.

Two younger boys wrestled first. They were just learning, and the match was long and sloppy. Finally, after it was over, the village chief walked to the middle of the ring. He called Jakate and Salue. Then he turned to the crowd and announced that the winner would carry the banner of Bikole. He turned back to the wrestlers.

"Start your combat," he commanded.

Salue crouched down low, until his head was only three feet from the ground. He pawed the air in front of him and moved smoothly sideways, circling his larger opponent like a cat.

Jakate quickly knelt down and lit a match. He pulled the small sack of leaves from his waist and burned them.

"A special *gris-gris*," murmured the audience.

Then Jakate was ready. He bent his knees a little and began to circle after Salue.

Salue threw a quick punch, but the huge wrestler from the north brushed it away as if it were a mosquito. Suddenly, Jakate charged. Just as in all the rest of his matches, he seized Salue's legs and drove

the Serrer backward.

Salue tried to break away, but Jakate was too strong. Jakate continued to press Salue backward. As he felt himself start to fall, Salue desperately reached for something to hold. His right hand found the leather band around Jakate's waist. As Jakate started a last drive, Salue pulled with all his might on the band.

When he did that, Jakate seemed to

stumble. To steady himself, the big wrestler had to free one hand from Salue's legs. Salue felt his leg freed and, regaining his balance, pulled again on the band around his opponent's waist. Jakate reached again for Salue, but this time the Serrer was too fast for him. Salue slid his free leg between Jakate's as the big man made his charge. Jakate, feeling himself falling, let go of Salue entirely and tried to stop his

fall with both hands. Like a cat, Salue spun around behind the stumbling giant and dove onto his back. With the added weight, Jakate could not catch himself and fell to the ground.

For a second, there was silence in the ring. Then the crowd let out a deafening roar, and Salue's friends ran to him. They put the smiling boy on their shoulders and, cheering wildly, they carried him all

the way back to his father's compound.

Latik could hear the crowd coming. From the noise they made, he knew that his son had won. Finally, at the entrance to his father's household, the happy crowd lowered Salue.

Salue held out his hand to his father. In it was a broken leather band. It was the same leather band Jakate had bought from the holy man.

"Father," said the tired and dirty wrestler, "I did not understand your story until today. I know now who the young boy was."

READING COMPREHENSION

Summarizing. Choose the best phrase to complete each sentence. Then write the complete statement on your paper.

1. The wrestling match between Jakate and Salue was _____ (the most exciting, an ordinary, a violent) event in the village of Bikole.

2. To be sure of winning the match, Jakate bought a _____ (small sack of leaves and a leather band with special powers, blessed house, car) from a holy man.

3. Instead of giving money to buy a gris-gris, Salue's father told him a story about a boy who _____ (sacrificed his gris-gris money to help a poor woman, never won a wrestling banner, did not believe in magic).

4. Salue won the match _____ (by magic, by his own skill, by mistake).

Interpreting. Write the answer to each question on your paper.

1. Why did Jakate buy the gris-gris from the marabout?

2. Why did Salue visit Latik Dione?

3. What was Latik Dione's reason for telling the story about a young wrestler who almost bought a gris-gris?

For Thinking and Discussing. Why did the wrestlers believe that they needed a gris-gris to win? What special power did it really give Jakate? Find examples in the story to support your answers.

UNDERSTANDING LITERATURE

Theme and Characterization. Sometimes the thoughts and actions of the people of a story are the important theme. The way the people or characters of a story think and act is the *characterization*.

Through their thoughts and actions, the characters in "The Wrestling Match" tell about this theme: The key to success is believing in yourself and doing what is right.

Match each character and action from the list below. Then write a sentence to explain how the action helps to show the theme.

Jakate, Salue, Latik Dione, Marabout, Blind Woman

1. Gave his gris-gris money to a blind woman.

2. Tripped his opponent when he saw an opening.

3. Blessed the young man for not thinking only of himself.

4. Stumbled when he realized that he was losing his gris-gris.

5. Became rich by selling special gris-gris.

WRITING

Suppose you are a television sports reporter. You are covering the wrestling match between Salue and Jakate. List three questions you will ask Salue after the match, and three questions you will ask Jakate. Then write the answers you think they will give for each question.

Precious Jade

A Chinese folktale retold by Toni McCarty

Precious Jade may be only a peasant, but she is very wise. This tale tells how she uses her wisdom, and what it brings to her and those she loves.

Plum Blossom and Peony grew up in the same village in China. When they were of age, they married two brothers of the Cheng family and left their village to live with their husbands' family.

There they grew homesick and would often beg their father-in-law to let them visit their mothers. Usually he gave his permission. After several of these visits, however, he grew impatient.

"You may make this journey to your village on one condition: When you return you must bring me two things. Plum Blossom, you must carry fire wrapped in paper. And Peony, you must bring me the wind on paper. If you fail, don't bother to return to our household." The old man thought his impossible requests would make the two women give up their desire to leave. But so excited were they at the prospect of going home, they agreed to his conditions without thinking.

They had not gone far, however, when they realized what they had promised. "What have we done?" said Peony.

A peasant on a water buffalo came riding by. She stopped and looked at the two well-dressed women who sat weeping at the side of the road.

"What's the matter?" she asked. Peony and Plum Blossom told her.

"Follow me," said the young woman, and she took them to her hut.

"Fire wrapped in paper. Light the candle inside and give it to Cheng." She handed a lantern to Plum Blossom.

"Wind on paper," she said, and gave a fan to Peony with a smile.

The young wives were delighted and thanked the young woman. "And what is your name?" asked Peony.

"I'm Precious Jade," she answered with a bow.

Peony and Plum Blossom continued happily on their way and had a splendid time visiting their families. When they returned to the Cheng family home, they handed their father-in-law the lantern and the fan.

"I can't believe you two could have figured this out yourselves," the old man said.

"We were helped by Precious Jade," they confessed.

"This woman is just what we need," Cheng said. He hoped her brains would help his family grow richer. He found Precious Jade, and before too long his

youngest son was married to her.

"You shall be the head of the household," Cheng told Precious Jade, and he bid the rest of the family follow her instructions.

"Never go to or from the fields empty-handed," she said to the sons. After that, they made sure they carried something to the fields each day — seeds, tools, or fertilizer. On the way back to the house, they filled their arms with sticks or stones.

Never before had the fields received so much care. Soon lush crops grew. The sticks the sons carried home each day kept the hearth fires blazing. The stones they gathered were stacked in a huge pile behind their house. "Someday we will use them for building," Precious Jade explained.

One day, Ku Yai, a dealer in precious stones, was traveling along the road that bordered the Cheng land. Seeing the pile of stones in the yard, he ventured closer to take a look. A glint caught his eye: A valuable stone was half buried among the rest. It was a chunk of unpolished jade.

He called for the head of the household. When Precious Jade appeared, he told her he would like to buy the pile of stones. "I need these rocks to build a bridge," he said.

Precious Jade did not believe him. "You offer too little for such a fine pile," she said. They began to bargain. When a final price was set, Ku Yai said, "I'll return with the money in two days and cart the stones away."

After he was gone, Precious Jade stared at the pile, wondering. But the rough jade remained hidden to her untrained eye.

She went to her father-in-law and asked him to invite Ku Yai to a feast the next day. "When he has eaten and drunk to his heart's content, ask him about precious stones — and how one may recognize them," she said.

Precious Jade made certain that the very best wines were served at the feast the next day. Ku Yai drank greedily. Finally Cheng said, "It's a wonder to me that you can ever tell one stone from another. To me, they always look the same. You must be a clever man, indeed, Ku Yai! Tell me, how do you do it?"

Flattered, Ku Yai explained how he recognized various types of stones. Precious Jade listened closely to every word.

At dawn she was up and looking over the pile. "Aha!" she exclaimed at last. "Look at this chunk of green jade!"

Later, when Ku Yai came to collect his stones, he was dismayed to find Precious Jade holding the jade in her arms. She smiled and said, "Perhaps you would also like to buy this jade?" Ku Yai was forced to give her a good price for the jade — in addition to the price he had already promised for the pile of rocks.

Now the Cheng family was wealthy. Precious Jade had a fine ancestral hall built on the property. When it was completed, she hung a sign over the door that read, "No Sorrow."

One day, a mandarin, a person of high rank, passed by the Chengs' ancestral hall. After he read the sign, he ordered his servants to set down his traveling chair and sent for the head of the household.

Precious Jade greeted him politely. The mandarin was gruff. "How dare you hang

'No Sorrow' over your door! No family is free from sorrow and it is arrogant of you to put up such a sign. For your pride I will make you pay a heavy fine, young woman. You must weave a piece of cloth as long as this road!"

Precious Jade bowed. "I will begin at once, Honorable Sir. Please measure the road."

The mandarin shouted at her. "For that impudence, I'll increase your fine. Deliver to me as much oil as there is water in the Eastern Sea!"

"I will begin pressing oil from the beans of my fields immediately," she replied. "How much water is in the sea?"

The mandarin narrowed his eyes. "You think you're clever. Answer this: I hold my pet quail in my hand. Will I keep hold of it or will I let it go? If you answer correctly, I will forget your fines. But if I do

the opposite of what you guess . . . ha!"

Meeting his angry eyes squarely, Precious Jade replied, "Your Honor is a learned man and I was raised an ignorant peasant. You must not levy fines against me unless you are wiser than I. First you must answer my riddle before I answer yours: You see me standing over the threshold to the house, one foot inside and one foot outside. Will I go in or will I go out? If you guess wrong, you are no wiser than I and must not judge me."

The mandarin laughed and gave up. "Now I see the meaning of 'No Sorrow.' The spirits of sorrow could never enter your door. They would have to get past you — and that's impossible!" He signaled his servants to lift his chair, and he left the Cheng household in peace.

Precious Jade remained the family treasure.

READING COMPREHENSION

Summarizing. Choose the best phrase to complete each sentence. Then write the complete statement on your paper.

1. Carrying fire wrapped in paper and bringing wind on paper was not hard when Precious Jade gave Plum Blossom and Peony _____ (a candle and a blower, a painting and a brush, a lantern and a fan).

2. Precious Jade was able to make Ku Yai explain _____ (how he knew precious stones, how to buy and sell rocks, the value of jade) and make him pay for the jade in the pile of rocks.

3. Precious Jade did not pay a fine for her "No Sorrow" sign because she proved that she was _____ (stronger, wiser, older) than the mandarin.

Interpreting. Write the answer to each question on your paper.

1. Why did Cheng decide to make Precious Jade the head of the household?

2. How did Precious Jade make the Cheng family wealthy?

3. What quality did Precious Jade have that made her "the family treasure"?

4. The mandarin called Precious Jade arrogant and impudent. How did Jade really answer the mandarin?

For Thinking and Discussing. If Precious Jade were living in today's world, what jobs could she do best? Why?

UNDERSTANDING LITERATURE

Theme and Humor. Sometimes the theme, or the main idea of the story, is shown through the use of humor. *Humor* is the way something can be funny.

The theme of "Precious Jade" is cleverness can solve any problem. Three humorous events show you the value of being clever. On your paper, answer the questions about these events.

1. First, Precious Jade shows she is more clever than Cheng by fulfilling his impossible requests. Later she beats Ku Yai, the dishonest jade dealer, at his own game. Finally Precious Jade shows she is more clever than the mandarin with her riddles. Which of these events seems funniest to you? Why?

2. Word play can be funny. A word can have two meanings, or, double meaning. In this story, Precious Jade is the name of a young woman. Precious jade is also a valuable stone that is used to make jewelry and statues. Explain the double meaning in the last sentence of the story: "Precious Jade remained the family treasure." How does this sentence tell about the theme of the story?

WRITING

Imagine what it would be like to have Precious Jade as a sister. Write a paragraph describing what your life with Precious Jade would be like. Make up a humorous event that happens between you and Precious Jade.

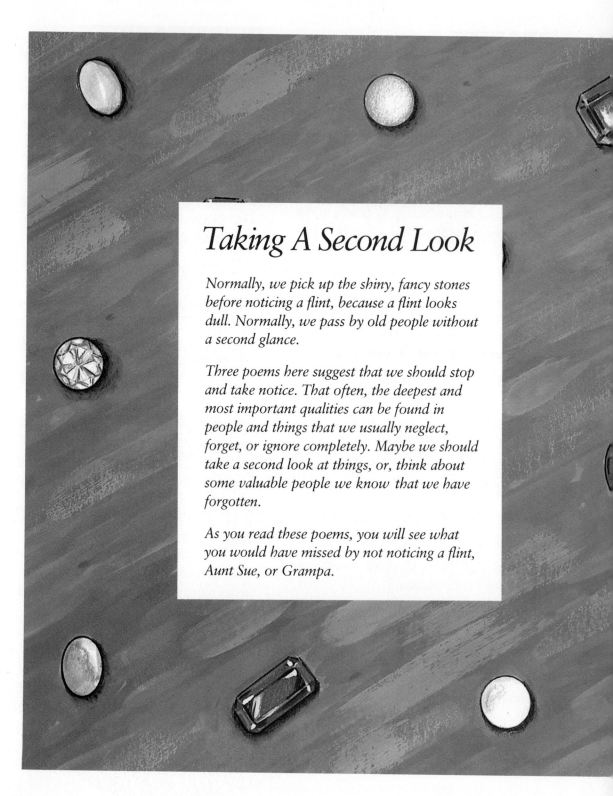

Taking A Second Look

Normally, we pick up the shiny, fancy stones before noticing a flint, because a flint looks dull. Normally, we pass by old people without a second glance.

Three poems here suggest that we should stop and take notice. That often, the deepest and most important qualities can be found in people and things that we usually neglect, forget, or ignore completely. Maybe we should take a second look at things, or, think about some valuable people we know that we have forgotten.

As you read these poems, you will see what you would have missed by not noticing a flint, Aunt Sue, or Grampa.

Flint

by Christina Rossetti

An emerald is as green as grass,
  A ruby red as blood;
A sapphire shines as blue as heaven;
  A flint lies in the mud.

A diamond is a brilliant stone,
  To catch the world's desire;
An opal holds a fiery spark;
  But a flint holds fire.

Aunt Sue's Stories

by Langston Hughes

Aunt Sue has a head full of stories.
Aunt Sue has a whole heart full of stories.
Summer nights on the front porch
Aunt Sue cuddles a brown-faced child to her bosom
And tells him stories.

Black slaves
Working in the hot sun,
And black slaves
Walking in the dewy night,
And black slaves
Singing sorrow songs on the banks of a mighty river
Mingle themselves softly
In the flow of old Aunt Sue's voice,
Mingle themselves softly
In the dark shadows that cross and recross
Aunt Sue's stories.

And the dark-faced child, listening,
Knows that Aunt Sue's stories are real stories.
He knows that Aunt Sue never got her stories
Out of any book at all,
But that they came
Right out of her own life.

The dark-faced child is quiet
Of a summer night
Listening to Aunt Sue's stories.

Birdfoot's Grampa

by Joseph Bruchac

The Old Man
must have stopped our car
two dozen times to climb out
and gather into his hands
the small toads blinded
by our lights and leaping
like live drops of rain.

The rain was falling,
a mist around his white hair,
and I kept saying,
"You can't save them all,
accept it, get in,
we've got places to go."

But, leathery hands full
of wet brown life,
knee deep in the summer
roadside grass,
he just smiled and said,
"They have places to go, too."

READING COMPREHENSION

Summarizing. Choose the best phrase to complete each sentence. Then write the complete statement on your paper.

1. In "Flint," a flint is valuable because it _____ (is as brilliant as diamond, lies in the mud, is used to make fire).

2. In "Aunt Sue's Stories," Aunt Sue tells stories about _____ (her past, her future, her dreams).

3. In "Birdfoot's Grampa," the old man stops the car two dozen times to _____ (wipe off the windshield, save the toads, pull out the roadside grass).

Interpreting. Write the answer to each question on you paper.

1. According to the poem "Flint," why is flint more valuable than a ruby, a diamond, or an opal?

2. In "Aunt Sue's Stories," why is the child quiet when he listens to the stories?

3. In "Birdfoot's Grampa," explain what the old man meant when he said "They have places to go, too."

For Thinking and Discussing. Think of a reason why you would rather have a diamond than a flint. Explain why the diamond is more valuable in this situation. Now describe a reason why you would rather have a flint than a diamond.

UNDERSTANDING LITERATURE

Meaning in Poetry. Poets often use *imagery*, words that you can see, hear, taste, touch, or smell. Imagery uses your senses. For example, "an emerald is as green as grass" is an image that you can see. From this line, you might think the poem "Flint" is about how different stones look. It is only when you read all the images in the poem that you can understand the full meaning of the poem.

Write the answers to parts A and B below on your paper.

A. Which sense does each image below uses?
   1. ruby red as blood
   2. singing sorrow songs
   3. hands full of wet, brown life

B. Match each title below with the most important idea in that poem.
   "Flint"
   "Aunt Sue's Stories"
   "Birdfoot's Grampa"

1. It is important for young people to understand their family's past.

2. Something that looks dull and unimportant may be valuable.

3. All life, even a small toad, is important.

WRITING

Write a short poem or paragraph telling about something you think is of value. Use imagery — words that use the senses.

VOCABULARY

Antonyms. *Antonyms* are words that have opposite meanings. *Happy* and *sad* are antonyms.

The sentences below are from the selections you have just read. Write each italicized word on your paper. Then write its antonym from the following list.

boring	command	light
fullness	stupid	ugly
clean	well	lowered
ordinary		

1. "That feeling of *emptiness* is the mood you should try to give your desert."

2. "Those torn old curtains and *dirty* papers are waving at us"

3. "I like her dreams — even if they are *weird*."

4. "I'd like to know how he taught you to see this block as *beautiful*."

5. "Nothing is more *exciting* than the wrestling match."

6. "He is *sick* and will surely die."

7. "The woman stopped crying and *raised* her head."

8. "There they grew homesick and would often *beg* their father-in-law to let them visit their mothers."

9. "You must be a *clever* man."

10. "For your pride I will make you pay a *heavy* fine."

READING

Predicting Outcomes. In the plot of a story many things, or events, happen. Knowing the order in which these events happen helps you to understand the story. The order in which things happen is called *sequence*.

When you read, keep in mind the sequence of events in the story. As you read, think about what might come next in the sequence. This is called *predicting outcomes*. When you are predicting outcomes, you are guessing what is going to happen next.

Each paragraph below tells the sequence of events from the stories in "Something of Value." Complete the last sentence in each paragraph to predict what is going to happen next.

1. In the beginning of the story "The Vision of Lucila Godoy," Jimmy thinks the building across the street is ugly. Then Lucila teaches him about "seeing with his heart." At the end of the story, Jimmy is at the window waving. In the future, Jimmy will _____ (imagine a garbage dump, see the warmth of his neighborhood, feel ashamed) whenever he looks at the "crummy" red apartment house.

2. In "The Wrestling Match," Salue fears he will lose the match because he has no gris-gris. His father tells him a story about a boy who won a match without a gris-gris. Salue goes on to try his best, and to win the match. Salue tells his father that he finally understands the story of the young boy. Before he fights in another important wrestling match, Salue will _____ (do without, search for, ask his father for) a gris-gris.

3. In "Precious Jade," Precious Jade helps the Cheng family to get money or wealth. They are so happy that a "no sorrow" sign is hung over their house. A mandarin is angered when he sees the sign. He tries to think of a way to punish Precious Jade. Precious Jade finds ways to outwit the mandarin each time he asks for something impossible. Finally the mandarin leaves the Cheng household in peace. In the future, Precious Jade brings _____ (all kinds of trouble, wealth and wisdom, many surprises) to the family.

QUIZ

The following is a quiz for Section 4. Write the answers in complete sentences on your paper.

Reading Comprehension

1. In the play "The Vision of Lucila Godoy," how does Lucila change the way her classmates see things?

2. In "The Wrestling Match," Latik tells his son a story about a young wrestler. Who was the young wrestler in the story?

3. In "Precious Jade," what did Precious Jade send Cheng when he asked for fire wrapped in paper and wind on paper?

4. If flint is a stone that lies in the mud, how can it be valuable, according to the poem "Flint"?

5. In the poem "Birdfoot's Grampa," what would have happened to the toads if the old man had not picked them up?

Understanding Literature

6. Why is scene three of "The Vision of Lucila Godoy," the most important scene for understanding the theme of the play?

7. Each event in "Precious Jade," leads the reader towards the discovery that Precious Jade is a "treasure." List three events in the story that help to show this theme.

8. Imagine that at the end of the story "The Wrestling Match," Salue had lost the match, and thanks to the magic of his gris-gris, Jakate had won. How would this change the theme of the story? Write a sentence that describes what the new theme of the story would be.

9. The theme "your own ideas and skills can help you solve problems" may be in more than one story in "Something of Value." Pick one story and explain why it fits this theme.

10. The poem "Aunt Sue's Stories," has the lines, "Black slaves/Working in the hot sun,/ And black slaves walking in the dewy night." What kind of picture does this imagery give you. Which of your five senses does this imagery reach?

WRITING

A Persuasive Letter. An *opinion* is a person's belief or feeling about something. Your opinions might be strong and important, and you want other people to share them. One way to tell a person your opinion is to write a letter to the person. A letter that will cause a person to know about, or share your opinions is a *persuasive letter*.

Read each step below to help guide you in writing a persuasive letter.

Step 1: Set Your Goal
Choose one of the following topics for a persuasive letter.

☐ Pretend you are Lucila from the story, "The Vision of Lucila Godoy." Write a persuasive letter to Jimmy. You want him to stop making fun of the way you see. Your opinion is that most people

see things with their hearts, but might not know that is what they are doing.

☐ Imagine that the building you live in has a yard that is filled with trash and overgrown weeds. Write a persuasive letter to your neighbors. Your opinion is that the trash and weeds are unclean and ugly. A garden that everyone could help plant would make the yard useful and beautiful.

Step 2: Make a Plan
Plan what you are going to say. It is not enough to state your opinions when you write a persuasive letter. You must show your opinions are correct. You must use facts and examples that show your opinion is correct.

Here is one way examples and facts help an opinion. Think back to the story, "The Wrestling Match." Imagine that a village chief writes a letter to cause the people to stop buying gris-gris. In his letter, the chief would state his opinion that the gris-gris have no special powers. Then he would support his opinion by telling them facts about Salue, Jakate, and Salue's father. He might use the following facts and examples:

☐ Salue has won wrestling matches without gris-gris.

☐ Salue's father learned from a poor old woman that you don't need to buy special powers in order to be successful. You only need to do what is right and believe in yourself. Salue's father, like

155

Salue, won wrestling matches without gris-gris.

☐ A gris-gris makes you lose belief in yourself. When Jakate lost his gris-gris, he no longer believed he had a chance to win, and so he lost the match.

Now make a list of facts and examples that support your letter.

Step 3: Write Your First Draft

Your persuasive letter should contain three paragraphs. The first should state your opinion. The second should be your supporting facts and examples. The third should restate your opinion and tell your reader what you want him or her to do.

1. Begin your paragraph by stating your opinion. For example, the chief might begin his letter this way:

   > Dear Villagers,
   > I am writing to you because I am worried that many of you are wasting your money buying gris-gris. I believe that gris-gris are worthless, and you should not buy them.

2. Next write a paragraph using your lists of facts and examples.

3. End your paragraph by reminding the reader of your opinion and tell the reader what you want him or her to do. The chief from "The Wrestling Match" might end his letter by saying:

   > For these reasons I do not believe gris-gris have special powers. In fact,

gris-gris have a bad effect on people. Gris-gris make people lose faith in their own abilities. I urge you, my people, to stop buying gris-gris.

> Sincerely,
>
> Your Chief

Step 4: Revise Your Letter

Check your letter one more time. Have you stated your opinion clearly? Make sure the facts and examples you give support your opinion. Make sure you have told your reader exactly what you want him or her to do based on your opinion. Correct any errors in spelling, grammar, and punctuation you find. Make a final neat copy of your letter.

ACTIVITIES

Word Attack. Look at these two words: *surely, badly.* Each word ends with the suffix -ly. The suffix -ly makes the sounds *lee*.

Add the suffix *-ly* to each word below where it is needed as you copy them on your paper. The completed words will be words from the story "The Wrestling Match." Practice pronouncing each word.

1. When Jakate wrestled, he charged his opponent immediate _____ ; all his matches were over in less than a minute.

2. "They have gone to see the holy man," said the old men knowing _____ .

3. All during his father's story, Salue listened attentive _____.

4. As he felt himself start to fall, Salue desperate _____ reached for something to hold.

5. Usual _____ they cost a lot of money: They are said to have special powers.

Speaking and Listening. Many times important lessons are told through stories. Look back to the story Latik tells his son in "The Wrestling Match." Practice reading the story aloud so that you will be able to share it with someone. When you feel that you know the story well enough, re-tell it in your own words

Researching.

1. The poem "Aunt Sue's Stories" talks about the value of understanding one's own family history or roots. Find a true story that shows how one person or group of people from your family history faced a problem with strength or courage. You may interview older people in your family to find information. Stories like this are often passed on from generation to generation. A family passes the story on to their children, and they pass it on to their children and so on.

Write at least one paragraph explaining this story. Tell what the problem was and how it was solved. Include the following information in your paragraph:

☐ The name of the person

☐ The relationship of the person to you. Is the person related on your mother's or father's side?

☐ Where did the person live?

☐ In what year did this take place?

☐ How many generations back does this take place?

2. Visit an art museum to look at some paintings. Or, find a library book that contains photographs of paintings. Choose five paintings. For each painting look at its different parts as listed below. What does each part make you think or feel? Fill in the chart.

Parts of a Painting	Your Reactions
Colors Size Subject or Form Title Materials	

Creating. Imagine that you can create your own treasure chest, filled with the ten things that you think are most valuable. The things you have may be objects such as a diamond or a flint, people such as Lucila's uncle or Jimmy's grandmother, or qualities such as cleverness or beauty. Make a list of the ten things you pick. Then, for each thing on your list, write a sentence telling why it is something of value.

AFTER DARK

The lights begin to twinkle
from the rocks;
The long day wanes; the slow moon climbs;
The deep
Moans round with many voices.

—Tennyson

Introduction

When most people think of nighttime, they think of quiet, calmness, and sleep. Night is when the hustle and bustle of day stops and most people rest safely inside their houses.

But outside the shuttered houses, danger may be lurking on deserted street corners. Night watchmen guard over towns and warn of fire or attack.

Midnight ambushes are not the only activities disturbing the silence of night. Many nocturnal creatures prowl in the dark; they sleep all day and wake at night. The night is more alive than you may suspect!

In this section you will read stories describing nightime activity.

"Janey By Moonlight" is the story of a girl locked out of her house and desperate for a way to wake her father from sleep.

In the poem "The Bat," a bat may look like an upside-down mouse with wings, but it flies around when no mouse is awake.

Longfellow's famous poem "Paul Revere's Ride" tells of the danger this hero risked in order to warn sleeping colonists of a British raid. But "What About the Midnight Ride of William Dawes?" wonders why no one remembers Revere's equally courageous partner.

The king and his wise men are faced with a dilemma in "Many Moons." The king's daughter has set them an impossible task: she wants nothing less than the moon itself!

Janey by Moonlight

by Eleanor Cameron

Do you sometimes hear strange sounds in the dark when you are trying to go to sleep? In this story Janey hears spooky noises and finds herself in a silly predicament when she tries to fix things. Read to see how she deals with the unexpected.

Janey woke with a start. She stared down at the oblong of brilliant moonlight on the carpet. What had woken her? Yes, the cats. Owwwr-rrr-rrr — low and menacing. Then, still together, soaring onto a higher note, rrr-owwwwwwww-rrrr. The sound changed suddenly into a spitting, snarling explosion of fury as they fought. The cats kept it up for at least half a minute. Janey was sure they were tearing one another to pieces.

Then silence, deep, deep silence. They went at it again. The sound was low to begin with. Then it rose into that hating double yowl. Moonlight moggies, Mama called them.

Janey bounced out of bed. She trotted along the hall to her mother and father's bedroom. Daddy could go outside and stop them. There was a light under the door but no voices. That was because Mama was away visiting Aunt Lydia. Gently, Janey knocked, then called — no answer. She pushed open the door. There was Daddy. His book had slipped down onto his stomach. His eyes were closed, head dropped over to one side. He breathed in a slow and peaceful snore. He hated being woken. He was a deep, solid sleeper. If he was brought wide awake all of a sudden, instead of being allowed to come half awake himself (just enough to snap out the light, turn over, and go right off again,) he'd be awake for hours.

Janey closed the door. Then went into the living room. She listened. Yes, the cats were at it. She opened the front door, went out onto the porch. She yelled, "SCAT!" — and away shot two black shadows.

She stood there a moment, sniffing in the sharp, spicy smell of dry eucalyptus and pine needles. Janey and her mother and father lived up in the Berkeley Hills, where the pine and oak and eucalyptus woods begin. Then she looked up and saw the moon, rather low in the sky, shining across Berkeley and the bay. Never had she seen such a moon! Why did it sometimes seem so much bigger and

brighter when it was full than at other times? It was a mystery. She had just decided to go inside and get Daddy's binoculars from his desk drawer, when —

CLICK.

Her heart jumped. She didn't have to turn and look. She knew exactly what had happened. The minute she'd left the door open as she stepped out onto the porch, it had begun swinging closed, very, very slowly. Now when the door had finished its swing, the tongue of the lock slipped into place.

Every summer it was the same. That old door stuck stubbornly all through the winter, when it was rainy and the wood swelled. During late summer and fall, when the weather turned dry, the wood shrank. Then the door swung to, as if its hinges were oiled.

Janey knew it would be no use, but she went over and tried it. Not a hope. She rang the bell, good and long. But she knew quite well Daddy wouldn't hear. The little bell was up over the kitchen door, on the side of the house opposite to his bedroom. Mama would have — she always heard everything — but not Daddy.

She stood thinking. What could she do? She ran down the steps, along the driveway to the back. Then she went around into the garden and over to Mama and Daddy's bedroom. The windows here at the back would be closed and locked, she knew. To be on the safe side, Daddy said. There were two windows around the corner, which he always opened a little at night. But there were so many big, thick, scratchy bushes under them. No one could possibly push a way in.

Quietly, quietly, like a little animal, she scratched at the window screen. She could just reach it. "Daddy!" she hissed, not very loudly. "Daddy — it's me, Janey, I'm locked out!"

Why so quiet? Because of old Mrs. Leather Lungs, right on the other side of the fence. She lived back up there in her apartment over the garage of the house next door. Old Mrs. Leather Lungs, the kids called her. She was someone who always knew what her neighbors were doing, back and front and either side. And she'd go on and on about these doings at the top of her voice to whoever would listen.

Rats! If Janey called really loud to Daddy now, old Leather Lungs would hear. She would come charging out and begin managing everything the way she always did. Soon the whole neighborhood would know Janey had been careless and stupid.

Janey kept on scratching and calling as loudly as she dared. But Daddy went right on snoring.

What could she do? She could go to the Pearsons, the nice, kind couple in the house on the other side and ask them to phone Daddy? But the phone was in the dining room — he'd never hear. Could they call the landlady to come with a key? Oh, no, no! She lived clear over on the other side of Berkeley. And besides, Janey couldn't wake the Pearsons. It would be too mean — and too embarrassing. She wouldn't have the nerve.

On she went working at Daddy's window. She got a stick and forced it through the fragile, weathered screen. Then she began pushing it hard, back and forth, so that it made a thumping on the window.

Immediately, Daddy's snoring stopped. She thumped hard, twice. Silence. He was listening, trying to think. She could just see him. he'd be blinking, trying to get his wits together. "Daddy!" she called. "Let me in — "

She heard a thump. That was his feet coming down on the floor. Silence again. Then, "Who — what is it? What's going on?" She bet he was still half asleep.

"It's me, Daddy—Janey. I'm out here." Another silence. He must have been

trying to make sense of this. "Janey? Out where?"

"Outside — "

"Outside! Where outside?"

"In the garden — "

"In the garden!" And he came over and unlocked the window and pulled it up. "What," he demanded "are you doing out in the garden at this time of night? Why, it must be 2:00 in the morning —"

"I know. But some cats woke me up. I went to chase them away. I stopped to look at the moon and then the door closed on me. Now I'm locked out."

Daddy groaned. "You crazy kid. Looking at the moon at 2:00 in the morning. I've told you time and again to watch that door if you don't have your key. And I was fast asleep —"

He put down the window, latched it, and went off. Naturally she expected him to come to the back door, but she waited and he didn't. Oh, of course — he'd just gone right on through the living room to the front as his quickest way to let her in. So she raced around the side, along the drive, and up onto the porch. And there he was, standing at the door.

"Janey, Janey!" he said. "What if you hadn't been able to wake me up? Your mother says there could be an explosion and I'd sleep right through it."

Janey went to him and threw her arms around him. Then she took his hand and pulled him onto the porch. "Look!" she said. "Just look! Did you ever see such a beautiful moon in your life?"

Daddy stood there with her at the railing. Together they looked out at that incomparable moon. And behind them, the door went — CLICK.

READING COMPREHENSION

Summarizing. Choose the best phrase to complete each sentence. Then write the complete statement on your paper.

1. Janey, wakened by fighting cats, had gone out and was looking up at the full moon when _____ (the door shut, the cats returned, someone yelled "SCAT!").

2. Because her father was a sound sleeper, Janey had to _____ (knock on the kitchen door, get a neighbor's help, thump on his bedroom window with a stick) to let him know she was locked out.

3. When Janey's father went out to let her in, he too _____ (saw the fighting cats, locked the window, got locked out).

Interpreting. Write the answer to each question on your paper.

1. Why did Janey go out instead of her father?

2. What did Janey see outside and why was it interesting to her?

3. Why was Janey trying to be quiet outside in the night?

For Thinking and Discussing. What do you think happened to Janey and her father after the story ended? What did they do to get help? Do you think they were able to get into the house that night? Explain your answer.

UNDERSTANDING LITERATURE

Plot With a Surprise Ending. An author carefully plans the *plot*, the important events of the story from the beginning to the end. Sometimes the author plans the plot to have a surprise ending. "Janey by Moonlight" has a surprise ending. Neither Janey nor the reader expects what happens.

On your paper, write a sentence to describe the surprise ending of "Janey by Moonlight." Then write the events below in the order that led up to the ending.

1. Janey and her father stand at the porch railing to look at the moon.

2. Janey scratches at the bedroom window.

3. Janey's father wakes up and opens the door.

4. Janey forces a stick through the window screen and pushes it back and forth to make noise.

5. The front door swings shut, locking Janey out of the house.

6. Janey goes onto the porch to chase the cats and stops to look at the moon.

WRITING

Sometimes when people hear noises at night, their thoughts go wild! Write a paragraph describing what Janey's father might have thought or imagined when he woke up to a thump on his window at 2:00 A.M.

The Bat

by Theodore Roethke

By day the bat is cousin to the mouse.
He likes the attic of an ageing house.

His fingers make a hat about his head.
His pulse beat is so slow we think him dead.

He loops in crazy figures half the night
Among the trees that face the corner light.

But when he brushes up against a screen,
We are afraid of what our eyes have seen:

For something is amiss or out of place
When mice with wings can wear a human face.

1. What is the bat like by day?
2. How does the bat spend the night?
3. According to the poem, what about the bat makes it a scary creature?

Paul Revere's Ride

by Henry Wadsworth Longfellow

Listen, my children, and you shall hear
Of the midnight ride of Paul Revere,
On the eighteenth of April, in Seventy-five;
Hardly a man is now alive
Who remembers that famous day and year.

He said to his friend, "If the British march
By land or sea from the town tonight,
Hang a lantern aloft in the belfry arch
Of the North Church tower as a signal light, —
One, if by land, and two, if by sea;
And I on the opposite shore will be,
Ready to ride and spread the alarm
Through every Middlesex village and farm,
For the country folk to be up and to arm."

Then he said, "Good night!" and with muffled oar
Silently rowed to the Charlestown shore,
Just as the moon rose over the bay,
Where swinging wide at her moorings lay
The *Somerset*, British man-of-war;
A phantom ship, with each mast and spar
Across the moon like a prison bar,
And a huge black hulk, that was magnified
By its own reflection in the tide.

Meanwhile, his friend through alley and street
Wanders and watches, with eager ears,
Till in the silence around him he hears
The muster of men at the barrack door,
The sound of arms, and the tramp of feet,
And the measured tread of the grenadiers,
Marching down to their boats on the shore.

Then he climbed the tower of the Old North Church,
By the wooden stairs, with stealthy tread,
To the belfry-chamber overhead,
And startled the pigeons from their perch
On the sombre rafters, that round him made
Masses and moving shapes of shade, —
By the trembling ladder, steep and tall,
To the highest window in the wall,
Where he paused to listen and look down
A moment on the roofs of the town
And the moonlight flowing over all.

Beneath in the churchyard, lay the dead,
In their night-encampment on the hill,
Wrapped in silence so deep and still
That he could hear, like a sentinel's tread,
The watchful night-wind, as it went
Creeping along from tent to tent,
And seeming to whisper, "All is well!"
A moment only he feels the spell
Of the place and the hour, and the secret dread
Of the lonely belfry and the dead;
For suddenly all his thoughts are bent
On a shadowy something far away,
Where the river widens to meet the bay, —
A line of black that bends and floats
On the rising tide, like a bridge of boats.

Meanwhile, impatient to mount and ride,
Booted and spurred, with a heavy stride
On the opposite shore walked Paul Revere.
Now he patted his horse's side,
Now gazed at the landscape far and near,
Then, impetuous, stamped the earth,
And turned and tightened his saddle girth;
But mostly he watched with eager search

The belfry's tower of the Old North Church,
As it rose above the graves on the hill,
Lonely and spectral and sombre and still.
And lo! as he looks, on the belfry height
A glimmer, and then a gleam of light!
He springs to the saddle, the bridle he turns,
But lingers and gazes, till full on his sight.
A second lamp in the belfry burns!

A hurry of hoofs in a village street,
A shape in the moonlight, a bulk in the dark,
And beneath, from the pebbles, in passing, a spark
Struck out by a steed flying fearless and fleet;
That was all! And yet, through the gloom and the light,
The fate of a nation was riding that night;
And the spark struck out by that steed, in his flight,
Kindled the land into flame with its heat.
He has left the village and mounted the steep,
And beneath him, tranquil and broad and deep,
Is the Mystic, meeting the ocean tides;
And under the alders that skirt its edge,
Now soft on the sand, now loud on the ledge,
Is heard the tramp of his steed as he rides.

It was twelve by the village clock,
When he crossed the bridge into Medford town.
He heard the crowing of the cock,
And the barking of the farmer's dog,
And he felt the damp of the river fog,
That rises after the sun goes down.

It was one by the village clock,
When he galloped into Lexington.
He saw the gilded weathercock
Swim in the moonlight as he passed,
And the meeting-house windows, blank and bare,

Gaze at him with a spectral glare,
As if they already stood aghast
At the bloody work they would look upon.

It was two by the village clock,
When he came to the bridge in Concord town.
He heard the bleating of the flock,
And the twitter of birds among the trees,
And felt the breath of the morning breeze
Blowing over the meadows brown.
And one was safe and asleep in his bed
Who at the bridge would be first to fall,
Who that day would be lying dead,
Pierced by a British musket-ball.

You know the rest. In books you have read,
How the British Regulars fired and fled, —
How the farmers gave them ball for ball,
From behind each fence and farmyard wall,
Chasing the redcoats down the lane,
Then crossing the fields to emerge again
Under the trees at the turn of the road,
And only pausing to fire and load.

So through the night rode Paul Revere;
And so through the night went his cry of alarm
To every Middlesex village and farm, —
A cry of defiance, and not of fear,
A voice in the darkness, a knock at the door,
And a word that shall echo for evermore!
For, borne on the night-wind of the Past,
Through all our history, to the last,
In the hour of darkness and peril and need,
The people will waken and listen to hear
The hurrying hoof-beats of that steed,
And the midnight message of Paul Revere.

READING COMPREHENSION

Summarizing. Choose the best phrase to complete each sentence. Then write the complete statement on your paper.

1. A lantern or two at the North Church tower would signal that the British were _____ (coming by land or sea, defeated, marching through town).

2. Paul rode through villages and farms to tell people to _____ (run to the hills, hide in their houses, prepare for battle).

3. The British left because _____ (the people were ready for them, the village was empty, Paul Revere chased them out).

Interpreting. Write the answer to each question on your paper.

1. Why did Paul Revere see so much going on in the river?

2. What did the author mean when he said that Paul Revere's alarm was "a cry of defiance and not of fear"?

3. Explain the meaning of the lines, "Through all our history, to the last, / In the hour of darkness and peril and need,/ The people will waken and listen to hear/The hurrying hoofbeats of that steed,/ And the midnight message of Paul Revere."

For Thinking and Discussing. "Paul Revere's Ride" is famous. Your parents and grandparents probably studied it. Why do you think this poem is so well known?

UNDERSTANDING LITERATURE

Plot in a Narrative Poem. A *narrative poem* tells a story. Just like a story, a narrative poem has a plot. The plot is how the story happens from the beginning, to the middle, to the end.

The following events are from the narrative poem "Paul Revere's Ride." Use them to write a paragraph telling what happens in the poem. When you write your paragraph, be sure to put the events in the order in which they happen in the poem.

1. Paul Revere asked a friend to send him a signal about British troop movements.

2. The villagers were prepared for the British.

3. Paul Revere rode through the night to warn the villagers to arm themselves.

4. Paul Revere waited for the signal on the Charlestown shore.

5. Paul Revere's friend spied on the British and found out that they were planning to go by sea.

6. The British fled.

7. Paul Revere's friend gave the signal.

WRITING

"Paul Revere's Ride" describes sights and sounds at night each hour as Paul Revere rode. Imagine you are taking a midnight ride. Write a paragraph telling what you see and hear at midnight, 1:00 A.M. and 2:00 A.M.

What About the Midnight Ride of William Dawes?

Based on an article from
The People's Almanac *by Charlie Jones*

*Is William Dawes an unsung hero? Charlie Jones thinks so.
Read his essay to find out who William Dawes was and why he
is a hero.*

In January, 1861, Henry Wadsworth Longfellow wrote the poem he would call "Paul Revere's Ride." Yet, he was one person who failed to remember what really happened on that famous day and year. Longfellow created a poem that was filled with false information. In doing so, he created a new hero. Because of Longfellow's poem, Paul Revere was given all the credit for a daring deed. But there was another hero who ever-after was ignored and forgotten by American history.

In Longfellow's poem, complete credit was given to Paul Revere for alerting the American colonists to the coming of the British troops. Actually, on that day in April, 1775, two young men were sent out on horseback to alert the American rebels between Boston and Lexington, Massachusetts. One, of course, was Paul Revere. The other was a young shoemaker named William Dawes. Here is what really happened . . . .

Preparing for Battle

It was the spring of 1775, and British troops were pouring into Boston. Day after day, tensions grew between British and American colonists. The Sons of Liberty, a rebel group, was preparing for a War of Independence. This group stored weapons and gunpowder in the nearby village of Concord. There they also trained troops and prepared for the war they felt was soon to begin.

The Sons of Liberty worried that the British Army would find out where they hid their weapons, and try to take them. So, thirty Sons of Liberty, under the command of Dr. Joseph Warren, were assigned to keep a constant watch on British troop activity. Dr. Warren picked two young men as his special messengers. They were Paul Revere, a silversmith, and William Dawes, a shoemaker.

On April 15, Dr. Warren received a midnight report of British troop movement. The British Royal Fleet had launched all of its small boats. A number of British soldiers had been relieved of their everyday duties. Based on these facts, Dr. Warren felt sure that the British were getting ready to sneak into Concord.

Dr. Warren sent Paul Revere to Lexington to warn Sam Adams and John Hancock. Their writings, speeches, and demonstrations against the British had placed them on top of His Majesty's Most Wanted List. Adams and Hancock called on other leaders of the Sons of Liberty. They decided to raise a "home guard." The American army—called Minutemen because they claimed they would fight the British at a minute's notice — was asked to gather at Concord four days later, on the nineteenth of April.

On the way back to Lexington, Revere stopped to warn Colonel Conant, the leader of the Charlestown Minutemen. Revere told Conant that the British might soon be coming through Charlestown. Conant wanted to know how he would be alerted to the enemy troops' approach.

Revere pointed across the Charles

River, toward the steeple of Christ's Church. "One lantern means they are marching overland through Cambridge," he said. "Two lanterns will shine if the British come across the river."

The Eighteenth of April, 1775

On April 18, Dr. Warren began hearing bits of gossip that made him sure that the British attack was coming very soon. He learned that British soldiers had been complaining about an upcoming night march. All the places that housed British soldiers seemed unusually active.

Warren's most valuable spy confirmed his suspicion. The order to move on Concord had been given. The British warship *Somerset* was moving down the river as if to protect a ferry full of soldiers. So, Dr. Warren guessed the British would cross the water.

Quickly, Dr. Warren contacted William Dawes. He sent Dawes along the land route (see map on page 177) to spread the word. When the young shoemaker came across the British troops assembling for the march, he rode slowly, looking like a good-natured country fellow. He mixed in with a bunch of farmers. The British guards set up a barrier across the road. When they saw Dawes, they studied his calm, innocent-looking face. They judged him a harmless "country bumpkin" and sent him on his way. Once out of their sight, Dawes began galloping furiously. Soon he was racing through Cambridge yelling "The British are coming."

It was not until late that evening that Warren was able to contact Paul Revere. Revere was sent by the water route (see map, p.177) with a special message for Conant. Revere knew the British troops would be following closely behind him. He lined up several other rebels to help him on his ride. Revere asked his friend John Pulling to give the promised signal from the church steeple. Pulling got the church sexton Robert Newman to do the actual signalling while he stood guard in the street below.

Two lights beamed briefly from the church tower, and Conant spotted them. The British were crossing the river.

Revere rode towards the docks. His route required that he, too, cross the river. He asked two friends, Josh Bentley and Tom Richardson, to meet him there and row him across. The plan called for the boatmen to wrap cloth around the oars to muffle the sound of the oars hitting the water. After all, they did not want to be discovered by the Royal Fleet. However, the boatmen had forgotten to bring anything with which to wrap their oars. Revere waited while one of the boatmen borrowed some cloth from a friend who lived near-by. She gave a petticoat to the Rebel cause.

At last the boat delivered Revere safely to Charlestown. There, Colonel Conant and some of his men were waiting for the news. After delivering his message, Revere was warned that there were already British troops between Charlestown and Lexington. Nevertheless, Revere decided to go on. He asked for a fresh horse. Soon

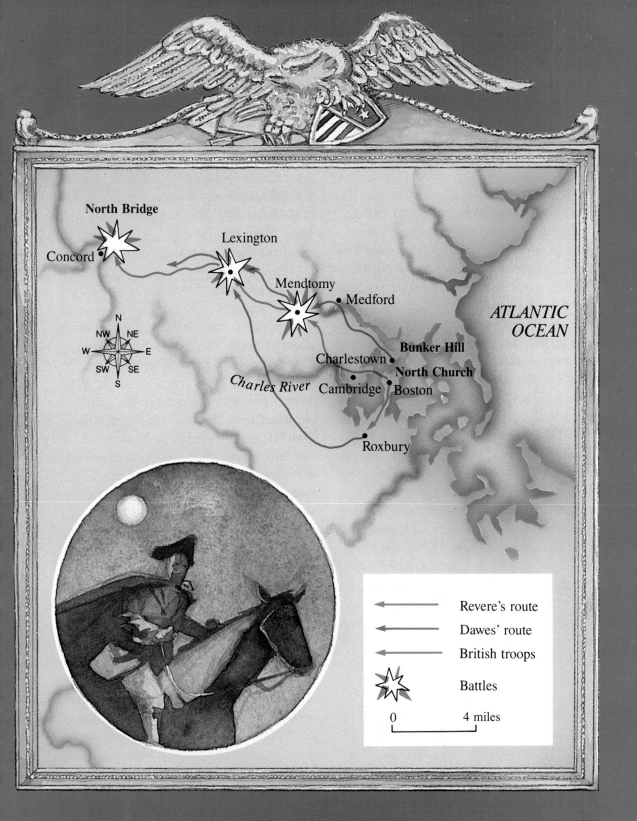

North Bridge

Concord

Lexington

Mendtomy

Medford

ATLANTIC OCEAN

N
NW NE
W E
SW SE
S

Bunker Hill

Charlestown

North Church

Charles River

Cambridge

Boston

Roxbury

⟵ Revere's route

⟵ Dawes' route

⟵ British troops

✦ Battles

0   4 miles

he was off, galloping in the bright moonlight.

The News Reaches Lexington

When Paul Revere reached Lexington, he went to find Sam Adams and John Hancock. Hancock picked up a gun. He said he wanted to stand his ground and fight the British. But Adams convinced him to put down his gun and escape into hiding. They would be of more use to the Rebel cause if they were able to escape from Lexington alive.

Paul Revere rode through Lexington. He yelled his news as he thundered through town. Lights went on everywhere. Church bells began to sound frantically. Drum rolls called men to gather in the town common. It was midnight. In the midst of this terrible excitement and fear, William Dawes arrived on his horse. He had ridden most of the day and most of the night. He was bone-tired. After all, he had come the long way, by land.

Revere suggested to Dawes that they continue to Concord to warn the rebels there. Dawes nodded and climbed wearily back into the saddle. Dr. Sam Prescott, another member of the Sons of Liberty, joined them. The three riders proceeded towards Concord. They took turns riding off the road to warn people who lived in farm houses along the way. As Revere rode off on one of these side missions, he was surprised by two British soldiers.

Revere yelled to Dawes and Prescott for help. But by the time Prescott reached the spot, two more British soldiers had arrived. Prescott managed to escape from the British, and went on to Concord. But Revere was captured. Revere called to Dawes: "Back to Lexington, Billy!"

Dawes disappeared into the woods and avoided the British. He followed Revere's instructions and set off for Lexington.

Throughout the Boston area, hundreds of Minutemen were gathering. They had heard the news, and they were ready to fight the British. By the time William Dawes returned to Lexington, a battle was in progress.

Paul Revere and the British soldiers who held him heard the shots coming from Lexington. The quick-thinking Revere told his British captors that the Rebel forces were certain to cut His Majesty's Army to pieces. The soldiers became frightened. They released Revere and retreated towards Boston.

Many years later, Henry Longfellow wandered through the scenes of all this Revolutionary excitement. He thrilled to the memory of the "Midnight Ride of Paul Revere." He even imagined Revere thundering all the way through to Concord, a point he never reached that night.

Why was it Revere he remembered and not Dawes? Perhaps it was because Paul Revere became famous for the silverware he made after the war. Longfellow had seen the gleaming stuff in the best homes in Boston. But little is known about what happened to William Dawes after April 18, 1775. Certainly, no one ever bragged that they owned a pair of shoes made by William Dawes — no matter how good a shoemaker he was.

READING COMPREHENSION

Summarizing. Choose the best phrase to complete each sentence. Then write the complete statement on your paper.

1. Joseph Warren was asked to _____ (watch the British troops, lead the Minutemen into battle, write articles against the British).

2. William Dawes _____ (called Joseph Warren, took the land route, went by the water route) to spread the word that the British were coming.

3. The author thinks Paul Revere was remembered and William Dawes was forgotten because_____ (Revere later became a general, Longfellow knew of Revere's work as a silversmith, Revere was braver).

Interpreting. Write the answer to each question on your paper.

1. In what way was William Dawes's job harder than Paul Revere's?

2. Why was Dawes a good messenger?

3. Why might the Midnight Ride be described as a group effort rather than the work of any one person?

For Thinking and Discussing. Paul Revere is remembered for his midnight ride and for the beautiful silverware he made. What would you rather be remembered for: a brave thing that you did or something beautiful that you made? Explain your answer.

UNDERSTANDING LITERATURE

Personal Narrative Essay. An *essay* is a short discussion of a subject or idea. "What about the Midnight Ride of William Dawes?" is a *personal narrative essay*. In this kind of essay, the author tells his or her own beliefs about the subject. Then the author gives examples to support those beliefs.

Write the events below that support Charlie Jones's belief that William Dawes was as important as Paul Revere.

1. Dr. Warren's spy found out that the British were moving.

2. Dr. Warren sent William Dawes through the countryside to spread the word.

3. Dawes rode among British troops and was not discovered.

4. Dawes raced through Cambridge yelling, "the British are coming."

5. Dr. Warren was not able to reach Paul Revere until late in the evening.

6. Although he rode all night to reach Lexington, Dawes agreed to ride on to Concord.

7. William Dawes alone escaped from British capture.

WRITING

Paul Revere became famous and William Dawes did not. Write how you would feel if you were William Dawes.

Many Moons

by James Thurber

Scientists may tell us the facts about the universe around us, but those facts don't change what we imagine and dream. In this special fable, the moon is a different place to every single person who beholds it.

Once upon a time, in a kingdom by the sea, there lived a little Princess named Lenore. She was ten years old, going on 11. One day Lenore fell ill of a surfeit of raspberry tarts and took to her bed.

The Royal Physician came to see her and took her temperature and felt her pulse and made her stick out her tongue. The Royal Physician was worried. He sent for the King, Lenore's father, and the King came to see her.

"I will get you anything your heart desires," the King said. "Is there anything your heart desires?"

"Yes," said the Princess. "I want the moon. If I can have the moon, I will be well again."

Now the King had a great many wise men who always got for him anything he wanted, so he told his daughter that she could have the moon.

Then he went to the throne room and pulled a bell cord, three long pulls and a short pull, and presently the Lord High Chamberlain came into the room.

The Lord High Chamberlain was a large, fat man who wore thick glasses which made his eyes seem twice as big as they really were. This made the Lord High Chamberlain seem twice as wise as he really was.

"I want you to get the moon," said the King. "The Princess Lenore wants the moon. If she can have the moon, she will get well again."

"The moon?" exclaimed the Lord High Chamberlain, his eyes widening. This made him look four times as wise as he really was.

"Yes, the moon," said the King. "M-o-o-n, moon. Get it tonight, tomorrow at the latest."

The Lord High Chamberlain wiped his forehead with a handkerchief and then blew his nose loudly. "I have got a great many things for you in my time, your Majesty," he said. "It just happens that I have with me a list of things I have got for you in my time." He pulled a long scroll of parchment out of his pocket. "Let me

see, now." He glanced at the list, frowning. "I have got ivory, apes, and peacocks, rubies, opals, and emeralds, black orchids, pink elephants, and blue poodles, gold bugs, scarabs, and flies in amber, hummingbirds' tongues, angels' feathers, and unicorns' horns, giants, midgets, and mermaids, frankincense, ambergris, and myrrh, troubadours, minstrels, and dancing women, a pound of butter, two dozen eggs, and a sack of sugar — sorry, my wife wrote that in there."

"I don't remember any blue poodles," said the King.

"It says blue poodles right here on the list, and they are checked off with a little check mark," said the Lord High Chamberlain. "So there must have been blue poodles. You just forget."

"Never mind the blue poodles," said the King. "What I want now is the moon."

"I have sent as far as Samarkand and Araby and Zanzibar to get things for you, your Majesty," said the Lord High Chamberlain. "But the moon is out of the question. It is 35,000 miles away and it is bigger than the room the Princess lies in. I cannot get the moon for you. Blue poodles, yes; the moon, no."

The King flew into a rage and told the Lord High Chamberlain to leave the room and to send the Royal Wizard to the throne room.

The Royal Wizard was a little, thin man with a long face. He wore a high red peaked hat covered with silver stars, and a long blue robe covered with golden owls. His face grew very pale when the King told him that he wanted the moon

for his little daughter, and that he expected the Royal Wizard to get it.

"I have worked a great deal of magic for you in my time, your Majesty," said the Royal Wizard. "As a matter of fact, I just happen to have in my pocket a list of the wizardries I have performed for you." He drew a paper from a deep pocket of

his robe. "It begins: 'Dear Royal Wizard: I am returning herewith the so-called philosopher's stone which you claimed — ' no, that isn't it." The Royal Wizard brought a long scroll of parchment from another pocket of his robe. "Here it is," he said. "Now, let's see. I have squeezed blood out of turnips for you, and turnips out of blood. I have produced rabbits out of silk hats, and silk hats out of rabbits. I have conjured up flowers, tambourines, and doves out of nowhere, and nowhere out of flowers, tambourines, and doves. I have brought you divining rods, magic wands, and crystal spheres in which to behold the future. I have compounded philters, unguents, and potions, to cure heartbreak, surfeit, and ringing in the ears. I have made you my own special mixture of wolfbane, nightshade, and eagles' tears, to ward off witches, demons, and things that go bump in the night. I have given you seven-league boots, the golden touch, and a cloak of invisibility."

"It didn't work," said the King. "The cloak of invisibility didn't work."

"Yes, it did," said the Royal Wizard.

"No, it didn't," said the King. "I kept bumping into things, the same as ever."

"The cloak is supposed to make you invisible," said the Royal Wizard. "It is not supposed to keep you from bumping into things."

"All I know is, I kept bumping into things," said the King.

The Royal Wizard looked at his list again. "I got you," he said, "horns from Elfland, sand from the Sandman, and gold from the rainbow. Also a spool of thread, a paper of needles, and a lump of beeswax

— sorry, those are things my wife wrote down for me to get her."

"What I want you to do now," said the King, "is to get me the moon. The Princess Lenore wants the moon, and when she gets it, she will be well again."

"Nobody can get the moon," said the Royal Wizard. "It is 150,000 miles away, and it is made of green cheese, and it is twice as big as this palace."

The King flew into another rage and sent the Royal Wizard back to his cave. Then he rang a gong and summoned the Royal Mathematician.

The Royal Mathematician was a bald-headed, nearsighted man, with a skullcap on his head and a pencil behind each ear. He wore a black suit with white numbers on it.

"I don't want to hear a long list of all the things you have figured out for me since 1907," the King said to him. "I want you to figure out right now how to get the moon for the Princess Lenore. When she gets the moon, she will be well again."

"I am glad you mentioned all the things I have figured out for you since 1907," said the Royal Mathematician. "It so happens that I have a list of them with me."

He pulled a long scroll of parchment out of a pocket and looked at it. "Now let me see. I have figured out for you the distance between the horns of a dilemma, night and day, and A and Z. I have computed how far is Up, how long it takes to get to Away, and what becomes of Gone. I have discovered the length of the sea serpent, the price of the hippopotamus. I know where you are when you are at Sixes and Sevens, how much Is you have

to have to make an Are, and how many birds you can catch with the salt in the ocean — 187,796,132, if it would interest you to know."

"There aren't that many birds," said the King.

"I didn't say there were," said the Royal Mathematician. "I said if there were."

"I don't want to hear about seven hundred million imaginary birds," said the King. "I want you to get the moon for the Princess Lenore."

"The moon is 300,000 miles away," said the Royal Mathematician. "It is round and flat like a coin, only it is made of asbestos, and it is half the size of this kingdom. Furthermore, it is pasted on the sky. Nobody can get the moon."

The King flew into still another rage and sent the Royal Mathematician away. Then he rang for the Court Jester. The Jester came bounding into the throne room in his motley and his cap and bells, and sat at the foot of the throne.

"What can I do for you, your Majesty?" asked the Court Jester.

"Nobody can do anything for me," said the King mournfully. "The Princess Lenore wants the moon, and she cannot be well till she gets it, but nobody can get it for her. Every time I ask anybody for the moon, it gets larger and farther away. There is nothing you can do for me except play on your lute. Something sad."

"How big do they say the moon is," asked the Court Jester, "and how far away?"

"The Lord High Chamberlain says it is 35,000 miles away, and bigger than the

Princess Lenore's room," said the King. "The Royal Wizard says it is 150,000 miles away, and twice as big as this palace. The Royal Mathematician says it is 300,000 miles away, and half the size of this kingdom."

The Court Jester strummed on his lute for a little while. "They are all wise men," he said, "and so they must all be right. If they are all right, then the moon must be just as large and as far away as each person thinks it is. The thing to do is find out how big the Princess Lenore thinks it is, and how far away.

"I will go and ask her, your Majesty," said the Court Jester. And he crept softly into the little girl's room.

The Princess Lenore was awake, and she was glad to see the Court Jester, but her face was very pale and her voice very weak.

"Have you brought the moon to me?" she asked.

"Not yet," said the Court Jester, "but I will get it for you right away. How big do you think it is?"

"It is just a little smaller than my thumbnail," she said, "for when I hold my thumbnail up at the moon, it just covers it."

"And how far away is it?" asked the Court Jester.

"It is not as high as the big tree outside my window," said the Princess, "for sometimes it gets caught in the top branches."

"It will be very easy to get the moon for you," said the Court Jester. "I will climb the tree tonight when it gets caught in the top branches and bring it to you."

Then he thought of something else. "What is the moon made of, Princess?" he asked.

"Oh," she said, "it's made of gold, of course, silly."

The Court Jester left the Princess Lenore's room and went to see the Royal Goldsmith. He had the Royal Goldsmith make a tiny round golden moon just a little smaller than the thumbnail of the Princess Lenore. Then he had him string it on a golden chain so the Princess could wear it around her neck.

"What is this thing I have made?" asked the Royal Goldsmith when he had finished it.

"You have made the moon," said the Court Jester. "That is the moon."

"But the moon," said the Royal Goldsmith, "is 500,000 miles away and is made of bronze and is round like a marble."

"That's what you think," said the Court Jester as he went away with the moon.

The Court Jester took the moon to the Princess Lenore, and she was overjoyed. The next day she was well again and

could get up and go out in the gardens to play.

But the King's worries were not yet over. He knew that the moon would shine in the sky again that night, and he did not want the Princess Lenore to see it. If she did, she would know that the moon she wore on a chain around her neck was not the real moon.

So the King sent for the Lord High Chamberlain and said, "We must keep the Princess Lenore from seeing the moon when it shines in the sky tonight. Think of something."

The Lord High Chamberlain tapped his forehead with his fingers thoughtfully and said, "I know just the thing. We can make some dark glasses for the Princess Lenore. We can make them so dark that she will not be able to see anything at all through them. Then she will not be able to see the moon when it shines in the sky."

This made the King very angry, and he shook his head from side to side. "If she wore dark glasses, she would bump into things," he said, "and then she would be ill again." So he sent the Lord High Chamberlain away and called the Royal Wizard.

"We must hide the moon," said the King, "so that the Princess Lenore will not see it when it shines in the sky tonight. How are we going to do that?"

The Royal Wizard stood on his hands and then he stood on his head and then he stood on his feet again. "I know what we can do," he said. "We can stretch some black velvet curtains on poles. The curtains will cover all the palace gardens like a circus tent, and the Princess Lenore will not be able to see through them, so she will not see the moon in the sky."

The King was so angry at this that he waved his arms around. "Black velvet curtains would keep out the air," he said. "The Princess Lenore would not be able to breathe, and she would be ill again." So he sent the Royal Wizard away and summoned the Royal Mathematician.

"We must do something," said the King, "so that the Princess Lenore will not see the moon when it shines in the sky tonight. If you know so much, figure out a way to do that."

The Royal Mathematician walked around in a circle, and then he walked around in a square, and then he stood still. "I have it!" he said. "We can set off fireworks in the gardens every night. We will make a lot of silver fountains and golden cascades, and when they go off, they will fill the sky with so many sparks that it will be as light as day and the Princess Lenore will not be able to see the moon."

The King flew into such a rage that he began jumping up and down. "Fireworks would keep the Princess Lenore awake," he said. "She would not get any sleep at all and she would be ill again." So the King sent the Royal Mathematician away.

When he looked up again, it was dark outside and he saw the bright rim of the moon just peeping over the horizon. He jumped up in a great fright and rang for the Court Jester. The Court Jester came bounding into the room and sat down at the foot of the throne.

"What can I do for you, your Majesty?" he asked.

"Nobody can do anything for me," said the King, mournfully. "The moon is coming up again. It will shine into the Princess Lenore's bedroom, and she will know it is still in the sky and that she does not wear it on a golden chain around her neck. Play me something on your lute, something very sad, for when the Princess sees the moon, she will be ill again."

The Court Jester strummed on his lute. "What do your wise men say?" he asked.

"They can think of no way to hide the moon that will not make the Princess Lenore ill," said the King.

The Court Jester played another song, very softly. "Your wise men know everything," he said, "and if they cannot hide the moon, then it cannot be hidden."

The King put his head in his hands again and sighed. Suddenly he jumped up from his throne and pointed to the windows. "Look!" he cried.

"The moon is already shining into the Princess Lenore's bedroom. Who can explain how the moon can be shining in the sky when it is hanging on a golden chain around her neck?"

The Court Jester stopped playing on his lute. "Who could explain how to get the moon when your wise men said it was too large and too far away? It was the Princess Lenore. Therefore the Princess Lenore is wiser than your wise men and knows more about the moon than they do. So I will ask *her*." And before the King could stop him, the Court Jester slipped quietly out of the throne room and up the wide marble staircase to the Princess Lenore's bedroom.

The Princess was lying in bed, but she

was wide awake and she was looking out the window at the moon shining in the sky. Shining in her hand was the moon the Court Jester had got for her. He looked very sad, and there seemed to be tears in his eyes.

"Tell me, Princess Lenore," he said mournfully, "how can the moon be shining in the sky when it is hanging on a golden chain around your neck?"

The Princess looked at him and laughed. "That is easy, silly," she said. "When I lose a tooth, a new one grows in its place, doesn't it?"

"Of course," said the Court Jester. "And when the unicorn loses his horn in the forest, a new one grows in the middle of his forehead."

"That is right," said the Princess. "And when the Royal Gardener cuts the flowers in the garden, other flowers come to take their place."

"I should have thought of that," said the Court Jester, "for it is the same way with the daylight."

"And it is the same way with the moon," said the Princess Lenore. "I guess it is the same way with everything." Her voice became very low and faded away, and the Court Jester saw that she was asleep. Gently he tucked the covers in around the sleeping Princess.

But before he left the room, he went over to the window and winked at the moon, for it seemed to the Court Jester that the moon had winked at him.

READING COMPREHENSION

Summarizing. Choose the best phrase to complete each sentence. Then write the complete statement on your paper.

1. When Princess Lenore became ill, the King promised to give her _____ (raspberry tarts, anything she wanted, many moons).

2. The Lord High Chamberlain, the Royal Wizard, and the Royal Mathematician all tried to tell the King that _____ (Lenore was too sick to save, the moon was impossible to get, Lenore should be given something else).

3. Finally the Court Jester gave the Princess exactly the kind of _____ (music she needed, moon she described, raspberry tarts she wanted).

Interpreting. Write the answer to each question on your paper.

1. Why did the King tell the Princess that she could have the moon?

2. How did the Court Jester figure out what to give the Princess?

3. What else worried the King after the Princess got her wish?

4. Who solved the second problem, and how?

For Thinking and Discussing. How were the answers the King got from his four men both the same and different? Whose answers were most wise? Support your ideas with details from the story.

UNDERSTANDING LITERATURE

Four Parts of Plot. The plot is the events in a story. Usually the plot has four parts:

1. *The Problem.* First the reader learns that the characters have a problem.

2. *Rising Action.* Next the characters try to solve the problem. The story becomes more exciting.

3. *Turning Point.* After that, the action reaches its highest point. Just as you think that the characters may never solve their problem, they find a way.

4. *Resolution.* The problem is solved. You learn how the solution affects the characters.

Write the following statements on your paper the way they happen in the plot of "Many Moons." Then write the part of the plot to which each belongs.

1. The Princess explains her ideas about the moon.

2. The King talks with his Chamberlain, Wizard and Mathematician.

3. The King makes a promise to Princess Lenore that he cannot fulfill.

4. The Jester talks to the Princess.

WRITING

Asking for the moon means asking for something impossible. Write a paragraph telling what you would request and why if you could *ask for the moon.*

VOCABULARY

Using Context Clues in Poetry. You can learn the meaning of many new words when you read by using *context clues*. Context clues are the other words in a sentence, a paragraph, or lines of poetry that help you figure out the meaning of a word you may not know.

Although there are words you may not know in the poem "Paul Revere's Ride" you can use context clues and what you do know about Paul Revere's ride to figure out the meaning of these words.

For example, can you tell what *belfry chamber* means in these lines? "Then he climbed the tower of the Old North Church . . . To the belfry-chamber overhead?" There are clues in the lines that help you guess what *belfry-chamber* means. The words *climbed, tower, Old North Church*, and *overhead* are all clues to help you know that a belfry-chamber is a room on the top of the bell tower in a church.

The following lines are taken from "Paul Revere's Ride." Use the context clues in each line to choose the best meaning for each italicized word or group of words. Write the italicized word or words and the meaning you choose on your paper. Then list the clue words that helped you make your choice.

1. "And lo! As he looks, on the belfry height/ A *glimmer*, and then a gleam of light!" (small light, church bell)

2. "Hang a lantern *aloft* in the belfry arch/ of the North Church tower as a signal light." (down, up high)

3. "Then he said, 'Good night!' and with *muffled* oar/ Silently rowed to the Charlestown shore," (quieted, scarf-like)

4. "And the measured *tread* of the grenadiers marching down to their boats on the shore" (footsteps, part of a tire)

5. "Through all our history, to the /last In the hour of darkness, and *peril* and need," (celebration, danger)

READING

Making Inferences or Reading Between the Lines. Sometimes an author does not put all his or her ideas in words. Instead, the author tells you just enough so that you can have your own ideas about the people in a story. For example, the author of "Many Moons" does not tell you if the Court Jester is wise or not. You must decide that for yourself from reading the story. When you decide for yourself what the author might be saying you are making an *inference*. Making an inference is also called *reading between the lines*.

Read the following parts from the stories in this section. On your paper, write the inference you think is best for each.

1. "If Janey called really loud to Daddy now, old Leather Lungs would hear and come charging out. She would begin managing everything the way she always did." You can infer that _____.
   a. Janey could not hear as well as her neighbor.
   b. Janey did not like her neighbor.
   c. Janey lived in a very friendly neighborhood.

2. "Hancock picked up a gun. He said he wanted to stand his ground and fight the British. But Adams convinced him to put down his gun and escape into hiding." You can infer that _____.
   a. Hancock had a quick temper, and Adams was more practical.
   b. Hancock wanted to join the army, but Adams talked him out of it.
   c. Hancock and Adams always agreed on everything.

3. " 'The moon'?" exclaimed the Lord High Chamberlain, his eyes widening. . . . 'Yes, the moon,' said the King. 'M-o-o-n, moon. Get it tonight, tomorrow at the latest.' " You can infer that _____.
   a. The Lord High Chamberlain is pleased that the King is asking for his help.
   b. The King enjoys spelling words aloud.
   c. The King expects to get whatever he asks for, whenever he asks for it.

4. "Who could explain how to get the moon when your wise men said it was too large and too far away? It was Princess Lenore. Therefore the Princess Lenore is wiser than your wise men and knows more about the moon than they do. So I will ask her." You can infer that _____.
   a. Princess Lenore will grow up to become a space scientist.
   b. The wise men did not really undersatnd what Princess Lenore wanted.
   c. Princess Lenore should run the kingdom, because she is wiser than any wise men.

5. After Princess Lenore explained how a new moon grows, the "Court Jester went over to the window and winked at the moon, for it seemed to the Court Jester that the moon had winked at him." You can infer that _____.
   a. The Court Jester had trouble seeing in the bright moonlight.
   b. The Court Jester understood that the moon was always growing and changing.
   c. The Court Jester was happy that Princess Lenore had come to her own understanding about the moon.

QUIZ

The following is a quiz for Section 5. Write your answers on your paper in complete sentences.

Reading Comprehension

1. In "Janey by Moonlight," why did both Janey and her father get locked out?

2. According to the author of "The Bat," how is the bat by night different from the bat by day?

3. According to the author of "Paul Revere's Ride," what route did Paul Revere take?

4. In "Many Moons," how does the Princess describe the moon?

5. What facts in "What About the Midnight Ride of William Dawes?" explain why neither Paul Revere nor William Dawes ever reached Concord on April 18, 1775?

Understanding Literature

6. What is the problem in the plot of "Janey by Moonlight"?

7. What two living things is the bat compared to in the poem "The Bat"?

8. What is the turning point in "Paul Revere's Ride"?

9. What does the author of "What About the Midnight Ride of William Dawes?" believe that Longfellow did wrong? Name one example he gives in his essay to support his beliefs.

10. How would you describe the ending of "Many Moons" — as an expected ending or a surprise ending? Explain your answer.

WRITING

A New Ending. You have learned that the plot of a story has a beginning, a middle, and an end. Many times when you know the beginning and the middle of a story, you can guess how it will end. At other times, the ending is unexpected. The ending must make sense with the other events in the story.

On your paper, write a new ending to "Janey by Moonlight" or "Many Moons." Read each step to help guide you in your writing.

Step 1: Set Your Goal
Choose one of the following suggestions and write a new ending for the story. If you wish, you may make up your own idea.

☐ In "Janey by Moonlight," Janey wakes her father to let him know she is locked out of the house. Suppose that he did not wake up. Rewrite the ending telling how Janey spent the night.

☐ In "Many Moons," Princess Lenore believes that the moon can replace itself. Suppose that she could not explain why the moon still shines at her window. Rewrite the ending of the story describing how the Jester solves this problem.

Step 2: Make a Plan
Plan what you are going to say.

Find the main idea of the story and the events that develop the plot. Anything that you add should make sense with the beginning and middle of the story. Then make a list of the possible actions your character might make. Keep in mind that the actions should show the problem or situation the author has set up.

For example, imagine that in "Many Moons" the Lord High Chamberlain decides to get the moon for Princess Lenore. Remember, he believes the moon is 35,000 miles away, but he is good at getting things for the King. Here is a list of actions he mights take.

He might try to invent a ladder tall enough to reach the moon.

He might have every tree in the Kingdom cut to make the ladder.

He might put every citizen of the kingdom to work building the ladder.

Step 3: Write Your First Draft

Your ending should have at least five paragraphs. The first should state the new situation, the middle ones should give the characters' actions, and the last paragraph should state the effects of the actions.

☐ Begin by stating the new situation. For example, if you were writing about the Lord High Chamberlain's efforts, you might begin:

"Your Majesty, I can help you!" exclaimed the Lord High Chamberlain. "I can build a ladder to the moon!"

☐ Next write the paragraphs using your list of actions.

☐ End by stating the effects of the ac-

tions. The Lord High Chamberlain's story might end this way.

The ladder grew taller and taller, but the moon remained out of reach. However, Princess Lenore was so delighted with the enormous ladder outside her window that she completely recovered from her illness.

Step 4: Revise Your Ending

Check your ending one more time. Does your ending make sense with the beginning and middle of the story? Correct any errors in spelling, grammar, and punctuation you find. Make a final neat copy of your ending.

Word Attack. What do the three words below have in common? What is different about them?

jumped ruled planted

All the above words end with the suffix *-ed*, but the suffix is pronounced differently in each. In jumped, *-ed* sounds like *t*. In *ruled, -ed* sounds like *d*. In *planted*, the suffix stands for the *-ed* sound. If you know the base word, you can figure out which sound *-ed* has.

In each sentence below, pronounce the word that ends in -ed. Copy them on your paper and write *t, d,* or *ed* according to the sound *-ed* makes in each.

1. The sound changed suddenly into a spitting, snarling explosion of fury as they fought.

2. Janey bounced out of bed.

3. He breathed in a slow and peaceful snore.

4. He hated being waken.

5. She listened.

6. She knew exactly what had happened.

7. Then the door swung to, as if its hinges were oiled.

8. The windows here at the back would be closed and locked, she knew.

9. She got a stick and forced it through the fragile, weathered screen.

10. He put down the window, latched it, and went off.

Speaking and Listening. Storytelling can be fun for both the storyteller and his or her audience. Practice telling the story "Janey by Moonlight" in your own way. Remember to keep what happens at the end a surprise until your very last words. Then tell the story to your family or some students in your school who haven't read it.

Researching
1. Paul Revere was a famous silversmith as well as a Revolutionary hero. Write the following words in alphabetical order on your paper.

silversmith   goldsmith   locksmith
blacksmith   tinsmith   smith

Look each word up in a dictionary and write the definition next to the word on your paper. Use the definitions to write a paragraph explaining the work of the different kinds of smiths.

2. As the moon travels around the earth, the sun strikes the face of the moon differently. At new moon, no sunlight strikes the face. At full moon, the whole face is lit. Use the chart to watch for the changes of the moon. Write the days you notice the changes.

Creating. "The moon is a different place to every single person who beholds it." What do you see when you look at the moon? Make up a drawing or diagram of the moon from your own imagination. Label all the important details that you see or imagine when you look at the moon. Make up a title for the diagram that expresses your idea of the moon.

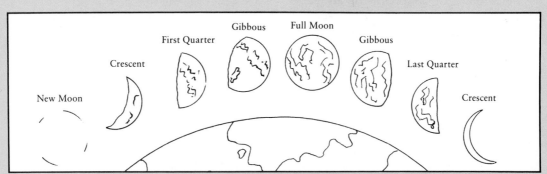

New Moon   Crescent   First Quarter   Gibbous   Full Moon   Gibbous   Last Quarter   Crescent

JANE YOLEN

Like a kite
Cut from the string,
Lightly the soul of my youth
Has taken flight.

—Ishikawa Takuboku

Introduction

by Jane Yolen

Rhymes and verse, non-fiction or informational books, and fairy tales—I have written them all. And I have also written mystery novels, science fiction novels, fantasy books, song books, adventure stories, ghost stories, short tales and long ones, three different musical plays, and historical novels. I like to think that every morning when I wake up and get to my typewriter I am there to discover a new story or poem that no one in the world has ever read before.

Beginning With Rhyme

The poems from "How Beastly" on page 200 for example, come from the light, humorous side of my personality. I have been writing in rhyme since I was very young. I have to admit that my first efforts were terrible. (From first grade, comes this scrap my mother saved: "Bus, bus/ wait for us/ we were going to school/ and we knew the rule. . ." Warning: don't let your parents save everything. Someday those scraps of paper will turn into flapping ghosts that will haunt you!) In junior high and high school I wrote many of my term papers in rhyme. I even wrote a 20 page poem about the New York State centers of manufacturing. This poem contained quite a splendid rhyme for Otis Elevators which we are all lucky I have forgotten. And in college I wrote a final exam in American History in rhyme. I received an A+ from the professor who was very impressed that I could do it. To be honest, I only knew about a C− worth of work. I simply enjoy rhyming, and I adore puns. Many of the poems for "How Beastly" I spoke into a tape recorder as I was driving in my car. I did a lot of polishing at home afterwards on the typewriter.

World On a String

Another interest I have had for many years is in kites. My father was first Western and then International Kite Flying Champion. He was in both *Ripley's Believe It Or Not* and the *Guiness Book of World Records*. I, on the other hand, could not get a kite into the air. But I was fascinated by kite history. The very first book I ever worked on was my father's book, *The Young Sportman's Guide To Kite Flying*. I did the research and a great deal

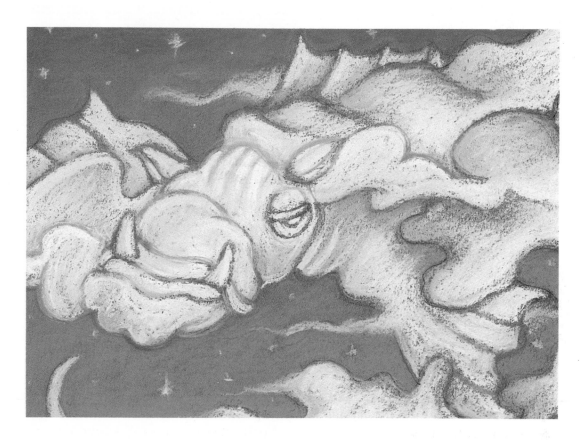

of the writing. He liked to fly kites and I like to write. It worked out wonderfully. But I wanted to learn more about kites. Eventually I did much more research and wrote my own kite book, *World On A String* from which the essay on pages 204–209 is taken. So curiosity and an on-going family interest motivated me to write about kites.

World of Imagination

Writing was also a family interest. My father was a newspaperman, my brother is now the editor-in-chief of a newspaper in Brazil. And at one point I wanted to be a journalist. But after a while I realized that writing for newspapers and magazines, reporting on things that were, was not enough for me. I wanted to write about "things that never were but always are." Some wise person once said that in the world of the imagination, magic works as easily and as regularly as gravity works in ours. I wanted to write fantasy novels and wonder tales. "The Seventh Mandarin" is a good example of that kind of writing. It also incorporates the love of kites. (In my kite research I learned about the Thai belief that the emperor's soul was bound fast to the wings of a kite at night and flown high above the terrors of the dark.) If you read the story aloud, you will hear the poetry in the lines. The lines don't rhyme—but as poet Eve Merriam once pointed out, "It doesn't always have to rhyme . . ." to be a poem.

How Beastly

Poems by Jane Yolen

*You might not want to meet up
with any of four unusual beasts.
But, you might not notice the
beasts, at first. Read these four
poems to find out if the alligate,
walrust, shirk, and porcupin are
really what their names may lead
you to think they are.*

The Alligate

If you come to my house for a visit,
Be warned of a hideous fate,
For there in the alley before you
A terrible beast lies in wait.

Its head is just like a veranda.
Its mouth like a cavernous door,
And people who enter that gateway
Are never heard from any more.

So if you come over to see me,
Remember that hideous fate,
And whatever you do, do not come by
The jaws of the fierce Alligate.

The Porcupin

Oh, do not needle Porcupin,
His rage is long, his patience thin,
A flight with him no one can win,
So don't get in the way.

His hair he wears both straight and long,
Each hair is like a sharpened prong,
So never do this beastie wrong
But let him have his say.

For when he gets into a fight
He doesn't throw a left or right,
He simply sews his foes up tight
And makes his getaway.

The Walrust

Do not leave him out at night
Or near some dampish drains,
And never take him for a walk
On any day it rains
Because his baggy, wrinkled skin
Which looks like well-done crust
Is iron-hard and very thick
And is inclined to rust.

201

The Shirk

The toothy Shirk swims lazily
Beneath the rainbow-colored sea.
It rarely has to move because
Its dinner swims into its jaws.

Upside-down or rightside up
It does not have to work to sup.
And since it never has to work,
There is no one who likes the Shirk.

READING COMPREHENSION

Summarizing. Choose the best phrase to complete each sentence. Then write the complete statement on your paper.

1. In "The Alligate," when people enter the alley they _____ (open a door, visit Jane Yolen, are eaten by a beast).

2. The Walrust shouldn't be out at night because _____ (his skin will rust, he is afraid of the dark, he is noisy).

3. Nobody likes the Shirk because it ____ (has sharp teeth, never has to work, swims upside down).

4. When a porcupin gets into a fight he _____ (throws a left, throws a right, sews up his enemy).

Interpreting. Write the answer to each question on your paper.

1. How is the alligate like an alligator?

2. What is rusty about the Walrust?

3. To *shirk* means to avoid work. How does this word describe the animal in the poem? What real animal is the beast like?

For Thinking and Discussing. The artist drew the animals in these poems the way she imagined them. Do these illustrations match your idea of what these animals look like? Explain your answer.

UNDERSTANDING LITERATURE

Style and Form in Poetry. The words a poet uses are part of the poet's *style*. Jane Yolen uses *word play*, a funny use of words, and rhyme in her poems. She gives her beasts names with double meanings by making up nonsense names with parts of real names. For example, the walrust, a baggy creature who is inclined to rust, is made up of the name *walrus* and the word *rust*.

The *form* a poet uses is the way the poet chooses to write a poem. Jane Yolen's poems are fun because of the form she uses. The short sentences and ending rhymes give the poems a light bouncy sound. The rhyme can best be enjoyed when the poems are read aloud.

Answer the questions below.

1. To needle can mean to bother or annoy. Why is the use of the word needle good in the first line of "The Porcupin"?

2. Which pair of ending words in "The Shirk" are spelled in a similar way and rhyme exactly? Which pairs are spelled differently? Do these lines still rhyme?

3. What real animal is the Alligate like?

WRITING

Write a paragraph about an animal to entertain readers. Use words that are scary or funny.

Kites

by Jane Yolen

Flying a kite may be just a fun game to some of us, but to many people it is much more meaningful and special than that. The author tells us in this article about the magical importance of the kite in many countries around the world.

For millions of people in the world, the kite long stood for the human soul.

In Polynesia, which includes New Zealand and Micronesia, as well as the Hawaiian Islands, kite-flying grew up first as part of a religion. Rehua, the god of the highest heaven, often called the "sacred bird," was a kite flier, like the twin gods Rongo and Tane. The Hawaiians loved telling stories about Maui, a hero whose favorite kite-flying field was by the boiling pools of the Wailuku River.

Kite-flying was so much a part of the Polynesian religions that *karakias,* special kite songs, were sung as the kites rose. Only the right hand was used for holding the kite line. And special tribesmen were chosen as the official kite fliers.

To the Polynesians, the kite was not a toy. It was a symbol of the soul of its owner. Often a chief was referred to in terms of the form of his kite, the way a medieval knight was sometimes known by the color or shape of his crest.

In New Zealand, the Maori said: "The flying kite foretells a person's luck. If it swoops, it is bad luck. If it is steady, then truly the sun shines before."

Sometimes the *manu taratahi,* a specially made Maori kite, was used as a crime detector. When murder was suspected in connection with the death of a person, the kite was given the dead man's name. This tradition arose more than 400 years ago, when two young brothers were missing from their home. The unhappy mother finally consulted a priest. He decided to use two kites to discover the whereabouts of the missing boys. Each kite was named after one of the boys and immediately flown. They rose steadily and then suddenly swooped toward a neighboring village. There they righted themselves and hovered over a single dwelling — the home of the chief. It soon came out that the chief had murdered the two boys, and he was found guilty and quickly punished. After that, the Maoris often used kites to find missing people or to decide who was guilty of a crime.

The Hawaiians said that Maui — who was supposed to be the common ancestor of all the brown people of the Pacific — once made a kite larger than a house. But the kite rose too slowly for the impatient Maui. Then he remembered an old priest named Kaleiioku who owned a magic calabash. With this calabash, Kaleiioku could summon the winds whenever he wished. So Maui traveled to Waipio, where the old priest lived. He persuaded the old man to lend him the calabash. Then Maui sang:

Oh, winds, winds of Waipio,
In the calabash of Kaleiioku,
Come from the calabash,
Come quickly, come with power.

And the winds came, roaring and surging. They ripped the kite from Maui's hands and tossed it far over the volcanoes of Hawaii to the other side of the mountains. Angrily, Maui leaped over the mountains to find his giant kite. But when he finally caught up with it, his anger was gone. Ever after, according to the legend, he was more respectful of the winds. And, too, the Hawaiians said that when Maui died, his kite fell from the sky. It landed far up on the top of a mountain, where it may be seen to this very day. They point to a flat plot of land between Mauna Kea and Mauna Loa, which they call Maui's Kite.

In China, too, the flying kite was regarded as a symbol of the human soul. The Chinese say, "The soul is like a flying bird," and kites were thought to bring

good luck. Each kite in ancient China was specially decorated, and each decoration had a meaning. A kite sacred to a certain god or warrior would carry his or her picture or symbol high toward the heavens.

The most famous of the Chinese religious kite festivals took place on the ninth day of the ninth month. It was known as *Ch'ung-yang* — the "Festival of Climbing the Heights," or the "Festival of Ascending on High." On this day, until very recently, all manner of kites were

flown throughout the country, with figures of men and women, of birds, of centipedes, of giant dragons or groups of fierce hawks. Some particularly interesting kites were made of bands of colored papers and were known as "women's robes." There were also singing kites that had strips of rawhide stretched tightly on their bamboo frames. The wind played across these strips like a violinist.

According to tradition, the Festival of Ascending on High began many centuries ago when a man received a strange warning. He was told that on the ninth day of the ninth moon a great calamity would befall his house and all within. So that day he took his family and servants on an all-day picnic to the countryside. They spent the whole day flying kites. Upon their return, they discovered their house in ruins and their animals all killed by invaders. Thanking the gods for the warning, each year on the same day the man — with all his household — went back to the hills to picnic and fly kites.

The festival grew and grew until it was

celebrated in almost all of China. In fact, every year there would be a special proclamation warning against the "tumult" caused by the 30,000 to 40,000 people who took to the hills that surround the city of Canton to fly their kites. And a special mandarin and policemen were assigned to keep peace there.

Prayer kites were once very popular in ancient Korea. Such kites still may be found in parts of the countryside. Korean mothers wrote prayers on the kites asking that the evil of the year might be caught by the wind and made to vanish. Then the kites were set free.

In Thailand, not only was the kite considered a person's soul, but the king of Siam had a special kite and a group of special kite mandarins. These men would take turns flying the king's kite all night long, to keep his soul high and safe from the dark and evil night while his body lay below in sleep. At other times, large paper kites were sent up in the Thai countryside to help the crops grow by calling to the gods of wind and rain.

It is not surprising that the kite should be thought of as a symbol for the human soul. It is made of the crude materials of earth — sticks and cloth and vines and paper. Yet it dares to fly up to the heavens, where, traditionally in almost all religions, the god or gods dwell.

READING COMPREHENSION

Summarizing. Choose the best phrase to complete each sentence. Then write the complete statement on your paper.

1. Polynesians, Chinese, and Thais believed that kites _____ (should only be flown on sunny days, are like birds, stand for the human soul).

2. After Maui's death, his _____ (friends destroyed the mountain, kite fell from the sky, neighbors leveled his house creating a flat plot of land).

3. The Chinese "Festival of Climbing the Heights" _____ (brings good luck, brings the winds, brings the gods).

4. To ward off evil, Korean mothers _____ (wrote prayers on kites, collected the ashes of burned kites, gathered flower seeds).

Interpreting. Write the answer to each question on your paper.

1. How is a kite like a human being?

2. Why have kites been thought of as symbols of the soul?

3. Why is the soul thought of differently in the daytime than at night?

For Thinking and Discussing. *Myths* and *legends* are stories that try to explain how or why something in nature came to be. Every country or group of people has its own myths and legends. What do the myths and legends in "Kites" try to explain? Do you know any other myths or legends that try to explain similar things?

UNDERSTANDING LITERATURE

Style and Form in Nonfiction. *Nonfiction writing* tells about real people and real events. In "Kites" Jane Yolen uses the form of essay to write about real events. The style she uses is to state the main idea and give examples that support that main idea.

Write the following statements from "Kites" in the order in which they occur in the essay. Underline the statement that tells the *main idea*. Write *supporting detail* next to each statement that gives an example of the main idea.

1. "The king of Siam had a special kite and a group of special kite mandarins."

2. "And, too, the Hawaiians said that when Maui died, his kite fell from the sky."

3. "Sometimes. . . . a specially made Maori kite was used as a crime detector."

4. "Each kite in ancient China was specially decorated, and each decoration had a meaning."

5. "For millions of people in the world, the kite long stood for the human soul."

WRITING

Imagine you are a giant kite drifting above your neighborhood. Write a paragraph about what you see. Underline the sentence that tells the main idea.

The Seventh Mandarin

by Jane Yolen

There are many ways to be wise. This tale tells of the very serious "mistake" of the seventh, and youngest, adviser to the king — and of how that mistake·teaches some very learned men about a whole new world right outside their door.

Once, in the East, where the wind blows gently on the bells of the temple, there lived a king of the highest degree.

He was a good king. And he knew the laws of his land. But of his people he knew nothing at all, for he had never been beyond the high stone walls that surrounded his palace.

All day long the king read about his kingdom in the books and scrolls that were kept in the palace. And all day long he was guarded and guided by the seven mandarins who had lived all their lives, as the king had, within the palace walls.

These mandarins were honorable men. They dressed in silken robes and wore embroidered slippers. They ate from porcelain dishes and drank the most delicate teas.

Now, while it was important that the mandarins guarded and guided their king throughout his days, they had a higher duty still. At night they were the guardians of the king's soul.

It was written in the books and scrolls of the kingdom that each night the king's soul left his body and flew into the sky on the wings of a giant kite. And the king and the seven mandarins believed that what was written in the books and scrolls was true. And so, each mandarin took turns flying the king's kite through the long, dark hours, keeping it high above the terrors of the night.

This kite was a giant dragon. Its tail was of silk with colored tassels. Its body was etched with gold. And when the sun quit that kingdom in the East, the giant kite rose like a serpent in the wind, flown by one of the seven mandarins.

And for uncounted years it was so.

Now, of all the mandarins, the seventh was the youngest. He was also the most simple. While the other mandarins enjoyed feasting and dancing and many rich pleasures, the seventh mandarin loved only three things in all the world. He loved the king, the books and scrolls of the law, and the king's giant kite.

That he loved his king there was no doubt, for the seventh mandarin would not rest until the king rested.

That he loved the books and scrolls there was also no doubt. Not only did the seventh mandarin believe that what was written therein was true. He also believed that what was not written was not true.

But more than his king and more than the books and scrolls of the law, the seventh mandarin loved the king's kite, the carrier of the king's soul. He could make it dip and soar and crest the currents of air like a falcon trained to his hand.

One night, when it was the turn of the seventh mandarin to fly the king's kite, the sky was black with clouds. A wild wind like no wind before it entered the kingdom.

The seventh mandarin was almost afraid to fly the kite, for he had never seen such a wind. But he knew that he had to send it into the sky. The king's kite must fly, or the king's soul would be in danger. And so the seventh mandarin sent the kite aloft.

The minute the giant kite swam into the sky, it began to rage and strain at the string. It twisted and turned and dived and pulled. The wind gnawed and fretted and goaded the kite, ripping at its tender belly and snatching at its silken tail. At last, with a final snap, the precious kite string parted.

Before the seventh mandarin's eyes, the king's kite sailed wildly over the palace spires, over the roofs of the mandarins' mansions, over the high walls that surrounded the courtyards, and out of sight.

"Come back, come back, O Magnificent Wind Bird!" cried the seventh mandarin.

"Come back with the king's soul, and I will tip your tail with gold and melt silver onto your wings."

But the kite did not come back.

The seventh mandarin ran down the steps. He put his cape about his face so that no one would know him. He ran through the echoing corridors. He ran past the mandarins' mansions and through the gates of the high palace walls. Then he ran where he had never been before — past the neat houses of the merchants, past the tiny homes of the workers, past the canals that held the peddlers' boats, past the ramshackle, tumbledown huts and hovels of the poor.

At last, in the distance, hovering about

the hills that marked the edge of the kingdom, the seventh mandarin saw something flutter like a wounded bird in the sky. And though the wind pushed and pulled at his cape and at last tore it from his back, the seventh mandarin did not stop. He ran and ran until he came to the foot of the mountain.

There he found the king's kite. But what a terrible sight met his eyes. The wings of the dragon were dirty and torn. Its tail was shredded and bare. The links of its body were broken apart.

It would never fly again.

The seventh mandarin did not know what to do. He was afraid to return to the palace. It was not that he feared for his own life. He feared for the life of his king. For if the king's soul had flown on the wings of the kite, the king was surely dead.

He carried the king's kite past the canals and the ramshackle, tumbledown huts and hovels of the poor. And as he passed with the broken kite in his arms, it came to him that he had never read of such things as these huts and hovels in the books and scrolls of the kingdom. Yet the cries and groans he heard were not made by the wind.

At last, as the first light of the new day touched the gates of the high palace walls, the seventh mandarin entered the courtyard. He climbed the stairs to his chamber and placed the battered, broken kite on his couch.

Then he sat down and waited to hear of the death of the king.

Scarcely an hour went by before all seven of the mandarins were summoned

to the king's chamber. The king lay on his golden bed. His face was pale and still. His hands lay like two withered leaves by his side.

Surely, thought the seventh mandarin, I have killed my king. And he began to weep.

But slowly the king opened his eyes. "I dreamed a dream last night," he said, his voice low and filled with pain. "I dreamed that in my kingdom there are ramshackle hovels and huts that are falling down."

"It is not so," said the six mandarins, for they had never been beyond the high palace walls and so had never seen such things.

Only the seventh mandarin was silent.

"I dreamed that in my kingdom," continued the king, "there are people who sigh and moan — people who cry and groan when the night is dark and deep."

"It is not so," said the six mandarins, for they had never read of such things in the books and scrolls.

The seventh mandarin was silent.

"If it is not so," said the king, slowly raising his hand to his head, "then how have I dreamed it? For is it not written that the dream is the eye of the soul? And if my soul was flying on the wings of my kite and these things are not so, then how did my dream see all this?"

The six mandarins were silent.

Then the seventh mandarin spoke. He was afraid, but he spoke. And he said, "O King, I saw these same things last night, and I did not dream!"

The six mandarins looked at the seventh mandarin in astonishment.

But the seventh mandarin continued. "The wind was a wild, mad beast. It ripped your kite from my hands. And the kite flew like an angel in the night to these same huts and hovels of which you dreamed. And there are many who moan and sigh, who groan and cry beyond the high palace walls. There are many — although it is not written in any of the books or scrolls of the kingdom."

Then the seventh mandarin bowed his head and waited for his doom. For it was

death to fail the king. And it was death to damage his kite. And it was death to say that what was not written in the books and scrolls was so.

Then the king spoke, his voice low and crackling like the pages of an ancient book. "For three reasons that you already know, you deserve to die."

The other mandarins looked at one another and nodded.

"But," said the king, sitting up in his golden bed, "for discovering the truth and not fearing to reveal it, you deserve to live." And he signaled the seventh mandarin to stand at his right hand.

That very night, the king and his seven mandarins made their way to the mountain at the edge of the kingdom. There they buried the king's kite with honors.

And the next morning, when the kingdom awoke, the people found that the high walls surrounding the palace had been leveled to the ground.

As for the king, he never again relied solely upon the laws of the land, but instead rode daily with his mandarins through the kingdom. He met with his people and heard their pleas. He listened and looked as well as read.

The mandarins never again had to fly the king's kite as a duty. Instead, once a year, at a great feast, they sent a giant dragon kite into the sky to remind themselves and their king of the folly of believing only what is written.

And the king, with the seventh mandarin always by his side, ruled a land of good and plenty until he came to the end of his days.

READING COMPREHENSION

Summarizing. Choose the best phrase to complete each sentence. Then write the complete statement on your paper.

1. At night, the seven mandarins flew the king's kite to _____ (entertain themselves, guard the king's soul, test the strength of the wind).

2. When he followed the runaway kite, the seventh mandarin saw _____ (huts and hovels, gardens and valleys, empty deserts).

3. The king learned the truth about his kingdom when he _____ (read a scroll, was visited by a prince, saw the kingdom through his soul).

Interpreting. Write the answer to each question on your paper.

1. Why was it more important to guard the king's kite at night than to guard the king by day?

2. The seventh mandarin told the king the truth even though it could have cost him his life. What can you tell about the mandarin from this?

3. Why did the king decide it was a mistake to believe only what was written?

For Thinking and Discussing. Why do you think the mandarins did not believe the king's dream? Remember that they had not seen much of the country outside the king's walls. Do people sometimes believe only what they want to? Explain your answer.

UNDERSTANDING LITERATURE

Style and Form in Fiction. There are many ways to tell or write a story. The *form* of a story is the particular way an author chooses such as a play or a poem. The words an author uses and the type of sentences he or she writes make up that author's *style*.

"The Seventh Mandarin" is a modern story, but its author, Jane Yolen, has chosen to write it in the form of a folktale. A *folktale* is a story that has been passed down for many years.

a. It happens long ago.

b. It happens far away.

c. It has unusual characters.

d. There is a moral, or lesson, to be learned from the story.

On your paper, copy each statement below about "The Seventh Mandarin." Next to each, write the letter of the thing it has in common with a folktale.

1. In the East, temple bells blew gently.

2. The king found he could not depend only on books.

3. Once upon a time, there lived a king.

4. A king of high degree had never been outside the palace walls.

WRITING

Imagine that you rule this king's country. Think about five changes you would make. Write a paragraph to explain how the country would be different with your changes.

VOCABULARY

Figurative Language. Sometimes authors use words in special ways to help readers get a good picture in their minds. For example, an author might say, "The cat's fur was silk," or "The cat's fur was like silk." Readers understand that the cat's fur was not really silk. The author is just using silk to give a better idea of what it was like. If an author says, "The sun smiled on the fields," readers know that a person's smile is like sunshine.

Words that reach the imagination are a form of *figurative language*.

Read each example below of figurative language from this section. On your paper, write a complete sentence to answer the question following each example.

1. "The wind gnawed and fretted and goaded. . . ."

   How would it feel to be outside in this kind of wind?

2. "His hands lay like two withered leaves by his side."

   How would his skin feel?

3. "The wind played across these strips like a violinist."

   What sounds would a wind that played like a violinist make?

READING

Sentence Meaning. Sometimes when sentences are taken out of the context of a story they can have different meanings. Each of the following passages is from "The Seventh Mandarin." Think back to the story and select the correct meaning for each passage. Write the answer on your paper.

1. "Once, in the East, where the wind blows gently on the bells of the temple, there lived a king of the highest degree."
   a. The king had a high degree from college.
   b. The king had a fever and always felt warm.
   c. The king was one of the most powerful rulers in the East.

2. "Now, while it was important that the mandarins guarded and guided their king throughout his days, they had a higher duty still."
   a. The mandarins had another job that was even more important than guarding and guiding the king throughout his days.
   b. The mandarins hoped to get a better job after they finished guarding the king.
   c. It was harder for the mandarins to pay duty, or taxes, than to guard the king.

3. "Now, of all the mandarins, the seventh was the youngest. He was also the most simple."

   a. The seventh mandarin was not as smart as the other six.

   b. The seventh mandarin had few needs.

   c. The seventh mandarin's character was the easiest to understand.

4. "The wings of the dragon were dirty and torn. Its tail was shredded and bare. The links of its body were broken apart. It would never fly again."

   a. The mandarin had killed the fire-breathing dragon.

   b. The dragon would have to walk in the future, since it could no longer fly.

   c. The kite was destroyed.

QUIZ

The following is a quiz for Section 6. Write the answers in complete sentences on your paper.

Reading Comprehension

1. In "The Seventh Mandarin," what did the seventh mandarin think when he saw the broken kite?

2. How did the king in "The Seventh Mandarin" change after his strange dream?

3. In "Kites," why did Maui want the magic calabash?

4. In "The Alligate," what hideous fate can a visitor to the poet's house expect?

5. Why doesn't the animal in "The Shirk" have to work?

Understanding Literature

6. Which event or events from "The Seventh Mandarin" could not happen in real life? Which could really happen?

7. How is the form of "The Seventh Mandarin" different from the form of "Kites"?

8. Is the purpose of "Kites" to entertain readers or to give them information?

9. How are the poems in "How Beastly" similar? Use examples from the poems to support your answer.

WRITING

A Poem. Poets paint pictures with words. They use words to help readers see a picture in their minds of the subject of the poem.

Many poets use *sensory imagery*, words that reach the readers' senses. Here are some examples.

sense of sight: rainbow, blue sea

sense of hearing: thunder, buzzer

sense of taste: lemon, honey

sense of touch: snow, hot sand

sense of smell: sea air, baking bread

220

Another use of words in many poems is rhyme. For example, the following lines from "The Shirk" rhyme:

"The toothy Shirk swims lazily
Beneath the rainbow-colored sea."

There are many different ways a poet can use rhyme. Look back at the poems to find examples of different *rhyme schemes*, or ways of using rhyme.

You have already learned that poets may use *comparisons*. Comparison shows how one thing is like something else. An example is in these lines from "The Alligate":

"Its head is just like a veranda.
Its mouth like a cavernous door."

Use sensory image, rhyme, or comparison to write a poem about an imaginary animal. Read each step to help guide you in your writing.

Step 1: Set Your Goal
Write a poem about an imaginary animal.

☐ Make up a name for your animal. Here is an example: a snapperflap.

☐ Think about what your animal is like.

Step 2: Make a Plan

☐ Make a list of words and phrases to describe the animal you have created in your mind. For example, the following list describes a snapperflap:
slinky way of moving, staring eyes, fire hose tail, green all over, not thin, not fat

☐ Plan what you are going to say and decide which style or form of poetry you want to use. For example, you might use comparison and rhyme.

Step 3: Write Your First Draft
Your poem should be eight to sixteen lines long. Use your list of words and phrases to write the lines of the poem. Notice how this poem about the snapperflap uses comparisons and rhyme.

The snapperflap is not thin nor fat.

It walks by moving like a cat.

Its staring eyes can never close,

Its tail looks like a fire hose.

The snapperflap is very shy

And hides from every passerby.

Although its body is grassy green,

A snapperflap is rarely seen.

Step 4: Revise Your Poem
Check your poem one more time.

Make sure you have described your animal well. Read your poem aloud to yourself. If you do not like the way it sounds, try changing some words until the rhymes and rhythms in your poem sound just right.

Finally, correct any errors in spelling, grammar, and punctuation that you find. Make a final, neat copy of your poem. If you wish, draw a picture of your animal to illustrate your poem.

ACTIVITIES

Word Attack. Each word below ends with the letters *ous*. When the letters *ous* are at the end of a word, they usually make the same sound as the word *us*.

dangerous   famous

Some words that end with *ous* such as those above, are a root word with a suffix.

Notice that the final *e* was dropped from the word *fame* before the suffix *-ous* was added to make the word *famous*.

Practice saying the words in the sentences below that end with *ous*. Which ones are made of a root word with a suffix? Write the root words on your paper

1. At last, with a final snap, the precious kite string parted.

2. Be warned of a hideous fate.

3. Its mouth is like a cavernous door.

4. The kite rose over mountainous land.

5. The six mandarins were not as adventurous as the seventh.

Speaking and Listening. Read "The Alligate" aloud. Pay special attention to the words ending in *-ous*. Pause for a moment, and then read "The Shirk" aloud. Think about how your voice sounded as you read each poem. What happened to the tone of your voice and the speed of your reading? Do you think there is a difference in the sound of each poem? Explain your answer.

Researching

1. Biographies are listed on subject cards in the library's card catalog by the last name of the person the biography is about. Look in the *F* drawer of the card catalog to find the names of biographies of Benjamin Franklin and the numbers of the shelves where these books are located.

Take out one of the biographies of Benjamin Franklin, or use it in the library. An *index* is a section in the back of a book that lists topics in alphabetical order and tells what pages they are on. Look up "kite" in the index. Turn to the pages given, and read about Benjamin Franklin and kites.

If your book does not have an index, or if the index does not list "kite" or "kites," turn to the table of contents at the front of the book. The *table of contents* lists the chapters in the order in which they appear in the book. Look for a chapter about science or electricity.

Use the information you find to write a paragraph explaining the use Benjamin Franklin made of a kite.

2. Now look in the *K* drawer for "kite". You will find out that kites have been used for many different reasons. Find out the answers to these uses of kites.

☐ How were kites used in Chinese battles?

☐ How was a kite used to help build the first suspension bridge?

☐ How were kites used to measure weather?

3. Flying a kite depends on the wind speed which is measured in miles per hour. Use the chart below to check your wind speed. List the days of the week. Record the wind speed for each day. Were any days right for a kite?

Creating. Jane Yolen tells us that "often a chief was referred to in terms of the form of his kite." From this, we may think that if a chief's kite was in the shape of a dragon, the chief might be known as "the dragon chief." If the kite was in the shape of a fish, perhaps the chief would be called "the fish chief."

Write a short paragraph explaining what you would like to be known as, and what your symbol would be. Your symbol may be anything you choose. It does not have to be a kite.

Illustrate your paragraph by drawing a picture of your symbol.

Wind Speed	
less than 1 mile per hour	calm, smoke rises straight up, kites will not fly
1-3 miles per hour	light breeze, weather vanes still, smoke drifts
4-6 miles per hour	light wind, leaves rustle, vanes move
7-10 miles per hour	gentle wind, twigs move, wind extends flag, perfect for most kites
11-15 miles per hour	moderate wind, branches move, raises dust and paper
16-21 miles per hour	windy, small trees sway
22-27 miles per hour	strong wind, umbrellas difficult to use, large branches moving

DECISION MAKERS

The door must either be shut or be open.

—Goldsmith

Once the what is decided, the how always follows.

—Pearl Buck

van GOGH, Vincent. *Hospital Corridor at Saint Rémy.* (1889). Gouache and Watercolor, 24 ⅛ × 18 ⅝″.
Collection, The Museum of Modern Art, New York. Abby Aldrich Rockefeller Bequest.

Introduction

You make thousands of decisions each day although you probably do not know you are making them! From the moment you swing your legs out of bed and decide where to land them to the moment you crawl back into bed and choose a position to sleep, you are faced with many choices.

Some of the decisions you make happen daily, like deciding what to wear to school or what to bring for lunch. But sometimes you may be faced with a larger decision such as choosing with whom to side when two friends are fighting, or whether to tell your teacher that you saw a classmate cheating on a test.

Some decisions have to be made quickly such as braking your bike when a squirrel runs into the road. But some decisions involve plans that require years of practice such as taking guitar lessons so you can eventually become a professional rock musician. In this section, you will read about both sudden decisions and long-term goals.

In "Ribsy's Return," a lost dog tries to find his owner but friendly strangers lead him further astray. When Ribsy is trapped on a fire escape, it seems as if no one, not even his owner, can figure out a way to rescue him. So Ribsy has to take matters into his own hands . . . or paws.

"Skeeter" overcomes a crippling child-hood disease to become an Olympic gold medalist runner. She had a goal that she was determined to realize . . . and she did.

"The Bookman" takes place during the

Revolutionary War. In this story, a boy must decide whether to remain loyal to his country or to protect the man his sister loves.

In "The Most Marvelous Thing," a princess must choose among three handsome princes and the wondrous gifts they have brought to try to win her love.

Ribsy's Return

by Beverly Cleary

What would you do if you lost the dog you loved? Henry Huggins searches for his lost dog Ribsy, and in his own way Ribsy searches for Henry. Read the story to find out how Henry and Ribsy finally find each other.

Henry Huggins was zigzagging down Klickitat Street on his bicycle delivering Journals. Out of habit he glanced back over his shoulder to see what Ribsy was doing. Of course, Ribsy was not there. It had been a month since he last had loped after Henry's bicycle. Still Henry could not get over the feeling that Ribsy was following him. A dull, heavy sensation filled Henry, as it always did when he forgot and looked back for Ribsy.

Henry pedaled slowly, leaning to the right and then to the left, as if pushing bicycle pedals was hard work. Ribsy was not coming back. He knew it now. He might as well stop telephoning the Humane Society and leaving food in the dish on the back porch. He might as well throw away the old tennis ball.

While the piano in the Saylors' living room went plink, plunk, plunk, Ribsy sat down in front of the refrigerator in the Saylors' kitchen. Joe, who was turning out to be the kind of boy Ribsy expected him to be, obligingly opened the refrigerator door and, after looking around, helped himself to a handful of raw hamburger, which he held out to Ribsy.

Mrs. Saylor's voice came from the living room. "Is that you, Junior?"

"Yeah," answered Joe above the *plink, plunk, plunk,* of the piano. Then he remembered to slam the refrigerator door.

Ribsy was curious about the people in the living room, so he followed Joe to investigate. A girl a couple of years younger than Joe was sitting on a round piano stool. She was a thin, wiry girl, who appeared to be all knees, elbows and ponytail. Her hair was full of plastic — a plastic bandeau, plastic barrettes, and a plastic clasp around her ponytail. Mrs. Saylor was standing beside her pointing to the music on the piano and saying, "Here I scrimp and pinch to give you piano lessons —" Then she saw Ribsy. "Joe Saylor, Junior! What is that dog doing in my house?" she demanded.

Ribsy knew from the way she pointed at him that she was talking about him. He distrusted the tone of her voice, and his tail drooped.

"I dunno." Joe shrugged his shoulders. "He just followed me." He was watching his sister Darlene twirl around the piano stool with her ponytail flying. If she twirled in the same direction long enough, the top of the stool would come unscrewed and she would fall over. Darlene, however, had it nicely timed. Just as the stool was about to topple she began to twirl in the opposite direction.

"Well, he can just follow you right out," snapped his mother, who was finding her son exasperating.

Joe heaved a gusty sigh. "Oh, all right. Come on, dog."

Obediently Ribsy followed Joe to the back door and allowed himself to be let out. "Don't mind her," whispered Joe. "She just talks that way when she's trying to make old Darlene practice."

The hamburger in Ribsy's stomach was filling but cold. Not having anything better to do, he sat down on the back porch. He liked Joe and he liked hamburger, so he decided he might as well stay for another meal. If he sat by the door long enough, the boy was sure to come out again.

The next morning Joe barged out the back door with his lunchbag in hand. He was going so fast he fell over Ribsy and dropped his lunch, which Ribsy began to sniff. His nose detected the fragrance of bologna.

Joe picked himself up and rescued his lunch. "You still hanging around?" he asked, as he started off to school.

Ribsy followed close to Joe with his nose against the lunch bag.

Joe understood. He opened the bag and took out half a bologna sandwich, which he handed to Ribsy, who wolfed it down before he caught up with Joe. He enjoyed following a boy to school again, and pranced along with his ears and tail erect. When they reached the school, Joe pointed to a sign on the metal fence around the school yard. "See? It says: 'No Dogs Allowed'." He stooped to pet Ribsy before he went through the gate.

Ribsy then explored the neighborhood by daylight, napped by the school yard fence, and spent recess and lunch period watching the boys and girls. Several times Joe spoke to him through the fence. The day seemed familiar to Ribsy, because he had followed its same pattern with Henry Huggins so many times. After school he followed Joe home just as he had followed Henry many times. It all seemed so natural that Ribsy was beginning to forget Henry and to feel that he belonged to Joe.

Joe seemed pleased to have Ribsy at his heels. Before he opened the back door he whispered, "Come on in, and let's see what happens."

Ribsy followed Joe into the kitchen, where Mrs. Saylor was ironing. "Junior, is that dog still here?" she demanded.

"I guess he likes it here," said Joe.

"Don't you think he belongs to someone?" asked Mrs. Saylor.

"He sure didn't act like it when he started following me around yesterday," said Joe.

Ribsy wagged his tail. Mrs. Saylor did not sound as cross as she had the day before, when she was worn-out trying to get Darlene to practice.

"Are we going to get to keep him?" asked Darlene, when she came home from school a few minutes later and found Ribsy in the kitchen.

"Ask your father," answered her mother. "Now wash your hands and practice your piano lesson."

That evening Ribsy was served a supper of beets, cold, leftover macaroni and cheese, and a crust of bread and margarine that Darlene had refused to eat. Ribsy, who was not a choosy dog, had eaten meals that he had enjoyed more. After supper, he slipped into the living room and curled up on the carpet. He might as well assume he was welcome until someone told him he was not.

Mr. Saylor settled back in his favorite chair, the one with the sagging springs, to read the evening paper, while Mrs. Saylor occupied herself with a book. Joe sat down on the floor in front of the television set to watch a detective program. Darlene chose that moment to practice the piano.

"Dad, make her stop," said Joe. "She hasn't practiced all day, and the minute I want to look at TV she has to start banging."

"I'm not banging," said Darlene, and added, Your old program bothers *me* when I'm practicing."

Plink, plunk, plunk. "Dad, Juney's bothering me when I'm practicing." Darlene knew it especially annoyed her brother to be called Juney.

"Cut it out, you kids." Mr. Saylor was paying very little attention to his children. He was used to bickering.

Ribsy did not care for the piano-playing, but he did not mind the bickering. He had heard the boys and girls in his neighborhood talk in the same tone of voice many times.

Suddenly Mr. Saylor looked up from his paper. "Well, what do you know!" he said. "That mutt you picked up has his picture in the paper. Right here in the sports section."

"Hey, let me see." Joe leaped to his feet and peered over his father's shoulder. There was his dog — just as he had found him the day before, photographed at the moment he tripped the football player. It was all in the picture — the running dog, the falling player, the rolling ball.

By now, Mr. Saylor was reading the story under the picture. "It says the dog belongs to Joe Saylor, and gives our address. Did you tell them that, Junior?"

"Sort of, I guess," admitted Joe. He felt embarrassed to be found out, but at the same time he was pleased.

He stooped to pet the dog he was now sure belonged to him. It said so right there in the newspaper. That ought to convince his family. Ribsy looked up gratefully and thumped his tail on the floor.

Then the telephone rang. "I'll get it,"

shrieked Darlene, who always liked to get to the telephone first. "It's for you, Dad," she said, disappointed.

"Who is it?" her father asked.

"I don't know. Some boy asked for Joe Saylor."

Mr. Saylor sank back in his chair. "You get it, Junior. It's probably some kid from school."

"Oh, that's right," said Darlene. "Some people do call Juney, Joe. I forgot."

Joe tried to trip his sister on the way to the hall to answer the telephone. "Hello?" he said.

"Hello," answered a strange boy's voice. "Uh . . . Joe Saylor?"

"Yes."

"Well . . . uh, my name is Henry Huggins," said the boy. "Your dog . . . I mean, how long have you had him?"

"Awhile," said Joe cautiously. "Why?"

"He's my dog," said Henry. "I lost him over at the shopping center about one month ago."

"Who is it, Junior?" asked Mrs. Saylor.

"A boy," Joe told his mother, and the answer seemed to satisfy her. "The shopping center," repeated Joe into the telephone, hoping to gain time to think. "That's way on the other side of town."

"I know," admitted Henry, "but my dog got into the wrong car by mistake, and some people took him home, and by the time they saw my advertisement in the paper he had run off, because they gave him a bubble bath, and then they couldn't find him."

Joe had no way of knowing whether what Henry was saying was true or not.

It sounded peculiar, that part about giving a dog a bubble bath. He certainly did not want to believe what he was hearing, not when it was beginning to look as if he might get to keep the dog. "Lots of dogs look like my dog," he said. "I don't think he's your dog at all."

"Yes, he is," insisted Henry. "I know he is. I could tell by the picture in the paper."

"Prove it," challenged Joe.

There was a silence from Henry's end of the line. Joe had a feeling Henry wanted to say something like, "Oh, a wise guy." Joe looked down the hall at Ribsy, lying on the carpet, and said, "O.K., if he's your dog, why doesn't he have a license tag?"

"He does have one," said Henry, "but when he got lost he wasn't wearing his collar. I took it off, so he could scratch his neck."

"You still haven't proved he is your dog," said Joe. Even though he had given out more information than he intended, he felt he had an advantage in the conversation. He could always hang up if he wanted to.

"My dad says he'll drive me over to your house," said Henry. "You'll see. Ribsy will know me."

"Ribsy," said Joe. "That's a dumb name for a dog."

At the sound of his name Ribsy picked up his ears. He had not heard the word Ribsy for weeks.

"When I first got him he was so thin his ribs showed," explained Henry. "So I called him Ribsy."

"They don't show now," said Joe. "It can't be the same dog. Well, so long."

"Wait!" The boy on the other end of the line sounded desperate. "My dad said

he'd bring me over tonight. We're offering a reward for Ribsy."

"How much?" Joe felt it could not be much. Ribsy was no fancy poodle or German shepherd. He was just a mutt.

"Ten dollars."

Ten dollars! Ten whole dollars. Ten dollars was a lot of money to Joe, but he was not going to admit it to Henry, who, he decided, must have lots of money if he could offer a ten-dollar reward for a dog when he could get another just as good for free at the Humane Society. Mutts like Ribsy didn't cost anything.

Joe's silence must have worried Henry, because he raised the reward. "Ten dollars and my new flashlight. Can we come over now?"

Joe saw that he was gaining a new kind of advantage. After all, he could get another dog just as good as this one free of charge himself. If he stalled long enough, there was no telling what this boy might offer him. "I don't know," he said, not committing himself. "We're pretty busy. Anyway, I don't think he is your dog. He's happy here."

"I know he's my dog." Henry sounded worried. Then he seemed to have an idea. "Hey, I know. Let me talk to him."

This surprised Joe. "On the phone?"

"Sure," said Henry, sounding as if he talked to dogs on the telephone all the time.

Joe was scornful of this suggestion. He did not believe a dog would pay any attention to a voice on a telephone, so he did not mind letting the boy try. "Just a minute," he said.

Ribsy heard Joe's fingers snapping for

him to come. Obediently, he got up and trotted into the hall.

"Here, somebody wants to talk to you," said Joe, holding the telephone to Ribsy's ear.

"Hiya, Ribsy!" Henry's voice came clearly through the telephone so that Joe could hear, too, "How's Ribsy?"

It worked. Ribsy began to bark.

Ribsy barked harder. He could not understand where Henry could be, but he recognized the voice coming out of the black thing Joe was holding to his ear. Maybe if he barked hard enough, Henry would come out from wherever he was hiding.

"Ribs!" Henry shouted again. "Ribsy!"

Joe, who was now sure of a reward, felt that a conversation that consisted of barks and a dog's name yelled into a telephone was not getting any place. Ribsy's nose told him that Henry was not in the living room or even in the house. As Joe put the telephone back against his own ear, Ribsy ran to the front door. When it was not opened instantly, he began to bark wildly and scratch at the wood. Henry had to be someplace on the other side.

The startled Saylors stared at him until Darlene darted across the room and opened the door. Still barking, Ribsy ran out into the night. "Ribsy!" The boy's voice came faintly from the telephone in the hall. "Ribsy, what happened to you?"

Back on the Saylors' porch Ribsy heard Joe shouting to his sister, "What did you let him go for? There's a reward for him! Ten whole dollars!"

And Darlene answered, "When a dog wants out, you're supposed to let him go. How was I to know he was worth so much?"

Then Joe's feet came pounding down the sidewalk behind Ribsy. "Ribsy!" he called. "Ribsy! Come back here!"

Ribsy wasn't going back. Henry was somewhere close by, and he was going to find him.

Henry pressed the telephone against his ear as hard as he could. He heard a lot of barking, and then he heard Joe yell.

"I don't get it," said Henry to his mother and father, who had been following his side of the conversation. "There was a lot of barking, and now there isn't anyone on the line. "Anybody home?" he asked into the telephone in a loud voice. There was no answer.

"Hang on a minute and see what happens," said Mr. Huggins. "Now that we're this close to Ribsy we can't let him get away."

Henry strained to catch any sound that might come through the telephone. He heard barks that grew fainter, yelling, arguing and finally a click as someone in the Saylor household replaced the telephone receiver. That click was a final as a period at the end of as sentence. Slowly he replaced the receiver. He thought a moment, and then said, "At least Ribsy recognized me. That's something."

When Ribsy could run no more, he flopped down on the sidewalk, in the dark, to pant. As soon as he had caught his breath, he got up again and started off at a brisk trot with his nose to the ground. The trouble was, he did not know where he was going. It was all very puzzling. He had heard Henry Huggins' voice but he could not find Henry.	The sidewalk gave Ribsy the scent of many people and of a variety of dogs and of a cat or two, but it did not give him the scent of Henry. Ribsy became tired, confused, and bewildered. Late that night he gave up looking for Henry and went to sleep on the cold concrete in front of the Coffee Cup Cafe, where the lingering smell of hamburgers, fried during the day, gave him some comfort.

Early the next morning Ribsy woke up, feeling stiff and hungry. The Coffee Cup Cafe was not open, so he walked around to the back door, where he found a garbage can that smelled interesting. It must have smelled interesting to some other dog, too, because the can had been tipped over and garbage was strewn around the ground. Ribsy helped himself to some bits of bun, which were smeared with more relish than he cared for. He also ate the remains of a piece of pie. The best garbage had already been eaten, but at least his stomach was no longer completely empty.

Ribsy wandered aimlessly around the neighborhood, which did not look at all like Klickitat Street with its green lawns and white houses surrounded by shrubbery. Many of the buildings came right to the sidewalk, and most of them were made of brick and were three or four stories high.

It was in front of one of these buildings that Ribsy first saw the boy with the tennis ball. He was a thin boy, somewhat round-shouldered, who was sitting on the

front steps tossing the ball from one hand to the other. Naturally Ribsy was interested in a boy with a tennis ball.

While Ribsy was watching the boy, a young woman came out of the apartment house. She was wearing a black coat over the starched dress and apron of a waitress. "Now see here, Larry Biggerstaff," she said, "you keep out of trouble today, you hear?"

"Yeah, Mom." Larry quit tossing the ball.

"I don't want to hear any more complaints from the manager about you," continued his mother. "Last Saturday, Mrs. Kreech complained that you played a mouth organ in the hall, bounced a ball so that it disturbed the lady downstairs, and tried to climb down the fire escape. Keep it up, and you'll get us evicted, and then where will we go?"

Larry heaved a big sigh to show that he was disgusted with the whole situation. "But Mom, there's nothing to do. I don't even have a good ball to take to the playground."

"I don't have money to buy balls," said his mother. "At noon you come to the cafe and get your lunch. And in the meantime, keep out of trouble." She left the apartment house and hurried down the street toward the Coffee Cup Cafe.

Larry began to bounce the tennis ball, which was old and had lost much of its life. He had to throw it down hard to make it bounce at all. Nevertheless, the sight was a stimulating one to Ribsy. He pranced right up to Larry and wagged his tail to show that he was ready to play.

Larry dropped the ball. Ribsy picked it up.

"You give me back my ball," said Larry.

Ribsy dropped the ball and stood over it, wagging his tail.

Cautiously Larry advanced toward the ball, but when he was about to pick it up, Ribsy grabbed it in his jaws and went racing up the street.

"Hey!" yelled Larry.

Ribsy raced back, dropped the ball at Larry's feet, and stood waving his tail and looking hopefully up at the boy.

"Well thanks, pal," said Larry, surprised and pleased.

"Wuf!" answered Ribsy.

The boy finally understood. He threw the ball down the street, and Ribsy bounded after it, darting between the people who were walking along the sidewalk, and catching it on the first bounce. He was delighted, and so was

Larry. The boy threw the ball again and again for Ribsy to retrieve. Finally Larry sat down on the front steps of the apartment house, and Ribsy threw himself down at his feet to pant.

"You're a pretty nice dog," remarked Larry. "I'd sure like to keep you, but Old Lady Kreech would never let me."

Ribsy laid his nose on his paws and looked up at Larry, who returned Ribsy's gaze. "You hungry?" Larry asked.

"Come on then. I'll get you some cornflakes or a wienie or something," said Larry, and pulled a key out of his pocket. Ribsy followed him up the stairs, and Larry unlocked the front door. Inside he tiptoed past the door of the apartment occupied by the manager of the building to an old-fashioned elevator. Ribsy was ready to enjoy this new game the boy was playing. Larry opened a glass door and

folded back a metal gate. Ribsy followed him into what appeared to be a small square room without windows. Larry closed the gate and the door, and pushed a button on the wall.

There was a whirring noise, and suddenly Ribsy had a feeling he had never felt before. He felt as if he was going up while his stomach stayed down. He did not like the feeling one bit. He did not like this strange little room. He wanted out right now. He began to bark.

"Sh-h-h! She'll hear you."

The manager had already heard. A door on the first floor flew open, and a woman's cross voice called up, "Larry Biggerstaff. You get that dog out of this building at once!" It was the kind of voice that could make a dog slink away feeling guilty.

By that time the little room had stopped at the second floor. Larry slid back the gate and opened the glass door. Before he stepped out, he whispered, "You stay right here. I'll come back and get you in a minute." Then he left the frightened dog and shut him in the little room. Ribsy did not know what to do. He did not want to stay in the little room alone, but there was no way he could get out. He was even afraid to bark, so he made little anxious noises. Suddenly he felt himself beginning to rise again while his stomach seemed to stay behind. He barked for Larry to come and get him out of this place, but all he heard was the whir of machinery and the thump of Larry's sneakers running downstairs.

As the elevator stopped on the third floor and his stomach caught up, Ribsy heard Larry's frightened voice coming up the elevator shaft from the first floor. "Dog? What dog?" he said.

"Don't you lie to me," the manager said. "I know there's a dog in this building."

"It isn't my dog," said Larry.

Upstairs a woman opened the door to the elevator and pushed back the gate.

"Hello," said the woman to Ribsy, as if she met dogs in elevators every day.

"How did you manage to press the button?"

This time Ribsy was taking no chance of being left in this frightening room. He dashed past the woman and into the third-floor hall, while the door of the elevator closed behind him. Now he did not know what to do. He was in a long hall with a strip of worn carpet down the center and doors on either side. At one end of the hall was a staircase, and at the end of the hall was a window with a fire escape sign over it. Nothing looked familiar to Ribsy. He had never been in an apartment house before.

Larry's voice came up the stairwell. "But I don't have a dog."

Ribsy did the only thing he could think of. He started down the stairs toward Larry's voice.

"You took a dog into that elevator," said Mrs. Kreech. "You can't fool me."

Ribsy hesitated. He did not like this woman's voice. It reminded him of too many voices that had yelled, "You get off my lawn!" to him.

Ribsy heard the elevator door open down on the first floor and the manager say in quite a different voice, "Oh, good morning, Mrs. Berg. I was looking for a dog in the elevator."

"There's no dog in the elevator," said Mrs. Berg, who was a friend of Larry's and who understood the situation. "I have come to pay my rent."

"Certainly," said the manager. "Just step into my apartment while I write your receipt."

Ribsy stood listening at the steps, but all he heard was the elevator door close and the machinery whir. As the elevator rose, Ribsy started cautiously down the steps. He did not know what to expect in this strange building where rooms went up in the air. The second floor looked exactly like the third, which Ribsy had just left — the same strip of carpet, the same doors on either side, the same window with a sign over it at the end of the hall.

Ribsy felt confused. He was even more confused when he heard a whispered, "P-s-s-t!" It was Larry, who was supposed to be down below but who was now up above. While Ribsy had walked down to the second floor Larry had ridden up to the third.

"Wuf!" answered Ribsy, who wanted to get out of this place.

"Sh-h-h!" Larry's worried face appeared in the stairwell above Ribsy. He came tiptoeing down the steps. "I've got to get you out of here," he whispered. "Come on." He started to lead Ribsy down the steps, when the door of the manager's apartment opened on the first floor.

"Thanks, Mrs. Berg," said the manager.

"We can't go down that way,"

whispered Larry. "Come on, this way."

Ribsy obeyed, because he did not know where to go by himself and because he wanted to stay away from the woman with the angry voice. Larry led him down the hall toward the back stairs, which were near the window with the sign over it. He was about to start down with Ribsy when he heard someone coming up.

"I don't know who it is, but I'm not taking any chances," Larry muttered, looking around wildly. He saw the window at the end of the hall and opened it.

Ribsy found himself being picked up, thrust through the window, and dropped onto the fire escape. The window was closed behind him and a curtain pulled. Ribsy's feet slid through the metal bars of the fire escape and stuck down in empty space.

Ribsy soon discovered that a fire escape was not only frightening, it was uncomfortable. He had to move his feet carefully on the cold metal or they would slip through. It made him uneasy to see the ground so far below him. There was an opening in the fire escape big enough to jump through, but the ground was too far down.

Since Ribsy could not go down, he did the next best thing. He climbed up cautiously, one step on the steep slanting ladder at a time. Unfortunately, when he reached the next level of the fire escape, things were worse. The good solid ground was farther away. Ribsy peered into the window, but the third floor hall was empty.

With his tail drooping, Ribsy looked around. The view was better, but there was nothing a dog would be glad to see — only some old fenders and wrecked cars behind the body-and-fender shop below. He could look out over the roof of the shop and see the cars and buses on the busy street on the other side of the block. He tried whimpering at the window, but no one came. He gave an experimental bark, but there was so much banging in the body-and-fender shop that no one heard him.

A half hour went by and then an hour. Larry did not come back, and the building was silent, because the apartments overlooking the body-and-fender shop were rented to people who were out all day and did not have to listen to the noise. Ribsy grew cold and stiff. His body hurt from the iron bars that pressed into him. Things were not getting any better. Ribsy would have to do something.

Ribsy got up and managed to shake himself without having his feet slip through the fire escape. Cautiously, he put one forepaw and then the other on the window ledge once more and whimpered at the empty hall. The doors remained closed. No rescuer appeared.

Ribsy became frantic. He felt as if the whole world had gone off and left him. He barked and barked. There must be somebody someplace who would come and get him off this thing.

And there was somebody. Somebody way down below on the next street. "Ribsy!" It was Henry Huggins' voice coming from the new station wagon, which was moving along with the rest of the traffic. "Ribsy!" Henry had his head out of the window and was pointing up at the fire escape.

At the sound of the voice he loved Ribsy went wild. He barked so wildly that even the body-and-fender men heard him.

One of them came to the back door of the shop and looked up at the dog on the fire escape. "Well, I'll be doggoned," he said.

"Hey, Bert," the body-and-fender man called to someone in his shop. "There's a dog on the fire escape."

"No kidding?" Bert appeared and looked up at Ribsy. "Well, what do you know? How do you suppose he got up there?"

Ribsy tried to tell the men that he had to get down, that he had to run down the street and find Henry Huggins before he got so far away he could never find him again.

"What do you think we should do?" asked the body-and-fender man.

Bert shrugged. "Probably some kid put him there. Most likely it was Larry. He'll probably get him down again."

"Yeah. I guess you're right." The two men knew Larry, who often came into the shop to admire the wrecked cars.

Suddenly Ribsy saw Henry Huggins coming closer to the side of the building. "Ribsy!" the boy shouted. "I've found you!"

This time Ribsy barked for joy at the sight of the boy down below.

"Funny place to lose a dog," remarked the body-and-fender man.

"I didn't lose him there," explained Henry, his eyes on his dog. "I lost him a month ago at the shopping center."

So why is he up there?" the man asked.

"Search me," said Henry. All that really mattered was that he had found his dog at last. "All I know is I was talking to him on the telephone, and he started running, and nobody saw him after that."

The two men looked at one another, shook their heads, and went back into the shop. One of them said something that sounded like, "Poor kid. Too much TV."

Next, Ribsy saw Henry's mother and father come around the corner of the apartment house. "I finally found a parking space," remarked Mr. Huggins, and looked up at Ribsy. "Hello there, fellow."

Ribsy made eager, anxious noises.

Surely his family would not go off and leave him here.

By this time, Larry Biggerstaff arrived. He had been sitting on the front steps worrying about how he was going to get rid of the dog, when he noticed three people hurrying to the side of his apartment building, and overheard the words "dog" and "fire escape."

"That's easy," Mr. Huggins was saying. "I'll just go ring the bell and tell the manager we want our dog back."

"Please don't do that," begged Larry, bursting into the conversation. "The dog isn't supposed to be there, and I'll catch it if the manager finds out about him. She might even evict me and my mother. She always says she's going to."

Ribsy barked to remind the people below that he was still up here.

"Sh-h-h," hissed Larry.

"I don't get it," said Henry. "What's he doing up there?"

"Well, I was playing out in front with this old tennis ball I have." From the way Larry spoke of the tennis ball, it was easy to tell he did not think much of it. "This dog came along and wanted to chase it. And, well, I got to thinking he might be hungry, and so I started to take him inside, and the manager started chasing me, and I shoved him out on the fire escape to hide him. And, well, I have been sitting out on the front steps trying to figure out how I was going to get rid of him without the manager seeing me."

"Well, you just get him down," said Henry. "Fast."

"I didn't put him out on the third floor," said Larry, as if this helped the situation. "I put him out on the second, and he climbed up to the third."

"We seem to have a problem," said Mr. Huggins, looking up at the dog on the fire escape.

"Maybe you could boost me up to that little ladder that sticks down from the bottom part, and then I could climb up and carry him down," offered Larry, who was glad someone had arrived to help him with his problem.

"Oh, no," said Mrs. Huggins hastily. "We couldn't let you climb down those steps with a dog. You might slip."

Ribsy could not be patient any longer. He put his paw on the top step.

"Maybe we could call the Fire

Department and they could bring a net and he could jump," suggested Henry.

"Don't do that! Please don't do that." Larry objected strenuously. "The manager really gets excited when she sees a fire engine in front of the building."

Ribsy was beginning to think the people below had forgotten all about him. He put a second paw on the steps. He wanted so much to get down. He wanted to feel Henry petting him again and to lick his face. Even though he was afraid, he was going to try.

"This is ridiculous," said Mr. Huggins. "I'll just go in the back door and up the back stairs, and bring him through the window."

"And have someone mistake you for a burglar?" asked Mrs. Huggins. "Oh, no!"

"You go," Henry said to Larry. "You got him up there."

Larry looked frightened. "The manager might catch me."

"Then I'll go," said Henry.

Ribsy reached for the second step and at the same time brought his hind feet down to the top step.

"No, you won't," said Henry's mother. "You can't go roaming around in a strange building."

"But we can't just leave him —" Henry began.

Ribsy had started down the steep steps. It was too late to turn back, even if he wanted to, and he did not want to. He found himself coming down the stairs faster that he expected. The metal was slippery to his paws. Halfway down, he slipped and tumbled, yelping, to the bottom, and there he was with his feet dangling in space again.

"Hey, look!" Henry pointed unnecessarily. Everyone was looking at Ribsy. "He got down by himself! That proves he wants to come home to us."

Ribsy got up and scrambled around trying to find places to set his feet.

"Smart dog, Ribsy!" said Henry. "Now how do we get him down from there?"

The two men from the body-and-fender shop came out once more to see what the commotion was about. "I hear that dog talks on the telephone," remarked Bert.

"He did once," said Mr. Huggins absentmindedly. He was wondering how they were going to get Ribsy down to the ground.

The two men exchanged a glance. "There's a ladder in the shop that should reach almost to the bottom of the fire escape," one of them said. "I'll get it." He returned in a moment with a paint-spattered stepladder, which he set up under the fire escape. It almost reached the metal ladder that extended down from the fire escape.

Mr. Huggins climbed the stepladder and then the short ladder that was part of the fire escape. He crawled through the opening in the lower level of the fire escape and picked up Ribsy. "Hold still, boy," he said, as Ribsy gratefully tried to lick his face.

"You'll fall," worried Mrs. Huggins. "You can't climb down the fire escape ladder and the stepladder with a dog."

"Don't drop him," begged Henry.

"I'm afraid that's what I will have to do," said Mr. Huggins.

"Go ahead," said one of the body-and-fender men. "We'll catch him."

Ribsy felt himself being lifted over the railing of the fire escape, and then he experienced a terrible moment of panic as he fell through the air. Suddenly, everything was all right. Four strong hands caught him. Ribsy wriggled out of the grasp of the body-and-fender men and sprang into Henry's arms, where he licked Henry's face for joy.

"Ribsy!" said Henry. "Ribsy, old boy!" he put the dog down at last, and Ribsy was so happy he waggled all over. Henry sank to his knees and hugged his dog.

"Whew! That's a relief," said Larry.

"And now I think we'd better go home before Larry's manager catches us," said Mr. Huggins, as the men took down the ladder and carried it into the body-and-fender shop.

"I wonder if that dog knows how to dial the telephone, too," remarked Bert.

"If he does he ought to be on TV," answered the other man.

Henry, his parents, and Larry walked along the side of the apartment house with Ribsy bounding along beside them. In front of the building they ran right into Mrs. Kreech, who was sweeping the front steps.

"I knew you had a dog, Larry Biggerstaff," she said triumphantly. "Wait till I talk to your mother about this!"

"There must be some mistake," said Mr. Huggins politely. "This is our dog. He never belonged to Larry."

"But —" began Mrs. Kreech.

"No," said Mr. Huggins firmly. "The dog is ours, and has been for several years. We just — misplaced him for a while."

READING COMPREHENSION

Summarizing. Choose the best phrase to complete each sentence. Then write the complete statement on your paper.

1. Henry Huggins was feeling sad because _____ (his bicycle was broken, he lost his tennis ball, his dog was lost).

2. Ribsy was in the Saylor's home after _ (Joe took him from the shopping center, he followed Joe, he got into Larry's car).

3. The _____ (ad in the paper, dog's picture in the paper, telephone call from the Humane Society) led Henry to believe that Joe had Ribsy.

4. Henry spotted Ribsy _____ (in Joe Saylor's yard, on the fire escape, in the schoolyard) while driving down the street with his parents.

Interpreting. Write the answer to each question on your paper.

1. What were Henry's feelings toward his dog, Ribsy?

2. How did Joe feel about giving Ribsy to Henry?

3. What did Larry think of Ribsy?

4. How can you tell that Ribsy loved Henry?

For Thinking and Discussing. Suppose Henry never found Ribsy. Do you think Ribsy could easily get used to having a new owner? Find examples in the story.

UNDERSTANDING LITERATURE

Characterization through Description. How do you get to know the people in a story? The ways an author presents the people, or characters is *characterization*. An author can use description to tell you how a character looks, speaks, feels, and acts. A good description helps you to see the character in your mind.

Read each description from "Ribsy's Return." Write the answers to the questions on your paper.

1. "Henry pedaled slowly, leaning to the right and then to the left, as if pushing bicycle pedals was hard work. Ribsy was not coming back. He knew it now."

   How does Henry feel?

2. "Ribsy felt as if he was going up while his stomach stayed down. He did not like the feeling one bit. He did not like this strange room. He wanted out right now. He began to bark."

   Describe how you see Ribsy in your mind.

3. "Ribsy heard Joe shouting to his sister, 'What did you let him go for? There's a reward for him! Ten whole dollars!'"

   What can you tell about Joe from his actions and his speech?

WRITING

Write a newspaper ad to help Henry find Ribsy. Describe what Ribsy looks like, tell how to reach Henry, and offer a reward.

Skeeter

by Michael Bonner

This play tells the true story of a great athlete named Wilma Rudolph. Wilma wore a leg brace as a child but she decided that nothing would stop her from participating in sports. Wilma proved that in becoming a champion, a strong spirit is as important as strong muscles.

CHARACTERS:
Wilma Rudolph
Mrs. Rudolph, *her mother*
Westley, *her brother*
Clinton Gray, *Wilma's high school coach*
Ed Temple, *Wilma's college coach*
Announcer
Reporter
Narrator

Scene One

Narrator: The year is 1944. The place is Clarksville, Tennessee. Young Wilma Rudolf has been very sick. Her sickness has left her with a bad leg. At first, doctors say she may never walk again. But Wilma's parents do not give up.

Wilma *(crying):* Stop fussing with my leg, Mama!

Mrs. Rudolph *(scolding):* Listen to me. The doctors say that there's still a chance to save your leg. But it's going to take time. We have to work with it four times every day. We have to move it and turn it to help it grow strong again. So stop crying!

Wilma: I'm sorry. It's just that I get so tired. Besides, maybe the treatments won't work.

Mrs. Rudolph: They'll work. We just have to try our hardest and make you better.

Wilma: But how? We don't have much money. You and Dad work hard enough just to keep this big family going.

Mrs. Rudolph: Don't worry, Wilma. Everything will work out. I know it.

Narrator: Wilma's leg starts to get a little stronger. But Wilma's parents are not satisfied. They know they must work harder than before. They teach Wilma's brothers and sisters how to work on her leg.

Wilma: Ouch! Stop hurting my leg!

Mrs. Rudolph *(to Westley):* Listen to me, Westley. Do it right this time. Do it the way I showed you.

Westley: Sorry, Mom. *(To Wilma)* The kids are waiting outside. We're going to play basketball. You can watch!

Mrs. Rudolph *(smiling):* Wait. Finish your job here, children. Then you can play.

Scene Two

Narrator: A few years go by. Wilma's leg gets stronger and stronger. A special leg brace helps Wilma walk. Now, even though she limps, she never wants to sit still.

Westley (to his brothers): Oh, no! Here comes Wilma again. Hide that basketball, or no one will get a chance to play.

Wilma: I heard that, Westley. I may limp a bit. But I try harder than any of you. So give me the ball, and let's play.

Narrator: One day, Wilma's mother looks out the window and sees Wilma playing basketball by herself. Suddenly, she noticed that Wilma is not wearing her special brace. She is not limping.

Mrs. Rudolph (worried): Wilma! What are you doing?

Wilma: What does it look like I'm doing? I'm playing basketball.

Scene Three

Narrator: Wilma is now in high school. She is one of the top players on the girls' basketball team. One day in practice, she trips and falls.

Coach Gray: Are you all right, Wilma?

Wilma (getting up): I guess I wasn't looking where I was going.

Coach Gray (laughing): You're a "skeeter" all right, Wilma. You're little. You're quick. And you buzz all over — just like a mosquito!

Narrator: Before long, Wilma sets a school basketball record — 803 points in 25 games. Soon, everybody has heard of "Skeeter," including Ed Temple, a college track coach. One day, he comes to watch her play.

Coach Temple: Look at her move! You know, that girl could be a runner.

Coach Gray: Do you think so?

Coach Temple: Let me put it this way. If you start a girls' track team, you already have a star.

Narrator: Soon, Wilma is winning race after race for the new track team. In her junior year, coach Temple invites her to work out with the college team. But things do not go well.

Wilma (upset): I knew I wasn't any good. I came in last in every race! I'll never get that scholarship.

Coach Temple: Listen, Wilma. You have been running against some of the best runners in the country. If you work as hard as they do, you'll be that good, too — maybe better. I know you will. And you know it, too.

Narrator: Wilma trains very hard all summer. All her works pays off. At the age of 16, Wilma qualifies for the 1956 Olympic team. At the Games she wins a bronze medal. But, in her mind, Wilma knows she can do better.

Scene Four

Narrator: Wilma is now 20. With the help of Coach Temple, she has won a college scholarship. Wilma has become the fastest woman runner in America. Is she the fastest anywhere? At the 1960 Olympics, Wilma faces the best runners in the world.

Announcer: The winner of the 200-meter dash is ... Wilma Rudolph of the U.S.A.!

Reporter: Wilma, this is your second gold medal. On Thursday you race in the relay. What can we expect?

Wilma *(smiling):* I don't know. Just keep your eyes on the U.S. team.

Narrator: The 400-meter relay is about to start. In the race, four women run as a team, taking turns. Wilma runs with the U.S. team with her teammates from college.

Announcer: They're off . . . The U.S. is in the lead . . . Wait! The last runner for the U.S. got off to a bad start. It's Wilma Rudolph! The German runner has passed her . . . But look! Rudolph is catching up . . . She's pulling even . . . Now she's ahead . . . She did it! THE U.S. TEAM HAS JUST SET A NEW RECORD!

Narrator: The crowd goes wild. Wilma

wins her third gold medal in the Olympics. No American woman has ever done better. After the race, Wilma goes over to Coach Temple.

Wilma *(in tears):* Thank you, Coach. Thank you for everything.

Coach Temple: You don't have to thank me, Skeeter. All I ever did was make sure you did your best. *(He smiles.)* You did most of the work.

Narrator: It took Wilma Rudolph only an instant to cross the finish line that day. But her race to the top started years before. Finally, at the age of 20, she proved herself a true champion.

READING COMPREHENSION

Summarizing. Choose the best phrase to complete each sentence. Then write the complete statement on your paper.

1. The doctors thought that Wilma's sickness could _____ (come back again, keep her from growing, keep her from walking).

2. Wilma was able to walk without a brace by _____ (resting, a miracle, trying harder).

3. Wilma became a top basketball player because her family helped her by _____ (playing basketball with her, exercising her legs, getting her on the team).

4. In the 1960 Olympics, Wilma set a record in the _____ (meter relays, basketball playoffs, swimming race).

Interpreting. Write the answer to each question on your paper.

1. Why did Mrs. Rudolph not want to stop exercising Wilma's leg?

2. What did Wilma learn about herself? How does she act when she falls in practice?

3. Why was Mrs. Rudolph worried when she saw Wilma without her brace?

4. How did Coach Temple help Wilma win?

For Thinking and Discussing. Do you think that Wilma was able to use her leg again because her mother believed she would? Does believing in something help you get it? Why or why not?

UNDERSTANDING LITERATURE

Characterization through Actions. One way to learn about characters is by their *actions*, or what they do. For example, if you are reading a story in which a boy gets two books as a present and gives one to his friend, you know from this action that the boy is generous.

The following statements are about the characters from "Skeeter." On your paper, write a sentence to describe what the action shows about the character at that point in the story.

1. Mrs. Rudolph works on Wilma's leg four times a day.

2. Wilma plays basketball even with a leg brace.

3. Wilma's brothers joke about hiding the basketball from Wilma.

4. Wilma gets up after she trips and falls in practice.

5. Wilma comes in last in the high school track meet and decides she will never get a scholarship.

6. Wilma trains very hard during the summer when she is 16.

7. Wilma wins the 400-meter race and thanks Coach Temple.

WRITING

Imagine that Wilma is going to speak at your school, and it is your job to introduce her. Write what you will say about her. Include her childhood, her success as an athlete, and her personality.

The Bookman

by Howard Fast

In this story of Colonial America, a boy and his sister fall under the charm of a mysterious traveler with books to sell and fantastic tales to tell. Their love for the bookman makes it all the more difficult to accept the disturbing truth they learn about him.

We were very poor, but we were never so poor as the soldiers. Before the war, it had been different. As the war went on, we got poorer and poorer. Yet we were never so poor as the soldiers.

I think it was in the fall of 1780 that the soldiers were all encamped down in the valley beyond our house. It was just at the beginning of the winter. The day they came, a film of snow covered the whole valley down to the river, which you could see from our house. Our house stood on a hill, overlooking the valley and the river and the plain beyond it. Mother always watched the valley. She said that when father came back, we should see him riding up the valley all the way from the river. Father was with the Third Continentals, a captain. But this was before he was killed.

The soldiers came marching down the riverside. They came along the dirt road. Then they turned up the valley, where they prepared to encamp. They were part of the New Jersey line. All of them looked very tired and were very thin. We ran down to meet them, and they all waved to us. I was ashamed of myself. I was so fat and healthy.

An officer on a horse was riding in front. An aide was riding a little way behind him. When the officer saw me, he came over. He was drawing up his horse close beside me and leaning over the front of his saddle.

"Hello there, sonny," he said.

I didn't say anything. I thought that maybe he would be thinking of how fat I was, he being so thin. His uniform was all torn and dirty. His cocked hat flapped wearily. But I liked his face. It was hard and thin, but it had small, dancing blue eyes.

However, I didn't want him to think me entirely a dunce. I saluted him smartly.

"Well, well," he smiled, "you've the markings, haven't you, sir? And how old might you be?"

"I'm eleven, sir."

"And what might be your name?"

"Bently Corbatt, sir."

"And I suppose you live in the big

house on the hill? Is this your sister?"

"Yes, sir," I replied, a little ashamed because Ann was so small. "But I've got another, sir."

"Another house?" he questioned, still smiling.

"No, sir. Another sister, who's much bigger than Ann here. And won't you come up to the house, sir?"

"Well — you're not Tories, then?"

"Oh, no, sir," I said quickly, and then added: "My father's with the Third Continentals. He's a captain."

"Well," he said, not smiling now. He stared at me thoughtfully. Then he shifted his gaze to our house. "Well," he said again. Then: "I'm General Wayne. I suppose you'll be very kind and introduce me to your mother?"

"She's dead sir."

"I'm sorry. Then your sister, if she's the lady of the house."

I nodded. Bending over, he grasped me about the waist, lifting me to the saddle in front of him. Then he motioned for the aide to do the same with Ann. Then we all set off for the house.

"When did your mother die, sonny?" he asked me, as we rode along.

"Only about three weeks ago." I told him about how she used to watch the valley all the time. "You see, Father doesn't know yet," I said. "Sis thought it would be best not to let him know."

"I see," he said gravely. But his blue eyes were warm and merry. I don't think his eyes ever lost that merry look. I twisted around him. That way I could see the troops marching into the valley. Now they were passing through our orchard, and many stooped to pick up rotten apples from the ground. His eyes followed mine. "It's pretty hard, this business of war, isn't it — for soldiers?" He seemed to include me in the last part.

"Not too hard," I answered evenly, "for soldiers."

Jane was waiting for us on the porch, looking very grave, the way she looked since mother had died. We rode up, and the general lifted me down to the porch. Then he dismounted himself. He bowed very nicely to Jane, sweeping off his hat with a graceful gesture, just as if it wasn't so battered and torn.

"Miss Corbatt?" the general said.

Jane nodded.

"I am General Wayne of the Continental Army, Pennsylvania line. I have 2,000 troops. I would like to encamp them in that valley. I hope it will be for just a few weeks, but possibly for a good part of the winter. I presume this property is yours?"

"Yes." Jane curtsied to him. "Yes, the property is my father's. Won't you come inside? We can talk about it there."

General Wayne entered the house after Jane. His aide followed, and I followed his aide. Ann tried to follow me but I pushed her back. "This is no place for little girls," I warned her.

In the living room, I wasn't noticed, and I made myself small in the corner. Jane sat in a chair. The two officers stood in front of her.

"You see," General Wayne was saying, "we can't be too far from the British — and we can't be too near. This spot is ideal."

"I think I understand."

"But you know what soldiers are — 2,000 half-starved soldiers."

"My father is with the army, sir."

"Thank you. You are very brave girl."

"No, no," Jane said quickly. "I'm doing nothing. Don't you see that it is safer with the troops here?"

General Wayne smiled sadly. "I'm afraid not. It is not very nice to have one's home turned into a battleground. Yet war is a bitter business all around."

"I know," Jane said.

"We should want to use your home as general headquarters. It will mean quartering myself and two or three officers. And a room to undertake business."

Jane bent her head. "I hope you will be comfortable," she said.

"You are very kind. And now, if you will excuse me, you can make all arrangements with Captain Jones here."

The general left the room, and I followed him. Outside, he looked at me curiously.

"I suppose," he said thoughtfully, "that you will want to be a soldier someday?"

"Yes, sir."

His face was very grave, his mouth as thin as a thread. With one hand, he shook out my long hair and the other was clasping and unclasping itself nervously. "Suppose," he considered, "suppose I make you sort of general's special aide. That way you could look after things I miss on?"

I was thrilled with pride. I could hardly keep from bursting into shouts of pure joy. However, I managed to stand very still, saluting him. "That will be very fine, sir," I said. And I stood looking after him as he rode down into the valley.

I couldn't go in just yet. I had to stand there for a while, and be alone in my glory. So I remained as he left me, very still, looking over the valley. The sun was setting, making the river a band of gleaming red. Then, after a little time, I went inside.

I heard Jane laughing in the parlor, and it surprised me. It was the first time she had laughed since mother died. I went in, and there she was, standing with the aide. She was laughing at something he had said. When she saw me, she stopped. Captain Jones came forward, offering me his hand.

"How do you do, sir," I said, with dignity. After all, I was in the army now.

"How do you do," he answered.

"Captain Jones and General Wayne and some others will live at the house, Bently," Jane told me.

"I know," I replied.

I turned to go, and as I left the room, I heard Captain Jones saying, "I must apologize for my men. We're pretty close to being beggars now — all of us."

The next few days were as exciting as any I had known. I had always considered our house a very lonely place. There was nobody I could play with outside of Ann and Jack, the caretaker's boy. And now, all of a sudden, there were 2,000 men. They were encamped in a sprawling fashion through the apple orchard, over the hayfields, and down the long slope to the river. Almost overnight, bubbles of tents had sprung up all over the place. In

and around our sheds a hundred horses were quartered. On the lawn, in front of our house, there were 16 cannons, ugly, frightening things, but oh, how fascinating!

And the soldiers — I made great friends with many of the soldiers. That was before the bookman came. I will get to the bookman later. I guess General Wayne spread word around, about the commission he had given me. The men took to calling me lieutenant, which I was very proud of, though I tried not to show it. I stole cakes and bread for them from the kitchen — not that we had so much, but they had almost nothing at all. And all the time I had to myself, I spent down in their camp. They were always telling me stories. Some of them never knew my father. Sometimes, they would let me handle a musket. But the muskets were taller than I, and so heavy I could hardly lift them. What I saw in the camp used to make me sick sometimes. The men were always cold, because they were short of clothing and blankets. Hardly any of them had shoes. Most were terribly thin. It would make me sick. Then I didn't know whether I wanted to be a soldier or not. But the men were always talking about their pay. They said their pay was to come from Philadelphia someday, and how much better all things would be after that.

The winter passed slowly. The men remained in the valley. More men came, until there were almost 3,000 of them. At night, their fires twinkled like glowworms. In the daytime they were always drilling and parading. I didn't know why they drilled so much, but one day Captain Jones told me the reason. He said it was to keep them knowing that they were soldiers, and to make them forget that they were starving. I wondered how men could starve, yet live so long. War is very strange, and you do not understand all the parts of it.

Our house became a busy place. In the parlor, General Wayne set up his main headquarters. Sometimes he sat there all day writing at his desk, receiving messengers and sending messengers, too. I knew that most of his writing was for pay and food for his soldiers, because that was the main topic of talk. All day, men rode up to our house and away from it. Many times in the night I woke to hear a horse stamping his hooves in front of the door.

I guess during that time Jane came to sort of like Captain Jones. I guess she couldn't help it. He was such a handsome young gentleman. He was not at all thin and worn, like General Wayne.

Then the bookman came, after the troops had been in the valley for almost three weeks. They don't have many bookmen any more. Bookmen are men who wander around the country, stopping at houses to peddle books and give away news. Many of them write their own books, publish them, and peddle them. That is what Parson Weems did with his stories of General Washington.

Well, the bookman came early one evening. He came not from the river valley, but instead he rode the trail that trickled over the hills. He was dressed in worn, rough clothing. He had an old broadbrimmed hat on his head, and a

great pack of books on either side of his saddle. He didn't come to the house. He had stopped at the barn, and I ran over to see what he had to sell. I knew he was a bookman, and I knew how rarely bookmen came nowadays.

"Hello," I called. "Hello, there, you bookman, you!"

He looked at me very gravely, and right there I liked him, from the beginning. He had little blue eyes, like General Wayne's, always sparkling, and long yellow hair that fell to his shoulders. He seemed very old to me then, as most grown-ups did. But he couldn't have been much past 30.

"Hello, sir," he said. He had a funny accent. It,was vaguely familiar, and I took it to be back-country talk. "Yes," he went on, "how do you do?"

"Fine," I answered. "And I hope you have English books, though Jane says I shouldn't read them now."

"And why shouldn't you read them now?" he asked.

"You know we're at war."

"Oh, yes, I do know it. I had a devil of a time getting through the sentries." He spoke as if he didn't approve of the sentries, or war. And then his eyes looked past me, down into the valley. He seemed surprised when he saw all the tents and soldiers.

"That looks like a big encampment," he said.

Yes," I said, nodding proudly, "most all of the New Jersey line."

But he did not seem to wish to speak of the troops or the war. "What kind of books do you like?" he asked, measuring me with his eyes.

Then I remembered my manners. "Won't you come in," I asked him, "and have something hot to drink? I am sure my sister would like your books, too."

Picking up his packs, he followed me into the kitchen. While Mary, the cook, put up the kettle, I ran to call Jane. Jane liked bookmen, because they made things less lonely. "I'm sorry," she told him, "that you have to eat in the kitchen, but our house has become a regular military station. I should like to offer you tea, but you know that we have none now."

"You are a very loyal family, aren't you?" the bookman said.

"My father is with the Third Continentals," Jane said quietly.

The bookman looked at her, as though he knew what Jane was thinking. After all, it was much more likely that a strong man like him would be in the army than wandering around with a pack of books. And then he said, a slow smile coming to his lips, "But somebody has to sell books. They are as necessary as war."

"Perhaps," Jane answered him.

I went out then, because Ann was calling me. Together we walked down into the valley. When I came back the bookman was showing Jane his books.

He and Jane were close together. They were kneeling on the floor, where the books were spread out. There, in the fading twilight, his yellow head made a very nice contrast to Jane's dark one. When I came in, Jane glanced at me.

"Don't you want to look at the books, Bently?"

"I was down in the valley," I said importantly. "There's a great battle there. I think that the troops are going to move soon, maybe at the end of the week or before that."

The bookman was looking at me very curiously. I thought his interest strange for a person who had so little interest in war. But a moment later, I had forgotten that, and I was looking at the books with Jane. He had a great many books for children. They were fascinating books full of pictures. The kind of books we saw very little of at that time. He seemed to have read every book, for he spoke of them in a way different from any other person I had ever known. He spoke of the books Jane wanted, too. I could see that there was a lot in him that fascinated Jane, the same way it fascinated me.

I had my dinner, and after dinner, Jane was still with the bookman. They were talking about books and other things. I went out on the porch where Captain Jones was sitting.

"Who is that tattered wreck?" Captain Jones asked me.

"Oh, he's just a bookman."

"Just a bookman, eh?"

"Yes." I nodded, and then I sat down to keep him company.

That evening, I sat in the kitchen, listening to the bookman. His stories weren't like the soldiers'. His stories were not about war, but about strange, distant lands. I could see right away that he liked me, and I was drawn to him more than I had ever been drawn to a stranger before. Later, Jane sat before the fire with us. Then most of the talk was between her

and the bookman. I remember some of the things he said.

"Egypt — like an old jewel in the sand. There are three of the great pyramids, and they stand all together, and if you watch the sun set behind them — " And that sort of thing. There seemed to be no land that he had not visited. Although how this should be so with a bookman, neither of us knew.

"And the war — ?" Jane once asked him.

"I sometimes wonder about the war," he answered. "But I don't know whether it is right or wrong. This new land is so big, so wild — why should anyone fight about it?"

"It is a very beautiful land, this America of ours," Jane said.

"Yes, with beautiful women."

I don't know whether Jane liked that or not, but she said nothing.

"Brave men and beautiful women," the bookman went on. "Oh, don't I know — how those men in the valley are so slowly starving. As ugly as war is, it makes more than men of us."

"Yet you do not believe enough to fight?"

"Are there not enough men — shedding blood?"

"I suppose so."

"I love books," the bookman said. "I used to dream of a great house, where I could live out my days comfortably and slowly. I would have many books around me — and peace. I used to dream of that."

"I know." Jane nodded.

"Funny, how you dream, isn't it?"

When I went up to bed, Jane was still there with the bookman, talking. Jane said, "Good night, Bently," and the bookman shook hands with me. "Don't love war too much, boy," he said.

That night I dreamed of the things the bookman told me. He was to sleep in the barn, since there was no more room in the house. I hoped I should see him the next morning.

The following day, there was more bustle than ever in the camp. All morning it snowed; but the men were out. They were drilling in the snow, and new troops were trickling in all the time. At the house, General Wayne was in a fury of excitement. I didn't dare go into the parlor. Once, a tall, tired-looking man rode up with a couple of aides. He was with General Wayne for more than an hour. I heard sentries whispering that it was General Washington. But he did not seem to be at all the great man I had heard of, only a tall, tired-looking person in a uniform covered with patches.

I went to the kitchen, to examine the books the bookman had left, and while I was there he came in. I was glad he had not gone. I hoped Jane would like him a great deal, perhaps convince him to remain awhile. I would have been content to listen forever to his smooth, enchanting voice.

"I want you to read this," he said. It was Malory's book on King Arthur, and I curled up before the fire with it.

Two more days went by, while the bookman remained. I noticed that Jane was spending more and more time with him. Captain Jones did not enjoy this. Once, I had seen the captain in the tearoom, with Jane in his arms, and I know that whenever Jane spoke of him,

there was a funny, far-off look in her eyes. Even now, with the bookman there, Jane grew more and more downhearted as the time came for the troops to leave.

"But the bookman may remain," I once said to her.

"Yes," Jane answered.

The troops were to leave in the morning. That day they began to break camp. The cannons were wheeled off our lawn, onto the river road. General Wayne was clearing his things from the parlor. I could see he was more excited than usual.

"The old fox has something up his sleeve," one of his sentries told me.

"It wasn't for nothing he was holding that meeting with General Washington," another said.

There was nothing much for me to do. Everyone else was busy, so I went to look for the bookman. I climbed to the little room he had, over the hayloft in the barn. I thought I would surprise him. There was a crack in the door, and I looked through it. There was the bookman, sitting on the floor. He was writing in a little pad he had on his knee. Then I knocked. He seemed to stiffen suddenly. The paper he was writing on, he folded and thrust into the crack in the floor. Then he covered his writing materials with hay. At last he sauntered to the door. When he saw it was only I, he appeared to be relieved.

"Yes," he said when he had opened the door, "I should be settling things with your sister. I'm to leave soon, and I want to find out what books she'll take."

"You're going?" I said.

"You don't want me to, do you, laddie? But we must all go on a-wandering.

259

Perhaps I'll come back someday . . . "

Walking over to the house with him, I almost forgot about the paper. Then I remembered and excused myself. Without thinking of what I was doing, I ran back to the barn. I went into his room. I was all trembling with excitement now. I had quite decided to find out who our bookman really was. I dug up the paper and began to read:

"Your Excellency,"

"I have done my best, yet discovered precious little. There are all of 3,000 troops here now, with 22 cannons. They will be moving north the morning you receive this, possibly to connect with General Washington . . . "

I read on, but my eyes blurred. First I was crying. I was good and ashamed of myself. Then I realized that the bookman must not find me there. I stumbled down from the loft. I ran out into the snow, the cold air stinging me into awareness, the paper clutched in my hand. The whole world was reeling around me.

"Why did it have to be him?" I said.

I guess I went to the kitchen to look at him again. I had to see whether it really was my own, my splendid bookman who had done this. I opened the door quietly. There was the bookman kissing Jane.

"Go away from here?" she whispered to him. "I don't know — I don't know."

"Then I'll tell you. You do love me, but you have too much pride in that glorious little head of yours. I'm a tattered wanderer. I have fascinated you with tales. You certainly would be a fool to throw yourself away on someone like me. But you do love me."

"Yes."

Jane nodded, and I remembered that even then I thought Jane was splendid.

"I'm not sorry," she said. "Why should I be sorry? I love you. That's all there is to it."

"Then you know. In the few days I've been here, you know."

"Yes, I know."

I could see the bookman's face from the side. I don't think I ever saw a sadder face than that. And beautiful, too, with all his yellow hair falling to his shoulders. I don't know how, knowing what I knew, I could have stood there, watching all this.

"If you knew all — but thank God you don't. Listen, Jane. I kissed you once. I shan't kiss you again — unless someday I come back. Would you wait?"

"I love you," Jane said. "I know I'll never love anyone else the way I love you."

I couldn't stand any more of that. I went up to my room and cried. Then I remembered that a Continental doesn't cry. I think I remembered my commission.

General Wayne was in the parlor when I came in. I could see that he was annoyed, being so busy. But he nodded to me.

"What is your business, sir?" he asked.

"Can I ask you something?"

The general pushed his papers aside. Now his eyes were twinkling, and I knew he would take some time with me. He had always liked me.

"Suppose a soldier runs away?" I said.

"There are times when the best do — have to." the general smiled.

"But suppose he knows his duty is to advance?"

"Then he's a coward — and a traitor," the general said slowly, staring at me very curiously.

"He's a coward, sir?"

"Yes."

I gave him the crumpled piece of paper. But I didn't cry then. I looked straight at him.

"What's this?" He read through it. Then he puckered up his lips, and read through it again. "My God," he whispered, "where did you get this, child?"

I told him. I told him where he could find the bookman. Then I said: "Will you excuse me now, sir?" I knew that something would happen inside me, if I didn't get away very quickly.

They shot the bookman that evening. Captain Jones tried to keep Jane in the house. "You mustn't see it," he pleaded with her. "Jane, why on God's earth should you want to see it?"

"Why?" She looked at him wonderingly. Then she put both hands up against his face. "You love me, don't you, Jack?"

"You know it by now."

"And you know what funny things love does to you. Well, that is why I must see it — must."

But he didn't understand. Neither did I, just then.

General Wayne came by while they were talking. He stopped, at the group of us. Then he said, "Let them see it, Captain, if they want to. I don't think it will hurt Bently. This spy is a brave man."

They stood the bookman up against the side of the barn, up against the stone

foundation. He smiled when they offered to blindfold him, and he asked not to have his hands tied.

"Could I talk to him?" I asked.

"Very well, but not for long."

The bookman had a tired look on his face. Until I was close to him, he had been watching Jane. Then he glanced down at me.

"Hello, laddie," he said.

My eyes were full of tears, so I couldn't see him very well at this point.

"A good soldier doesn't cry," he said, smiling.

"Yes, I know."

"You want to tell me you saw me hide the paper, don't you, laddie?"

"Yes,"

"And you're sorry now?"

"I had to do it."

"I understand. Give me your hand, laddie."

I went back to Jane after that. She put her arm around me, holding me so tight that it hurt. I was still watching the bookman.

"Sir," the bookman called out, "you will see that my superiors are informed. My name is Anthony Engel. My rank is Brevet Lieutenant Colonel."

General Wayne nodded. The rifles blazed out. The bookman was dead.

READING COMPREHENSION

Summarizing. Choose the best phrase to complete each sentence. Then write the complete statement on your paper.

1. During the winter _____ (the bookman, the general, Continental soldiers) camped in the valley owned by the Corbatt family.

2. Bently found out that _____ (Captain Jones, the bookman, General Wayne) was a spy.

3. Bently had to choose between loyalty to a friend and loyalty to the Continental cause. He decided to _____ (turn the spy in, hide the note, help the spy).

Interpreting. Write the answer to each question on your paper.

1. How would you describe Bently's feelings about the soldiers and war?

2. Why was Jane polite to General Wayne?

3. What did the bookman mean when he said, "But somebody has to sell books. They are as necessary as war."?

4. Why did Bently give General Wayne the note?

5. Why did Bently want to see the bookman before he was shot?

For Thinking and Discussing. Bently made a choice when he gave the note to General Wayne. What would you do if you were in Bently's position?

UNDERSTANDING LITERATURE

Direct and Indirect Characterization. Sometimes an author describes a character directly. For example, in "The Bookman," the author says, "Jane sat in a chair, looking very pretty." This remark tells the reader *directly* that Jane was pretty.

At other times, instead of saying what a character is like, the author lets the reader form an opinion about a character from that person's thoughts, speech, and actions in the story. This is called *indirect characterization*.

For example, Bently took cakes and breads from the kitchen to give to the soldiers. He did this even though his family did not have much food. You can say that Bently is not selfish and has feelings for other people. The author does not say Bently is not selfish, you know this indirectly.

Which statement below is indirect characterization?

1. But his blue eyes were warm and merry.

2. Jane bent her head. "I hope you will be comfortable," she said.

Find three things in the story you learn directly and indirectly.

WRITING

If you were Bently and you kept a diary of daily events, how would you describe the soldiers? How would you feel about their camping in your valley?

The Most Marvelous Thing

A Puerto Rican folktale retold by Ricardo E. Alegría

Can you decide which of the three young men in this tale the king should choose to marry his daughter? He has declared that the suitor who brings him the most marvelous gift will win her. But what happens if all three gifts seem equally marvelous?

Once upon a time, in a distant country, there was a king with an only daughter, and she was very beautiful. Three princes, who were brothers, were in love with her. Each one wanted her for his wife. Neither the king nor the princess knew which one to choose, as all were good men, handsome, brave, and true.

Not knowing what else to do, the king called the three brothers to the castle. He explained that, because he had only one daughter and did not know which one of the young men to choose as his son-in-law, he had decided to test them. Each was to go out into the world. At the end of a year each was to return, bringing as a gift to the king the most marvelous thing he had found during his travels. The one who brought the most marvelous thing in the world was to marry the princess. The other two would be awarded other kingdoms to rule.

This sounded fair enough to the three young men. They accepted the king's conditions. That very day, after receiving the king's blessing and a handkerchief each from the princess, they mounted their horses and rode off in search of the most marvelous thing in the world.

After many days they came to a place where the road branched out in three directions. Here the brothers parted. They said good-bye to each other and agreed to meet in the same place at the end of ten months to return home together. Each one set out by a different road.

The eldest brother took the road to the left. He crossed many countries and had many adventures, without finding anything marvelous enough to bring to the king.

Then, as he was crossing a desert, he came upon an old woman. She asked him for water. The youth had very little water left, but out of kindness he gave her all that he had. She took a long drink and asked the youth what he was doing in the desert. He told her his story.

The old woman then revealed she had magical powers. She told the young man that, since he had been so generous, she would help him find the most marvelous thing in the desert region — a magic carpet.

Not far away, the woman explained, there lived a dwarf who owned the carpet. He never slept. He stayed awake all day and all night, guarding his prized carpet. Then the old woman took some magic powder out of her bag and gave it to the young man. She told him to throw it into the dwarf's well when the dwarf wasn't looking.

Overjoyed at the thought of obtaining the magic carpet, the young man thanked the old woman for her help. Then he galloped off.

Before he reached the dwarf's house, the youth made a large figure of straw, dressed it in his own cloak and cap, then mounted it on his horse. When he neared the house, he sent the horse galloping by while he hid behind a tree.

When the dwarf heard the horse, he rushed out with his dogs. He was worried that someone had come to steal his magic carpet. He raced after the horse and its rider. The youth took advantage of the dwarf's absence to put the magic powder into the well. Then he climbed a tree to wait for the dwarf to return with the dogs.

When they did return, both the dwarf and his dogs were exhausted by the chase. They went straight to the well for a drink of water. As soon as the water touched their lips, they fell to the ground in a deep sleep.

Quickly the youth climbed down from the tree and went into the dwarf's house to search for the magic carpet. He found it in a box under the dwarf's bed and carried it outside. There he spread it out, sat down upon it, and told it to carry him to the fork in the road where he was to meet his brothers. At once the magic carpet rose and flew through the air.

In just a few minutes the young man reached the meeting place. He was a few days early, so he built a little straw house and waited there for his brothers to arrive.

Meanwhile, the second brother had taken the middle road. He had traveled through many strange countries full of new and different sights, sounds, and people. Although he had had many interesting adventures and seen many curious and wonderful things, he had not found anything marvelous enough to bring to the king.

Then one day, as he was passing through the woods, he was met by a large crowd of people who warned him not to advance any farther. Fearfully they explained that he was entering the territory of the Snake-of-the-Marvelous-Eye. The snake would eat him, they said, for with one marvelous eye he could see anyone who drew near his territory.

The youth felt that such a marvelous eye would indeed be the prize he was searching for. He told the people not to worry, that he would fight and kill the Snake-of-the-Marvelous-Eye.

With that the young man pushed his way deeper into the woods. He had not gone far when he heard the hissing of the fearsome snake. The youth, like his two brothers, was brave and unafraid. But he was sensible. He climbed onto a rock that was surrounded by water. There, his sword in hand, he awaited the snake.

The snake wasn't long in coming. But, since it had only one eye, it could not tell which was the young man and which was

his reflection in the water. The youth fought the snake and soon killed it. Then he cut off its head, and with the point of his sword lifted the marvelous eye from the snake's forehead.

The eye was like a crystal lens with which one could see everything at any distance. The youth was overjoyed. This was indeed the marvelous thing to bring to the king. He set out immediately for the place where he was to meet his brothers.

In the meantime, the youngest brother

had taken the right-hand fork in the road. He had reached a land of Oriental people, and there he had seen many rare and curious things; yet he had not found anything marvelous enough to bring to the king. He was worried, for he knew that there was little time left before he would have to return to his brothers.

One day as he was walking through the high mountains, he came upon an old man who was dying. Although the youth was pushed for time, he did not want to leave the old man there alone. He stayed and fed the fellow, and talked with him of many things.

The old man grew fond of the youth and told him that he would reveal a secret he had been keeping all his life. He was a hundred years old, he said, and for all that time he had been looking for the Tree of Marvelous Fruit. He knew now where the tree was. Since he could not get there in the few hours left to him, he was going to tell where it was so that the youth might succeed where he had failed.

The man pointed over to the highest mountain. At the top, he said, was a cave. And in the cave was a clearing, where the Tree of Marvelous Fruit stood blooming. Any sick person who tasted that fruit would be cured, no matter how serious his illness might be.

The cave was guarded by a ferocious eagle, the old man said. The eagle caught in its claws anyone who came near. Then the unlucky victim was carried off to the eagle's nest in the Tree of Marvelous Fruit — and was fed to her babies.

Just as he finished his story the old man died. The youth grieved for him and buried him on the side of the road. Then he climbed up to the highest mountain, to the cave where the tree grew.

As he drew near the cave, he shot two deer. One of them he cleaned so that he could hide inside it; the other he opened and filled with stones. In the morning, before the sun rose, he hid in the deer's body and waited for the eagle.

It wasn't long before the youth heard a screech. Through a hole in the deer's body he watched the eagle soar high overhead. Not long afterward he felt himself being lifted through the air, as the eagle carried him, inside the deer, to the nest and left him there. The youth crawled out and hid himself in the tree. The eaglets began picking away at the food.

He knew the eagle had gone to get the other deer, so he climbed down through the branches until he came to the marvelous fruits themselves. They looked like golden pears, but much larger. The youth took one. Then, very quietly so as not to attract the eagle's attention, he climbed out of the tree.

The eagle was trying with all her might to lift the other deer. But the stones inside the body were so heavy that it could not be moved. While the eagle continued to struggle, the youth escaped with the marvelous fruit. He ran to where he had left his horse and hurried to the fork in the road where he was to meet his brothers.

The eldest brother, with his magic carpet, and the middle brother, with his magic crystal, had been waiting for him. It was the last day of the time period they had set for the meeting, and both were very sad, for their youngest brother had not come and they feared that some misfortune had befallen him. But at the last minute, they saw him coming. He was half dead from the long and hard ride he had had.

The three brothers were very fond of one another and rejoiced to be together again. After the youngest had recovered,

each one told of his adventures and showed the marvelous thing he had found to bring to the king. Each one thought that his gift would win the princess, whom they all loved.

The brothers were very anxious to see the princess. So, before leaving for the king's castle, they decided to look through the middle brother's magic crystal to find out how she was. When they looked, they discovered that everyone in the castle was weeping, because the princess lay in her bed at the point of death.

The young men were heartbroken. But then the youngest brother reminded them of his marvelous fruit that could save the princess's life if they could reach her in time. The eldest brother said they could do just that if they rode on his magic carpet. It would carry them instantly to the castle and the princess.

All three sat on the carpet. It rose through the air and in a few minutes reached the king's castle. Everyone there was happy to see the brothers, but told them that the princess might die at any moment.

The three raced up the castle stairs. They quickly told the king that one of their marvelous things would cure his daughter. The grieving man led them to the princess's bedroom, where she lay very ill. When he told her that the three brothers were in the room, she recovered enough to open her eyes a little. But only tears came from them, for the princess knew she would soon die.

Then the king put the marvelous fruit to her lips and told her to bite into it. She managed to do so. Immediately, the color came back to her cheeks. She opened her eyes again and smiled at the brothers. It was not long before she sat up in bed and laughed joyfully.

The news of the princess's recovery brought joy to the whole castle. Everyone celebrated. The only one who remained quiet and thoughtful was the king.

In spite of his great happiness at his daughter's recovery, he had a problem that he could not solve. He had promised that the princess should marry the one who brought him the most marvelous thing. But all the brothers had brought marvelous things! Which brother should his daughter wed?

The king called his wise counselors together to help him solve the problem. Some of them thought that the princess should marry the youngest brother. He had brought the marvelous fruit that cured her.

Others judged that the princess should marry the middle brother. After all, it was he, with his magic crystal, who had discovered she was dying. The magic fruit would have been of no use had they not known she needed it.

Still other counselors thought that the princess should marry the eldest brother. Had it not been for his magic carpet, they would not have arrived in time.

The king's counselors and the people were divided among these three groups. Each one thought the princess ought to marry a different brother.

But no one ever knew which one of the three the princess did finally marry. If you had been the king, which of the brothers would you have chosen?

READING COMPREHENSION

Summarizing. Choose the best phrase to complete each sentence. Then write the complete statement on your paper.

1. The one brother who could find the most marvelous thing in the world would _____ (rule other kingdoms, marry the princess, be given the crown).

2. The three brothers each found a marvelous thing because each one was kind, _____ (handsome, evil, clever), and brave.

3. Together the magic carpet, the marvelous eye, and the healing fruit _____ (saved the dying princess, won the kingdom, decided which brother married the princess.)

Interpreting. Write the answer to each question on your paper.

1. How did each brother get his marvelous thing?

2. What was marvelous about each thing that they found?

3. How did each marvelous thing help save the princess?

4. Why was it hard for the king to decide which brother was to marry the princess?

For Thinking and Discussing. Do you think this story could ever really have happened? Why or why not?

UNDERSTANDING LITERATURE

Characterization. Sometimes story characters seem like real people. This happens when an author includes details that help you understand how the character thinks, acts, looks, and feels. A character that is described fully is called a *round character*.

At other times, an author does not tell you much about a character. A briefly described character is called a *flat character*. Flat characters are often found in folktales such as "The Most Marvelous Thing." The author wants you to think about the meaning of the story instead of the characters.

"The Most Marvelous Thing" has flat characters. The author does not tell you much about what the princess is like.

Decide whether each description below would help make a flat character or a round character. Write your answer on your paper.

1. The princess listened quietly.

2. The princess's few words were filled with wisdom.

3. The king's eyes twinkled as he watched his daughter try to decide which prince she would marry.

4. The king was the head of the country.

WRITING

If you had been the king, which of the brothers would you have chosen? Explain your choice. Use descriptions of each of the princes in your answer.

VOCABULARY

Compound Words. A *compound* word is a word made up of two or more smaller words. When the words are put together, they have a meaning different from that of each word alone. For example, the word *candle:* "a molded piece of wax that is burned," and the word *stick:* "something that resembles a long thin piece of wood," make up the compound word *candlestick:* "a holder with a socket for a candle."

Read each sentence below and decide which compound word will best complete the sentence. Write the complete sentence on your paper. Then write the meaning of the compound word.

easygoing	heartache
schoolyard	teamwork
firemen	

1. You could tell Bently was filled with __ when he had to turn the bookman over to the general.

2. The princes were all _____ to set off on the quest to find the most marvelous thing without a fuss.

3. It takes _____ to win a basketball game.

4. Ribsy followed Joe to the _____ and took a nap by the fence.

5. Larry was afraid that Mrs. Kreech would find out about Ribsy if Henry called the _____ to get Ribsy off of the fire escape.

READING

Cause and effect. Some sentences show cause and effect. A *cause* is what makes something happen. The *effect* is what happens.

Words and phrases such as *because, since, so that, as a result of* and *for this reason* may show that there is cause and effect in the sentence. Look at this sentence: Because Mrs. Rudolph did not give up massaging Wilma's leg, Wilma's leg was saved.

That Mrs. Rudolph did not give up massaging Wilma's leg is the cause.

That Wilma's leg was saved is the effect.

Make two columns on your paper. Label one *Cause* and the other *Effect*. Then write the cause and effect in each sentence below in the correct column.

1. As a result of a terrible sickness, Wilma was left with a bad leg.

2. Since Wilma did not want to suffer with her bad leg, she tried harder than the other children to play a good game of basketball.

3. Because he was loyal to the Continental's cause, Bently let the soldiers use his house.

4. As a result of the eldest brother's kindness, the old woman told the brother where he could find a magic carpet.

5. The princess did not die since the princes brought the healing fruit.

6. Both Larry and Mr. Huggins had a problem as a result of Ribsy going out on the fire escape.

7. Because Bently was made a lieutenant by General Wayne, he told the General what he knew about the Bookman.

8. Ribsy followed Joe and did not leave the Sayler House. For this reason Joe thought the dog didn't belong to anyone.

9. Because Ribsy heard Henry's voice on the telephone, he began to bark and look for him.

QUIZ

The following is a quiz for Section 7. Write the answers in complete sentences on your paper.

Reading Comprehension

1. In "Ribsy's Return," how did Ribsy get lost?

2. In "The Most Marvelous Thing," how did the eldest brother get the magic carpet away from the dwarf?

3. In the "The Bookman," to what cause was the Bookman loyal?

4. In "Skeeter," what did Wilma Rudolph do that no other American woman had done?

5. How are Henry Huggins from "Ribsy's Return" and Wilma Rudolph from "Skeeter" similar?

Understanding Literature

6. In "Skeeter," what are the three things the reader learns directly about Wilma?

7. Which character from "Ribsy's Return" would you consider a "flat" character? What could you do to "round" the character out?

8. In "The Most Marvelous Thing," the author gives some information about what all three princes are like. List three characteristics that all the brothers have.

9. In "The Bookman," how can you tell how Bently feels about giving the Bookman's note to the general? Describe the way he feels.

10. Think back to all the stories in this section. List three characters you would consider "flat" and three you would consider "round." Do not choose the princes in "The Most Marvelous Thing." Explain your choices.

WRITING

A Summary. A *summary* is a short description of a story. It tells the main events. In order for another person to understand the story, the events must be in the correct order. If you wanted to tell people about a story you had read, you could write a summary. Read each step to help guide you in your writing.

Step 1: Set Your Goal
Choose one of the following topics for a summary.

☐ the story "Ribsy's Return"

☐ the story "The Bookman"

☐ the story "The Most Marvelous Thing"

Step 2: Make a Plan
Plan what you are going to say. Make a list of the important events in the story.

Suppose you were going to write a summary of "Skeeter." You would probably list these important events:

Wilma's childhood sickness leaves her with a weak leg.

Wilma's family helps her strengthen her leg by exercising with her four times a day.

Wilma becomes a high school basketball star.

Wilma becomes a runner.

Wilma won three gold medals in the 1960 Olympics.

Step 3: Write Your First Draft
Your summary should contain three paragraphs. The first paragraph should introduce your topic and give the main events from the beginning of the story. The second should tell the main events from the middle of the story, and the third should summarize the story's ending.

☐ Start by introducing the topic. Then use your list of important events to summarize the beginning of the story. A summary of "Skeeter" might begin this way:

> The play "Skeeter" is about a girl named Wilma who was very sick when she was a child. The sickness left her with a weak leg. Her family believed they could help her, so they would exercise her leg four times a day. The exercise worked and Wilma's leg became better.

☐ In your next paragraph, continue to use your list of important events as you summarize the middle of the story:

> Wilma was always interested in playing basketball. When she got to high school, she became a basketball star. In fact, her coach nicknamed her "Skeeter" because she reminded him of a mosquito. Wilma, like a mosquito, was little and quick.

☐ End with a paragraph about the important happenings in the last part of the story:

> One day Coach Temple, a college

track coach, came to see Wilma play basketball. He decided she had what it takes to become a great runner. Through his encouragement, Wilma became a runner. In 1960 she entered the Olympics. She won three gold medals and set a new record for American women runners.

Step 4: Revise Your Summary

Check your summary one more time. Have you left out any important events? Correct any errors in spelling, grammar, and punctuation. Make a final, neat copy of your summary.

ACTIVITIES

Word Attack. What letters do the words below end with? What sounds do those letters make?

invention   direction

Each word ends with the letters *tion*. The letters *tion* almost always make the sound *shun*. The sound *shun* rhymes with *run*.

Find the words that end with *-tion* in the sentences below and write them on your paper.

1. A dull, heavy sensation filled Henry, as it always did when he forgot and looked back for Ribsy.

2. Mr. Saylor was paying very little attention to his children.

3. Even though he had given out more information than he intended, he felt he had an advantage in the conversation.

4. Joe was scornful of this suggestion.

5. Larry heaved a big sigh to show that he was disgusted with the whole situation.

Speaking and Listening. In "Ribsy's Return," Henry makes a telephone call to Joe. Imagine that you are Joe and ask a friend to be Henry. Read Henry and Joe's conversation including the author's narration. Pay special attention to words ending in *-tion*. Use details from the author's description of Joe to help you talk in a way that reflects Joe's feelings.

Researching

1. *Almanacs* are books containing many facts. They are published every year.

Look up *Olympic Games* in the index of an almanac in your library. You will find many lists of Olympic events. Look for the women's track and field records. Then answer the following questions on your paper.

☐ The play "Skeeter" tells you that Wilma Rudolph won the 200-meter dash and was a member of the winning 400-meter relay team in the 1960 Olympics. What other events did she win that year?

☐ What was Wilma's time in the 200-meter dash?

☐ Who won the 200-meter dash in 1956? What country was she from?

☐ In what year did the women's 400 meter relay become an Olympic event? What country had the winning team that year?

☐ What was the best time ever recorded in the Olympics for the women's 400-meter relay? In what year was that time scored? What country scored it?

2. The story "The Bookman" takes place during the Revolutionary War. Many battles were fought during the war. Some people look to see who won and what was won in battle. Other people look to see how many men were lost. Charts of information from encyclopedias can tell you results of battles. Read the chart below. Then decide what you think and feel about the battles listed. Write a paragraph explaining your thoughts.

Creating. Think of an invention that could be the most marvelous thing in the world. Make a model of the invention out of paper, clay, or wood. Write instructions explaining how to use the invention. Then write an advertisement telling people why it is the most marvelous thing in the world.

Revolutionary War Battle Results

Name of Battle	Approximate Casualties		Results
	American	British	
Bonhomme Richard vs. *Serapis*	300	120	The British warship *Serapis* surrendered.
Brandywine	700	540	The British occupied Philadelphia.
Guilford Court-house	250	650	The British gave up most of North Carolina.
Camden	1,000	300	An entire American army was almost destroyed.

ROBERT LOUIS STEVENSON

*Adventure is the
vitiminizing element in histories
both individual and social.*

—William Bolith

*The most beautiful adventures
are not those we go to seek.*

—Robert Louis Stevenson

279

Introduction

Life is a journey, beginning at birth and ending at death. Robert Louis Stevenson's journey through life was short, but marked by many adventures and accomplishments. Robert Lewis Balfour Stevenson was born in Edinburgh, Scotland in 1850. He was the only child of Thomas Stevenson, a lighthouse builder, and Margaret Balfour, a minister's daughter.

Early Travels and Writings

Stevenson had serious problems with his lungs all his life. When he was too sick to go to school, Stevenson wrote stories filled with the adventures he could not have. His family took him on trips to improve his health. These travels helped shape his writing.

In 1867, he began studying to be a builder like his father. But writing interested him more. He moved to France in 1875, where he lived with other artists and began writing essays for magazines.

The next year, he and a friend traveled through Belgium and France by canoe. His first book was about that trip.

The same year, he fell in love with Fanny Osbourne. They married in 1880, and their marriage was a very happy one. They often helped each other as writers. Together they traveled in search of a climate good for Stevenson's health. They went to England, France, Switzerland, and America. Then they sailed to Hawaii, Tahiti, Australia, and finally Samoa. The play *The Bottle Imp* (p.298) is based on a Stevenson short story that takes place in Hawaii and reflects Stevenson's love of sailing and the South Seas — as well as his love of mystery and adventure.

One day in 1883, Stevenson saw his young stepson draw a map of an island. That same day he began his famous book, *Treasure Island*. In 1885, he wrote the collection of poems called *A Child's Garden of Verses*. These poems still guide children on wonderful voyages of the imagination. The poem *Windy Night* (p.313) is from this famous book.

In 1886, he wrote two more classics, *The Strange of Dr. Jekyll and Mr. Hyde*

and the novel that is retold in this unit, *Kidnapped* and *The End of the Journey*.

In *Kidnapped*, Stevenson chose his own family name, Balfour, for the novel's hero. Young David Balfour resembles the author in many ways. Stevenson, whose grandfather was a minister, made his hero a minister's friend. David Balfour also travels and faces a serious illness. Stevenson wrote of this from experience.

Kidnapped is historical fiction, but it is based on fact. Alan Breck Stewart and many other characters actually existed. Many of the events in *Kidnapped* really happened, but Stevenson himself created the character David Balfour and his adventures.

Kidnapped and many other Stevenson novels are filled with narrow escapes from death, just as his own life of poor health was. The success of these books allowed him to escape to a better climate for his lungs.

In 1888 Stevenson fulfilled a lifelong dream and sailed his own boat to the South Seas. For three years Stevenson and his family sailed the Pacific Ocean. Finally they settled on the island of Samoa. He wrote many works there, including *Catriona*, a sequel to *Kidnapped*. He loved the island, where he was known as *"Tusitala"* — "Teller of Tales" — and he asked to be buried there.

In a twist of fate as strange as any in his stories, he did not die of the disease that he had suffered from all his life. A blood vessel burst in his brain, killing him within a few hours. He died when only 45 years old. Years earlier, he had written a poem called *Requiem,* (p.314) that told how he wanted to be remembered. As he had indicated in this poem, he was buried "under the wide and starry sky" on a mountaintop. Stevenson's journey is over. But his work continues to carry readers of today to unexpected worlds of adventure.

Kidnapped, Part One

by Robert Louis Stevenson

Here begins the story of David Balfour, whose wicked Uncle Ebenezer does everything possible to rob him of his inheritance. In the seafaring world of the late 1700s, David finds he must face many evils.

I will begin the story of my adventures with a morning in June, 1751. It was then that I took the key for the last time from the door of my father's house. The sun began to shine upon the hills as I went down the road. By the time I reached the minister's house, birds were singing in the lilacs.

Mr. Campbell, the minister, waited by his garden gate. We walked in silence until he asked, "Are you sorry to leave?"

"If I can better myself where I am going," I said, "I will go with a good will."

"Aye, Davie?" said he. "Then let me tell you your fortune. Before he died, your father gave me this letter. He called it your inheritance."

On the envelope of the sealed letter was written: "To the hands of Ebenezer Balfour, of the Shaws, this will be delivered by my son, David Balfour."

My heart beat fast. What bright future lay before this lad of 17? To the Shaws I would go.

Mr. Campbell embraced me with a sob. He was so sad at my leaving, my conscience ached. I was happy to leave the quiet countryside. I wanted to go to a great house and be with rich people of my own name. I took a last look at the churchyard where my parents rested and set off.

I walked for two days before I neared the house of Ebenezer Balfour. Before dark, I met a woman coming down a hill. I asked her if she knew the Shaws. She pointed toward a big house in a valley. The land around it was beautiful, but the house itself was an old ruin. No smoke rose from the chimney.

My heart sank. "That is the Shaws?"

"Yes!" she cried. "With blood it was built, and blood shall bring it down."

In a moment, she was gone. My knees grew weak. What sort of man was

Ebenezer Balfour? I sat down and stared at the Shaws.

After sunset, smoke began rising from a chimney. It meant a bit of warmth and perhaps some cooking. Feeling better, I made my way toward the house. But the nearer I got, the worse it looked. Many windows were broken, and bats flew in and out.

I knocked on the door, but no one stirred, so I banged with all my might. Finally, an old man with a thin, mean face unlocked the door. He pointed an old, rusty gun right at me. He said, "What do you want?"

"My name is David Balfour," says I. "I have a letter for Ebenezer Balfour from my father."

"Is your father dead?" he asked. Before I could answer, he went on, "Of course he's dead. That's why you're here. Give Alexander's letter to me."

I did not trust the old man. "How do you know my father?" I asked him.

"It would be strange if I didn't," he replied. "I am Ebenezer Balfour. Alexander was my brother."

I was surprised. I said, "I never knew he had a brother."

My uncle said, "So give me the letter, and sit down and fill your stomach."

There was one bowl of porridge on the table. I said I was afraid it was his own supper.

"Oh," said he, "I can do without."

The house and my uncle were so dreary, I felt ill. Was this the palace I was to come to? Was this where I would find my rich friends and my fortune? I watched my uncle break the seal and read the letter.

Then he asked me, "Have you read this?"

"It has been read by you alone," I said.

My uncle grunted and put the letter away. When he saw I had no appetite, he took the bowl of porridge from me and ate hungrily. After he had finished, he said, "Now I will show you to your bed."

To my surprise, he did not light a candle, but climbed upstairs in the dark. I followed as best I could. Then he

unlocked a door and told me to enter. I asked for a candle to see by. He said, "Lights in a house cause fires. The moon will give you light enough. Good night."

Then I heard him lock me in. I didn't know whether to laugh or cry. The bed was so damp, I slept on the floor.

In the morning, I banged on the door until my uncle let me out. I told him, "I am leaving at once."

"Hoot toot, be patient, laddie," he said. "We'll soon get on better."

In the kitchen, he had lit a fire. On the table were two bowls and spoons, but only one cup. He asked if I would take something to drink. I said not to bother.

"I'll deny you nothing in reason," he said. Then he poured exactly half from his cup into another. My uncle made being a miser seem almost a fine thing.

That night he spoke to me kindly. "David, my lad, I mean to help you all I can. To prove it, here are 40 gold coins for now."

I could not find words to thank him.

"I want no thanks," said he. "It is a pleasure to help my brother's son."

I said, "And I will help you if I can."

"Oh, you can," he said. "I have need of the papers in a chest at the top of the tower. I'm too old to climb the stairs. Would you bring the chest to me?"

"Of course," I said. "May I have a light?"

"No," he said. "Lights cause fires. I will have no lights in my house."

There was a great rain that night. Inside the tower it was pitch-dark. I felt the wall with my hands and climbed the stairs. It was slow work. I was almost at the top

when lightning flashed. In that moment, I saw that the stairs came to a sudden end. If I had gone on, I would have fallen to my death. My uncle had sent me there to die!

Very slowly, I made my way back down the stairs. I entered the house quietly. When he saw me, my uncle fell into a faint. I threw water on his face and he opened his eyes. He cried out in terror, "Are you alive?"

"I am," I said. "And no thanks to you." I demanded to know why he had tried to kill me, but he was too weak to speak. He begged me to let him go to bed, saying he would explain all in the morning. To make sure, I locked him in his room.

In the morning, I brought him down to the kitchen. Then I asked, "Why do you plot against my life?"

Before he could answer, there was a knock at the door. It was a sailor with a letter from a Captain Hoseason. He was at a nearby port and had business with my uncle.

Uncle Ebenezer's eyes lit up. "David, my lad, how would you like to visit a ship? After that, I'll take you to my lawyer, Mr. Rankeillor. He knew your father and can explain everything to you."

My uncle could not harm me at the busy port, I thought, and then I would insist we see the lawyer. In truth, I wished to see the sea. "Let us go," says I.

On the way to the port, the young sailor told me his name was Ransome. He boasted of the many wild and bad things he had done. He said Captain Hoseason was fierce and mean, yet he seemed to love the man and his ship, the *Covenant*. Then he turned down his stocking and showed me an ugly red wound. The poor lad seemed almost proud when he said, "Mr. Shuan done it!"

"Is there no one to protect you?" I asked.

"Oh, there's worse off than me," said he. "The ship carries criminals to slavery in the Carolinas. And for a price, Hoseason kidnaps innocent people and sells them as slaves."

I believed Ransome, and yet when I met the captain at the inn, I felt sure the boy was mistaken about him. He seemed an upright man. While Captain Hoseason and my uncle talked, I went for a walk.

In the bay, the *Covenant* was shaking out her sails. I longed to sail for far places. But the rough language of the sailors made me think better of it.

Back at the inn, I asked the landlord if he knew Mr. Rankeillor the lawyer.

"Aye," says he, "and a very honest man he is."

Then I said, "I see Mr. Ebenezer is not much liked."

"Hoot no lad," said the landlord, who did not know my identity. "Many has he ruined, the miser. Yet, he was once a fine fellow. But that was before word got out that he had killed Mr. Alexander his brother," said the landlord.

"And what would he kill him for?" I asked.

"The Shaws. Why else?" The landlord left.

I sat stunned. These people thought my father had died long ago. And somehow the Shaws had belonged to my father. At his death, the Shaws had become mine! I would have to think hard before I told my uncle what I knew. Just then, I heard my uncle call. He was with Captain Hoseason.

"Sir," Hoseason said to me, "your uncle tells me good things of you. I wish I could know you better, but my ship sails soon. Why not come aboard and drink some punch with me?"

He seemed so friendly that I agreed. We rowed to where the *Covenant* was moored. I was whipped into the air on a tackle sent down from the main mast, and set upon the deck. The strange sights excited me. Then it struck me. I cried, "Where is my uncle?"

"There," Hoseason said, pointing to a boat heading toward land. My uncle's cruel face was the last thing I saw. Lightning seemed to strike me. I knew no more.

I woke up in darkness and knew not where I was. I was in great pain and could not move. I found that I had been tied hand and foot. My whole world moved up and down; I knew I must be aboard the ship. Rats pattered across my body. I

felt sick and afraid. Day and night were the same to me. I do not know how long it was before I had a visitor. He came to bandage the wound on my head. His bright lamp hurt my eyes.

"Cheer up, lad," he said. Then he gave me water and left me in darkness.

Later, the man returned with the captain. He told him, "I want this lad taken out of here, or he will die."

Hoseason argued, but soon my hands and legs were untied. I was taken to the sailor's bunkroom. The crew was a rough lot, but I learned they could be kind. I soon had my health back. The man who had helped me was Mr. Riach, the second mate. The chief mate was Mr. Shuan. The sailors warned me of his horrible temper; poor Ransome had already proved it to me.

One night about midnight, there began a whisper that "Shuan had done for Ransome at last." We hardly had time to speak of it, when Captain Hoseason entered. He said to me, "My man, we need you to serve in the roundhouse. You and Ransome are to change berths."

When I entered the roundhouse, Mr.

Shuan did not look up. Later, Mr. Riach came in and shook his head. Ransome was dead.

"You murdered the boy!" the captain shouted at Mr. Shuan. Then his anger died. "What happened tonight must be kept secret. The boy fell overboard. That is what our story will be."

But the shadow of Ransome was upon all, especially upon me. It was I who did his work, slaving for the captain and mates in the roundhouse. I did not care much, for the work kept my mind from the slaving I would do at my journey's end.

More than a week passed. The luck of the *Covenant* grew worse. The weather turned foul; the wind drove us back. On the tenth day, a thick, wet, white fog hid one end of the ship from the other. At 10:00 that night, the ship struck something with a great sound. We had run down a boat in the fog. It had gone to the bottom with all crew aboard but one.

The survivor looked about 25 years old. His clothes were wet but very fine. He wore a blue coat with silver buttons and a red vest. At his belt were a pair of silver pistols and a sword.

The captain said to him, "You're wearing a French soldier's coat, yet you speak like a Scot. You must be a rebel against King George."

The man did not deny it. Many Scots did not accept George as their king. In 1745 they had risen up against him. Their revolt was crushed, and many fled to France.

The rebel offered to pay Hoseason to take him to France. That was impossible, the captain said. Then the man took off a money belt filled with gold coins. The captain looked at the coins, then at the gentleman's face.

"For 60 of the coins," Hoseason said, "I'll put you ashore in Scotland."

The rebel agreed, and the two men shook hands. When the captain left, the rebel asked for wine. I went on deck to ask the captain for the key to the wine closet. The captain was talking to two officers. I suspected they were up to no good, so I hid and listened. Hoseason was saying, "While I talk to the man, you grab his arms. Then I finish him with a pistol."

I pretended I had not heard anything and asked for the key. Suddenly, Hoseason became very nice to me. "David," he said, "you're a good lad and I know you will help me. The man in the roundhouse is an enemy of the king and all our pistols are under his nose. Now, if you would pick up a pistol or two, he would never notice. Then bring them to me. I'll see you get your share of his gold."

These men had kidnapped me. They had killed Ransome. Now, was I to hold a candle to another murder? But the fear of death was plain before me. What could one man and a boy like me do against the whole crew?

When I entered the roundhouse, I told the rebel, "The crew has already murdered a boy. Now it's you they want."

"Aye, but they haven't got me yet," he said. "Will you stand by me?"

"Yes," I said. "I'm no murderer."

The rebel said his name was Alan Breck Stewart, and that he came from the Highlands. The Highlanders had fought against English rule for many years. Now he prepared to fight against Hoseason and his crew.

The roundhouse had two doors. It also had a window in the roof to let in light. Alan would guard one door with his sword against the main attack. I would guard the other door and window with two pistols.

My heart beat like a bird's, both quick and little. The attack came suddenly, with a rush of feet and a shout from Alan. I turned to see him crossing swords with Mr. Shuan.

"He killed the boy!" I shouted.

"Watch your door!" Alan warned. He stabbed Shuan with his sword.

Then I heard the men trying to smash my door. I had never fired a pistol before. Without thinking, I shot at the door. I heard a cry of pain. I fired two more shots and heard the men run away. Alan's attackers also fled, dragging Mr. Shuan's body with them.

"Reload your pistols," Alan said.

Minutes later, I heard footsteps creeping to Alan's door. Then I heard a whistle, a signal. The glass in the window above was smashed and a man jumped through to the floor. I froze. But when the man came at me, I cried out in terror and shot him. Another man was about to jump through the window. I shot him in the leg and he fell back.

Meanwhile, Alan was charging his attackers like a bull. One by one, they turned and ran.

The thought that I had killed a man made me suddenly burst into tears. Alan put his hand on my shoulder and said I was a brave lad. He cut a silver button from his coat and said, "Whenever you show this, friends of Alan Breck Stewart will help you."

There were no more attacks that night. In the morning, Captain Hoseason called to ask Alan's terms for peace. Alan described an inlet on the Scottish coast where he wanted to be put ashore. Hoseason said it was too rocky to land, but when Alan offered him money, he said he would try.

Later, I told Alan everything that had happened since I had left home. He listened patiently, until I mentioned my friend Mr. Campbell, the minister. Then he became angry. He said, "I hate all people of that name.

"The Highland people are divided into clans. Each clan is usually made of people with the same name. The Campbells are enemies of my clan, the Stewarts. They are trying to drive the Stewarts off their land. The worst is Colin Roy Campbell, the Red Fox. He is an agent of King George."

"But why were you going to France?" I asked.

"Our clan chief fled to France in 1745. Each year, the clan collects money for him and I carry it back to France. I was on my way back there when my boat was rammed. I am a wanted man in Scotland. I must get back to France."

But we were still far from France. That night, Captain Hoseason steered the ship toward the Scottish coast. The sea was rough. The ship was tossed about by strong winds. Suddenly, we struck some rocks with great force. Waves began pounding the ship to pieces. We were readying the lifeboat when a giant wave came at us, sweeping me into the sea.

I do not know how many times I sank beneath the surface. I felt half drowned when I saw a large piece of wood from the ship. I grabbed it and held on for dear life.

READING COMPREHENSION

Summarizing. Choose the best phrase to complete each sentence. Then write the complete statement on your paper.

1. David Balfour went to the Shaws to _____ (find his father, meet Mr. Campbell, find his inheritance).

2. After tricking David into going on the ship, his uncle _____ (gave him his inheritance, had him kidnapped, entertained him).

3. When David heard the captain's plan for Alan Breck, he decided to _____ (warn Alan, help the captain, pretend he didn't hear anything).

4. The ship _____ (glided onto the beach, crashed on the rocks, got stuck in the sand) when Captain Hoseason steered it towards the Scottish coast.

Interpreting. Write the answer to each question on your paper.

1. Why didn't David's uncle want lights in his house?

2. Why did David help the rebel even though he felt they did not have a chance against the ship's crew?

3. What is the meaning of the silver button Alan gave to David?

For Thinking and Discussing. What is your opinion of David's Uncle Ebenezer? If Ebenezer did not have David's inheritance, do you think he would have treated David the same way? Explain your answer.

UNDERSTANDING LITERATURE

Conflict. A *conflict* is a struggle or fight between two sides. In "Kidnapped, Part One," the Campbell clan and the Stewart clan have a conflict. They both want to live on the same land.

Read the following statements. Then decide which ones are the conflict of a person against another person or group of people. Write your choices on your paper. Then write who is having the conflict.

1. "The bed was so damp, I slept on the floor."

2. "When I entered the round house, I told the rebel, 'The crew has already murdered a boy. Now it's you they want.'"

3. "The rebel said his name was Alan Breck Stewart and that he came from the Highlands. The Highlanders had fought against English rule for many years. Now he prepared to fight against Hoseason and his crew."

4. "We were readying the lifeboat when a giant wave came at us, sweeping me into the sea."

5. "I demanded to know why he had tried to kill me, but he was too weak to speak."

WRITING

Imagine you are David. Write a letter to your friend Mr. Campbell. Tell about your problems and ask for help.

Kidnapped, Part Two

In this dramatic conclusion, the bravery and daring of Robert Breck Stewart come once again to the rescue of young David Balfour. However, David must still endure many hardships to recover what is rightfully his.

I hung on to the wood until I began to feel a man can die of cold as well as drowning. I had no skill of swimming, but I found that when I kicked with both feet, I moved. Hard work it was, and slow. At last, the sea was quiet and the moon shone bright. I had never seen a place so desolate, but it was dry land. I cannot tell if I was more tired or grateful.

In the morning, it started to rain. I climbed a hill to look around, but saw no sign of the ship. I was all alone on a small island. There was a larger island nearby, with smoke rising from it, so someone lived there. But it was too far to swim.

For days it streamed rain. I was cold and wet, but I did not starve. I found shellfish among the rocks. Sometimes they made me sick, but I knew I must eat. By the third day, my clothes were rotting, my throat sore and my strength gone.

Then the sun came out. The comfort of the sun is a thing I cannot describe. It was then that I saw a fishing boat. I waved, but it kept going. I thought my heart would burst with anger.

But the next day, it came back. The fishermen spoke an old Scottish language I could not understand. They kept pointing to the nearby island. Then I understood. It was low tide, and the water between the islands was so low that I could walk across. A boy born by the sea would not have spent a day on the island. But, if not for the fishermen to show me, I would have left my bones there.

When I crossed over to the larger island, it seemed deserted at first. I walked toward the place where I had seen the smoke before. I finally found the house. An old man sat outside it. He said my shipmates had landed in the lifeboat and that he had given them food.

"You must be the lad with the silver button," he said. When I agreed, he told me to follow my friend to Torosay, then take a boat to the coast. I was to look for him among the Stewarts.

It was a two-day walk to Torosay. There I boarded a boat for the mainland. The captain, a member of Alan's clan, told me how to reach the Stewarts' land.

He warned me to speak to no one on the road. The redcoats, British soldiers, were looking for rebels. I did not tell him I was not a rebel. Alan had helped me; now I would help him. Then I would find Mr. Rankeillor and claim my fortune.

The next day, I was stopped by men on horses. One was a big, proud man with a red beard. I knew he was the Red Fox.

"Who are you?" he asked.

"An honest subject of the king," I said.

"I am Colin Roy Campbell, the king's agent. I have soldiers to support me."

It was then I heard a rifle shot. With the very sound of it, the Red Fox fell. I

saw a man in a dark coat holding a rifle. I ran toward him crying "Murderer!"

A redcoat shouted, "Capture the lad! He helped the murderer by stopping us!"

The soldiers ran after me, pausing only to shoot. I knew not which way to run.

"Duck in here among the trees," a voice said. It was Alan Breck Stewart. "Follow me," he said.

We ran until we had circled behind the redcoats. We were safe for a time. When I had caught my breath, I said, "Alan, we must part. I will not be party to murder."

"If I were to shoot a man," Alan said, "I would need a gun. I haven't got one. I swear I had no part in it."

"I believe you!" I cried.

"But the redcoats won't," he said. "We must flee the Highlands or we both shall hang. We will go to your country, the Lowlands. You will be safe; then I shall return to France."

That night we came to the house of James Stewart, half brother of the clan's exiled leader. He gave us food, money, and clothes. He told us we must leave quickly, as the redcoats were nearby.

We traveled over mountains, hiding among rocks and in caves. We often saw the redcoats on our trail. When we came to land with few trees, we crawled from one low bush to another. The pain was almost unbearable, but Alan would not stop — not even to sleep. I began to hate this man who had involved me in this cause not my own. My sickness and anger made me find a way to stop this endless journey.

"Mr. Stewart," says I, "I have met many members of your clan, and there isn't one who could not use a good washing." I knew these were fighting words and drew my sword.

"I cannot fight you," he cried. "It would be murder!" He threw down his sword.

At once, my anger left. I remembered how brave and kind he was, and that I owed my life to him. "Alan," I said, "what makes you put up with me?"

"Well," he said, "I thought I liked you because you never quarreled. Now I think I like you even better."

Alan and I braved the wilds of Scotland until we reached the port where I had been kidnapped. Alan hid while I searched for Mr. Rankeillor. Once I told the lawyer my name, he listened carefully to the story of my kidnapping and escape. To my surprise, he believed me.

He said, "Your friend Mr. Campbell worried when you did not write him. He asked me to find you. When your uncle said you had gone away, I could not prove he lied. Then Captain Hoseason said you had drowned at sea. What could I do?"

Mr. Rankeillor told me of my father and uncle. "When they were lads, they fell in love with the same lady. She loved your father, and he, being the older brother, was to inherit the Shaws by law. But he felt sorry for Ebenezer. So, he married the lady, gave Ebenezer the property, and left. Those in the neighborhood who knew what had happened gave Ebenezer the cold shoulder. Those who didn't know the story decided Ebenezer must have murdered his brother in order to steal his property. Ebenezer became a lonely miser."

"What is my position now?" I asked.

"The Shaws is yours," he said. "That was why Ebenezer had you kidnapped. You could sue for the property through the courts, but your friendship with a rebel would become known. Also, we cannot prove your uncle had you kidnapped. I suggest we bargain with Ebenezer."

I told Mr. Rankeillor my secret plan.

It was night when we arrived at the Shaws. Mr. Rankeillor and I hid near the door. Alan knocked loudly.

"Who are you?" my uncle asked.

"I won't say my name," said Alan, "but David Balfour brings me here."

My uncle said, "Tell me your business."

Alan said that after the ship went down, David had been found on an island. Alan's friends were holding him prisoner. If Ebenezer wanted to see him again, he must give him money.

"I care not what you do to him," Ebenezer said. "You'll get no money here."

"If you won't pay to save him, then you must pay us to keep him," said Alan.

Ebenezer said, "How much?"

"How much did you pay to have him kidnapped?" asked Alan.

Ebenezer said, "I gave Captain Hoseason 20 gold coins. He was to keep the money he made from selling David as a slave, too."

Just then Mr. Rankeillor stepped to the

door. "Good evening, Mr. Balfour. Do you know you can go to jail for kidnapping?"

"Good evening, Uncle," said I.

It did not take my uncle long to sign an agreement with me. He gave me most of the money he had hoarded, and I gave him the Shaws. At last, I could begin the life I had set out to lead the day I bid Mr. Campbell good-bye. But there was one thing left undone. I had to get Alan safely from Scotland.

Alan told me of a lawyer who belonged to his clan, who could get him aboard a ship to France. I met the lawyer and arranged for Alan's passage.

I walked with my friend part of the way toward the port. Then the time came for us to part. Alan held out his hand.

"Good-bye," he said.

"Good-bye," I said, shaking his hand.

We could not look at each other. We were both afraid we might cry if we did. We owed each other our lives. And we knew we would never see each other again.

READING COMPREHENSION

Summarizing. Choose the best phrase to complete each sentence. Then write the complete statement on your paper.

1. David was on an island until some fishermen pointed out that David could _____ (easily swim, walk in low tide, rent a boat) to the larger island.

2. Alan and David traveled through the wilds of Scotland because _____ (Captain Hoseason's crew, the Redcoats, the Scottish fishermen) were looking for them.

3. By telling Ebenezer Balfour that David was being held for ransom, Alan got Ebenezer to _____ (confess his plan, pay the ransom, plan an escape) for David.

Interpreting. Write the answer to each question on your paper.

1. Why did David pick a fight with Alan?

2. How did Ebenezer's neighbors feel about him?

3. How did David's actions towards his uncle show what kind of person he was?

4. How did Mr. Rankeillor's story explain the conflict between Alexander and Ebenezer Balfour?

For Thinking and Discussing. Imagine you are a lawyer representing David. Who would you call as witnesses to prove that Ebenezer withheld David's inheritance? What questions would you ask them?

UNDERSTANDING LITERATURE

Conflict. Conflict does not only happen between people. It can also be a struggle against the environment. This type of conflict is that of a person against nature.

Read each of the following situations from "Kidnapped, Part Two." Decide whether the conflict is that of a person against another person (or group of people) or a person against nature. Write your answers on your paper.

1. "I had no skill of swimming, but I found that when I kicked with both feet, I moved."

2. " 'I cannot fight you,' he cried. 'It would be murder!' "

3. "For days it streamed rain. I was cold and wet . . . ."

4. "When we came to land with few trees, we crawled from one low bush to another. The pain was almost unbearable, but Alan would not stop—not even to sleep."

5. "Alan, we must part. I will not be a party to murder."

6. "I was cold and wet, but I did not starve. I found shellfish among the rocks. Sometimes they made me sick."

WRITING

Write a paragraph about Ebenezer Balfour. Tell if you think he got what he deserved at the end of "Kidnapped." Give reasons to support your opinion.

The Bottle Imp

by Robert Louis Stevenson

Here's the offer. You can have anything you wish, except eternal life. In return, the devil gets your soul when you die!

This theme — selling a soul to the devil — is often called "the Faust theme." It has been an important idea in literature for a long time. Faust, a real person, was a magician. He lived in Germany during the late 1400's. He claimed he got his magical powers from the devil. After his death, many stories were written about him.

The following play also has a Faust theme. In this play, an imp lives inside a bottle. The imp is a creature who works for the devil. What happens when Kea and Loa, two young sailors, get the bottle? Will evil . . . or goodness win out in the end?

CHARACTERS

Narrator
Kea, a young Hawaiian sailor
Loa, his friend
Old Man
Woman at Party
Chang, Kea's servant
Kokua, a young woman
Man in Singapore
Lawyer
Keone
Young Woman
Young Man
Elderly Man
Sailor

Scene One

A street in San Francisco in the late 1800's.

Narrator: It all began one day when Kea and Loa left their ship to walk around San Francisco. . . .

Loa: Wait, Kea. Rest for a minute. That wasn't a hill we just climbed. That was a mountain.

Kea: It was a hill, Loa. Look down at the ocean. It spreads as far as we can see — all the way home to Hawaii. And over there, look at the most beautiful houses in San Francisco.

Loa: And next to you is the tiredest sailor

who ever spent a day of his leave climbing hills.

Kea: You haven't any imagination. Here we are, two sailors with a month's pay in our pockets. And we can walk along and look into the windows of the richest people in America.

Loa: I'd rather be sitting in their chairs.

Kea: So would I, if they were my chairs. Look at that house right across from us. The steps shine like silver. The windows sparkle like diamonds.

Loa: It's very pretty, except for the old man frowning at us from the doorway.

Kea: Shhh. He's calling us.

Old Man *(calling):* Young gentlemen! Please come here!

Kea *(to Loa):* Let's see what he wants.

(He and Loa walk to the man's doorway.)

Old Man: I noticed you were interested in my house.

Kea: Yes. We've never seen anything like it before.

Old Man: I suppose you'd like to own a house like it.

Kea *(laughing):* Who wouldn't, if they could?

Old Man: There's no reason why you can't. You have some money, don't you?

Kea: Only $50.

Old Man: Well, it's too bad you don't have more. But I'll let you have it for $50.

Kea: The house?

Old Man: No, of course not. The bottle.

Kea *(laughing):* You want me to pay $50 for a bottle? You've got an odd sense of humor.

Old Man: This is no joke. This house and everything in it came out of a bottle. It is a little bottle that won't hold more than a pint. Would you like to see it?

Kea: You bet I would!

Old Man: Wait right here. I'll get it for you. *(He goes.)*

Loa: Kea, let's go. This man is crazy.

Kea: Maybe not. The world is filled with strange things.

Loa: If he's crazy, it's even worse. We'd better get out of here.

Kea: Shhh. He's coming back.

Old Man: Here is the bottle.

Kea: How odd-looking it is. What's inside it that flickers like a flame?

Old Man: That is the imp.

Loa *(whispering):* Come on, Kea. Let's get out of here.

Kea: No, wait. What kind of imp can live in a glass bottle?

Old Man: The glass in this bottle was heated in the flames of hell. If you buy the bottle, the imp is at your command. You can have anything — money, fame, whole cities. When you sell the bottle, the power goes.

Kea: If I were you I wouldn't want to sell it.

Old Man: I have everything I want. But I'm growing old.

Kea: Why don't you ask the imp to let you live forever?

Old Man: That's the only thing the imp can't do.

Kea: Even so, you could try to get more than $50 for the bottle.

Old Man: I'd like to, for the good of the buyer.

Kea: I don't understand.

Old Man: There are two things about this bottle you must know. Once it's yours, you can't get rid of it, except by selling it. And it can only be sold for less than it was bought for. I paid $90 for it. If I sold it for more than $89.99, the imp would come right back to me.

Kea: I wouldn't worry about that.

Old Man: Oh, yes, you would. Anyone who dies still owning the bottle will burn in hell forever.

Kea: No wonder you want to get rid of it. I wouldn't touch it, not even for $50.

Loa: That's the first sensible thing you've said, Kea. Now, let's go.

Old Man *(desperately):* Don't you want a fine house like mine?

Kea: Not if it costs me my soul!

Old Man: But it won't! You can buy the bottle from me and get all you want from it. Then sell it!

Loa: We've got to get away from here, Kea.

Kea: We're in no danger, Loa. We haven't bought the bottle. Besides, how do we know he is telling the truth?

Old Man: I can prove it! The bottle is glass, isn't it? And glass breaks — ordinary glass, that is. But I can throw this on the pavement, and it won't break. *(He throws the bottle down.)* See? It bounces right back into my hand.

Kea: That still doesn't mean the bottle

can do all the things you say it can do.

Old Man: I'll make a bargain with you. Give me your $50. Take the bottle. Then wish the $50 back in your pocket. If it doesn't work, I'll give you your money back.

Loa: Don't take the risk, Kea.

Kea: Are you trying to trick me, old man?

Old Man: No, I swear it!

Kea: All right. *(He gives the man his money.)* Here's my money. Give me the bottle. Now imp of the bottle, I want my $50 back.

Loa: You're a fool, Kea. You've lost a month's pay for a piece of glass.

Kea: No! Look, Loa! My $50! It's back in my pocket, just as he said.

Old Man: I wish you luck with it.

Kea: Oh, no. Here, take it back. I don't want to fool around with anything like this.

Old Man: You bought it for less than I paid for it. It's yours now. That's the end of it as far as I'm concerned. Good day, young gentlemen. *(He goes into his house.)*

Loa: Now you've done it, Kea. Why didn't you leave when I wanted to?

Kea: How did I know he was going to trick me into buying the bottle? Well, he won't get away with it. I'm going to leave the bottle right here. Let's get out of sight before he comes back.

Loa: All right. Only maybe now you'll listen to me when I try to keep you out of trouble. *(He and Kea start to walk away.)*

Kea: Don't give me a lecture. Look, we've got a good story to tell back on the ship. Turn around. Is the bottle still on the doorsteps of the house?

Loa *(surprised):* No! The old man must have taken it.

Kea *(worried):* No, he didn't. Do you remember what he said? When the bottle belongs to you, you can get rid of it only by selling it.

Loa: Then where is it?

Kea *(feeling sick):* In my coat pocket.

Scene Two

A restaurant in San Francisco. Loa and Kea are sitting at a table.

Loa: Is the bottle still in your pocket, Kea?

Kea: It's still there. Loa, I'm beginning to be glad we met that old man. I want many things. If what he said is true, the bottle will give all of them to me. I'm going to be a happy man!

Loa: What would you wish for?

Kea: First, a house in the islands. Let's see, I want 17 rooms and three porches — overlooking Kona Bay.

Loa: You'd better wish for enough money to keep it in good shape.

Kea: Of course. I want enough money so I'll never have to work again.

Loa: Why don't you try it?

Kea: I don't want to take a chance until I'm sure the bottle works. I'm going to try to sell the bottle for $60. If it comes back to me, I'll believe the old man. And I'll use the bottle to get the things I want.

Loa: Good idea.

Kea: Let's get out of here. We'll sell the bottle for $60. Then we'll go back to the hotel and see what happens.

Scene Three

The stairs that lead to Kea and Loa's room at a hotel.

Kea: If my bottle comes back, this will be the last time I have to climb creaky stairs.

Loa: Even if the bottle doesn't come back, you've got $60 in your pocket. That's $10 more than you had before.

Kea: I was afraid that storekeeper wouldn't pay it. He was a pretty careful man.

Loa: He'd have been even more careful if he knew what kind of bottle it's supposed to be.

Kea: Well, the bottle hasn't come back yet. *(He and Loa enter their hotel room.)*

Loa: Somebody has pushed a letter under our door — it's for you. It's a letter from home.

Kea: From Hawaii? Let me see it. *(He opens it and reads it.)* Loa, my uncle is dead.

Loa: I'm sorry. That's really rough.

Kea: It's not rough for me Loa. I've never even met this uncle. But he has left me his fortune.

Loa: Wow!

Kea: The lawyer says it's enough money so I won't ever have to work again. I've also been given some land overlooking Kona Bay. That's just what I've wanted. I'm sorry that my uncle had to die. But now I've got everything I've ever wanted! Aren't you going to congratulate me? Loa, what are you staring at?

Loa: Kea. The bottle is back. It's on the chest of drawers. As you spoke just now, the flame in it flared up. The bottle turned bright red.

Kea: Oh, I see now. This letter brings me all the things I said I wanted this afternoon.

Loa: Then it's true, Kea.

Kea: It's true. I have everything I want. Now I must sell the bottle for less than I paid. Loa, I don't want it near me any longer!

Loa: Kea, I'll buy it from you. I'll take the chance. I'll ask for a little boat. Then I can set up my own business sailing around the islands. I'll buy the bottle from you for $49.99. Then as soon as I get my boat, I'll sell it for a penny less.

Kea: You'll be able to find plenty of buyers, Loa. Give me the money, and take the bottle.

Loa: All right. Here. What are you going to do now?

Kea: I'm going back to the islands. I'll live in luxury in my house on Kona Bay.

Scene Four

Kea's house on Kona Bay. A party is going on.

Woman: This is a wonderful party, Kea. There's no place on the island like your house and its gardens. Your house needs only one thing.

Kea: What is that?

Woman: A wife.

Kea: You are right.

Woman: You must look around. Many women would like to live in a house like this.

Kea: I don't doubt it. But when I meet the woman meant to be my wife I shall know her.

Scene Five

Kea and his servant, Chang, are walking along the beach.

Kea: Wait, Chang.

Chang: Yes, sir?

Kea: You know everyone on the island. Who is that young woman — down there by the sea?

Chang: The one who has just been swimming? That is Kokua, the daughter of Kiano.

Kea: There is something about her. . . . Go on home, Chang. Don't fix dinner for me. I'm not sure when I'll be home.

Chang: Very well, sir. *(He goes.)*

Kea *(calling):* Kokua! Kokua!

Kokua: Who are you?

Kea *(walking over to her):* I'm Kea.

Kokua: Kea of the Great House?

Kea: Yes.

Kokua: My father has spoken of you. How do you know who I am?

Kea: Does it matter? Here is the plain truth, Kokua. I have only just met you. But your eyes draw me toward you. My heart has gone to you, as swiftly as a bird.

Kokua: Kea has said the same to many young women.

Kea: No, I have not, Kokua. If you want nothing to do with me, say so. But if you find me no worse than any other man, say that. And I will go to your father's house and ask him for your hand.

Kokua: My father's house is this way.

Scene Six

Kea's house.

Kea *(entering):* Chang! Chang! We will

be busy these next few days. We must get the house ready for a bride.

Chang: You are to be married?

Kea: To Kokua, daughter of Kiano. I spoke to her father. Life can be not better than this, Chang.

Chang: Sir! Look at your arm!

Kea: My arm? There's a speck of something on it. What is it?

Chang *(frightened):* Come no closer, sir!

Kea: Chang, what do you mean?

Chang: The speck on your arm is the — the evil.

Kea: What? You mean leprosy? Oh, no,

Chang! Don't stare at me like that! Go away! Leave me alone!

Chang: Yes, sir. *(He goes.)*

Kea: So, now it all ends. I must go to the settlement of lepers and live there. I could do this bravely, had I not met Kokua. Why did I have to meet her before this came upon me? Now I may never marry her. I may never see her again. Wait — the bottle! If I could buy it back again, I could ask the imp to cure me. Yes. That is what I must do. I risked facing the devil once to get a house. I will certainly risk facing him again for Kokua. Chang! Chang!

Chang *(entering):* Yes sir?

Kea: Where was Loa when I heard from him last?

Chang: Singapore.

Kea: Pack my clothes, and get me a ticket to Singapore. I must get back the bottle I wanted so much to get rid of.

Scene Seven

Kea is at a doorway in Singapore.

Man in Singapore: Loa is not at home. He has left for a long trip to the Indies.

305

Kea: Isn't there any way I can reach him?

Man: Maybe through his lawyer. I will give you his name.

(Kea stands at another doorway.)

Lawyer: Loa didn't leave me an address. He did not know exactly where he would be stopping during his trip. Is it important?

Kea: Yes. He bought something from me. I want very much to buy it back.

Lawyer: Don't say it! It is an evil thing! Loa sold it. I probably should say no more about it. But you look desperate. If you call at the house of Keone, you may be able to trace it. I'll give you his address.

(Kea is at another doorway.)

Kea: Keone?

Keone: What can I do for you?

Kea: I am tracing an article sold to you by Loa, and —

Keone: Yes, of course. I haven't got it any longer. But I'll tell you the name of the person I sold it to.

(Kea is at another doorway.)

Young Woman *(whispering):* Yes, I had it for a while. But it has passed from my hands.

Kea: Where? Where is it now?

Young Woman: I'm not sure. I can give you an address. But I'm not sure whether or not the man still lives there.

(Kea at another doorway.)

Kea: I have come to buy the bottle.

Young Man: What?

Kea: To buy the bottle. Don't pretend you don't know what I mean.

Young Man: No, there is no need for that.

Kea: All right, then. What is the price?

Young Man: I bought the bottle for two cents.

Kea *(with a gasp):* Oh! Then the price is one cent.

Young Man: I can't sell it for more.

Kea: And I won't be able to sell it at all. All right. Let's have it.

Young Man *(amazed):* You're going to buy it?

Kea: Yes, rather than die in loneliness.

Scene Eight

Kea is on a ship, going back to Hawaii.

Kea: Bottle imp, make me a healthy man again. Take the illness away from me. Let me marry Kokua!

Scene Nine

Kea and Kokua's house.

Kokua: Chang, did Kea say when he would be home for dinner?

Chang: No, ma'am.

Kokua: Was my husband always like this, Chang? He is so moody. He speaks so sharply. Did he always go out for so long in the evenings?

Chang: It was after his trip to Singapore that he changed.

Kokua: That's when we were married. Chang, do you think he is tired of me?

(As she begins to cry, a door opens.)

Kea *(entering):* Is there no one in this house to help me with my horse? What are you waiting for, Chang? Get to work!

Chang: Right away, sir. *(He goes.)*

Kea: And you, Kokua! Can't I have some cheerfulness when I come home?

Kokua *(crying):* Oh, Kea, I have tried. If I only knew what is making you unhappy.

Kea: Ha! What if I told you I had sold my soul to the devil for you? What would you think then?

Kokua: Kea! No!

Kea: Listen to my story. Then you'll see who should be weeping in this house.

Scene Ten

An hour later.

Kea: And so, I love you dearly. But my mind is always on the bottle that I can never sell. I bought it for a cent. There is nothing less than that.

Kokua: Oh, Kea! Why didn't you tell me all this before? In France, there is a coin called a *centime*. It takes five of them to make a cent.

Kea: Are you sure, Kokua?

Kokua: I have seen the coin myself. We will go to the French islands. There we will have four centimes, three centimes, two centimes, one centime.

Kea: That means four possible sales!

Kokua: Let's leave right away. Soon we'll be happy, with our minds at peace.

Scene Eleven

Outside Kea and Kokua's rented house on the island of Tahiti.

Kea: Let's go back inside the house.

Kokua: No. Let's stay in the moonlight a while longer.

Kea: We have to pack. We must go home. We've been gone too long.

Kokua: But we can't leave yet! We haven't sold the bottle.

Kea: We've tried for six months. We're never going to sell it.

Kokua: But we can't give up, Kea.

Kea: I made the bargain, Kokua. I'll stick by it. That's why I want to go home. I want to end my days near the hills of my ancestors. I don't want to die in a strange land.

Kokua: Kea, I won't let you.

Kea: Don't worry. Look, there's an old man coming this way. I don't want him to hear us. We'll talk more when you come in. *(He goes inside the house. Kokua begins to cry.)*

Elderly Man *(approaching Kokua):* Can I help you, young lady?

Kokua: No, thank you. *(Pause.)* Wait! There's a bottle that I want to buy. It's — very pretty. The man who just went inside this house owns it. He won't sell it to me. But maybe he'd sell it to you.

Elderly Man: But I don't need a bottle, pretty or not.

Kokua: Look, I'll give you the money. He'll sell you the bottle for four centimes. He won't take a centime more. Then, you bring the bottle to me. And I'll buy it from you for three centimes.

Elderly Man: For such a cheap bottle, you're going to a lot of trouble.

Kokua: There is a lot that I can't explain. Will you do this for me?

Elderly Man: Well, all right.

Kokua: Here are four centimes. While you speak to the man in this house, I'll wait over there for you.

Scene Twelve

A few minutes later.

Elderly Man: Young lady, here is your bottle.

Kokua: Thank you. And here are your three centimes. I'll hide the bottle in my pocket. Now, you must go quickly!

Elderly Man: I'm going. *(He hurries off.)*

Kea *(appearing):* Kokua! Guess what happened!

Kokua: Tell me.

Kea: An old fool came and bought the bottle. I don't know how he heard about it. But I didn't ask any questions. He seemed to think he could sell it for three centimes when he wanted. But he'll never be able to sell it for four centimes. *(He laughs.)*

Kokua *(suddenly unhappy):* Kea, it is a terrible thing to save yourself at the expense of another person's soul. I could never laugh about it. I would be so sad.

Kea *(angry):* Be sad then. No good wife would feel that way. You should be ashamed. *(Pause.)* Let's forget it. It's a beautiful night. Let's take a boat ride.

Kokua: I can't. I'm ill. I feel so unhappy.

Kea: So this is the way you love me! Your husband is saved from the devil — a risk he took for you! Instead of being glad, you are unhappy. You are a disloyal wife. I'm going out. *(He goes.)*

Scene Thirteen

Several hours later. Kea and a sailor appear back at Kea and Kokua's rented house.

Sailor: So this is your house, my friend? Quite a fancy place. How did a former sailor like you get a place like this?

Kea: Never mind. It gives me no satisfaction. I might as well be back at sea. Just before I met you tonight, I had a wonderful piece of luck. But would my wife help me celebrate? She would not!

Sailor: That's too bad.

Kea: Let's go in. We can sneak in without her hearing us. *(He looks in one of the windows.)* There she is. Oh! She has the bottle!

Sailor: She has it? You mean we can't have a drink?

Kea: It's not that kind of bottle. I understand now. She bought the bottle to save me. She sent the old man to buy it from me.

Sailor: Who cares how she got the bottle? Let's go in and have a drink out of it.

Kea: This is a bottle with an imp of the devil in it. It gives you anything you ask for.

Sailor: I've heard about it. I don't believe stuff like that.

Kea: It's true. I owned it until tonight. That's how I got my house. Then I sold the bottle to an old man so I could be free. My wife, dear Kokua, bought it from him. There she sits, staring at it, knowing.

Sailor: Let's go in and surprise her. We'll cheer her up.

Kea: No. Look, here are two centimes. Go in and buy the bottle from her. Bring it to me, and I'll buy it back for one centime. Just promise you won't tell her that you know me.

Sailor: Are you trying to make a fool of me?

Kea: No. You can prove it. When you get the bottle, wish for something. Wish for a pocketful of money — or anything. You'll see. . . .

Sailor: All right. But you'll be sorry if this turns out to be a big joke and you're making fun of me. *(He knocks on the door. Kokua opens it.)*

Kokua: Who are you? What do you want?

Sailor: I want to buy that bottle of yours. I have two centimes to pay for it.

Kokua: Do you mean that?

Sailor: Are you going to sell it to me or not? *(He holds out the money.)*

Kokua: I don't understand. But yes, take it! *(She gives him the bottle and takes the money.)* Take it, and I will pray for you. *(She closes the door.)*

Sailor: And now, I wish for a bottle of rum. *(A bottle of rum appears.)* Well, I'll be! A bottle of rum!

Kea: You got it! You got the bottle with the imp!

Sailor: If you come any closer, I'll knock you out. You thought you could make a fool of me, didn't you?

Kea: What do you mean?

Sailor: This is a pretty fancy bottle. If you think you can have it for one centime, you're crazy!

Kea: You mean you won't sell it?

Sailor: No, I won't sell it.

Kea: But I told you — whoever owns it goes to hell.

Sailor: I reckon I'm going there anyway. So I might as well go in style. This bottle is the best thing I've ever met up with. I'm keeping it. Get yourself another one.

Kea: For your own sake, sell it to me.

Sailor: Try and get it! *(He goes off, laughing.)*

Kea: Kokua! We're saved! *(He goes into the house.)*

Narrator: So they lived a life of peace and plenty in the islands of Hawaii. Or so the story was told to me.

READING COMPREHENSION

Summarizing. Choose the best phrase to complete each sentence. Then write the complete statement on your paper.

1. The old man tricked Kea into _____ (buying his house, buying the bottle, selling the bottle to Loa).

2. In order to marry Kokua, Kea _____ (bought the bottle a second time, moved to the island of Tahiti, gave the bottle to Kea's father).

3. Kokua bought the bottle because she wanted to _____ (be rich and famous, save Kea and make him happy, see the imp inside the bottle).

4. The sailor would not sell the bottle back to Kea because he _____ (wanted to sell it to Kokua, wanted to save Kea, was a greedy person).

Interpreting. Write the answer to each question on your paper.

1. Why was it very important for the buyer to know that the bottle could be sold only for less money than it was bought?

2. Why did Kea buy the bottle a second time?

3. How did Kokua feel about trying to sell the bottle to another in order to save herself?

For Thinking and Discussing. If you had the opportunity to buy the bottle imp, would you? Why or why not? If you bought it, what would you wish for?

UNDERSTANDING LITERATURE

Conflict. Conflict, or a struggle, makes a story exciting. Sometimes the conflict is between different feelings within one person. This kind of conflict is called an *inner conflict*. For example, if you want to go to a movie with a friend, but you have promised to help your brother study for a test, you have an inner conflict. In order to *resolve*, or end the conflict, you must make a decision and act on it.

Each statement below describes a character's action in "The Bottle Imp." The action suggests that the character has made some kind of decision. On your paper, write *yes* or *no* to show whether the decision was made to resolve an inner conflict. If your answer is yes, explain what the conflict was.

1. Loa and Kea left their ship to walk around San Francisco.

2. Kea was afraid to buy the bottle but agreed to give the old man $50 to see if his claims were true.

3. Kokua agreed to marry Kea and brought him home to meet her father.

4. Kea bought the bottle a second time.

5. The sailor would not sell the bottle back to Kea.

WRITING

Suppose you had something that would magically grant you anything you wanted. Write a paragraph telling what you would wish for and why.

Windy Nights

Whenever the moon and stars are set,
Whenever the wind is high,
All night long in the dark and wet,
A man goes riding by.
Late in the night when the fires are out,
Why does he gallop and gallop about?

Whenever the trees are crying aloud,
And ships are tossed at sea,
By, on the highway, low and loud,
By at the gallop goes he;
By at the gallop he goes, and then
By he comes back at the gallop again.

---

1. Do you think the poem is really about
a man riding a horse? What else could it
be about?
2. How does the poem make you feel?
What words does the author use to set the
mood of the poem?

Requiem

Under the wide and starry sky
Dig the grave and let me lie.
Glad did I live and gladly die,
And I laid me down with a will.

This be the verse that you grave for me:
Here he lies where he longed to be,
Home is the sailor, home from sea,
And the hunter home from the hill.

---

1. Why do you think the speaker of the
poem is ready to die?
2. Why do you think the speaker of the
poem wants to be buried "Under the wide
and starry sky"?

*Grave of
Robert Louis
Stevenson
in Samoa*

314

VOCABULARY

Prefixes. A root word is a word from which other words can be made. When you put a word part called a *prefix* before a root word, you change the meaning of the word. If you do not know the meaning of a word, you can look at its word parts to help you. For example, the word *unhealthy* is made up of a prefix and a root word. The prefix *un-*means "not," and the root word *healthy* means "to be well." By looking at the prefix and the root word, you can tell that *unhealthy* means "not being well."

Look at the following prefixes and their meanings. Read each sentence below, paying careful attention to the root word. On your paper, write each sentence, filling in the prefix that would best complete the root word. Then write a sentence of your own using the word you put together.

pre-	before
re-	again
un-	not

1. David and Alan decided to _____ turn to the port where David was kidnapped.

2. Kea thought the old man's story about the bottle imp was _____ believable.

3. David and Alan became _____ united after Red Fox was killed.

4. Uncle Ebenezer said he would not allow lights in his house as a _____ caution against fires.

5. David was _____ comfortable using a pistol.

6. Uncle Ebenezer _____ paid the Captain to kidnap David.

READING

Drawing Conclusions. In some stories, an author will tell you what he or she wants you to conclude about a story and its characters. In other stories, an author will give you facts and details but let you make your own decisions or *draw your own conclusions* about a story and its characters. For example, in "The Bottle Imp" Kokua tells the elderly man, "He'll sell the bottle to you for four centimes . . . . And I'll buy it from you for three centimes." From these statements, you can conclude that Kokua is willing to risk her own future for her husband, but that she would not trick anyone else into becoming the bottle's owner.

On your paper, write the conclusions you can draw from the facts below.

1. In "The Bottle Imp," the sailor knows that he will burn in hell if he dies owning the bottle, yet he refuses to sell it. Tell what you can conclude about the sailor from this fact.

2. In "Kidnapped, Part Two," Mr. Rankeillor tells David how he thinks he

should go about getting his inheritance. He says David can take his uncle to court, but he suggests David bargain with his uncle instead. What could you conclude Mr. Rankeillor feels about going to court?

3. In "Kidnapped, Part One," the captain asks David to help him get the pistols away from the rebel. What might the captain have concluded about David?

4. In "Kidnapped, Part Two," you learn that David's father married the lady that Ebenezer loved as well. David's father gave Ebenezer the property where Ebenezer lived as a lonely miser. What can you conclude about David's father and Ebenezer?

QUIZ

The following is a quiz for Section 8. Write the answers on your paper in complete sentences.

Reading Comprehension

1. In "The Bottle Imp," what was the only wish that the bottle imp could not grant?

2. In "The Bottle Imp," what happened if someone bought the bottle for more money than the last person who bought it?

3. In "Kidnapped," why did David's uncle try to kill him?

4. In "Kidnapped," how did the captain plan to get rid of David?

5. In "Kidnapped," how did Alan come to be on Captain Hoseason's ship?

Understanding Literature

6. In "The Bottle Imp," Kea faced an inner conflict when he wanted to buy the bottle from the young man. What was the conflict and what action did he take to resolve it?

7. Give an example about a person against nature conflict in "Kidnapped." Was the character able to resolve the conflict? How?

8. At the end of "Kidnapped," David discovered a conflict that existed between his father and his uncle. What was it, and how was it resolved?

9. In the poem "Windy Nights," what kind of sound does "whenever the trees are crying aloud" suggest?

10. Robert Louis Stevenson's poem "Requiem" contains the line "Home is the sailor, home from the sea." What do you think the poet means when he refers to "home"?

WRITING

A Comparison and Contrast of Two Characters. To *compare* means to say how two or more people or things are alike. To *contrast* means to say how they are different. Comparing and contrasting characters can help you understand them better.

On your paper, write a comparison of two of the characters you have read about in this section. Read each step to help guide you in your writing.

Step 1: Set Your Goal
Choose one of the following topics to write about.

☐ Both the Old Man from "The Bottle Imp" and Uncle Ebenezer from "Kidnapped" tricked another person. How are these characters alike? How are they different?

☐ Both Kea and Kokua in "The Bottle Imp" bought the bottle to save another person. How were their feelings about buying the bottle alike? How were their feelings about selling different?

☐ In "Kidnapped," certain character traits helped both David and Alan survive. In what ways are David and Alan alike? In what ways are they different?

Step 2: Make a Plan
Plan what you are going to say. Make a list of examples from the story that show how the characters are alike. Make another list to show how they are different.

Suppose that you were comparing David and the young sailor named Ransome from "Kidnapped, Part One." Your two lists might look like this:

Similarities
☐ Both were young.

☐ Both had bad experiences on the ship.

☐ David took over Ransome's work.

Differences

David	Ransome
☐ didn't do bad things	boasted of bad things he had done
☐ no experience on ship	experienced sailor
☐ didn't think the captain was bad at first	knew the captain was wicked
☐ disliked the ship	loved the ship
☐ escaped	was murdered

Now make lists of similarities and differences in the characters you have chosen.

Step 3: Write Your First Draft
Your comparison should contain three paragraphs. The first should introduce the characters. The second should tell how they are alike. The third should tell how they are different.

☐ Begin by introducing the characters. For example, if you were writing about David and Ransome you might begin this way:

David Balfour and Ransome, the young sailor, are alike in some ways and different in others.

317

☐ Next write a paragraph using your list of similarities.

☐ End by writing a paragraph using your list of differences.

Step 4: Revise Your Comparison
Check your paragraph one more time.

Make sure you have said what you want to say about each character. Correct any errors in spelling, grammar, and punctuation you find. Make a final, neat copy of your comparison.

ACTIVITIES

Word Attack. When the letter *i* is followed by a consonant and then a vowel, it usually stands for the long *i* sound:

    fine   bite

When *i* is followed by two consonants or by one consonant and no vowel, it usually stands for the short *i* sound:

    little   his

However, when *i* is followed by the letters *gh,* the *i* usually stands for the long *i* sound:

    right   light

Find all the words that have an *i* in the poem "Windy Nights." Then copy them on your paper and write *short i* or *long i* for each.

Speaking and Listening. Practice reading the poem "Windy Nights" aloud. Try to read in a way that will help your listeners

get a mysterious, spooky feeling from hearing the poem. Pay special attention to words containing the letter *i.*

Researching.
1. An *atlas* is a book of maps. Find an atlas in the library. In the index at the back of the atlas, look up Hawaii, where Kea and Kokua lived. The index will tell the number of the map that shows Hawaii. Use the map to answer the following questions on your paper.

☐ How many islands make up the Hawaiian Islands?

☐ What is the name of the largest island?

☐ In which ocean are the Hawaiian Islands?

☐ What is the capital of Hawaii?

☐ On which island is the capital located?

2. Use an atlas to help you draw a map of Hawaii, Samoa, Tahiti, or another island or group of islands that you would like to visit. Mark the capital city and other important features such as large cities, long rivers, and tall mountains. Write the name of the body of water in which the island is located. Use the island's name as the title of your map. Color the map. Write a paragraph explaining why you would like to visit the island.

3. David Balfour in the story "Kidnapped" did a lot of traveling from the time he set out for The Shaws until he returned. The map of Scotland shows

David's route. Look up Scotland in an encyclopedia or an atlas. Find answers to these questions:

☐ From what large city did David leave?

☐ On what bodies of water did David travel?

☐ Near which Island did David first meet Alan Breck Stewart?

☐ What two countries are near Scotland?

☐ In which direction did Alan go from Scotland to get to France?

Creating. Think about one small adventure that took place in your life. Tell the story about your adventure onto a tape recording, or in front of some of your friends. Include the following information in the tale of your adventure:

1. Where does it take place?

2. Who are the characters involved?

3. Were you searching for something, and if so, what was it?

4. Is there any conflict involved between you and the other characters?

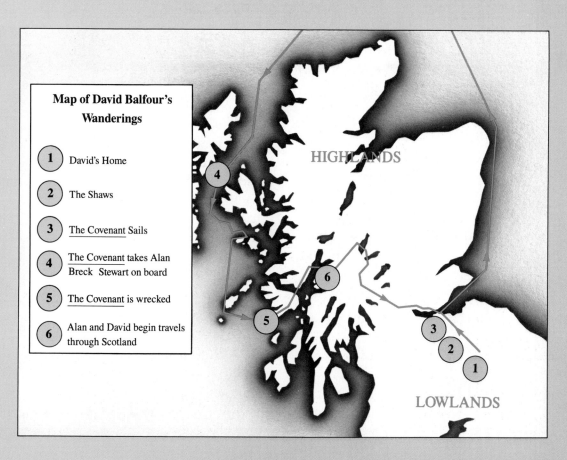

Map of David Balfour's Wanderings

1. David's Home

2. The Shaws

3. The Covenant Sails

4. The Covenant takes Alan Breck Stewart on board

5. The Covenant is wrecked

6. Alan and David begin travels through Scotland

HIGHLANDS

LOWLANDS

SECTION 9

MYSTERY

O'er all there
hung a shadow and a fear;
A sense of mystery
The spirit daunted, and said as plain
as whisper in the ear,
The place is haunted.

—Thomas Hood

Hopper, Edward. *House by the Railroad*. (1925). Oil on Canvas, 24 × 29″. Collection, The Musem of Modern Art, New York. Given anonymously.

Introduction

You want to know the answer to everything, don't you? Do you ever like *not* knowing something?

Not knowing what is happening, or what will happen can be a mystery that may make you wonder. Or, a mystery may make you curious enough to try to solve it. You will then need to find pieces of information, or clues, that fit together, because solving a mystery is like putting the pieces of a puzzle together to discover the picture. But, solving a mystery is really more difficult than a puzzle; clues are not always in a box! Sometimes clues are right in front of your nose. Other times you have to think carefully or you can be fooled.

Here is what one 11-year old said about a kind of mystery that she tried to solve:

"I like to know in advance about my birthday and Christmas presents. I don't like surprises that I don't know about, so, I have to figure out where they are hidden. First, I figure out where the places are that people think I don't usually go. Then, if I hear someone say, 'don't go in there,' I know that's a clue. Also, if I am told 'that's not for you, it's for your cousin,' I know that's a BIG clue that it's really for

me. I listen carefully to what is said."

Mysteries involve clues, hidden places, what people say that may or may not be true, and strange twists.

In these selections, you will have a chance to use your skills in mystery solving.

In "Sarah Tops," Larry's detective father is puzzled over the dead man's last words. Find out what Larry discovers that can teach his father something about being a detective.

In "The Redheaded League," Sherlock Holmes is given a very strange mystery to solve: Mr. Wilson first gets a job just because he has red hair, and then the job ends. Wilson's hair is still red, but something has happened that he did not know about. What could it be?

Read the poem, "The Way Through the Woods," to find out what things are really happening in the woods. Are there people and horses on a road, or not?

In "The Phantom Cyclist," a girl in all white named Sigrid whizzes along on her bicycle and disappears from sight. Where does Sigrid travel to so quickly, and where did she come from? Join Randy and Sara as they try to solve this mystery.

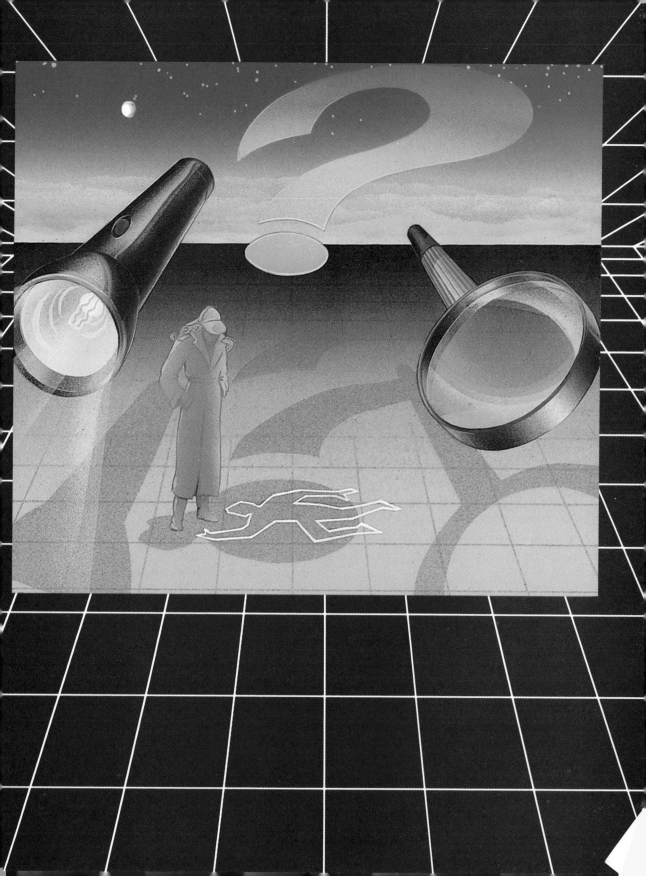

Sarah Tops

by Isaac Asimov

There's an art to solving mysteries. You have to be good at understanding clues. The clue left by the dead man in this story stumps all the crime solvers — except Larry, the son of a detective on the force. It seems Larry could teach his dad a thing or two.

I came out of the Museum of Natural History and was crossing the street on my way to the subway. Suddenly, I noticed the crowd and the police cars about halfway down the block. I could hear the whine of an approaching ambulance.

For a minute I hesitated. Then I walked on. The crowds of the curious just get in the way of officials trying to save lives. My dad is a detective on the force. He complains about that all the time. I wasn't going to add to the problem myself.

I just kept my mind on the term paper I was going to have to write on air pollution for my seventh-grade class. I thought about the notes I had taken on the subject at the museum.

Of course, I knew I would read about the incident in the afternoon papers. Besides, I would ask Dad about it. Sometimes he talked about cases without giving too many of the real security details. And Mom and I never talk about what we hear, anyway.

After dinner I described what I had seen outside of the museum. Dad knew all about it. A man had been murdered outside the museum!

I said, "I was working on my term paper. I was there first thing in the morning."

Mom looked worried. "There might have been shooting in the museum," she said.

"Well, there wasn't," said Dad soothingly. "This man tried to lose himself in the museum. But he didn't succeed."

"I would have," I said. "I know the museum, every inch."

Dad doesn't like me to boast, so he frowned at me. "The thugs who were after him didn't let him get away entirely. They caught up with him outside. Then they knifed him, and got away. We'll catch them, though. We know who they are."

He nodded his head. "They're what's left of the gang that broke into that jewelry store two weeks ago. We

managed to get the jewels back. But we didn't grab all the men. And not all the jewels either. One diamond was left. A big one — worth 30,000 dollars."

"Maybe that's what the killers were after," I said.

"Very likely. The dead man was probably trying to cheat the other two. He wanted to keep that one stone for himself. They turned out his pockets and ripped his clothes after they knifed him."

"Did they get the diamond?" I asked.

"How can we tell? The woman who reported the killing found him when he was just barely able to breathe. She said he said three words to her, very slowly, 'Try . . . Sarah . . . Tops.' Then he died."

"Who is Sarah Tops?" asked Mom.

Dad shrugged. "I don't know. I don't even know if that's really what he said. The woman was pretty upset. If she's right and that's what he said, then maybe the killers didn't get the diamond. Maybe

the dead man left it with Sarah Tops, whoever she is. Maybe he knew he was dying. Maybe he wanted to give it back and have it off his conscience."

"Is there a Sarah Tops in the phone book, Dad?" I asked.

Dad said, "Did you think we didn't look? No Sarah Tops, either one P or two. Nothing in the city directory. Nothing in our files. Nothing in the FBI files."

Mom said, "Maybe it's not a person. Maybe it's a company. Sarah Tops Cakes or something."

"Could be," said Dad. "There's no Sarah Tops company. But there are other kinds of Tops. We'll check them out for anyone working there named Sarah. It'll take days of dull routine."

I got an idea suddenly and bubbled over. "Listen, Dad, maybe it isn't a company either. Maybe it's a *thing*. Maybe the woman didn't hear 'Sarah Tops' but 'Sarah's top'. You know, a *top* that you spin. If the dead guy has a daughter named Sarah, maybe he made a hole in her toy top. Then he could have stashed the diamond inside and . . ."

Dad pointed his finger at me and grinned. "Very good, Larry," he said. "A nice idea. But he doesn't have a daughter named Sarah. Or any relative by that name as far as we know. We've searched where he lived. There's nothing reported there that can be called a top."

"Well," I said. I felt sort of disappointed, "I suppose that's not such a good idea anyway. Why should he say we ought to *try* it? He either hid it in Sarah's top or he didn't. He would know which. Why should he say we should *try* it?"

And then it hit me. What if . . .

Dad was just getting up, as though he were going to turn on the television, and I said, "Dad, can you get into the museum this time of evening?"

"On police business? Sure."

"Dad," I said, kind of breathless, "I think we better go look. *Now*. Before the people start coming in again."

"Why?"

"I've got a silly idea. I . . . I . . . "

Dad didn't push me. He likes me to have my own ideas. He thinks maybe I'll be a detective, too, someday. He said, "All right. Let's follow up your lead, whatever it is."

He called the museum. Then we took a taxi and got there just when the last purple bit of twilight was turning to black. We were let in by a guard.

I'd never been in the museum when it was dark. It looked like a huge underground cave. The guard's flashlight seemed to make things even darker and more mysterious.

We took the elevator up to the fourth floor. There the big shapes loomed in the bit of light that shone this way and that as the guard moved his torch.

"Do you want me to put on the light in this room?" he asked.

"Yes, please," I said.

There they all were. Some in glass cases. But the big ones in the middle of the large room. Bones and teeth and spines of dinosaurs that ruled the earth hundreds of millions of years ago.

"I want to look close at that one," I said. "Is it all right if I climb over the railing?"

"Go ahead," said the guard. He helped me. I leaned against the platform. I looked at the grayish plaster material the skeleton was standing on.

"What's this?" I said. It didn't look much different in color from the plaster on which it was lying.

"Chewing gum," said the guard, frowning.

"The guy was trying to get away. He saw his chance to throw this . . . He wanted to keep it away from *them* . . . " Before I could finish my sentence Dad took the gum from me. He squeezed it. Then he pulled it apart. Something inside caught the light and flashed. Dad put it into an envelope. "How did you know?" he asked me.

"Well, look at it," I said.

It was a magnificent skeleton. It had a large skull. There were two horns over the eyes, and a third one, just a bump, on the snout. The nameplate said *Triceratops*.

READING COMPREHENSION

Summarizing. Choose the best phrase and write the complete statement on your paper.

1. Larry went to the _____ (Department of Environmental Control, Museum of Natural History, City Library) to research his term paper.

2. Larry's dad believed that the man who was killed was a _____ (museum employee, member of a jewel thief gang, school librarian).

3. The man hid the diamond _____ (in his coat pocket, in his daughter's top, on the base of the dinosaur skeleton).

Interpreting. Write the answer to each question on your paper.

1. How did Larry's father determine that the thieves might have been looking for a diamond?

2. Why did the man say, "Try . . . Sarah . . . Tops," to the woman?

3. Why did Larry want to take his father to the museum at night?

4. What experience probably helped Larry to figure out the meaning of "Try Sarah Tops" before his father could figure it out?

For Thinking and Discussion. Do you think a story like this could really happen? Which events, if any, are realistic, and which, if any, are unbelievable?

UNDERSTANDING LITERATURE

Suspense in a Mystery. Plot is the order of events in a story. A mystery writer carefully presents things in the plot that build suspense. *Suspense* makes the reader ask questions and feel tense because he or she is not sure what will happen next.

The following quotations are from "Sarah Tops." Write a question that each quotation makes you want to ask.

1. "I came out of the Museum of Natural History and was crossing the street on my way to the subway. Suddenly I noticed the crowd and the police cars about halfway down the block. I could hear the whine of an approaching ambulance."

2. "The woman who reported the killing found him when he was just barely able to breathe. She said he said three words to her, very slowly, 'Try . . . Sarah . . . Tops.' Then he died."

3. "I'd never been in the museum when it was dark. It looked like a huge underground cave. The guard's flashlight seemed to make things even darker and more mysterious."

4. "The guy was trying to get away. He saw his chance to throw this . . . He wanted to keep it away from *them* . . ."

WRITING

Write a paragraph about walking around inside of a museum late at night. Use details in your paragraph that help create a feeling of suspense.

The Redheaded League

*adapted from the story by
Sir Arthur Conan Doyle*

*Mr. Jabez Wilson presents the detective Sherlock Holmes with a
very perplexing mystery. First, says the redheaded London
pawnbroker, he won a very well-paying — but meaningless —
job, simply because of his hair color. Then, all of a sudden, his
job simply ended, with no explanation. See if you can solve the
puzzle. Who was Mr. Wilson's boss? Why did he suddenly end
the job? And why had he hired Mr. Wilson in the first place?*

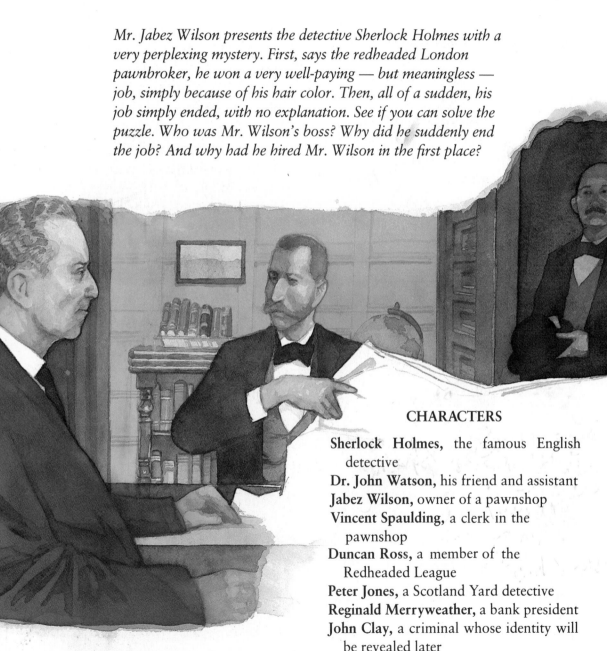

CHARACTERS

Sherlock Holmes, the famous English
   detective
Dr. John Watson, his friend and assistant
Jabez Wilson, owner of a pawnshop
Vincent Spaulding, a clerk in the
   pawnshop
Duncan Ross, a member of the
   Redheaded League
Peter Jones, a Scotland Yard detective
Reginald Merryweather, a bank president
John Clay, a criminal whose identity will
   be revealed later

Scene One

It is a Saturday morning in the summer of 1890. Dr. Watson enters Sherlock Holmes's sitting room. Holmes is there talking with a man who has bright red hair.

Holmes: Watson, you could not have come at a better time.

Watson: You seem to be busy. I can wait outside.

Holmes: Not at all. *(He turns to the man with the red hair.)* Dr. Watson has helped me in many of my cases, Mr. Wilson. I have no doubt he will be helpful in yours.

Wilson: How do you do?

Watson: How do you do, sir?

Holmes: Watson, I know you share my love of the unusual. Mr. Wilson has started to tell me one of the strangest stories I've ever heard. Mr. Wilson, will you be kind enough to begin your story again?

Wilson: Of course.

Holmes: I am sure, Watson, you can tell that Mr. Wilson has been in China.

Watson *(puzzled):* Well . . .

Holmes: And you can see that he has been doing a lot of writing.

Wilson *(amazed):* How did you know that?

Holmes: The cuff on your right sleeve is very shiny. Your left sleeve has a smooth patch at the elbow, where you rest it on a desk. It is clear that you've been writing a lot with your right hand, while leaning on your left elbow.

Wilson: That's true. But how did you know that I've been in China?

Holmes: There is a tattoo of a fish above your wrist. I have made a study of tattoos.

Only in China are the fish scales colored pink, as they are in your tattoo.

Wilson *(laughing):* I thought at first you had done something very clever. But I see now that it was really very simple.

Holmes: Perhaps, Watson, I should not give away my ways of drawing conclusions. I might lose my reputation as a genius. Now, Mr. Wilson, will you read us the newspaper ad that led to your adventure?

Wilson *(reading a newspaper ad aloud):* "There is a position open in the Redheaded League. According to the will of the late Elmer Hopkins, of the U.S.A., a League member will be paid a high salary for doing easy work. Redheaded men over the age of 21 may apply. See Duncan Ross at 7 Pope's Court, Monday at 11:00 A.M."

Watson: What on earth does this mean?

Holmes: Please note the paper and the date, Watson.

Watson *(looking at the ad):* It is from *The Morning Chronicle,* April 27, 1890. That was two months ago.

Holmes: Now, Mr. Wilson, tell us your story.

Wilson: I own a pawnshop on Coburg Square. It's a small business, and I don't make much money. In fact, I pay my assistant only half the usual salary. He was willing to take the job in order to learn the business.

Holmes: What is this young fellow's name?

Wilson: His name is Vincent Spaulding, and he isn't very young. He does his job well, but he has one fault. He spends too much time on his hobby, photography. He always seems to be down in the cellar, developing his pictures.

Watson: He doesn't sound very helpful.

Wilson: Oh, but he is. It was Spaulding who showed me this newspaper ad two months ago . . . .

Scene Two

The scene is Wilson's pawnshop, two months earlier. Spaulding enters.

Spaulding: Mr. Wilson, I wish I had red hair.

Wilson: Why?

Spaulding: There's another opening in the Redheaded League.

Wilson: What is that?

Spaulding: Haven't you ever heard of it? Why, you could apply for the job, with hair that color. You get paid well for doing very little work. You could handle that job — and still run this shop.

Wilson: I certainly could use the money. Tell me about this Redheaded League.

Spaulding: It was started by an American millionaire who was a bit odd. He was redheaded. When he died, he left his fortune to help redheaded men live an easy life.

Wilson: I'm sure that thousands of men will apply for the job opening.

Spaulding: No. You have to live in London. Elmer Hopkins lived in London for a while, and he wanted to do something good for the city. Also your hair cannot be light red or dark red. It must be as bright red as yours.

Wilson: Spaulding, let's close up the shop for an hour or so. We're going to visit the office of the Redheaded League.

Scene Three

Wilson and Spaulding join a line of redheaded men outside a small office. The line moves forward as the men ahead of them enter the office, one by one, then quickly come out again.

Wilson: Did all these men see the ad?

Spaulding: Oh, yes. The League is very well known.

Wilson: I don't have a chance of getting the job.

Spaulding: You do, sir. There aren't many men here with hair as bright as yours.

Now they are at the open door of the office. Duncan Ross, a man with bright red hair, is sitting at a desk. Another redheaded man is standing before him.

Ross *(to the redheaded man):* I'm sorry, sir. Your hair is a bit too orange for us. *(The man leaves.)* Next!

Spaulding *(leading Wilson forward):* This is Mr. Jabez Wilson. He is willing to join the League.

Ross: Well, he has a very fine head of red hair. *(He stands up and walks around Wilson, looking at his head. Suddenly he pulls Wilson's hair.)*

Wilson *(surprised):* Oww!

Ross: Good. That hair is real. We have to be careful. We've been tricked twice by wigs and once by boot polish. *(He shouts out the doorway.)* You men may all go home now! The job has been filled! *(He turns to Wilson.)* My name is Duncan Ross. I'm part of the League. When can you start working for us?

Wilson: Well, I have a business of my own already.

Spaulding: Never mind that, Mr. Wilson. I'll be able to look after the shop.

Ross: The hours here are from 10:00 in the morning until 2:00 in the afternoon.

Wilson: That's fine. Most of my business takes place late in the afternoon or early in the evening. Spaulding can handle anything that turns up in the morning. What is the work I'm to do?

Ross: It is very simple, but you must stay in this office the whole time. If you leave, you lose the job. The will of Mr. Hopkins states that very clearly. No excuse will be accepted, not even sickness.

Wilson: What is the work?

Ross: You copy an encyclopedia. Here is the first volume. *(He hands a volume to Wilson.)* You bring your own ink, pens, and paper. We provide this desk and chair. Can you start tomorrow?

Wilson: Yes.

Ross: Then let me congratulate you. You are lucky to be a member of the Redheaded League.

Scene Four

The scene is Holmes's sitting room once again. Wilson continues to tell his story to Holmes and Watson.

Wilson: I was sure the whole thing was a prank. I couldn't believe that anyone would pay a high salary for copying an encyclopedia. But I decided to go through with it. To my surprise, everything seemed to be in order.

Holmes: Were you paid?

Wilson: Yes.

Holmes: Was Mr. Ross always there?

Wilson: He dropped by the first few days. Then I saw less and less of him. But I never dared to leave the office. I never knew when he might appear. If he found I wasn't there, I would lose the job.

Watson: How long did this go on?

Wilson: For eight weeks. I wrote about abbots and archery and armor. Then, suddenly, it all came to an end.

Holmes: To an end?

Wilson: Yes, sir. At 10:00 this morning, I went to the office as usual, but the door was locked. This card was tacked on the door. *(He hands a card to Holmes.)* You can read it for yourself.

Holmes *(reading aloud):* "The Redheaded League no longer exists." What did you do after you found this card?

Wilson: I went to the landlord. He said he had never heard of the Redheaded League, nor of Mr. Duncan Ross, but he had rented the office to a redheaded man named Morris. Mr. Morris, he said, moved out yesterday.

Holmes: Did he give you Mr. Morris's new address?

Wilson: Yes, and I went there. No one there had heard of either William Morris or Duncan Ross.

Watson: What did you do then?

Wilson: I went back to my shop and talked to Spaulding. He said there was nothing I could do but wait to see if Mr. Ross would write me a letter. But I didn't want to lose a job like that without a struggle. I had heard that you, Mr. Holmes, give advice to poor people who need help. So here I am.

Holmes: You were wise to come here. I shall be happy to look into your case. This might be more serious than it seems at first sight.

Wilson: Of course it's serious! I've lost a good job. I want to know more about this Redheaded League. Why did they play this prank upon me? Or wasn't it a prank?

Holmes: We shall try to clear up these questions. First, tell me more about Spaulding. How long had he worked for you before he showed you the newspaper ad?

Wilson: About a month.

Holmes: Before you hired him, did anyone else apply for this job?

Wilson: Yes. There were several people.

Holmes: Why did you pick Spaulding?

Wilson: He was willing to accept half the usual salary.

Holmes: What does he look like?

Wilson: He is small and stout, about 30 years old. He has a white mark on his forehead from some acid.

Holmes: I thought so! Are his ears pierced for earrings?

Wilson: Yes. He said a gypsy pierced them for him when he was a boy.

Holmes: Does he still work for you?

Wilson: Yes, sir.

Holmes: That will do for now, Mr. Wilson. I will be happy to give you my opinion in two days.

Wilson: Thank you, Mr. Holmes. Good day, Dr. Watson. *(He leaves.)*

Holmes: Well, Watson, what do you make of all this?

Watson: I make nothing of it. It is a mysterious business. What are you going to do about it?

Holmes: I'm going to sit here and think. Please do not disturb me for an hour. At the end of that time, we shall go to Coburg Square.

Scene Five

An hour later, Holmes and Watson are outside Wilson's pawnshop on Coburg Square. Holmes knocks on the door, and Spaulding opens it.

Spaulding: May I help you?

Holmes: Can you tell me how to get to Fleet Street from here?

Spaulding: Take the third right and the fourth left. *(He goes back into the shop.)*

Holmes: Watson, Spaulding is the fourth smartest man in London. He is also one of the most daring. I have heard of him before.

Watson: You seem to think he matters a great deal in this mystery. I supposed you asked for directions so you could get a look at him.

Holmes: No, not at him. I wanted to see the knees of his trousers.

Watson: What did you see?

Holmes: What I expected to see. Now, Watson, we must study the buildings on this street. I wish to remember the order. On the corner is a tobacco shop. Next is a newspaper shop. Then there is Wilson's pawnshop. Next to that is the Coburg branch of the Bank of London. Then there is a restaurant. Finally, there is a tailor's shop.

Watson: Why is the order of the buildings important?

Holmes: A serious crime has been planned. I believe we still have time to stop it. I shall need your help tonight.

Watson: At what time will you need me?

Holmes: At 10:00 at my place. I warn you, though, there may be some danger.

Scene Six

At 10:00 that night, Watson enters Holmes's sitting room. Holmes is talking with two men.

Holmes: Ah, Watson, you know Peter Jones of Scotland Yard. Let me introduce you to Reginald Merryweather. He is the president of a branch of the Bank of London.

Watson: How do you do, sir?

Jones: Well, Watson, your friend Holmes is a wonderful man for starting a chase.

Merryweather *(frowning)*: I hope that a wild goose is not at the end of it.

Jones: You may trust Mr Holmes. His ways of solving mysteries are a little unusual. But now and then he does a better job than our police force.

Merryweather: All right, but I am missing my Saturday-night poker game. It is the first Saturday night in 27 years that I have not played poker.

Holmes: Mr. Merryweather, you will play for higher stakes tonight than you have ever done before. And the game will be more exciting. The prize for you is a huge amount of money. The prize for you, Mr. Jones, is John Clay.

Merryweather: Who is John Clay?

Jones: He is a murderer, thief, and forger. I would rather arrest him than any other criminal in London. He's the grandson of a duke. His brain is as swift as his fingers. We find signs of his evil work everywhere, but we've never found the man himself. I've been on his track for years.

Holmes: I hope that I may be able to introduce him to you tonight. Now, Mr. Merryweather, let us go to your bank on Coburg Square.

Scene Seven

The four men are now in the cellar of Mr. Merryweather's bank. Mr. Merryweather is carrying a lantern. The cellar is filled with crates.

Holmes *(looking at the ceiling)*: It doesn't look as if anyone could break in from above.

Merryweather: Nor could anyone break in from below. *(He hits the stone floor with his walking stick.)* Why, it sounds hollow!

Holmes *(taking the lantern from him)*: I must ask you to be more quiet. Please sit on one of those crates and don't interfere. *(He gets down on his knees, and examines the stone floor.)*

Watson: What are you doing, Holmes?

Holmes: I am checking these stones. *(He stands up.)* Well, we must wait until Mr. Wilson goes to bed.

Jones: What do you mean?

Holmes: Mr. Wilson owns the pawnshop next door. He lives above the shop. As soon as he is asleep, John Clay and his men will make their move. Mr. Merryweather can explain why John Clay would be interested in this cellar.

Merryweather *(whispering)*: It's the shipment of gold from France. We have thousands of pounds' worth of gold here. It's in these crates. Why, the crate I'm sitting on holds a fortune. We heard that an attempt might be made to steal it.

Holmes: I believe that this will happen soon. Mr. Merryweather, I must cover the lantern.

Merryweather: Must we sit in the dark?

Holmes: I'm afraid so. These are daring men. They will harm us if we are not careful. I shall stand behind this crate. The

rest of you hide behind those crates. When I flash the light upon the criminals, close in quickly.

Silence.

Merryweather: This waiting could drive me mad.

Holmes: Control yourself, Merryweather. Jones, I hope you did what I asked you to do.

Jones: Yes. Two officers are at the front door of the pawnshop.

Holmes: Good. That is the only way they could escape.

Watson *(quietly):* Look. Some light is shining between the stones on the floor.

Holmes *(calmly):* I see it. Be ready.

Suddenly a large stone is pushed up from the floor. Then two men climb up from the hole and into the cellar. One has red hair.

Clay *(to the redheaded man):* It's all clear. *(Holmes uncovers the lantern and grabs Clay.)* Jump, Archie!

The redheaded man jumps down through the hole in the floor. Jones grabs at his jacket, but the cloth rips.

Watson: Holmes, watch out for Clay's gun!

Holmes *(knocking the gun out of Clay's hand):* It's no use, John Clay.

Clay: So I see. At least my pal got away.

Holmes: I'm afraid not. Two officers are

waiting for him at the door to the pawnshop.

Clay: You seem to have handled everything very well. I must compliment you.

Holmes: And I compliment you. Your redheaded idea was very clever.

Jones: Clay, you and your partner are coming to the police station. Now, hold out your hands for these. *(He puts handcuffs on Clay.)*

Clay: Be careful with your filthy hands. You may not be aware that I have royal blood in my veins. Have the goodness to say "please" and "sir" when you speak to me.

Jones: All right. Would you please, sir, march upstairs?

Clay *(calmly)*: That is better. *(He bows to the others, then walks off with Jones.)*

Merryweather: Mr. Holmes, I don't know how my bank can repay you.

Holmes: I have had several scores to settle with Mr. John Clay. I shall expect the bank to pay my expenses in this case. Otherwise, I have already been well paid by having this adventure.

Scene Eight

Later, Holmes and Watson discuss the case in Holmes's sitting room.

Holmes: Why was the ad placed in the newspaper? And why was Mr. Wilson hired to copy an encyclopedia? It was to get him out of the way for four hours every day. Clay dreamed up the idea of the Redheaded League because his partner and Wilson both have bright red hair.

Holmes: Exactly. Clay, calling himself Vincent Spaulding, got himself hired by Wilson. We heard that he was working for Wilson for half the usual salary. I knew then that he had a strong reason for taking that job.

Watson: But how could you guess what that was?

Holmes: According to Wilson photography was Spaulding's hobby. He spent many hours in the cellar. I figured he was digging a tunnel to another building. So I went to the pawnshop to ask for some directions.

Watson: You said you wanted to get a look at Spaulding's — I mean Clay's — trousers.

Holmes: Right. I saw that the knees of his trousers were worn and dirty. That meant hours of digging. But what was he digging for? We saw that the Bank of London is next to Wilson's shop. That was the answer.

Watson: How could you tell that they would break in tonight?

Holmes: Well, they closed the Redheaded League office. That was a sign that they no longer needed Mr. Wilson out of the way. In other words, they had finished their tunnel. Saturday would be the best day to steal the gold. The bank would be closed, and they would have two days to escape. The theft would not have been discovered until Monday.

Watson: You thought it all out perfectly!

Holmes: Oh, these little problems keep me from being bored. And this case gave me the added satisfaction of seeing John Clay arrested. Perhaps now there will be a little less evil done in London.

READING COMPREHENSION

Summarizing. Choose the best phrase to complete each sentence. Then write the complete statement on your paper.

1. Mr. Wilson asked Sherlock Holmes to help him find out more about_____ (his assistant, the Redheaded League, finding a new job).

2. Sherlock Holmes stopped at the pawnshop in order to_____ (ask Spaulding about the league, look at the knees of Spaulding's trousers, ask to see Spaulding's photographs).

3. The thieves were caught as they attempted to steal_____ (piles of bank notes, precious stones, crates of gold).

Interpreting. Write the answer to each question on your paper.

1. What did Spaulding and Ross tell Jabez Wilson about the Redheaded League? What was the real reason the Redheaded League was formed?

2. Why was it a mistake for the thieves to close the office of the Redheaded League?

3. How do you know Holmes suspected Spaulding was not who he said he was?

For Thinking and Discussion. Sir Arthur Conan Doyle wrote many stories about Sherlock Holmes. The stories usually included Dr. Watson. How does the author use Watson to help the reader understand what Sherlock Holmes is doing?

UNDERSTANDING LITERATURE

Significant Details in a Mystery. Every story has details that help you understand what the story is about. In a mystery story, some of the *significant details* are important clues that help solve the mystery.

Sherlock Holmes from "The Redheaded League" used some of the following details as clues to solve the crime. List those details on your paper. For each detail you list, write a sentence explaining what the clue told Sherlock Holmes about the thieves' plans.

1. Mr. Wilson had a tattoo of a fish above his wrist.

2. Mr. Merryweather played poker on Saturday nights.

3. Mr. Wilson would lose his job at the Redheaded league if he left the office between 10:00 in the morning and 2:00 in the afternoon.

4. The knees of Spaulding's trousers were dirty.

5. John Clay was the grandson of a duke.

6. Spaulding agreed to work in the pawnshop for half the usual pay.

WRITING

Write a paragraph for a "Wanted" poster about John Clay, also known as Vincent Spaulding. Describe John Clay and tell the kinds of crimes he commits.

The Way Through the Woods

by Rudyard Kipling

They shut the road through the woods
Seventy years ago.
Weather and rain have undone it again,
And now you would never know
There was once a road through the woods
Before they planted the trees.
It is underneath the coppice and heath
And the thin anemones.
Only the keeper sees
That, where the ring-dove broods,
And the badgers roll at ease,
There was once a road through the woods.

Yet, if you enter the woods
Of a summer evening late,
When the night-air cools on the trout-ringed pools
Where the otter whistles his mate,
(They fear not men in the woods,
Because they see so few.)
You will hear the beat of a horse's feet,
And the swish of a skirt in the dew,
Steadily cantering through
The misty solitudes,
As though they perfectly knew
The old lost road through the woods . . . .

But there is no road through the woods.

1. Why can't you tell that there was once a road through the woods?

2. If there is no road throught the woods, how can you hear "The beat of a horse's feet, and the swish of a skirt in the dew . . . "?

The Phantom Cyclist

by Ruth Ainsworth

*In this tale a mysterious young stranger captures the imagination
of Randy and Sara, two close friends who live in a small town
by the sea. Who is this girl in white? Where does she come from?
And however did she learn to ride her bicycle at such high speeds?*

Randy and Sara were friends. They lived in the same village by the sea, surrounded by flat salt marshes and swept by a ceaseless wind. They spent every spare minute together. They found a surprising number of interesting, and even exciting, things to do in the small village in which they lived.

They lay in the reeds and watched wild birds through a pair of binoculars belonging to Sara's father. They knew where the sea asters grew, and the sea arrow-grass. They could find their way across the everchanging channels of water. Sometimes it was safe to wade, other times it was wiser to walk on a mile

or two and cross by a bridge, which was often only a slippery plank.

But, best of all, they each had a new bicycle. Their birthdays happened to be in the same month, so they got their bicycles almost at the same time. The bicycles differed in color; Randy's was pink and Sara's purple. But they were both racing bicycles, and each had a five-speed gear, cable brakes, and a horn guaranteed to scare stray chickens out of the way.

There were no movies, skating rinks, or other forms of entertainment for many miles around, so the girls' parents did not mind spending a great deal of money on the bicycles. Day after day, their daughters sped off, and seemed to be perfectly happy just cycling around the flat, deserted countryside.

One Friday after school, when the days were beginning to draw in, Randy suggested a quick spin to the tower and back. The whole ride was a distance of about four miles.

The wind was behind them, and they had a friendly race along the empty road. Sometimes Randy drew ahead, and then Sara would overtake her.

Suddenly, with no warning at all, a girl dressed in white — white shirt and white skirt — passed them on the road. She was riding an old-fashioned bicycle with upright handlebars. Both Randy and Sara put their heads down and pressed on with all possible speed, as being passed by another cyclist, especially another girl, challenged them to do their best. But the girl in white overtook them easily and raced ahead. They lost sight of her when the road curved inland and went over a bridge across a deep channel known as Devil's Dike.

As they crossed the bridge themselves, they looked for the cyclist on the other side. But they could see no trace of her.

"She can't have gotten so far ahead; it isn't possible," said Randy. The two stopped for a minute on the bridge. They leaned on the iron railings without getting off their bikes.

"White shows up so clearly. Look at that white cow over there. The cow must be a mile away or more and we can see her."

"That girl must have gotten off the road for some reason," said Randy. "Perhaps she's got a bad tire. This is a pretty rough, stony surface."

"I rather hope she has got into some trouble," said Sara. "I'd love to have a close look at that bike of hers. It must be a miracle."

"Yes, but I thought it looked kind of old-fashioned, what I could see of it."

"Let's go on. If she's having any trouble with her bike, we'll pass her between here and the tower. We must pass her. Perhaps we could give her a hand. Maybe her chain has come off. Remember how mine used to come off till Dad took a link out and tightened it?"

They rode on, no longer hurrying. They checked the grass as they went. Eventually the tower came into sight, a bare, circular building where they had often played and had picnics.

But it was too late to play now. They got off and walked around the tower and then turned back for home. The wind was in their faces this time, and they had to pedal harder. Conversation was almost impossible as the wind whirled their

words away. They reached Sara's house first.

"I can't understand it," said Randy. "I simply can't understand. I suppose a very good cyclist could have overtaken us — just barely — but where did she disappear to? We never saw her after she'd turned toward Devil's Dike Bridge. But she couldn't have gone any other way. There isn't any other way to go. The dike must be ten feet wide, perhaps more, and there's no side turning anywhere. The track to Devil's Farm doesn't lead off till just opposite the tower."

"She must be very eager to be training, if she's riding at this time of day and in this wind," added Sara. "Perhaps she's training to be a racer."

"I've never heard of a famous girl cyclist, though I don't see why girls shouldn't be famous racers. I'd like to be one. I may be when I'm grown up."

"I thought you were going to be a vet."

"Well, so I am, but I can do cycle-racing in my spare time."

"You won't get much spare time if you're studying to be a vet. Mother says it takes as long learning to be a vet as learning to be a real doctor."

"It is being a real doctor, silly, only you don't treat people. It's harder than being a people's doctor. You have to know about birds' skeletons and reptiles and everything. Think of all the creatures in a zoo and all the queer pets people keep. Vets must know how to treat them all."

Neither girl could forget the strange cyclist in white who had sped past them at such an amazing speed. The way she had disappeared into thin air was particularly puzzling. If only they'd had a proper look at her and her bicycle. But they hadn't had a chance.

Randy and Sara kept up their habit of riding around after school, but they never came across any strangers cycling on the road. An occasional van or a farmer in a Land-Rover sometimes passed them. The only regular cyclist was Meg, the postwoman, who cycled everywhere, in all weather, like themselves.

A week went by. Randy and Sara began to think less about the mysterious girl. Saturday was clear and sunny, and they decided to take a picnic to the old quarry. It had not been worked for many years, and was a good place to play in. They could climb on the rocks and sometimes find a stone marked long ago by the drill.

It was sheltered, too, and very fine blackberries could be found there. Their mothers had given them each a plastic bag on the chance that a few late berries would still be left, enough for a blackberry and apple pie on Sunday.

When they reached the quarry, they immediately noticed a bicycle propped against a rock. It was black and very out of date. They were not surprised to see the mysterious girl in white eating blackberries a few yards away. She was dressed in the same white short-sleeved shirt and rather long skirt.

"Are there many blackberries?" asked Randy.

"Quite a few, here and there."

"We're supposed to pick enough for a pie. Well, for two pies." She produced her plastic bag.

"I'll help you. They need searching for."

Sara got her bag out of her pocket, too, and the three girls picked steadily. The strange girl put a handful sometimes in Randy's bag and sometimes in Sara's. She was very fair and pale and thin. Her arms were like sticks and had no trace of tan on them. For an athletic type she appeared fragile.

"You get along fast on that bike of yours," said Randy. "Sara and I thought you were pretty good when you passed us on the road the other evening."

"We were going flat out," added Sara, "but you left us miles behind."

"Wherever did you get to when you rounded the bend to Devil's Bridge? You weren't in sight when we got there."

"I just went over the bridge and on," said the girl. "The way I always go."

"But you couldn't —" began Randy, and stopped. "I mean, it was odd how you disappeared. We waited on the bridge for ages."

The girl looked up with interest.

"You waited on the bridge?"

"Yes, we leaned against the railings and looked for you."

"But I don't see how you could have waited *on* the bridge, both of you. It's only a single plank. I get into trouble for riding over it instead of getting off and pushing my bike over."

"Trouble from your parents, you mean?"

"I haven't any parents. Trouble from my uncle and aunt who have brought me up. They don't want me to slip when the plank is muddy or frosty."

"I don't think we're talking about the same thing," said Randy. "The bridge we went over is quite wide — a car can go over — and there are railings on each side painted white. That's to help people to see them in the dark."

"No, we're not talking about the same thing," said the girl sadly. "We can't ever talk about the same thing."

She looked so upset that both Randy and Sara felt they must try to cheer her up. They could discuss the bridge — or was it the bridges? — afterward.

"Thanks awfully for the blackberries. I'm Randy and she's Sara. Who are you?"

"I'm Sigrid. My mother was Norwegian. That's why I'm so fair. And Sigrid is a Norwegian name."

"May we look at your bike, Sigrid? The brake looks strange to me. How does it work?"

Sigrid quickly showed them how the brake worked on the front wheel. But you had to pedal backward to stop the back wheel. "It's called a back-pedaling brake," she explained.

"Let's have a game, Sigrid. You and Sara go and hide, and I'll count to a hundred slowly and then come back and look for you. All right?"

Sigrid scaled the rocky face with such skill and speed that Sara found it was all she could do to follow. They flattened themselves in a crack and Randy passed them twice before she caught sight of Sigrid's white shirt.

"That was a fabulous place. I thought I

knew the quarry inside out, but I'd never noticed that crevice. Now Sara and I'll hide and you count to a hundred."

Randy and Sara hid in one of their favorite spots, a hollow filled with bushes. But they didn't fool Sigrid for long. She seemed drawn to the hollow like a dog following a scent.

"Have you been here before, Sigrid?"

"Yes and no."

"Well, it must be one or the other."

"Yes, then. But I couldn't go just anywhere, like we can today. Then, the men working here wouldn't let me."

Sigrid was as strong as an acrobat, and when the girls began to do cartwheels on a smooth stretch of turf, she outshone them both. Tricks that they had practiced for hours Sigrid learned at once and performed with ease. She seemed absolutely unaware of her talent. She became uncomfortable when the others praised her. She turned aside and a bit of color crept into her pale cheeks.

Randy and Sara shared their picnic with Sigrid, and she enjoyed the cheese sandwiches and apples and chocolate.

"My aunt never gave me anything like this," she said, biting into an apple. "Great slabs of dry bread and a sliver of meat, that's all I ever got."

"You've grown very strong on it," said Randy. "Your muscles must be terrific."

When they left to go home, Sigrid was unwilling to cycle with them.

"You go on," she said. "I've something I want to do to my bike."

"Then we'll wait," said Randy. "Are you coming our way? Back to Welland Village?"

"As a matter of fact, I don't think I am. My way home is different. Good-bye."

"Good-bye, Sigrid. We'll see you sometime."

"Good-bye. Thanks for the picnic."

Randy and Sara cycled slowly. They hoped that Sigrid might catch up to them. There were so many questions they wanted to ask. But they did not know if the questions could be answered.

That evening, when Randy's father had come home from work, Randy asked, "Was the quarry working when you were a boy, Dad?"

"No, Randy. It was as empty as it is now. A little less overgrown, perhaps. My pals and I played there like you and Sara do."

"Was it working when your father was a boy?"

Her father paused. "I believe it was, but my dad didn't work there. He went back to the land and was a stockman at Sunnyacre Farm. But when my granddad was a lad, he worked there. He worked there till he retired. Pretty well all the men around here had jobs in the quarry in those days. There wasn't anything else to do, except for farm work."

"Was that a hundred years ago?"

Again her father paused. "Not quite. I reckon it was about 80 years ago when he started working there. Children left school at 12 in those days."

"We've got an old photo of your granddad," said Randy's mother. "You know, the one taken when the men had a holiday for some occasion, like Queen Victoria's death. I'll get it."

She rummaged in a drawer and brought out a rather yellow print of a group of men. Many of them wore beards or moustaches, and they were arranged as if for a school photograph: Those in the back row stood on something, those in the next row stood on the ground, and those in the front row sat, or sprawled. In the center, on a chair, sat an old gentleman in a top hat and frock coat.

"Where's Great-grandfather?" asked Randy.

"He's the one in the back row with the very bushy beard."

"And who's the man in the middle in the funny hat?"

"Oh, I guess he was the owner of the quarry — the boss, in fact."

The next few weeks passed without either of the girls coming across Sigrid. They cycled to the tower and to the quarry, but they never met her. Yet they talked about her almost all the time they were together. Where had she gone the evening she'd passed them on the coast road? Where was the single plank that she had mentioned, crossing the Devil's Dike? How could she have visited the quarry and found it full of men working, when there hadn't been work done there for years and years? Although they came to no conclusions, they could not leave the subject alone. It fascinated them.

Every Thursday evening, after school, Randy cycled into the next village for her music lesson. The village lay between Welland and the big town of Queen's Lynn. It was getting dark earlier now, and she had to have her lights on for the homeward trip.

Her violin teacher was an old man who

had once been a professional violinist. But now the teacher was poor and forgotten. Randy's parents often told her how lucky she was to have such a famous musician for a teacher, and Mr. Pirelli agreed with them. He, too, thought Randy was lucky. The only person in any doubt about her good fortune was Randy herself. Mr. Pirelli had fierce white eyebrows and piercing black eyes that rolled in anger when Randy played a wrong note. He had a blistering tongue that almost reduced Randy to tears. No one likes to be called "a deaf donkey" and other such names. But Randy bore all this because she loved her violin and wanted to play well. She still had hopes of being a vet *and* a racing cyclist *and* a famous violinist.

On this particular Thursday Randy had passed the quarry on the way to Mr. Pirelli's cottage, and was about two miles from the cottage itself, when she made a terrible discovery. She had forgotten her music case. It was still on the chair in the hall at home. Her violin was safe enough, strapped on her back, but the thought of appearing before Mr. Pirelli without her music was frightening. Should she go home and say she was ill? Should she go back for her music and be late for her lesson? Should she just turn up without her music?

None of these possible courses of action appealed to her. Once before she had forgotten her music. Mr. Pirelli had been furious and made her play scales and exercises for the entire lesson.

Just then Randy found Sigrid beside her. She had not heard her coming but was delighted to see her. Randy poured all her troubles into Sigrid's sympathetic ear. Sigrid never hesitated a second.

"I'll go back and fetch your music. Then I'll catch up with you. You just ride on. You say it's the white cottage with the fir tree by the gate? I'll be there as soon as you are."

"But Sigrid, you can't be. It's at least two miles back. That's six all together. I'll be so late it won't be worth turning up at all."

"I'll be quicker than you think. Please trust me. Can I get your music easily?"

"Yes of course. Just open the door, and it's on the chair in the hall. But Sigrid —"

"No time for 'buts.' Now ride on and don't worry about me. I know a shortcut. Goodbye."

Sigrid was dressed in her usual outfit of white shirt and white skirt, and she flashed out of sight. Randy was puzzled but nevertheless relieved. She cycled on. As she reached the fir tree and propped up her bicycle, there was a rush of wind. Sigrid jammed on her brakes and drew up beside her. She handed over the music case, smiled, and rode away. Randy knocked on the door, her hand shaking slightly.

The lesson went unusually well. Mr. Pirelli actually said, "*Brava!* Not bad," when Randy played.

Randy could hardly wait to see Sara the next day and tell her of the incident. Sara was a real friend. She always listened and believed what she was told, however incredible it sounded.

The friends met up in the schoolyard. "So Sigrid cycled roughly four miles in the time you took to cycle two?" said Sara.

"Yes. I swear she did."

"And you didn't ride slowly?"

"No, I rode quickly. Quite up to my normal speed. That shortcut Sigrid mentioned — do you know where it could have been?"

"I've no idea. But I do know this: There's only one road between Mr. Pirelli's cottage and our house."

"But there may have been another road once. That's the point. Do you think we could get hold of some old maps? We might be able to find a footpath or something over the marshes."

"Yes, we might."

Just then the bell rang for the end of the morning break. The children ran in from the schoolyard, Randy and Sara with them.

"There's only one thing to do," said Randy after school. "We must go to see Mr. Penrose and ask if we can look at some of his old maps. He's got old maps simply everywhere. He's got one on the wall that shows wrecks and mermaids and a spouting whale."

All the village loved Mr. Penrose. He had been vicar of Welland Church some years ago, and had christened most of the children's fathers and mothers, and married them, too. He was gentle and friendly, with none of the alarming habits of Mr. Pirelli.

The two girls rang Mr. Penrose's bell

that very evening, having assured both sets of parents that they had done their homework. No one thought it at all strange that they should visit Mr. Penrose. He was an authority on birds' eggs, wild flowers, fossils — in fact on all subjects that interest young people.

At their request for old maps of the district, Mr. Penrose opened a cupboard door and revealed a wonderful collection, some in the flat binding of the Ordinance Survey Maps, and some on rolled sheets of paper.

"How far back do you want to go? The vicar before me was something of an expert on maps and he left me his collection. 1800? 1900?"

"Sort of in-between."

"What about this — printed about 1870. Let's spread it out on the desk."

Mr. Penrose soon saw where the girls' interest lay. Guided by him, they discovered a track from Mr. Pirelli's cottage to Welland. It went straight across the marshes, like the third side of a triangle, the present roads forming the other two sides. They found no sign of the coast road as they knew it. There was also a faint track that seemed to cross Devil's Dike.

"There must have been a footbridge here, perhaps just a plank," said Mr. Penrose, "because the track goes on on the far side. If you wanted to drive cows across, or a wagon, you'd have to go several miles inland and cross by the bridge we still use."

The girls studied the map with great care. They found familiar landmarks like the church and the tower, and they noticed paths and tracks that no longer existed.

"Why this sudden interest in maps?" asked Mr. Penrose casually. The girls knew he would not press them if they did not choose to answer.

"Let's tell him," said Randy suddenly.

"Yes, let's."

Between them, they told Mr. Penrose everything they knew about Sigrid, and of their three meetings with her. Each kept chipping in with some extra detail, and sometimes both talked together. Yet Mr. Penrose did not appear to find the story confusing. He just nodded encouragingly when there was a pause. At the end, he rolled up the map carefully before he spoke.

"Now I'm going to tell you a story, as strange and true as the one you have told me. You've seen the memorial stone in the seawall?"

"Yes, lots of times."

"What does it say?"

" 'This is a memorial to the men, women, and children who lost their lives in the high tide of 1898.' "

"Good, Sara. You've a useful memory that will serve you well. The tide became dangerously high two hours before it reached its highest point. The seawall broke and people living in the cottages in Fisherman's Row were drowned, whole families of them. The water was too rough anyhow for the boats to go out, and that's why men were at home. But the houses farther inland were on higher ground. The people fled and were saved. One young girl, whose name was Sigrid, volunteered to ride on her bicycle along the coast

road, which was only a rough track, to the tower. It was a lookout post in those days, and a warning could be flashed to neighboring villages. No one knows exactly what happened, but Devil's Dike must have been in flood, and Sigrid was swept away, perhaps while crossing the plank. They found her bicycle long afterward, but her body was never found, God rest her soul."

"So she never reached the tower?"

"No. She never got there. But the lookout man saw the danger and sent out warning messages."

"So she didn't actually save anybody?"

"It isn't known that she did. And she couldn't save herself. But no brave deed is ever done in vain."

The girls thanked Mr. Penrose and left for home. They could see the lights in the cottage windows and hear the sound of the waves in the darkness, the sound so familiar and yet so haunting, especially at night.

Randy and Sara hoped daily that they might meet Sigrid again. As the days grew shorter and the wind off the sea colder, there seemed fewer and fewer chances. When school let out for Christmas, they still had not come across her.

The first few days of the holidays were always the same. The girls felt restless and could not settle to anything. They went on the bus to Queen's Lynn and looked around Woolworth's.

One day, Sara suggested that they go watch the excavator that was working near Devil's Bridge. They walked, as the

wind made riding almost impossible, even for hardy cyclists like themselves.

It was very satisfying to watch the huge machine opening its steel jaws and grabbing up mouthfuls of marshland.

"Look," said Randy suddenly. "There's something lying beyond the dike. It looks like an old bicycle."

"Let's go and look."

They crossed the bridge and examined the shapeless tangle of bent iron that might once have been a bicycle. Just then the driver of the excavator stopped and took a break.

"Did you dig up that old bike?" shouted Sara.

"No. I only came on this morning. The fellow working yesterday must have found it. If it is a bicycle. It looks a mess to me."

"It's a bike, all right. I can see traces of a leather saddle, and this crumpled bit was the frame."

"Perhaps you're right. It must have been lying around for many years, buried under the mud. No one'll miss it. No one knew it was there, likely enough."

He prepared to make another grab at the newly deepened dike. The girls set off for home.

"Do you think it was Sigrid's bike?" said Sara.

"Yes, I do. Mr. Penrose said she was probably drowned somewhere near the bridge. I guess that when her bike was found, it was too rusty to be worth repairing. Someone just left it there, and it stayed there till yesterday getting covered with mud."

"Now it's gone forever. Not even a ghost could ride it."

"I don't think we'll ever see Sigrid again," said Randy. "Sigrid and her bicycle seemed to belong together."

"They did. And now she can't ride it anymore. She was a wonderful rider. What strength she had!"

"And what courage! I wonder what she thought about as she raced toward the tower, hearing the waves pounding on the seawall."

"And hearing the roar as they broke through."

"I expect she just thought about getting there, like us when we're racing. We only think about winning the race."

"I shall miss her," said Sara.

"So will I. It was exciting always thinking she might appear."

The girls plodded home with the wind in their faces. They knew that they would never see Sigrid again, with her fair hair and pale face and white clothes. And they never did, except sometimes in dreams, where the dead and the living meet.

READING COMPREHENSION

Summarizing. Choose the best phrase and write the complete statement on your paper.

1. Randy and Sara tried to outride the _____ (passing cars, girl on an old-fashioned bike, postwoman named Meg).

2. The girls could not believe that Sigrid _____ (rode her bike in, could have visited, picked blackberries in) the quarry when men worked there.

3. When the girls_____ (started summer vacation, saw the rusty bike, heard Mr. Penrose's story) they realized they would never see Sigrid again.

Interpreting. Write the answer to each question on your paper.

1. Why did Sigrid tell Randy and Sara they would never be able to talk about the same things?

2. Why did Randy ask her father if men worked in the quarry when he was a boy?

3. How can you tell that Mr. Penrose believed the girls' story?

4. Why did Sigrid volunteer to ride her bicycle along the coast road?

For Thinking and Discussing. Imagine you could meet a person who lived generations ago. Could you easily become friends? What things might you have in common? Would the person have problems adjusting to life today?

UNDERSTANDING LITERATURE

Foreshadowing. Sometimes a writer puts clues into a story to hint at what is to come at the end. This is called, *foreshadowing.*

At the end of "The Phantom Cyclist," Randy and Sara discover that Sigrid is a girl who lived in the past. On your paper, write the statements below that foreshadow, or give hints of, what the girls' discover.

1. Randy and Sara have birthdays in the same month.

2. Sigrid describes Devil's Bridge as one plank.

3. Sigrid talks about men working in the quarry.

4. Sigrid tells Randy and Sara that they can never talk about the same things.

5. Mr. Penrose is a map collector.

6. Randy and Sara notice that Sigrid's bike and clothing look very old-fashioned.

7. Randy, Sara, and Sigrid all like to eat blackberries.

8. Sigrid cycles four miles in the time it takes Randy to cycle two.

WRITING

An *epitaph* is a short statement written in memory of someone who has died. It often tells what the person should be remembered for. Write an epitaph for Sigrid.

VOCABULARY

Suffixes. A *suffix* is a word part added to the end of a word. When you put a suffix after a *root word*, you change the meaning of the word. If you do not know the meaning of a word, you can look up its word parts to help you. For example, the word *fearful* is made up of a root word and a suffix. The suffix is *-ful* and it means "filled with." The root word is *fear*. By looking at the root word and the suffix, you can tell that *fearful* means "filled with fear" or "afraid."

The left-hand column below lists some root words. The right-hand column lists some suffixes and their meanings. Decide which root word and suffix to put together to make a word that best completes each sentence. Write the completed sentences on your paper. Use each word only once.

Root words	Suffixes
detect	*-able:* able to be
skill	*-ful:* filled with
use	*-less:* without
meaning	
believe	
hope	

1. Larry was _____ that he would find the diamond.

2. The glint of the diamond was _____ in the gum.

3. Mr. Wilson felt that the job of copying an encyclopedia was _____.

4. Sherlock Holmes was _____ at solving crimes.

5. Randy and Sara realized it was _____ to try and outrace Sigrid.

6. Randy and Sara were afraid Mr. Penrose would not think that their story was _____.

READING

Critical Reading. The ability to read a story and make judgments about what you read is called *critical reading*. When you read critically, you try to uncover the author's message. You also try to understand how the characters think and feel. You gain this understanding through the author's descriptions and the characters' actions.

Read each statement below. Think back to the stories in this section. Use your judgement about the characters to decide which one could have made each statement. On your paper, write the name of the character next to the number of the correct statement and briefly explain your choice. Use each character only once.

Characters

Randy	Sigrid
Holmes	Spaulding
Wilson	Larry

1. All I need is an excuse to get him out of the shop so I can work on my secret plan.

2. The lighter patch of skin under his lip shows that he shaved off his mustache recently.

3. I would not get lost in a department store because I always remember the direction I walk in.

4. I can be an engineer and a lumberjack when I grow up.

5. "I'll save him!" she exclaimed as she rushed into the oncoming traffic.

6. I don't mind doing tasks as long as I get paid for them.

QUIZ

The following is a quiz on Section 9. Write the answers in complete sentences on your paper.

Reading Comprehension

1. In "Sarah Tops," how did Larry know where to look for the diamond?

2. In "The Redheaded League," how did Sherlock Holmes know that Spaulding was digging a tunnel?

3. In "The Redheaded League," how did Sherlock Holmes conclude that Spaulding had finished digging the tunnel?

4. What happened to the road in the poem "The Way Through The Woods"?

5. In "The Phantom Cyclist," what made the girls realize that they would never see Sigrid again?

Understanding Literature

6. List two details from "The Phantom Cyclist" that foreshadow the girls' conclusion that Sigrid lived in the past.

7. List four significant details from "Sarah Tops" that help you identify and solve the mystery.

8. Describe the most suspenseful scene in "The Redheaded League."

9. In "The Phantom Cyclist," Mr. Penrose had a map that showed a footbridge crossing Devil's Bridge. Is this a significant detail? Why or why not?

10. How can you compare Sigrid from "The Phantom Cyclist," and the person hinted at in "The Way Through The Woods"?

WRITING

An Explanation. An explanation clearly states step by step how or why something happened. When you write an explanation, the sequence of events is very important. Help the reader understand your explanation by putting the events in the correct order. Read each step to guide you in your writing.

Step 1: Set Your Goal

Choose one of the following topics for an explanation.

☐ Explain how Larry's father in "Sarah Tops" determined that the thugs were after a diamond.

☐ Explain how Randy and Sara decided that Sigrid lived in another time.

Step 2: Make a Plan

Plan what you are going to say. Make a list of the important events that will support your explanation. Remember to list the events in the order in which they occur in the story.

For example, if you were writing an explanation of Sherlock Holmes's method of solving the mystery and catching the criminals in "The Redheaded League," you might list the following events:

☐ Holmes listened to Wilson's story.

☐ Holmes asked Wilson questions.

☐ Holmes went to Wilson's pawnshop.

☐ Holmes met with Peter Jones and Reginald Merryweather.

☐ Holmes went to the bank.

Step 3: Write Your First Draft

Your explanation should have three para-graphs. The first should tell about the topic and the characters in the explana-tion. The second should list your events, giving details about each event. The third paragraph should sum up the explanation.

a. Begin by introducing the topic and de-scribing the characters involved in the explanation. For example, the expla-nation of Sherlock Holmes's method might start this way:

This will explain how Sherlock Holmes, a famous detective, discovered that a crime was being planned, and how he caught the criminals.

b. For your second paragraph, use your list of events and fill in the details as you write.

c. End with a concluding sentence that sums up your explanation. Here is an example:

Sherlock Holmes, with the help of Wat-son, Peter Jones, and Mr. Merryweather, caught the criminals during their attempt to rob the bank.

Step 4: Revise Your Explanation

Check your explanation one more time.

Add any important details you have left out. Make sure the events you described are in the order in which they occur in the story. Correct any errors in spelling, grammar, and punctuation you find. Make a final, neat copy of your explanation.

ACTIVITIES

Word Attack. What two letters are the same in each word below?

eat	bread
great	heard
bread	

The vowels *ea* are in each word above, but they stand for a different sound in each.

Usually when the vowels *ea* come together, they stand for the long *e* sound, as in *eat*. However, sometimes they stand for the short *e* sound, as in *bread*. Sometimes they stand for the long *a* sound, as in *great*. They may also stand for the vowel sounds in *her*, as in *heard*; or in *here*, as in *beard*.

If you are not sure which sound the vowels *ea* make in a word you are reading, try pronouncing the word different ways until one pronunciation sounds like a word you know.

Pronounce the following words from the poem "The Way Through the Woods":

1. weather	5. hear
2. underneath	6. beat
3. heath	7. steadily
4. fear	

Speaking and Listening. Read "The Way Through the Woods" aloud. When you read a poem aloud, you can appreciate the sound of the words as well as the meaning. Pay special attention to words in which the vowels *ea* come together. To help you enjoy your reading more, look up the following words to learn their pronunciation: *coppice*, *anemone*, and *solitude*.

Researching.

1. In a newspaper, find a true story about a crime that the police solved.

A newspaper article is supposed to answer these questions: *Who? What? When? Where? Why? How?* Read the article. Then answer the questions below on your paper.

1. What was the crime?

2. Who committed it?

3. When did it happen?

4. Where did it happen?

5. Why did the criminal or criminals do it?

6. Who solved the crime?

7. When was the crime solved?

8. How was it solved?

Then find another crime that has not been solved yet. Make a chart listing the eight categories above. Leave enough space to write. Fill in the spaces to the questions with clues that are needed. Try to think of possible answers. Look at the newspapers over the next few weeks to see if there is any more information.

2. The drawings show three dinosaurs: Triceratops, Stegosaurus, and Tyrannosaurus. Look up each name in a dictionary. The dictionary should give you enough information to identify each dinosaur. The definitions will give you some information. Look also at the meaning of the word parts. Pay attention to these word parts: stegos and sauros, tyrannos and sauros, and tri.

Creating. Imagine that Sherlock Holmes's associate, Dr. Watson, is on vacation. Sherlock decides to advertise for an assistant to help him solve crimes while Dr. Watson is away. Write the advertisement Sherlock Holmes would put in the newspaper. Be sure to include the personal qualities that are a must for an assistant in the crime detection business.

In writing your advertisement, you will need to use the following information:

1. Name of position

2. Place of work

3. Hours of work

4. Duties involved

5. Necessary skills

6. Salary

7. Who to contact, and where

THE MIRACLE WORKER

*The change which occurred after Anne Sullivan
began my education still causes me to thrill and glow.*

—Helen Keller

Things were first made, then words.

—Sir Thomas Overbury

Introduction

To the Scope *Readers of*
The Miracle Worker, *by William Gibson*

When I was about your age, everyone in my class was given a slim book as a reading text. It was *The Story of My Life,* by Helen Keller.

It was much fatter 30 years later, when I read it again, because I was reading the original edition. This included dozens of long letters about the child Helen written by her teacher, Annie Sullivan, and I fell in love with the young woman who wrote those letters. *The Miracle Worker* is my own love letter to her.

Annie's Gift to Helen

Annie graduated from a school for the blind in Boston — after many eye operations — and went off to her first job, which lasted all her life. It was as governess to a child who was a hopeless case.

Helen as a baby had lost not only her sight but, worse, her hearing. Why worse? Because with deafness she knew nothing of language, and language is what makes everything human possible. At six years old, she was more like an animal, but wild with very human rages of despair.

Annie arrived in Tuscumbia, Alabama, on March 3, 1887, charged with the task of putting this deaf, mute, blind bundle of flesh in touch with all human thought. Such a piece of teaching had never been done. Annie was 21 years old, which isn't as old as you think. And only six years earlier, when Helen was born, Annie had herself been sightless, living in the state poorhouse, and so unschooled she could not even write her name. One month after arriving in Tuscumbia, on April 5, she set into Helen's hungry hand the understanding of words, calling them "the key to everything she wants to know."

When Helen wanted to know her new friend's name, Annie spelled into her hand the word "Teacher." It became her name; everyone called her Teacher for 50 years.

Helen grew into a great woman. She graduated with honors from Radcliffe College, wrote several books, and toured the world giving lectures to large crowds,

with the help of a translator who spoke for her. She devoted her life to the blind, turning her affliction into a blessing for others. The lives of blind people around the world are now better because of her life. With Helen, until the day she herself died in 1936, was Annie Sullivan.

Mark Twain, the famous author, knew both Helen and her teacher. He said, "Helen Keller is a miracle, and Annie Sullivan is the miracle worker."

The Play

In what happened between them in that first month — battling day after day to answer one question, "What is a word?" — I saw the heart of their story. At that time I was myself a new father, with another child on the way, and because we needed money for baby shoes I wrote *The Miracle Worker* as a television play. It was aired in 1957, and two years later I turned it into a stage play, which is what you are now reading.

I took all the events from Annie's extraordinary letters, which someday you should read, too. What I had to make up was the talk, which means the *kind* of person I thought Annie — and the members of the Keller family — might have been.

The play has been translated into many languages. It is always on some stage somewhere, and for a good reason: It's one of the great stories of the world. And it was really written by Annie and Helen.

Nowadays Helen's book isn't given to students. But the story lives; you have it in your hands.

More About the Author

William Gibson was born in New York in 1914. During his writing career he has produced prize-winning poetry and a best-selling novel, *The Cobweb*, in addition to the play you will be reading. *The Miracle Worker* won the Sylvania Award in 1957 and has twice been made into a film.

The Miracle Worker

by William Gibson

In the 1880s, if you were a deaf-blind child, you were destined to live as an animal, completely unable to communicate with others. Helen Keller was such a child. How could young Annie Sullivan, a poor orphan who had once been blind and had been unable to read until her teens, tame the wild animal known as Helen?

CHARACTERS

Doctor

Kate Keller, Helen's mother and James's stepmother, in her twenties

Arthur Keller, Helen's and James's father, in his forties

Helen Keller, a deaf-blind child, seven

Aunt Ev, Helen's aunt

James Keller, Helen's half brother, a weak person who can't stand up to his strong father, in his twenties

Michael Anagnos, director of an institution for the blind

Annie Sullivan, Helen's teacher, 21

Children at the institution for the blind

Viney, the Keller's housekeeper

Narrator

Act One

Narrator: It is night, and we see a child's crib: What we see is the crib railings and three faces in lamplight, looking down. They have been through a long vigil; it shows in their tired eyes and disarranged clothing. One is a young gentlewoman with a kind face, **Kate Keller**; the second is a dry elderly **Doctor**. He has a stethoscope at his neck, and a thermometer in his fingers; the third is a dignified gentleman with chin whiskers, **Captain Arthur Keller.** Their dress is that of 1880, and their accents are Southern. The **Kellers'** faces are drawn and worried until the **Doctor** speaks.

Doctor: She'll live. *(Kate closes her eyes.)* You're lucky, Captain Keller. Tell you now, I thought she wouldn't.

Keller *(heavily):* Doctor. Don't spare us. Will she be all right?

Doctor: Has the constitution of a goat. Outlive us all. Especially if I don't get some sleep. *(He removes his stethoscope, his face leaves the railing; we continue to hear him, but see Keller's hand across the crib take and squeeze Kate's.)* You ran an editorial in that paper of yours, Captain Keller, wonders of modern medicine, we may not know what we're curing but we cure it. Well, call it acute congestion of the stomach and brain.

Narrator: Keller moves after the Doctor, we hear them; we see Kate's tearfully happy face hovering over us, her hand adjusting the blanket.

Keller: I'll see you to your buggy. I won't undertake to thank you, Doctor —

Doctor *(simultaneously):* Main thing is the fever's gone. I've never seen a baby with more vitality, that's the truth. By morning she'll be knocking down your fences again.

Keller: Anything that you recommend for us to do, we'll do —

Doctor: Might put up stronger fencing. Just let her get well; she knows how to do it better than we do. Don't poke at Providence — a rule I've always made it a practice to —

Narrator: Captain Keller walks the Doctor to the door.

Doctor: You're a pair of lucky parents, Captain Keller.

Keller *(with weight):* Thank you.

Narrator: The Doctor clicks a giddyyap; we hear the clop of hooves and the roll of wheels. Keller's eyes follow the buggy out of sight, then lift to the stars, thanking them, too. Suddenly from the house behind him comes a knifing scream. Keller runs back inside.

Keller: Katie!

Kate: Look.

Narrator: She makes a pass with her hand in the crib, at the child's face.

Keller: What, Katie? She's well, she needs only time to —

Kate: She can't see. *(She takes the lamp from him, moves it before the child's face.)* She can't see!

Keller *(hoarsely):* Helen.

Kate: Or hear. When I screamed she didn't blink. Not an eyelash —

Keller: Helen. Helen!

Kate: She can't hear you.

Keller: *Helen!*

Narrator: It is now five years later. The Keller family are gathered in their living room. There is a cradle with a sleeping infant; Helen now has a baby sister named Mildred. Captain Keller, in spectacles, is working over newspaper pages at a corner desk. Aunt Ev has a sewing basket on a sofa and is putting the finishing stitches on a big, shapeless, doll made of towels; a young man of Kate's age, James Keller, turns from the window to look at Helen. Kate turns Helen toward the Aunt, who gives her the doll.

Aunt *(turning to speak to Captain Keller)*: This Baltimore occulist I hear just does wonders. Why, lots of cases of blindness that people thought couldn't be cured, he's cured.

Keller *(patiently)*: I've stop believing in wonders, Aunt Ev.

Kate: But will you write to him, Captain?

Keller *(patiently)*: No.

James *(lightly)*: Good money after bad. Or bad after good —

Aunt: Well, if it's just a question of money, Arthur —

Keller: Not money. The child's been to every specialist in Alabama and Tennessee. If I thought it would do good I'd have her to every fool doctor in the country.

Kate *(simply and relentlessly)*: Will you write to him?

Keller: Katie. How many times can you let them break your heart?

Kate: Any number of times.

Narrator: While the others speak, Helen sits on the floor. She explores the doll with her fingers. Her hand pauses over the face: This is no face, but a blank area, and that troubles her. Her fingertips search for features. She taps questioningly for eyes, but no one notices. She then yanks at her Aunt's dress, and taps again vigorously for eyes.

Aunt: What, child?

Narrator: Of course Helen cannot hear the question. Helen begins to go around, from person to person. She is tapping for eyes, but no one attends or understands.

Kate *(no break)*: As long as there's the least chance for her to see, or hear, or —

Keller: I've done as much as I can bear, Katie.

James: You really ought to put her away, Father.

Kate: What?

James: Some asylum. It's the kindest thing.

Keller *(with force)*: She's your sister, Jimmie.

James *(retreats)*: Half sister, and half mentally defective. It's not pleasant to see her about all the time.

Kate: Do you dare to complain of what you *can* see?

Aunt: What does the child want, Kate?

Narrator: Helen walks back to her Aunt and yanks two beads off her dress.

Aunt: Helen!

Narrator: Helen pushes the beads into the doll's face. Kate comes to kneel in front of Helen, lifts the child's hand to her own eyes in question, and Helen nods energetically. Kate takes pins from the sewing basket and pins the beads on as eyes.

Aunt *(looking at her dress)*: My goodness.

Kate: She doesn't know better, Aunt Ev.

James: She'll never learn with everyone letting her do anything she takes a mind to. Might as well pamper a wild bearcub in the house here.

Kate *(closing her eyes, wearily):* I know, I know, what else can I do? If your father won't write to this Baltimore doctor, I will.

Aunt *(indulgently):* Why, it's worth a couple of beads, Kate, look.

Narrator: Helen now has the doll with eyes. And she cannot contain herself for joy. She rocks the doll, pats and kisses it.

Aunt: This child has more sense than all these men Kellers, if there's ever any way to reach that mind of hers.

Narrator: But Helen suddenly is scrambling toward the cradle and overturns it. The baby tumbles out. Captain Keller barely manages to dive and catch the baby in time.

Keller: Helen!

Narrator: All are in commotion. We hear the baby's screams, but Helen, calmly, is laying her doll in the baby's place in the cradle. Then Kate, on her knees, pulls Helen's hands off the cradle.

Kate: Helen, Helen, you're not to do such things, how can I make you understand?

James *(easily):* You've never trained an animal.

Kate: How can I get it into your head, my darling, my poor —

James: You teach them some discipline first thing by —

Kate *(angrily):* How can you discipline an afflicted child? Is it her fault?

Narrator: Helen's fingers move to her mother's lips. She tries to understand their movements.

James: You didn't hear me say it was her fault —

Kate: Then whose? I don't know what to do! How can I teach her — by beating her? She wouldn't have the faintest notion what it's about or for —

Keller *(shouldering the infant):* Katie, it's not fair to Baby Mildred here. We simply can't —

Kate: Are you willing to put her away?

Narrator: Now we see anger on Helen's face. Her hand strikes at Kate's lips. Kate catches her hand again and Helen begins to kick, struggle, twist.

James: Now what?

Kate *(in despair):* She wants to talk like — *be* like — you and me.

Narrator: Kate holds Helen. Helen struggles until we hear her first sound so far: a weird noise in her throat, like one an animal in a trap would make. Kate's eyes fill with tears. She releases Helen. The second she is free Helen puts herself back in her mother's arms, whimpering to be held. Kate embraces and soothes her.

Aunt: I've a mind to take her up to Baltimore myself. If that doctor can't help her, maybe he'll know who can.

Keller: I'll write the man, Katie. Today.

Narrator: Captain Keller writes to many doctors and receives many replies. Each doctor says he can do nothing for Helen, then suggests that the Kellers contact still another doctor. Finally the Kellers write to Mr. Michael Anagnos in Boston. He is the director of the Perkins Institution for the Blind. Mr. Anagnos has an idea, which he explains to a student of his named Annie Sullivan one morning at the Perkins Institution.

Anagnos: The child's name is Helen Keller. I then wrote her father saying a

Helen Keller at age ten.

governess, Miss Annie Sullivan, had been found. Well. It will be difficult for you there, Annie. But it has been difficult for you here, too. Hm? When you came to us you could not spell your name. You have accomplished so much here in a few years, yes. But not easily. There was always a battle. For independence.

This is my last time to counsel you, Annie. You do lack some — by some I mean *all* — tact, or talent to bend. To others. And what has saved you on more than one occasion here is that there was nowhere to expel you to. Hm? Do your eyes hurt?

Annie *(wickedly):* My ears, Mr. Anagnos.

Narrator: Annie opens her eyes. They had been closed as she listened to Mr. Anagnos. Light makes her eyes hurt, and they are red because of a disease. She often keeps them closed to shut out the pain of light.

Annie: What's the child like?

Anagnos: Like?

Annie: Bright, or dull?

Anagnos: Deaf, blind, mute — no one knows. She is like a little safe, locked, that no one can open. Perhaps it is empty. She is given to tantrums.

Annie: So am I.

Anagnos: Yes. Annie, you will find yourself among strangers now, who do not know your history.

Annie: Well, that's a kindness.

Anagnos: Perhaps you should tell it?

Annie *(angrily):* Why?

Anagnos *(teasing):* So they will understand. When you are so proud and determined to have things your own way.

Some must be content with only wealth or family. Not the fortune to be blind, orphaned, in a state poorhouse until 14. Such things go to a young girl's head. Hm? *(He turns serious.)* Annie, be —

humble. For your own sake. You will need their affection.

Annie *(dryly):* And pity, too?

Anagnos: Child, we can all use some pity. Not only the afflicted. *(Crisply)* Well. You are no longer our pupil, we throw you into the world, a working woman, governess, teacher. *If the child can be taught.* No one expects you to work miracles, even for 25 dollars a month. Now, in this envelope, a loan for the railroad. You can repay me when you have a bank account. In this box, a gift. With our love.

Narrator: Annie opens the small box he offers. Inside is a garnet ring. She looks up, blinking, and then down.

Anagnos *(He moves to open the double doors.):* Now I think other friends are ready to say good-bye.

Annie *(Her voice is trembling.):* Mr. Anagnos. Dear Mr. Anagnos, I — *(But she swallows, and cannot continue until she finds a joke.)* Well, what should I say, I'm an ignorant, opinionated girl, and everything I am I owe to you?

Anagnos *(smiles):* That is only half true, Annie.

Annie: Which half? I thought I died when my brother Jimmie died. I'd never again — Well, it's true, you say love, and I haven't *loved* a soul since and I never will. But this place did more than give me my eyes back, or teach me to spell, which I'll never learn anyway. It taught me what help is, and how to live again, and I don't want to say good-bye. Don't open the door, I'm crying.

Anagnos *(gently):* They will not see.

Narrator: Dr. Anagnos opens the door. Waiting outside is a group of girls, aged eight to 17. Doctor Anagnos guides them in with a hand. They are all blind.

A child: Annie?

Annie *(cheerfully):* Here, Beatrice.

Narrator: As soon as the younger girl locates Annie's voice the girls rush joyfully to her, speaking all at once. Annie bends down on her knees to the smallest.

Children: There's a present. We brought you a going-away present, Annie!

Annie: Oh, now you shouldn't have —

Smallest child *(sadly):* Don't go, Annie, don't go away.

Children: We did, we did bring you a present. Where is it? Alice has it. Alice! Where's Alice? Here I am! Where? Here!

Annie: I have it. I have it, everybody. Should I open it?

Children: Open it! Everyone be quiet! Do, Annie! She's opening it! Sssh!

Narrator: The children wait silently while Annie unwraps the present. It is a pair of dark glasses. She stands still, looking at them.

Children: Is it open, Annie?

Annie: It's open.

Children: It's for your eyes, Annie. Put them on, Annie! 'Cause Mrs. Hopkins said your eyes hurt since the operation. And she said you're going where the sun is *fierce.*

Smallest child *(sadly):* Don't go, Annie, where the sun is fierce.

Children: Do they fit all right? Did you put them on? Are they pretty, Annie?

Annie: I'm putting them on now. Oh, they fit fine. Why, my eyes feel hundreds of percent better already, and do you know how I look in them? Magnificent!

Children *(delighted):* There's another present! Beatrice! We have a present for Helen, too! Give it to her, Beatrice! Here, Annie!

Narrator: This present is an elegant doll. It has movable eyelids and makes a "mama" sound.

Children: It's for Helen. And we took up a collection to buy it. And Laura dressed it. So don't forget, you be sure to give it to Helen from us, Annie!

Annie: It's beautiful. I promise it will be the first thing I give her. If I don't keep it for myself, that is!

Smallest child *(sadly):* Don't go, Annie, don't go to her.

Annie *(her arm around her):* Sarah, dear. I don't *want* to go.

Smallest child: Then why are you going?

Annie *(gently):* I'm a big girl now, and big girls have to earn a living. But I'll write, and I'll come back. Someday.

Children: Will you surely, Annie? Is that a promise, too?

Annie *(hugging the smallest child):* That's a promise. But if Sarah here doesn't smile for me first, what I'll have to do is —

Smallest child: What?

Annie: Put *you* in my suitcase, instead of this doll. And take *you* to Alabama!

Narrator: This strikes the children as very funny. They begin to laugh and tease the smallest child, who after a moment does smile for Annie.

Shortly after that Annie leaves Boston to make her way by train to the Kellers' home. She spends many uncomfortable, tiring days and nights on trains. Often she must find trains on her own in strange cities. She travels through New York, Philadelphia, Baltimore, Washington, Roanoke, Knoxville, and Chattanooga. At last she arrives in Tuscumbia. James and Kate Keller meet her at the station. James comes toward her, to greet her and help with her suitcase.

James *(coolly):* Miss Sullivan?

Annie *(cheerfully handing him her bag):* Here! At last. Thank heaven.

James: I'm James Keller.

Annie: James? *(The name stops her, but her voice is gentle.)* I had a brother Jimmie. Are you Helen's?

James: I'm only half a brother. You're to be her governess?

Annie *(lightly):* Well, I'll try!

James *(eyeing her):* You look like half a governess.

Narrator: Kate has been sitting in a horse-drawn carriage watching Annie and James. She eagerly waits for them to approach. As they near, her face grows doubtful, troubled. But then she makes herself look pleasant and welcoming. James helps a stony-faced Annie, wearing her dark glasses, up to the carriage seat.

James: Mrs. Keller, Miss Sullivan.

Kate *(shaking Annie's hand):* We've met every train for two days.

Narrator: Annie looks at Kate's face and the stoniness goes out of her own. The good humor comes back to her mouth.

Annie: I had to change trains every time it stopped. The man who sold me that ticket ought to be tied to the tracks —

James: You have a trunk, Miss Sullivan?

Annie *(handing him the claim check):* Yes. Where's Helen?

Kate: Home.

Anne Sullivan

Annie: I can't wait that long.

Kate: Neither can she. There's been such a bustle in the house, she expects something. Heaven knows what . . . . You're very young.

Annie: Oh, you should have seen me when I left Boston. I got much older on this trip!

Kate: I mean, to teach her.

Annie: *I* mean to try.

Kate: Is it possible, even? To teach a deaf-blind child *half* of what an ordinary child learns — has that ever been done?

Annie: Half?

Kate: A tenth.

Annie *(a pause):* No. Dr. Howe began, but — as much as an ordinary child? No, never. But I think he made a mistake.

Kate: Mistake?

Annie: He never treated them like ordinary children. Don't lose heart, Mrs. Keller, I have three advantages over Dr. Howe that money couldn't buy for you. One is his work behind me. Another is that I am young. I've got energy to do anything and nothing else to do! The third is, I've been blind.

Kate *(a pause, then quietly):* These are advantages?

Annie: Well, some have the luck of the Irish, some do not.

Kate: What will you teach her first?

Annie: Language. I hope.

Kate: Language.

Annie: Language is to the mind more than light is to the eye. As Dr. Howe said.

Kate: Language. *We* can't get through to teach her to sit still. You *are* young, to

371

have so much confidence. Do you, inside?

Annie *(truthfully):* No, I'm as shaky inside as a baby's rattle!

Narrator: The two women smile at each other. Kate pats Annie's hand.

Kate: Don't be.

Narrator: James comes back and lifts a small trunk up behind them. Then he comes around and climbs into the driver's seat of the horse-drawn carriage.

Kate: We'll do all we can to help, and to make you feel at home. Don't think of us as strangers, Miss Annie.

Annie *(cheerily):* Oh, strangers aren't so strange to me. I've known some all of my life!

Narrator: Kate smiles again, Annie smiles back, James shakes the reins, and the carriage moves toward the Keller home.

When they arrive, Captain Keller is waiting inside the gate. Helen stands on the porch. Her hair is tumbled and her pinafore is soiled.

Keller: Welcome to Tuscumbia, Miss Sullivan. I take it you *are* Miss Sullivan —

Kate: My husband, Miss Annie, Captain Keller.

Annie: Captain.

Keller: A pleasure to see you, at last. You had an agreeable journey?

Annie: Yes, several! Where's Helen?

James: Where would you like the trunk, Father?

Keller: Where you can get at it, I imagine, Miss Sullivan?

Annie: If you can, yes —

Keller: In the hall, I think —

Kate: We've put you in the upstairs corner room, Miss Annie. If there's any breeze at all this summer you'll feel it —

Keller: *And* the suitcase —

Annie: I'll take the suitcase.

Keller: I have it.

Annie: I want it.

Keller: No, no —

Annie: Let me.

Keller: Not at all, Miss Selliv —

Annie *(impatiently):* I've got something in it for Helen. *(Captain Keller lets the bag go.)* Thank you. When do I see her?

Kate: There. There is Helen.

Narrator: Then Annie enters the yard, lugging her bulky suitcase, and begins the long, slow walk across it to the waiting child. When Annie finally reaches the steps she stops again, studying Helen for a last moment before entering her world. Then she drops the suitcase on the porch with intentional heaviness; Helen starts and comes to feel it. Annie puts out her hand and touches Helen's. Helen at once grasps it.

Then Helen's hand begins to explore Annie's, with its garnet ring, as if the child were reading a face. Afterward the hand moves on to Annie's forearm, and then her dress. Annie kneels to bring her face within reach of Helen's fingers. The fingers travel over it. Annie's face is calm until Helen's hand finds and removes the dark glasses. Annie's eyes look unpityingly at Helen.

Then Annie puts her hands on Helen's arms, but Helen at once pulls away. She returns to the suitcase. She tries to open it, but cannot. Annie points Helen's hand overhead. Helen pulls away, tries to open the suitcase again; Annie points her hand overhead again. Helen then points over-

Annie did not feel pity for Helen. She worked hard to teach Helen discipline.

head, asking a question, and Annie, drawing Helen's hand to her own face, nods. Helen now begins tugging the suitcase toward the door. When Annie tries to take it from her, she fights her off and backs through the doorway with it. Annie stands a moment, then comes through the doorway, her eyes following Helen upstairs. Then she climbs the stairs, too.

The Kellers have been watching. Captain Keller is frowning. We leave James unloading the trunk, and move with Captain Keller and Kate toward the house.

Keller: She's a little rough, Katie. How old is she?

Kate: Twenty-one.

Keller: A child. What's her family like, shipping her off alone?

Kate: She's very close-mouthed about some things.

Keller: Why does she wear those glasses? I like to see a person's eyes when I talk.

Kate: She was blind.

Keller *(stops):* Blind.

Kate: She's had nine operations on her eyes. One just before she left.

Keller: Blind, good heavens, do they expect one blind child to teach another? Has she experience, at least? How long did she teach there?

Kate: She was a pupil.

Keller: Katie, Katie. This is her first position?

Kate (defensively): She's quite old for her years —

Keller: Here's a houseful of grown-ups can't cope with the child, how can an inexperienced, half-blind Yankee schoolgirl manage her?

Narrator: James approaches with the trunk.

James: Great improvement. Now we have two of them to look after.

Narrator: Helen and Annie have reached the bedroom. In her own way, Helen helps Annie unpack. She tries on Annie's dark glasses, her bonnet, and a shawl. Annie smiles. She sits on the floor beside her open suitcase and watches Helen. Then Helen comes back to the suitcase and lifts out a pair of bloomers.

Annie: Oh, no. No you don't —

Narrator: Helen throws down the bloomers and comes to the elegant doll underneath. Her fingers explore its clothes, its hair, its features. Then she raises it and finds its eyes open and close. At first she is startled, then delighted. She picks it up, taps its head vigorously, taps her own chest, and nods questioningly. Annie takes hold of Helen's finger, points it to the doll, points it to Helen. Then she brings Helen's hand to her own face and nods.

Helen sits back on her heels, holds the doll to herself, and rocks it. Annie studies her and addresses her humorously, as one might talk to a kitten.

Annie (smiling and taking Helen's hand): Let's begin with doll. (In Helen's palm, Annie's forefinger points. Her thumb holds her other fingers down.)

D.

(Annie's thumb next holds all her fingers clenched, making a fist. She touches Helen's palm with the fist.)

O.

(Still in Helen's palm, Annie's thumb and forefinger extend.)

L.

(Annie repeats the motion.)

L.

(She puts Helen's hand to the doll.)

Doll.

James: You spell pretty well. Finding out if she's ticklish? She is.

Narrator: Annie gives him a cold stare. Helen tugs at her hand again, demanding attention. Annie repeats the letters, and Helen interrupts her fingers in the middle, feeling each of them, puzzled. Annie touches Helen's hand to the doll, then begins spelling into Helen's hand again.

James: What is it, a game?

Annie: An alphabet.

James: Alphabet?

Annie: For the deaf.

Narrator: Helen now repeats the finger movements in the air, correctly, her head cocked to one side, and Annie's eyes suddenly gleam.

Annie: How bright she is.

James: You think she knows what she's doing? She imitates everything. She's a monkey.

Narrator: Annie takes the doll from Helen, and reaches for her hand. Helen instantly grabs the doll back. Annie takes it again, along with Helen's hand, but Helen is angry now. Annie draws Helen's hand to her face to shake her head no, then tries to spell to her, but Helen scratches at Annie's face. Annie grasps Helen by both arms, and swings her into a chair, holding her pinned there, kicking. The doll and the glasses fly in different directions.

James *(laughing):* She wants her doll back.

Annie: When she spells it.

James: Spell! She doesn't know the thing has a name, even.

Annie: Of course she doesn't, who expects her to already? I want her fingers to learn the movements.

James: Won't mean anything to her.

Narrator: Annie tries to form Helen's fingers into the letters, but instead Helen swings a fist, which Annie barely ducks. Annie at once pins Helen down again.

James: She doesn't like that alphabet, Miss Sullivan. You invent it?

Annie *(struggling, dodging Helen's kicks):* Spanish monks invented it . . . under a . . . vow of silence. Which I wish *you'd* take!

Narrator: James smiles, bows his head, and leaves. Helen is now in a rage, fighting tooth and nail to get out of the chair. Annie looks around desperately. Seeing her purse on the bed, she suddenly releases Helen. She rummages in the purse, and comes up with a battered piece of cake wrapped in newspaper. Helen meanwhile has dropped to the floor and is groping for the doll.

Annie's foot moves the doll out of the way of Helen's groping. Then she goes on her knees and sets the cake on the back of Helen's hand. Helen freezes. She sniffs at it, then her other hand comes across for it. But Annie removes the cake and spells quickly into the reaching hand.

Annie: Cake. C, a, k, e. Do what my fingers do, never mind what it means.

Narrator: Annie touches the cake briefly to Helen's nose, pats her hand, then presents her own hand.

Helen spells the letters rapidly back. Annie pats her hand enthusiastically and gives her the cake. Helen crams it into her mouth with both hands. Annie watches her, with humor. She takes the doll, touches it to Helen's nose, and spells again into her hand.

Annie: D, o, l, l. Think it over.

Narrator: Helen thinks it over, while Annie presents her own hand. Helen spells three letters into Annie's hand. Annie waits for the fourth letter, then completes the word for Helen in her palm.

Annie: L.

Narrator: Annie hands over the doll, and Helen gets a good grip on its leg.

Annie: Imitate now, understand later. End of the first les —

Narrator: She never finishes the word, because Helen swings the doll hard. It hits Annie squarely in the face, and she falls back with a cry of pain, her knuckles up to her mouth. Helen waits, tensed for further combat. When Annie lowers her knuckles, there is blood on them. She works her lips, gets to her feet, coughs, spits something into her palm, finds the mirror, examines her teeth. Now she is furious herself.

Annie: You little devil, no one's taught you *any* manners? I'll —

Narrator: The door slams. Helen and the

doll are gone. Worse, the key is rattling outside in the lock. Annie darts over to open the door; nothing gives. She yanks again.

Annie: Helen! Helen, let me out of —

Narrator: Annie remembers Helen can't hear her. She rattles the knob, kneels, peers through the keyhole, gets up again. She hurries to the window, looks down, frowns. She comes back, takes a handkerchief, nurses her mouth. She stands in the middle of the room, staring at the door and the window in turn, and so catches sight of herself in the mirror. Her cheek is scratched, her hair is messy, her handkerchief is bloody.

Annie *(to herself in the mirror):* Don't worry. They'll find you, you're not lost. Only out of place.

Narrator: Soon Captain Keller discovers Annie's problem. He gets a ladder and helps her to escape through the bedroom window.

Keller: We've looked everywhere. I don't know what she could have done with that key. Steady, now —

Annie: I'd really like to —

Keller: No, no, hold tight. The last occasion she locked her mother in the pantry, Mrs. Keller was there pounding for three hours. I'll have to have that door taken down —

Annie: Captain Keller, I'm perfectly capable of going down a ladder myself.

Keller: I doubt it, Miss Sullivan. Simply hold on to my neck.

Narrator: Kate, James, and a couple of servants are all standing in a wide circle in the yard. They watch Captain Keller carry Annie down the ladder from the up-stairs window. Keller wobbles, and Annie grabs at his whiskers.

Keller: My *neck*, Miss Sullivan . . . .I'll have to have the lock replaced. Your tooth I believe will have to wait until morning, unless you are in such pain that —

Annie *(over his shoulder):* I'm not in any pain — comfortable as can be. I've had worse things —

Keller *(He reaches the ground, lets her down.):* There.

Annie: Thank you.

Narrator: She smooths her skirt, looking as unembarrassed as possible. Captain Keller shoos away the spectators.

Keller: Go, go, back to your work. There's nothing here to look at.

Narrator: They break up and move off.

Keller: Is dinner ready?

Kate: In a few minutes, Captain.

Keller: Well, let's go in.

Narrator: Everyone but Annie and James goes inside. He whispers to Annie, gesturing toward the window.

James: Might as well leave the l, a, d, d, e, r, hm?

Narrator: James goes in, too. Annie is alone in the yard. She moves back around the water pump, until at its base she sees Helen seated, happily playing with the doll. Then Helen's fingers find an opening in the doll's dress. She takes the key out of her mouth and she tucks it away in the doll.

Annie comes around, leans against a fence, and takes off her dark glasses to study the child. She shakes her head and cannot keep a faint smile from appearing on her lips. It is a smile of respect, humor, and acceptance of a challenge.

READING COMPREHENSION

Summarizing. Choose the best phrase to complete each sentence. Then write the complete statement on your paper.

1. Helen Keller became blind and deaf _____ (at birth, after a fever, through an accident).

2. The Kellers hired a governess, Annie Sullivan, who was _____ (a teacher, a student, a director) at the Perkins Institute for the Blind.

3. Annie Sullivan made finger movements on Helen's palm in order to _____ (teach her language, tickle her, keep Helen awake).

4. Helen locked Annie in her room to show she was angry that Annie _____ (would play with her, took her doll away, ate all the cake).

Interpreting. Write the answer to each question on your paper.

1. How did James feel about Helen and the way her parents treated her?

2. What was Annie's reason for dropping her suitcase near Helen?

3. Why didn't Annie get upset with Helen when she saw her hiding the key?

4. Why could Annie understand Helen better than most people could?

For Thinking and Discussing. Does the author want you to think that Helen is capable of learning? Give examples to explain your answers.

UNDERSTANDING LITERATURE

Setting. As in a story, *setting* in a play is the time when and the place where the events of the story happen. In the play "The Miracle Worker," the setting changes. You can tell what the setting is by looking for words or phrases that tell *when* and *where*. For example, the narrator says, "Their dress is that of 1880, and their voices are southern." This statement tells when (1880) and where (in the South) the event happens.

Number your paper from 1 to 5. Write *where* or *when* according to what each statement tells about the setting. Write *where* and *when* if the statement tells both time and place.

1. "Mr. Anagnos has an idea, which he explains . . . . to Annie Sullivan one morning. . . ."

2. "She spends many uncomfortable, tiring days and nights on trains."

3. "At last she arrives in Tuscumbia."

4. "The Keller family are gathered in their living room."

5. "He gets a ladder and helps her escape from the bedroom window."

WRITING

Imagine that the train Annie was on stopped for repairs. Write a paragraph telling *when* the train broke down, *where* it stopped, and *what* Annie did to pass the time.

Act Two

Narrator: Annie soon realizes Helen's biggest problem: No one has ever tried to control her. Annie works hard to teach Helen simple tasks that will give the girl discipline. She helps Helen to string beads and to use sewing cards. Annie hopes that learning to follow directions will help open Helen's mind to learning language. She continues to spell words into Helen's hand as they do these things. The morning after Annie's arrival, Kate and Captain Keller come in as teacher and pupil are working with sewing cards. Annie has just spelled something in Helen's hand.

Kate: What are you saying to her?

Annie: Telling her it's a sewing card.

Kate: But does she know?

Annie: No. She doesn't know what a word is yet.

Keller: It's like talking to the fence post, Miss Sullivan, what possible —

Annie: No, it's how you talk to Baby Mildred. Gibberish, she can't understand one word, till somehow she begins to.

Keller: Yes. After how many words, a million?

Annie: I guess no mama's ever minded enough to count!

Narrator: Annie's fingers meanwhile continue to spell, indicating the card, and Helen's fingers spell back.

Kate: What did she spell?

Annie: *I* spelled card. *She* spelled cake! It's only a finger-game to her now; she's got to learn that things have names first.

Kate: When will she learn?

Annie: Maybe after the millionth word.

Kate *(presently):* I would like to learn

Helen Keller's birthplace in Tuscumbia, Alabama.

those letters, Miss Annie.

Annie: I'll teach you this evening. That makes only half a million each!

Narrator: Annie shows the needle to Helen. Helen begins threading the card any which way, from hole to hole. Annie's hand tries to instruct hers; Helen's is impatient, and soon gets rid of Annie's by jabbing it with the needle. Annie gasps and jerks her hand away.

Kate: I'm sorry, Miss Annie. But that's how she is. There are times she simply will not be interfered with.

Viney (*calling from downstairs*): Breakfast's ready!

Annie (*to Kate*): Yes. I'm the same way myself.

Narrator: Everyone goes into the dining room and sits down. Captain Keller and James begin arguing about the Civil War. Annie sits behind her dark glasses and watches Helen. Helen has left her chair and is wandering around the table toward Viney and Annie. The child goes to her mother's plate, clawing her hand into some scrambled eggs. She takes what she wants, cramming it into her mouth. Kate smiles at Annie. Helen continues her way around the table. She grabs food from each plate. The Kellers take this for granted. They don't even seem to notice. But when she reaches for Annie's plate, Helen gets a surprise. Annie's hand promptly lifts and removes Helen's. The child's hand gropes toward the plate again, but Annie firmly pins her by the wrist and pulls her away.

Keller: What's the matter?

Kate: You see, Miss Annie, she's used to helping herself from our plates —

Annie: *I'm* not used to it!

Keller: No, of course not. No reason you should —

Kate: Perhaps you can give her something, Jimmie, to quiet her —

James: But her table manners are the best she has. Let's see if this —

Narrator: James pokes a chunk of bacon at Helen's hand, which Annie releases. But Helen knocks the bacon away. Stubbornly, she grabs at Annie's plate. Annie grips her wrists again. And the struggle continues.

Keller (*rising*): Let her, Miss Sullivan, it's the only way we get any peace. I'll get you another plate.

Annie (*gripping Helen*): I've got a plate, thank you.

Kate: Viney! (*Then, to Annie*) I'm afraid what Captain Keller says is true. She'll just keep on until she gets her own way. We find —

Keller (*at the door*): Viney, bring Miss Sullivan another plate —

Annie: I've got my own plate. I mean to keep it.

Narrator: There is silence for a moment, except for Helen's noises as she strains to get loose. The Kellers don't know what to do or say.

Keller (*uncertainly*): Miss Sullivan. One plate or another is hardly a matter to struggle with a deprived child about.

Annie: Oh, I'd sooner have a more glorious . . . issue myself —

Narrator: Helen bangs her toe on the chair. She sinks to the floor and cries with rage, pretending to be hurt. Annie keeps hold of her hands, gazing down. Kate gets up and hurries around to Helen.

Keller: She's hurt herself.

Annie: No, she hasn't.

Keller: I can't bear to hear her cry, will you please let her hands —

Kate: Miss Annie, you don't know the child yet, she keeps —

Annie: Well, I know an ordinary tantrum when I see one!

Keller *(angrily):* Have you no pity in you, girl?

Annie: *Pity!* For this *tyrant?* The whole house turns on her whims. Who's to teach her the sun doesn't rise and set for her? Of course I have no *pity.* You do, though, you do —

Kate *(troubled):* Miss Annie, please, it will do no good to —

Annie *(to Captain Keller):* — because it's easier to feel sorry for her than to help her, isn't it?

Keller *(stiffly):* I fail to see where you have helped her yet, Miss Sullivan.

Annie: I'll begin this minute, if you'll leave the room, Captain Keller.

Keller *(amazed):* Leave the —

Annie *(struggling with Helen):* Everyone, please.

Keller: Miss Sullivan, you were sent here as a paid teacher. Not as anything more. Not as a —

Annie: I can't unteach six years of pity if you can't stand one tantrum! Mrs. Keller, you promised me help.

Kate: I did, yes, but what can I —

Annie: Leave me alone with her.

Keller: Katie, will you come outside with me? At once, please.

Narrator: Everyone leaves the room. Annie releases Helen's hands, and the child sinks to the floor crying. Annie locks the door, reseats herself at the table, and very deliberately begins to eat the food on her plate.

Helen keeps pulling on Annie's chair, trying to knock it down. This doesn't work, so Helen puts her hand on Annie's fork and feels the movement of the fork to Annie's mouth. But as soon as Helen tries to grab food from Annie's plate, Annie firmly removes the girl's hand. Helen pinches Annie as hard as she can, then pinches her again. This time Annie slaps her. Helen is shocked. She feels her way around the room and realizes that she is alone with Annie.

There is no one to help her. The struggle goes on. After a while, Annie seats Helen at her place at the table. She makes her hold a spoon and use it to eat the food on her plate.

Viney *(outside the dining room):* What am I gonna do, Miss Kate? Almost lunchtime, I didn't get to them breakfast dishes yet.

Kate: I can't stand this a minute longer, Viney. I'm going in there.

Narrator: As Kate comes to the door, the key rattles on the other side and the door is opened. Helen stumbles out, falls against her mother's knees, and clutches them for dear life. Annie appears next in the doorway. Her glasses are in her hand. She looks as though she has just won a battle.

Annie: She ate from her own plate. She ate with a spoon. She folded her napkin.

Kate: Folded her napkin!

Annie: The room's a wreck, but her napkin is folded. I'll be in my room, Mrs. Keller.

Helen with "Teacher."

Viney: Don't be long, Miss Annie. *Lunch* be ready right away!

Kate: Folded her napkin. Viney, did you hear? Helen folded her napkin!

Narrator: Annie makes her way to her bedroom and closes the door. She is very tired. Tears begin to run down her cheeks. She falls across the bed and lies there, having a good cry.

Later that afternoon Annie is cheerful again when Kate Keller knocks at her door.

Annie: Come in!

Kate *(carrying a tray of tea things):* To mark your victory. The entire house is agog.

Annie: And Helen?

Kate *(handing Annie a cup of tea):* Very clinging. To me. I get the benefits. She's always been such an uncuddly child. And of course she's my first, and has my heart, in a way that — You should have seen her before her illness, what eyes she had! Always picking up needles and buttons that no one else could find. And so happy, Miss Annie, such a good-tempered child.

Annie *(dryly):* She's changed.

Kate: Do you know she began talking when she was only six months old? She could say "water." Not really— "wahwah, wahwah," was what she said, but she meant water, she knew what it meant, and only six months old. Miss Annie, put up with it. Please.

Annie (*slowly*): Mrs. Keller, Helen's worst handicap isn't blindness or deafness. It's your love. And pity. I'd burn them both out of the dictionary if it were up to me. All of you are so sorry for her you've kept her from becoming a human being.

Kate: I don't know what you —

Annie: I think what makes a human being is choosing, Mrs. Keller. Between the easy things and the hard things. You've always given Helen the easy things. She doesn't know what choice is. She won't come near *me* for days now. It's hopeless for me to try to teach her language or anything else here. I might as well —

Kate (*fearfully*): Miss Annie, before you came we spoke of putting her in an asylum.

Annie (*flatly*): What kind of asylum?

Kate: For the mentally handicapped. I visited one. There were *rats,* even in the — What else are we to do, if you give up? None of us can help her —

Annie: Give up? Who told you I was thinking of giving up? It never entered my head!

Kate: You said it was hopeless —

Annie: I said it was hopeless *here.* Give up? Why, I just now saw what has to be done. To begin!

Kate: What?

Annie: She has to depend on *me.* For everything. Food, clothing, fresh air — yes, the air she breathes. The one who lets her have it has to be her teacher. Not someone who *loves* her! You have so many feelings, they fall over each other like feet!

Kate: But how can she —

Annie: It's simple enough. I'll live with her somewhere else. Till she learns to depend on and listen to me.

Kate (*shocked*): For how long?

Annie: As long as it takes. Cheer up. I don't want her forever. I thought the garden-house in back would do. Change the furniture, take Helen there after a long ride so she won't recognize it, and you can see her every day. If she doesn't know. Well?

Kate (*slowly*): I'll have to talk it over with my husband.

Annie (*impatiently*): Mrs. Keller, I grew *up* in such an asylum. Rats, why, my brother Jimmie and I used to *play* with the rats! You're as innocent as a lamb to me, and Captain Keller too. Maybe he'd like to hear what it will be for Helen to live in such a place. The room we played in was the dead-house, where they kept the bodies till they could dig the —

Kate (*stricken*): Oh, my dear —

Annie: — graves. No, it made me strong. But Captain Keller wouldn't want to send Helen there. She's strong enough!

Kate (*after a minute, simply*): Is that who tried to burn it out of you?

Annie: What?

Kate: Love. They didn't burn it out of you, or else you wouldn't stay.

Annie (*in between sips of tea*): I didn't come here for love. I came for money! We'll talk to Captain Keller.

Narrator: That evening, Annie presents her plan to Captain Keller.

Keller: Take her away from us, Miss Sullivan? Do you know what it's like to take care of a child, single-handed, day and night?

Annie: I can use both hands, Captain Keller. You wouldn't prefer an asylum.

Kate: After all, she did fold her napkin, Captain. It's more than you got her to do.

Keller (*gloomily*): All right, Katie. I consent to the garden-house. We'll give them two weeks. It'll be a miracle if she lasts that long.

Kate: Two weeks! Miss Annie, can you get anything done at all in two weeks?

Keller: Anything or not, two weeks, then the child comes back. Two weeks. Yes or no, Miss Sullivan?

Annie: Fourteen days. Maybe it's enough. For only one miracle. Yes.

Narrator: Captain Keller and Kate bring Helen to the garden-house. Inside the one large room is a fireplace, a big bed, and a large window with a window-seat. Helen explores her new surroundings. She stumbles over a box on the floor. In it she discovers her dolls and other well-used toys. She is pleased, sits near the toys, then she becomes worried. She jumps up and runs back to her mother's knees. But Annie steps in, and it is her knee that Helen hugs. Helen pulls back and touches her cheek in a special gesture.

Annie: What's that mean?

Kate: It's her sign for me. Helen, dear —

Annie (*standing in her way*): No.

Narrator: Kate realizes that Annie is right, and she turns and hurries out. Captain Keller waits outside on the path. Kate joins him, then Annie closes the door. Helen rushes to the door but Annie holds her back. Helen kicks her, breaks free, and runs around the room like an imprisoned bird, bumping into furniture, grabbing the air wildly. Again and again she touches her cheek, growing more afraid. She begins her strange screaming.

Annie: Two weeks. Well.

Narrator: That day and night are hard for both Annie and Helen. Helen will not let Annie come near her. She keeps her hand in a fist when Annie tries to spell words to her. Helen stubbornly fights Annie's efforts to make her eat with a spoon, sleep in the strange bed, and dress herself. She throws her clothes all over the floor.

In the morning, Helen sits on the floor in her nightgown, with her clothes all around her on the floor. Her fists are closed tightly.

Keller (*looking in the window*): On my way to the office, I thought I'd see how you were getting along.

Annie: Fine!

Keller: Where is — What's wrong?

Annie (*cheerfully*): A difference of opinion. I thought she should dress herself, she thought she shouldn't.

Keller: Is this her breakfast?

Annie: Yes.

Keller: She wouldn't eat it?

Annie: Oh, she'd love to eat it.

Keller: But it's almost 10 o'clock. Why haven't you given it to her?

Annie: She understands I will. When she dresses herself. She's thinking it over. (*In a minute*) We've got a lot to think over, in two weeks.

Keller (*heavily*): Miss Sullivan.

Annie (*cheerfully*): You gave us two weeks.

Narrator: Captain Keller leaves. Soon after that Helen reaches thoughtfully for her

Helen learned to understand the meaning of words because of Annie's hard work.

shoe. In the end she does dress herself.

As the days go by Helen learns many things. She comes to accept Annie's being near her, although she is very cold to her. She eats with a spoon, she dresses herself, she strings beads. And she lets Annie spell words into her hand. She spells them back. But it is still just a game to Helen. She has no idea what the finger-spelled words mean.

One day Annie lets Helen hold an egg, just as a baby chick is hatching out of it.

Annie: E, g, g. It has a name, the name stands for the thing. Simple, it's as simple as birth — to explain. Helen, the chick *has* to come out of its shell, sometime.

Narrator: The shell is cracking. The chick is pecking its way out, and makes it. Helen's face shows she is amazed, delighted. Annie looks hard at Helen.

Annie: You come out, too. There's only one way out, for you, and it's language. To learn that your fingers can talk. And say anything. Anything you can think.

This is water. Water, Helen.

Narrator: Annie holds a glass and dips Helen's fingers in. She spells again, her voice weary.

Annie: Water. It has a *name*.

Narrator: The 14 days are almost up. Annie is frustrated. She writes to Mr. Anagnos at the Perkins Institution and describes her problem.

Annie:

Dear Mr. Anagnos:

I feel everyday more and more useless. My mind is full of skips and jumps, and a lot of things crowded together in dark corners. If only there were someone to help me! I need a teacher as much as Helen. I need —

(To herself) I need help too! Who, who? How do *I* learn? In all the world isn't there one person who can tell me how to reach Helen?

Narrator: Annie gets up and crosses the room. She goes over to Helen, who is sitting on a stool playing with a scarf.

Annie: How to tell you that this — *(she spells)* — means a *word,* and the word means this *thing,* scarf. How do I *reach* you?

Narrator: Annie yanks the scarf from Helen's face. Helen does not even react. Her face shows no emotion.

Later that day, Kate Keller comes for a visit. She sees Helen on the floor quietly stringing beads. Annie is bent over a dictionary. Her eyes look very red and tired.

Kate: What are you doing to your eyes?

Annie *(putting on her glasses):* Learning words.

Kate: You're not to overwork your eyes, Miss Annie.

Annie: Well, I wouldn't if I didn't have such an underworked brain! When I spell something to Helen I'd better spell it right.

Kate: How quiet she is. You've taught her that. I wish I could touch her.

Annie: She's learned two nouns since yesterday: key and water.

Kate: But not that they mean *things.*

Annie: No. It's still a finger game, without meaning. But she will learn.

Kate *(shaking her head in a hopeless way):* How? *How?*

Annie *(taking Kate's hand):* Let's play our finger game. She will understand. And when she does, you'll have a lot to tell each other.

Narrator: Annie keeps spelling words to Helen. But Helen does not understand. At last the two weeks are up. Captain Keller comes by. With him is the family pet, a dog named Belle.

Keller: Miss Sullivan! I've brought Helen a playmate.

Narrator: Annie gets up tiredly and sees Keller heaving the old setter through the window. Belle jumps to the floor.

Keller: I'll send Viney to help you pack, at the crack of dawn tomorrow. Mrs. Keller is so excited at having Helen home you might think it was a new baby in the house — you look very tired. You might be glad, too.

Annie: No. I need more time.

Keller: Miss Sullivan.

Annie: Another week.

Narrator: Helen scrambles off the chair where she has been sitting. She moves about the room. When she discovers Belle, she throws her arms around the dog's neck and squeezes her hard.

Keller: No. See how homesick she is? And we miss her too much. What would another week accomplish?

Annie: I can't promise anything, but —

Keller: An agreement is an agreement. You've done so much better than I thought was possible. Her manners are so much improved I —

Annie: She has to learn that everything has its name! That words can be her *eyes,* to everything in the world outside her. What is she without words? With them she can think, have ideas, speak, be reached. There's not a thought or fact in the world that can't be hers. You publish a newspaper. Do I have to tell you what *words* are? And she has them already —

Keller: Miss Sullivan.

Annie: — Eighteen nouns and three verbs, they're in her fingers now, I need only time to push *one* of them into her *mind!* One, and everything will follow. Give me time alone with her to —

Keller (*He points, and Annie turns.*): Look.

Narrator: Helen is playing with Belle's paws. She makes letters with her fingers and shows them to Belle, moving the dog's claws.

Keller: What is she spelling?

Annie: Doll.

Keller: Teaching a dog to spell. *(pause)* The dog doesn't know what she means, and she doesn't know what you mean. If God had meant Helen to have eyes, He would have given her eyes. *(pause)* I'll send Viney to pack in the morning.

Narrator: Captain Keller leaves. Annie looks at Helen. Then she closes her eyes.

Helen reading Braille during her second year at Radcliffe College.

She looks defeated.

Annie: I didn't do it. Didn't, and can't. I don't know how, Helen. Not a soul in the world knows how.

Narrator: That night, Annie has a terrible nightmare. She dreams about her childhood and her brother Jimmie. She wakes up yelling.

Annie: *Jimmie!*

James (*outside by the window*): Yes? You called me?

Narrator: Annie whirls and sees James at the window. He is looking in. Annie grabs a shawl, throws it around herself, and goes to the window.

Annie: No, no. What are you doing here?

James: I take a turn around here each night. See that all's well. Just a dream?

Narrator: Annie nods. After a moment James speaks quietly.

James: How old was your brother?

Annie: Seven. Helen's age.

James: How did he die?

Annie: He couldn't walk anymore. He had a bunch on his hip the size of a teacup — a tubercular hip, they said. It kept growing. We lived together in the women's ward of the poorhouse, to be near each other. Jimmie had to wear a girl's apron to stay. We were a pair, all right, me blind and him on a crutch in that apron. He kept saying about his hip, over and over, "It hurts, it hurts." Then he couldn't walk, even with the crutch. I was asleep when it happened, I didn't hear them roll his bed out, but I woke up and felt it wasn't there. So I went into the dead-house in the middle of the night and found his bed. And under the sheet I felt his skinny ribs and the bunch on his hip. When I screamed it woke everyone. They dragged me off him . . . . That's the part I dream.

James: How long?

Annie: Eleven years. This May.

James: And you've had no one to dream about since?

Annie: No. One's enough.

James: You don't let go of things easily, do you?

Annie: No. That's the original sin.

James: What?

Annie: Giving up. Jimmie gave up.

James: You'd be quite a handsome girl if it weren't for your eyes. No one's told you?

Annie (*grabbing to put on her glasses*): Everyone. *You'd* be quite a gentleman if it weren't for your manners!

James (*amused*): You wouldn't say that to me if you didn't have your glasses on . . . perhaps Helen will teach you.

Annie: What?

James: That there *is* such a thing as defeat. And no hope. And giving up. Sooner or later, we do. Then maybe you'll have some pity on . . . all the Jimmies. And on Helen, for being what she is. And even on yourself.

Narrator: Annie sits for a moment, then without another word gets up and closes the window on James. She turns her back, and he leaves. Annie begins to pace angrily in the darkened room. She comes to the bed and looks down at Helen.

Annie: No. I won't let you alone. No pity. I won't have it — either of us. If God didn't mean you to have eyes, I do. We're dead a long time. The world is not something to be missed. I *know*. And I won't let you alone till I show it to you. Till I put it in your hand.

Narrator: Annie puts her lips to Helen's hand. But Helen, even in her sleep, tugs it free and rolls away. Annie closes her eyes. She feels very much alone.

READING COMPREHENSION

Summarizing. Choose the best phrase to complete each sentence. Then write the complete statement on your paper.

1. Annie tried to teach Helen that she must not _____ (pour milk on the floor, grab food from anyone's plate, give the dog her breakfast).

2. To make Helen depend on her, Annie took Helen _____ (to live in the garden house, for a daily walk, on a vacation).

3. Annie keeps trying to teach Helen about words, that with words Helen could _____ (understand the world, be nice to her mother, play finger games).

4. When Annie told James about her brother, James suggested that she _____ (let him teach, give up on, talk to a doctor about) Helen.

Interpreting. Write the answer to each question on your paper.

1. Why did Annie think the Kellers were harming Helen, not helping her?

2. Why did Annie want Helen to become dependent on her?

3. How would Annie teach Helen to see the world?

For Thinking and Discussing. If all the members of your family had caught sore throats and could not speak, how could you communicate with each other? How would you feel about it?

UNDERSTANDING LITERATURE

Characterization. You can learn about characters in a play through what they say and what they do.

Read the questions and the quotations from "The Miracle Worker," Act Two.

1. How did Helen want people to react to her? How can you tell?

   "Helen bangs her toe on the chair. She sinks to the floor and cries with rage, pretending to be injured. . . . Kate gets up and hurries around to Helen."

2. How did Annie feel after she got Helen to eat from her own plate? Do you think she has given up?

   "Annie makes her way to her bedroom and closes the door. She is very tired. Tears begin to trickle down her cheeks. . . . Later that afternoon Annie is cheerful again. . . ."

3. How did Helen feel about Belle?

   "Helen scrambles off the chair where she has been sitting. She moves about the room. When she discovers Belle, she throws her arms around the dog's neck and squeezes her hard."

4. How does Annie feel about Helen?

   "Annie puts her lips to Helen's hand. But Helen, even in her sleep, tugs it free and rolls away."

WRITING

Pretend you are Annie Sullivan. Write a short letter to Mr. Anagnos telling how you felt about your first meal with Helen.

Act Three

Narrator: It is daylight on the day of Helen's homecoming. Kate is waiting eagerly in the yard outside the garden-house. Annie spells mother into Helen's hand. Then she moves the girl's hand to her cheek in Helen's own sign for her mother. She repeats both actions.

Kate: Let her *come!*

Narrator: Annie makes the sign again on Helen's cheek and gives Helen a little push. Now Helen understands, and begins groping, trembling herself. Kate rushes to hold Helen in her arms and kisses her. Helen clutches her as tight as she can.

Later that afternoon, Helen is comfortably settled back with her family. There are presents for her.

Annie has returned to her upstairs room. It is there that Captain Keller comes to speak to her. He knocks on the door.

Annie: Come in.

Keller (*entering, with an envelope in his hand*): Miss Annie, I've been waiting to give you your first month's salary. The first of many months', I trust. It doesn't express what we feel. It doesn't even pay for what you've done.

Annie: What have I done?

Keller: Taken a wild thing, and given us back a child. You've taught her so much that we couldn't.

Annie: I taught her two things: yes and no; can do and can't do.

Keller: It's more than all of us could, in all the years we —

Annie: I wanted to teach her what language is.

Keller: Perhaps you will.

Annie: I don't know how. I know without it she's in a dungeon. With it we're all kinfolk — at least we can talk. All I know is to go on, keep doing what I've done, and have some faith that inside she's — that inside it's waiting. Like water, underground. All I can do is keep on.

Keller: It's enough. For us.

Annie: You can help, Captain Keller.

Keller: How?

Annie (*her eyes filling with tears*): Even learning yes and no has been at a cost, of trouble and pain. Don't undo it. The world isn't an easy place. To let her have her way in everything is a terrible injustice to her! And I don't even love her, she's not my child! You've got to stand between that injustice and her. Because *I* will. As long as I'm here.

Keller: We will. We've learned something too, I hope. (*pause*) Won't you come down to us?

Annie (*waving the envelope, cheerfully*): Of course. I used to wonder how could I earn a living.

Keller: You do earn a living.

Annie: Yes, now the question is, can I survive it?

Narrator: Captain Keller escorts Annie downstairs for dinner. They join the family around the table.

Kate: Will you say the grace, Jimmie?

Narrator: They all bow their heads, except for Helen, who reaches to be sure her mother is there. James thinks a moment, then begins lightly.

James: And Jacob was left alone, and

wrestled with an angel until the breaking of the day; and the hollow of Jacob's thigh was out of joint, as he wrestled with him; and the angel said, Let me go, for the day breaketh. And Jacob said, I will not let thee go, except thou bless me. Amen.

Narrator: They lift their heads. James winks across at Annie, but Aunt Ev stares. Annie puts the napkin around Helen's neck.

Aunt: That's a very strange grace.

James: It's from the Good Book, isn't it?

Keller: Pass the bread, Kate.

Aunt: Well, of course it is. Didn't you know?

James: Yes, I knew.

Kate: Will you have some lamb, Miss Annie?

Aunt: Then why ask?

James: I meant it *is* from the Good Book, and therefore a fitting grace.

Aunt: Well, I don't know about *that*.

Annie: The water, Captain Keller, please.

Aunt: There's an awful *lot* of things in the Good Book that I wouldn't care to hear just before eating.

Narrator: Annie fills Helen's glass from the water pitcher. She sees the girl's napkin on the floor. She bends, picks it up, puts it around Helen's neck again. Helen deliberately yanks it off and throws it on the floor. Annie grows quiet, as does everyone around the table for a moment.

James: Well, fitting in the sense that Jacob's thigh was out of joint, and so is this lamb's.

Aunt: I declare, James!

Narrator: Annie, with all watching in silence, now picks the napkin up and puts it on Helen. Helen throws it down. Annie

Helen Keller with the author Mark Twain

rises and bears Helen's plate away. Helen, feeling it gone, begins to kick the table. Annie comes back, takes Helen's hand, and tries to lead her away. Helen grabs her mother's arm.

Kate: Miss Annie.

Annie: Yes.

Kate (*pause*)*:* It's a special occasion.

Annie (*hesitates, then*)*:* No.

Narrator: Annie tries to remove Helen's hand, but Kate stops her.

Kate: Please.

Annie: Captain Keller.

Keller: We had a little talk, Katie. Miss Annie feels that if we give in to Helen —

Aunt: But what's the child done?

Annie: She's too old to throw things on the floor.

Aunt: But only a napkin, it's not as if it were breakable!

Annie: I'm sorry, Mrs. Keller.

Kate: What is it you want to do?

Annie: Take her from the table.

Aunt: Oh, let her stay, my goodness, she's only a child. She doesn't have to wear a napkin if she doesn't want to —

Annie (*cutting in*)*:* You musn't interfere

Kate: This once, Miss Annie. I've hardly had a chance to welcome her home —

Annie: She's testing you.

James: Or you.

Keller: How?

Annie: She's home, she wants to see what will happen. Mrs. Keller, I know it hurts you, but to teach her that everything can't be as she wants is bound to be painful, to everyone. She'll live up to what you ask of her. Keep her to what she's learned, and she'll learn more.

Narrator: Kate releases Helen's hand. But the moment Annie takes it again, Helen begins to fight and kick.

Keller: All right. I'll keep her to it. Not by sending her from the table.

Narrator: Captain Keller comes around. He takes Helen's hand from Annie, pats it. At once Helen quiets down.

Keller: Bring her plate back. I won't see a child of mine deprived of food.

Annie: If she was a seeing child, none of you would put up with such —

Keller: She's not. Bring her plate, please.

Narrator: Annie looks angry but she gets the plate. Captain Keller fastens the napkin around Helen's neck and puts a fork in her hand.

Keller: There. It's natural enough, most of us don't like our teachers.

Narrator: Captain Keller returns to his seat. Helen is quiet for a moment. Then she flings the fork to the floor. After another moment's thought she plunges her hand into her food, crams a fistful into her mouth, plunges her other hand into Annie's plate. Annie moves in to grasp her wrist. Helen, flinging out her other hand, finds the water pitcher. She swings it at Annie, but the water flies over Annie and the pitcher tumbles to the floor. Annie gets her breath. Then she snatches up the pitcher in one hand, snatches up Helen in the other, and carries the kicking girl out of the room.

Annie: Don't interfere, Captain Keller.

Keller: Where are you going?

Annie: Don't undo what I do! I treat her like a seeing child because I *ask* her to see, I *expect* her to see! Don't —

Keller: Where are you taking her?

Annie: To make her fill this pitcher again!

Keller: Miss Sullivan, we have *servants* to fetch water —

Annie: Don't interfere with me in *any* way!

Narrator: Annie moves past him, with Helen under her arm, out the doorway.

Aunt Ev is shocked.

Aunt: You let her speak like that, a girl who *works* for you?

Keller *(angrily):* No, I don't.

James *(standing up):* Let her go.

Keller *(turning around):* What?

James: I said let her go. She's right — she's right and you're wrong.

Narrator: Outside the house, Annie pulls Helen toward the water pump. She puts Helen's hand on the pump handle.

Annie: All right. Pump.

Narrator: Helen touches her cheek, calling for her mother. She waits uncertainly.

Annie: No, she's not here. Pump!

Narrator: Annie forces Helen's hand to work the handle, then she lets go. Helen obeys. She pumps till the water comes, then Annie puts the pitcher in her other hand and guides it under the spout. The water, tumbling half into and half around the pitcher, falls on Helen's hand. Annie takes over the handle, pumping to keep water coming. Automatically, Annie does what she has done so many times before. She spells into Helen's free palm.

Annie: Water. W, a, t, e, r. Water, it has a —

Narrator: And now the miracle happens. Helen's face changes. She looks startled. Her lips tremble. She is trying to remember something. At last a sound finds its way out of her mouth. It is a baby sound,

The pump behind Helen Keller's birthplace, where she learned her first word "water."

buried under years of silence.

Helen: Wah. Wah.

Narrator: Helen drops the pitcher on the rock under the spout. It shatters. Annie freezes at the pump handle.

Helen: Wah. Wah.

Narrator: Helen plunges her hand into the dwindling water. She spells into her own palm. Then she gropes frantically for Annie's hand and spells into it.

Annie: Yes!

Narrator: Helen grabs at the handle, pumps more water, plunges her hand again into its stream, and grabs Annie's to spell it again.

Annie: *Yes!* Oh, my dear —

Narrator: Annie falls to her knees to clasp Helen's hand, but Helen pulls free, stands almost bewildered, then drops to pat the ground swiftly, and holds up her palm, demanding to know its name. Annie spells into Helen's hand.

Annie: Ground.

Narrator: Helen spells it back.

Annie: Yes!

Narrator: Helen whirls to the pump, pats it, holds up her palm, and Annie spells into it.

Annie: Pump.

Narrator: Helen spells it back.

Annie: Yes! Yes!

Narrator: Helen excitedly runs around the yard. She touches whatever she comes across and demands that Annie spell its name into her hand.

Annie: Mrs. Keller! *Mrs. Keller!*

Narrator: Helen scrambles onto the porch. She finds the bell string, tugs it. The bell rings, and at the same time she reaches out and Annie spells more quickly into her hand. The door opens. Kate and Captain Keller hurry out. Helen, still ringing the bell, with her other hand touches her mother's skirt, and Annie spells into her hand.

Annie: Mother.

Narrator: Captain Keller now grabs Helen's hand, and Annie again spells.

Annie: Papa. She *knows!*

Narrator: Kate and Captain Keller go to their knees. They clutch Helen to them. Annie steps back to watch the threesome. Helen spells wildly into Kate's hand, then into Captain Keller's hand. Kate spells back into Helen's. Then Helen turns all around, pulls free from her parents, and comes, with both hands groping, to find Annie. She touches Annie's thigh, and Annie kneels down in front of her. Helen's hand pats Annie's cheek impatiently, points a finger, and waits; and Annie spells into it.

Annie: Teacher.

Narrator: Helen spells it back, slowly; Annie nods.

Narrator: Annie holds Helen's hand to her cheek. But Helen withdraws it and retreats a step. She stands thinking it over. Then she turns again and stumbles back to her parents. They take her to them, and Helen now begins to weep, not weirdly, but softly, like an ordinary child.

In a moment, though, Helen begins hitting the pocket of her mother's dress. She wants the keys. Kate digs them out for her.

Annie has retreated toward the pump to sit. Kate touches Helen's hand questioningly, and Helen spells a word to her. Kate understands it. This is the first time

Helen Keller with blind children at an institution for the blind in Rome, Italy.

Helen has been able to use language to tell her mother anything. And what she has said is that she wants Annie.

Kate *(choked up):* Teacher?

Narrator: Kate points Helen in Annie's direction. Helen feels her way across the yard until her moving hands touch Annie's skirt. She stops and holds out the keys, placing them in Annie's hand. For a moment neither of them moves. Then Hel

en slides into Annie's arms and lifts away her dark glasses. She kisses her on the cheek and Annie hugs her in return.

Kate and all the others make their way into the house. Annie and Helen are alone in the yard. Annie has found Helen's hand, almost without knowing it. She spells slowly into it.

Annie *(in an unsteady whisper):* I . . . love . . . Helen — forever and ever.

READING COMPREHENSION

Summarizing. Choose the best phrase to complete each sentence. Then write the complete statement on your paper.

1. During her first meal at home, Helen's actions showed that she wanted to _____ (help serve dinner, test her family, drink cold milk).

2. When Helen _____ (called water "Wah, Wah," spelled dog into Annie's hand, gestured for a clean napkin) Annie knew that Helen understood language.

3. Helen demands that Annie spell names into her hand to know _____ (what everything is, the alphabet, how to spell).

4. Helen communicated to her mother that she wanted Annie by _____ (holding out Annie's glasses, using language, touching her cheek).

Interpreting. Write the answer to each question on your paper.

1. Why did Annie say that without language, Helen was in a prison?

2. How could you tell that James had changed his opinion about Helen?

3. How did Helen ask Annie questions?

4. Why did Helen bring Annie the keys?

For Thinking and Discussing. Do you think a person can be "free" without the use of language? Explain your answer.

UNDERSTANDING LITERATURE

Plot. As in a story, the plot in a play is the sequence of important events. The plot has a beginning, a middle, and an end, and, as in a story, it can be divided into four elements:

☐ *The Problem.* In "The Miracle Worker," Act One, we learn the problem: that Helen is an unruly deaf, blind girl.

☐ *Rising Action.* In Act Two, Annie tries to solve the problem.

☐ *Turning Point.* The action reaches its highest point in Act Three, when Helen realizes the meaning of language.

☐ *Resolution.* The problem is solved, and we learn how the characters react.

Write the following events from Act Three on your paper in the order in which they appear in the play. Write *turning point* next to the proper event, and *resolution* next to the events that show the resolution.

1. Annie spells water into Helen's hands, and Helen understands what water is.

2. Helen asks Annie the names of things.

3. Helen swings a pitcher at Annie.

4. Helen kisses Annie.

WRITING

Write a description of the things you did yesterday. Then list the three most important things in the order in which they happened.

VOCABULARY

Context Clues. One way to find out the meaning of a word is by looking it up in a dictionary. Another way is by using context clues. *Context clues* are the other words or phrases in a selection or a sentence. They help you figure out the meaning of the word you do not understand.

What is the meaning of the word *yanks* in this sentence: "Helen walks back to her Aunt and *yanks* two beads off her dress." The phrase *off her dress* is the clue in the sentence that helps you to figure out that to *yank* an object means "to pull it." Helen pulled the beads off her aunt's dress.

Number your paper from 1 to 6. Choose the correct meaning of the word in italics, and write it on your paper. Then write a new sentence using the italicized word.

1. "But Helen suddenly is scrambling towards the cradle and overturns it. The baby *tumbles* out." (jumps, falls, leaps)

2. "Here's a houseful of grownups can't *cope* with the child, how can an inexperienced, half-blind Yankee schoolgirl manage her?" (live, deal, play)

3. "Annie's hand promptly lifts and removes Helen's. The child's hand gropes towards the plate again, but Annie firmly *pins* her by the wrist and pulls her away." (hold, touches, pushes)

4. "Captain Keller *fastens* the napkin around Helen's neck and puts a fork in her hand." (attaches, admires, dislikes)

5. "James tries to convince Annie to give up but she turns her back on him and he leaves. Annie begins to *pace* angrily in the darkened room." (walk back and forth, smile sweetly, wait patiently)

6. "That night Annie has a terrible *nightmare*. She dreams about her childhood and her brother, Jimmie. She wakes up yelling." (stomach pain, high fever, bad dream)

READING

Cloze Exercise. The *cloze* method is used to test how well you understand what you read. In a cloze reading test, words are left out of a selection and you are asked to fill in the blanks. The words you fill in should make sense in the context of the selection.

Here are some lines from, "The Miracle Worker." Number your paper from 1 to 10. Write the missing words on your paper. If you cannot fill in the missing words, reread the play and try again. When you have finished the exercise, go back and see if the words you filled in are the same as those in the play.

1. "The Doctor clicks a giddy-yap, we hear the clop of hooves and the roll

of _____. Keller's eyes follow the buggy out of sight. . . ."

2. "Each doctor says he can do nothing for Helen, then suggests that the Kellers contact still another _____.

3. "Light makes her eyes hurt, and they are red because of a disease. She often keeps them _____ to shut out the pain of light."

4. "Annie hopes that learning to follow directions will help open Helen's mind to _____ language."

5. "The whole house turns on her whims. Who's to teach her the sun doesn't _____ and set for her?"

6. "She has to depend on me. For everything. Food, clothing, fresh air — yes the _____ she breathes."

7. "Helen stubbornly fights Annie's efforts to make her _____ with a spoon, sleep in the strange bed, and dress herself."

8. "Annie fills Helen's glass from the water _____."

9. "At last a sound finds its way out of her mouth. It is a baby sound, buried under years of _____."

10. "Helen whirls to the pump, pats it, holds up her palm, and Annie _____ into it."

QUIZ

The following is a quiz for Section 10. Write the answers on your paper in complete sentences.

Reading Comprehension

1. How did the Kellers find Helen a teacher?

2. What handicap did Annie and Helen have in common?

3. What did Helen's skill in imitating Annie's finger movements show Annie?

4. How did Annie get Helen to depend only on her?

5. How did Annie find out that Helen understood language?

Understanding Literature

6. What does the narrator's description of the Doctor leaving the Kellers house by horse and buggy tell you about the setting in the play?

7. Do you think the setting of the garden-house is an important part of the play? Could the actions that took place there happen in the Kellers living room? Why or why not?

8. How do Annie's actions show that she will be a good teacher for Helen? How can you describe Annie?

9. What can you tell about Helen's abil-

ity to learn by the way she acts with her family? Give an example of her actions to support your answer.

10. Choose four important events from the three acts of the play "The Miracle Worker." Write the events in the order in which they happen in the play.

WRITING

A Speech. When you speak formally, in public, to an audience, you are giving a speech. A speech can present your opinions or thoughts on a subject. It can also supply information, using facts. Read each step to help guide you in writing a speech.

Step 1: Set Your Goal

Write a speech that might have been given by one of the characters from "The Miracle Worker." Choose one of the following characters and topics.

☐ Pretend you are Annie Sullivan. Tell how you taught Helen Keller language.

☐ Pretend you are Helen Keller. Tell how your life has changed since you learned language.

☐ Pretend you are James Keller. Tell how you came to see that Helen was capable of learning.

☐ Pretend you are Mr. or Mrs. Keller. Tell why one should allow handicapped children to do things for themselves.

Step 2: Make a Plan

Review the play to gather facts to support the topic you have chosen. Add your own personal ideas to the list of facts you have gathered.

Here is an example of how you can use facts from the play and your own ideas. Imagine that Mr. Anagnos is going to give a speech explaining why he chose Annie to be Helen's teacher. For his speech, you might include the following facts and ideas:

Fact: Annie has accomplished much as a pupil at the school.

Ideas: Annie is smart. Annie tries hard.

Facts: Annie has trouble with her eyes. Annie has temper tantrums.

Idea: Annie will understand Helen's problems.

Now make a list of facts and ideas that support the topic you have chosen.

Step 3: Write your First Draft

Your speech should contain three paragraphs. The first should introduce the character you are pretending to be and the topic of the speech.

The second paragraph should contain your list of facts and ideas. The third paragraph should sum up your thoughts on the topic of your speech.

☐ Begin by saying who you are and what your speech is about. For example, Mr. Anagnos might begin his speech this way:

I am Michael Anagnos, director of the Perkins Institution for the Blind. For several years, Annie Sullivan was a pupil here. When Mr. Keller asked me for help with his daughter Helen, I decided to send Annie to be Helen's teacher.

☐ Next write a paragraph using your list of facts and ideas.

☐ End with a paragraph summing up your thoughts. Mr. Anagnos might say:

Annie proved to be the ideal teacher for Helen. She introduced Helen to language and enabled her to become the great woman she later was.

Step 4: Revise Your Speech
Check your speech one more time.

Have you stated your facts and ideas clearly? Add any information that you have left out. Make sure to correct any errors in spelling, grammar, and punctuation you find. Make a final, neat copy of your speech.

ACTIVITIES

Word Attack. The letter *g* does not always stand for the same sound. Usually, *g* stands for the sound you hear at the beginning of *girl* or the end of *ring*.

However, when *g* is followed by an *e, i,* or *y,* it may stand for the sound at the beginning of *gym* or the middle of *age*.

When a *g* and an *h* come together, they are often silent, although they influence the sound of the vowel in the word:

light   night

Pronounce the following words from "The Miracle Worker." Then copy them on your paper and write *girl, gym,* or *silent,* according to the sound of *g* in the word.

1. suggests
2. governess
3. light
4. bright
5. among
6. strangers
7. taught
8. garnet
9. blinking
10. ignorant
11. eight
12. guides

Speaking and Listening. Practice reading the speech you wrote in this section. Pay special attention to words containing the letter *g.* Then give your speech in front of other people who have read the play, if possible. Try to give the speech without reading it from your paper.

Researching
1. Dictionaries give a lot of helpful information besides definitions. For example, they tell you where many words come from. Look up the word *braille* in a dictionary. On your paper, write the meaning of *braille.* Then tell where the word comes from.

Next, look up *braille* in an encyclopedia. Use the information you find there to write a short paragraph about the invention of braille.

Then use the chart of braille symbols to

write a short message in braille. Be sure to include the meaning of the message in ordinary letters.

2. Annie Sullivan is called a miracle worker because of her help to Helen Keller and the Keller family. What can you do to help someone?

☐ Ask your parents what you could do to help in the house. Make a list of these things and the day when you will do them. Mark a check on your list when you have done the task.

☐ Make get-well cards for someone in the hospital.

☐ Make art work to cheer the elderly at a home or hospital.

☐ Donate toys or clothes to the needy.

☐ If there is a problem in your town or city that you wish were helped, write a letter to the correct official to tell him or her about the problem.

You can find out names, addresses, and telephone numbers of social service organizations, hospitals, or City Hall, in your telephone book. Look in the Yellow Pages section of your telephone book for these listings. The listings are in alphabetical order.

Creating. Have someone you know put an object in a paper bag. Do not watch the person choose the object. Then, put your hand in the bag and write a description of the object, telling what you think it is. Do not look into the bag until you have finished writing your description. In your last sentence, tell what the object really is.

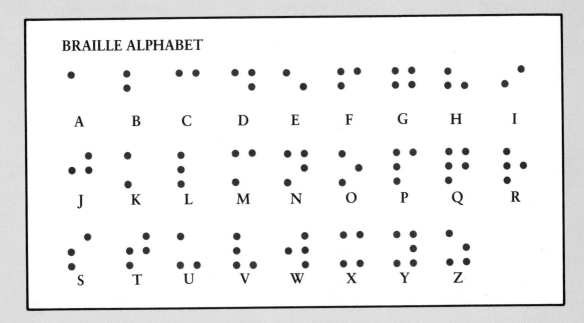

BRAILLE ALPHABET

A B C D E F G H I

J K L M N O P Q R

S T U V W X Y Z

LEVEL Z
Glossary

PRONUNCIATION KEY

ă	pat	j	judge	sh	dish, ship
ā	aid, fey, pay	k	cat, **kick**, pi**que**	t	tight
â	air, care, wear	l	lid, need**le**	th	path, thin
ä	father	m	am, man, mum	th	bathe, this
b	bib	n	no, sudden	ŭ	cut, rough
ch	church	ng	thing	û	circle, firm, heard, term,
d	deed	ŏ	horrible, pot		turn, urge, word
ĕ	pet, pleasure	ō	go, hoarse, row, toe	v	cave, valve, vine
ē	be, bee, easy, leisure	ô	alter, caught, for, paw	w	with
f	fast, fife, off, phase, rough	oi	boy, noise, oil	y	yes
g	gag	ou	cow, out	yōo	abuse, use
h	hat	o͝o	look	z	rose, size, xylophone, zebra
hw	which	o͞o	boot, fruit	zh	garage, pleasure, vision
ĭ	pit	p	pop	ə	about, silent, pencil, lemon,
ī	by, guy, pie	r	roar		circus
î	dear, deer, fierce, mere	s	miss, sauce, see	ər	butter

PART OF SPEECH LABELS

n.	(noun)	*conj.*	(conjunction)
adj.	(adjective)	*prep.*	(preposition)
adv.	(adverb)	*v.*	(verb)
pron.	(pronoun)	*interj.*	(interjection

The additional italicized labels below are used as needed to show inflected forms:

pl. (plural)   *sing.* (singular)

STRESS

Primary stress ′
  bi · ol′o·gy | bī ŏl′ə jē |
Secondary stress ′
  bi′o · log′i · cal |bī′ə lŏj′ĭ kəl |

In this glossary, definitions were chosen to show the meanings of the words as they are used in the selections. Unless otherwise indicated, entries based on © 1986 by Houghton Mifflin Company. Reprinted by permission from The Houghton Mifflin Student Dictionary.

ab·dom·i·nal | ăb dŏm′ ə nəl | *adj.* Of the stomach area.

ac·cus·tomed | ə kŭs′ təmd | *adj.* Used to; familiar with; in the habit of.

a·cute | ə kyoot′ | *adj.* **3.** Very serious; developing suddenly and reaching a crisis quickly: *An acute disease.*

af·flict | ə flĭkt′ | *v.* To cause distress to; cause to suffer; trouble greatly.

a·ghast | ə găst′ | or | ə gäst′ | *adj.* Shocked or horrified, as by something terrible.

a·gog | ə gŏg′ | *adj.* Full of eager anticipation; greatly excited.

al·der | ôl′ dər | *n.* Any of several trees or shrubs that grow in cool, damp places.

a·loft | ə lôft′ | or | ə lŏft′ | *adv.* **1.** In or into a high place.

a·miss | ə mĭs′ | *adj.* Wrong; faulty; improper.

an·ces·tor | ăn′ sĕs′ tər | *n.* **1.** Any person from whom one is descended, especially of a generation earlier than a grandparent.

as·sure | ə shoor′ | *v.* **3.** To give confidence to.

a·sy·lum | ə sī′ ləm | *n.* **1.** A hospital or shelter for the helpless or insane.

back·woods | băk′ woodz′ | or | -woodz′ | *pl. n.* Heavily wooded areas, usually isolated from populated areas.

badg·er | băj′ ər | *n.* **1.** A burrowing animal with short legs and thick, grayish fur.

ba·sin | bā′ sən | *n.* **1.** A round, open, shallow container often used for holding water to wash in.

bat·ter | băt′ ər | *v.* **2.** To injure or damage by rough treatment or hard wear.

bel·fry | bĕl′ frē | *n.* **1.** A tower or steeple in which one or more bells are hung.

be·lit·tle | bĭ lĭt′ l | *v.* To cause to seem small or unimportant.

berth | bûrth | *n.* **1.** A built-in bed or bunk in a ship or a railroad sleeping car.

be·wil·der | bĭ wĭl′ dər | *v.* To confuse greatly; puzzle.

bound | bound | *v.* **1.** To leap, jump, or spring.

brace | brās | *n.* **1.b.** A support, as a beam in a building. **2.** A medical device used to support a part of the body. **3.** *v.* To prop or hold firmly in place.

branch | brănch | or | bränch | *n.* **5.a.** A local unit or office of a business, institution, etc.

brood | brood | *v.* **1.** To sit on and hatch (eggs).

burr | bûr | *n.* A seed, fruit, nut, or flower head enclosed in a rough prickly covering.

cal·a·bash | kăl′ ə băsh | *n.* **1.** A large gourd with a tough shell-like rind. **2.** A bowl, ladle, pipe, etc., made from the hollowed-out shell of such a gourd or fruit.

can·ter | kăn′ tər | *n.* A slow, easy gallop. *v.* To ride or run at a canter.

cap·tor | kăp′ tər | *n.* Someone who takes or holds another as a captive or prisoner.

cas·cade | kăs kād′ | *n.* **1.** A small waterfall, usually one of many, that flows over steep rocks.

cav·ern·ous | kăv′ ər nəs | *adj.* Resembling a cavern or large cave; huge, deep, and hollow.

chan·nel | chăn′ əl | *n.* **1.** The depression or cut in the earth through which a river or stream passes.

clam·ber | klăm′ bər | *v.* To climb with difficulty, especially on all fours: *Clamber up a slope.*

clan | klăn | *n.* **1.** A group of families, as in the Scottish Highlands, claiming a common ancestor. **2.** Any group of relatives, friends, etc.

clasp | klăsp | or kläsp | *n.* **2.** To hold or embrace tightly.

com·mis·sion | kə mĭsh′ ən | *n.* **1.** The act of granting authority to someone to carry out a certain job or duty.

com·pound | kŏm′ pound′ | *n.* A group of houses enclosed by a wall or other barrier.

Con·es·to·ga wagon | kŏn′ ĭ stō′ gə | *n.* A heavy covered wagon, first built at Conestoga, Pennsylvania, used by American pioneers in their westward travel.

con·sti·tu·tion | kŏn′ stǐ too′ shən | or | -tyoo′ | *n.* **3.** The physical makeup of a person.

con·tem·pla·tion | kŏn′ təm plā′ shən | *n.* Thought.

cope | kōp | *v.* To deal with successfully.

cop·pice | kăp′ əs | *n.* **1.** A grove, or group of small trees.

coun·sel | koun′ səl | *v.* To give advice.

crest | krĕst | *v.* **1.** To reach the top of. **2.** To form into or rise to a crest.

dame | dām | *n.* **3.** Any lady or wife.

de·lib·er·ate | dǐ lǐb′ ər ǐt | *adj.* Done or said on purpose.

des·o·late | dĕs′ ə lǐt | *adj.* **1.** Empty of life. **2.** Deserted.

dew·y | doo′ ē | or | dyoo′ ē | *adj.* **1.** Moist with or as if with dew.

dig·ni·fied | dǐg′ nə fīd′ | *adj.* Having or expressing dignity; serious and stately; poised.

dis·ar·range | dǐs′ ə rānj′ | *v.* **dis·ar·ranged, dis·ar·rang·ing** To upset the order or arrangement of.

dis·mount | dǐs mount′ | *v.* **1.** To get off or down, as from a horse.

down·heart·ed | doun′ här′ tǐd | *adj.* Low in spirits; sad; depressed.

dwin·dle | dwǐn′ dəl | *v.* To waste away; become less and less.

ed·i·to·ri·al | ĕd′ ǐ tôr′ ēəl | or | -tōr′- | *n.* An article in a newspaper or magazine expressing the opinions of its editors or publisher.

em·brace | ĕm brās′ | *v.* **1.** To hug or hold with the arms as a sign of affection.

e·merge | ǐ mûrj′ | *v.* **1.** To come into view; appear.

en·camp | ĕn kămp′ | *v.* To set up or live in a camp.

en·chant | ĕn chănt′ | or | -chänt′ | *v.* **1.** To cast under a spell; **2.** To delight; charm.

es·cort | ĕs′ kôrt | *n.* **1.** One or more persons accompanying another to give protection or guidance or to pay honor.

es·cort | ǐ skôrt′ | *v.* To accompany as an escort.

eu·ca·lyp·tus | yoo′ kə lǐp t əs | *n.* Any of several tall trees with leaves that produce a strong-smelling oil.

e·vict | ǐ vǐkt′ | *v.* To put out (a tenant) from home or property by legal process.

ex·as·per·ate | ǐg zăs′ pə rāt′ | *v.* **ex·as·per·at·ed, ex·as·per·at·ing.** To annoy greatly; try the patience of.

ex·haust | ǐg zôst′ | *v.* **4.** To wear out completely; tire.

ex·tend | ǐk stĕnd′ | *v.* **5.** To straighten or reach out with: *Extend a hand.*

fal·con | făl′ kən | or | fôl′- | or | fô′ kən |*n.* Any of several long-winged, swift-flying hawks, especially one of a kind trained to hunt for and catch small animals and birds.

flare | flâr | *v.* **1.** To break into flame suddenly.

fod·der | fŏd′ ər | *n.* Food, such as chopped corn stalks or hay, for horses, cattle, etc.

foe | fō | *n.* An enemy.

fol·ly | fŏl′ ē | *n.* **1.** Lack of good sense or judgment; foolishness. **2.** A silly idea, plan, or action.

fore·paw | fôr′ pô′ | or | fōr′- | *n.* A front paw.

fork | fôrk | *n.* **3.a.** A separation into two or more parts, as of the branches of a tree, or two paths from one main road.

frag·ile | frăj′ əl | or | -īl′ | *adj.* **3.** Physically weak.

fra·grance | frā′ grəns | *n.* A sweet or pleasant odor; scent.

fran·tic | frăn′ tǐk | *adj.* Very excited with fear or worry.

fret | frĕt | *v.* **fret·ted, fret·ting 2.** To grow or wear away.

fume | fyoom | *v.* **fumed, fum·ing 3.** To feel or show anger or excitement.

fu·ry | fyoor′ ē | *n.* **2.** Violent and uncontrolled action; great anger and excitement.

ges·ture | jĕs′ chər | *n.* A motion of the hands, arms, head, or body used while speaking or in place of speech to help express one's meaning.

girth | gûrth | *n.* **2.** A strap encircling the body of a horse or pack animal to secure a load or saddle on its back.

gnaw | nô | *v.* **1.** To bite, or chew away with the teeth.

goad | gōd | *v.* To prod with, or as if with, a goad (a long stick with a pointed end).

grasp | grăsp | or | gräsp | *v.* **1.** To grab and hold firmly with or as if with the hands.

gren·a·dier | grĕn′ ə dîr′ | *n.* **2.** A soldier of the British Grenadier Guards, the first regiment of the royal household infantry.

grope | grōp | *v.* **1.** To reach about or search blindly or uncertainly.

grove | grōv | *n.* A group of trees with open ground between them.

grub | grŭb | *v.* **grubbed, grub·bing 1.** To dig in the ground.

hal·ter | hôl′ tər | *n.* **1.** A device of rope or leather straps that fits around the head or neck of an animal, such as a horse, and can be used to lead or secure it.

haul | hôl | *v.* **2.** To transport, as with a truck or wagon; cart.

heath | hēth | *n.* **2.** Low-growing plants and shrubs.

hid·e·ous | hĭd′ ē əs | *adj.* **1.** Horribly ugly; terrible.

hinge | hĭnj | *n.* **1.** A jointed device on which a door, gate, lid, etc., turns or swings.

hoard | hôrd | or hōrd | *v.* To save, keep, or store away, often secretly or greedily.

home·spun | hōm′ spŭn | *n.* **1.** A plain, coarse, loosely woven cloth made of yarn that is spun at home.

ho·ri·zon | hə rī′ zən | *n.* **1.** The line along which the earth and sky appear to meet.

hov·el | hŭv′ əl | or | hŏv′- | *n.* A small, miserable home or dwelling.

hov·er | hŭv′ ər | or | hŏv′- | *v.* **2.** To remain close by.

hud·dle | hŭd′ l | *n.* **2.** In football, a brief gathering of a team's players behind the line of scrimmage to prepare for the next play.

im·pet·u·ous | ĭm pĕch′ oo əs | *adj.* **1.** Tending toward suddenness and boldness of action.

in·cline | ĭn klīn′ | *v.* **2.** To be likely to, tend.

in·com·pa·ra·ble | ĭn kŏm′ pə rə bəl | *adj.* **2.** Above all comparison; the best.

in·jus·tice | ĭn jŭs′ tĭs | *n.* Lack of justice; unfairness.

in·land | ĭn′ lənd | *adj.* Away from the ocean or water; of or located in the interior of a country or region.

in·let | ĭn′ lĕt | or | -lĭt | *n.* **1.** A bay or other recess forming a body of water along the coast.

in·ten·tion·al | ĭn tĕn′ shə nəl | *adj.* Done on purpose.

in·ter·fere | ĭn′ tər fîr′ | *v.* To butt in or get in the way.

jag·ged | jăg′ ĭd | *adj.* **2.** Having uneven edges; irregular.

kin·dle | kĭn′ dl | *v.* **1.a.** To build and start (a fire).

kin·folk | kĭn′ fōk | *n.* Members of a family; relatives.

land·mark | lănd′ märk′ | *n.* **2.** A familiar or easily recognized object, feature of the landscape, etc.

lathe | lāth | *n.* A machine on which a piece of wood, metal, etc., is spun and shaped by a tool that cuts or wears it away.

league | lēg | *n.* **1.** A group of nations, people, organizations, etc., acting or working together.

lep·ro·sy | lĕp′ rə sē | *n.* A disease that destroys the skin and other parts of the body, eventually causing death.

lev·y | lĕv′ ē | *v.* **1.** To impose or collect (a tax, tariff, or other fee).

loft | lôft | or | lŏft | *n.* **2.** An open space under a roof; an attic.

loom | loom | *v.* **1.** To come into view or appear as a massive or indistinct image.

lope | lōp | *v.* **loped, lop·ing** To run or ride in a steady and easy way.

lush | lŭsh | *adj.* **1.** Having or forming a thick, plentiful plant growth.

lute | loot | *n.* A stringed musical instrument with a pear-shaped body.

mag·net·ic | măg nĕt′ ĭk | *adj.* **2.** Having the properties of a magnet that attracts iron and other substances.

main·land | **mān′** lănd′ | or | -lənd | *n.* The principal land mass of a country, territory, or continent as opposed to its islands or peninsulas.

make·shift | māk′ shĭft′ | *adj.* Serving as a temporary substitute.

mast | măst | or | mäst | *n.* **1.** An upright pole that supports the sails, rigging, etc., of a ship or boat.

mate | māt | *n.* **5.a.** An officer on a ship ranking below the captain.

me·di·e·val | mē′ dē ē′ vəl | or mĕd′ ē- | or | mĭd′ ē- | or | mĭ dē′ vəl | *adj.* Of or characteristic of the period in European history from the fall of the Roman Empire (about A.D. 500 to the rise of the Renaissance (about 1400).

med·i·ta·tion | mĕd′ ĭ tā′ shən | *n.* **1.** The act of thinking deeply and quietly.

me·mo·ri·al | mə môr′ ē əl | or | -mōr′- | *adj.* Serving to honor the memory of a person or event.

midst | mĭdst | *n.* In the middle of.

min·gle | mĭng′ gəl | *v.* **1.** To mix or become mixed; unite; combine, join.

moat | mōt | *n.* A wide, deep ditch, usually filled with water.

mock | mŏk | *v.* **1.** To make fun of.

moor·ing | moor′ ĭng | *n.* **2.** A place at which a vessel or aircraft may be secured.

muf·fle | mŭf′ əl | *v.* **muf·fled, muf·fling** **2.b.** To wrap up or pad in order to deaden the sound of.

mus·ket | mŭs′ kĭt | *n.* An old type of long-barreled gun, used before the invention of the rifle.

mus·ter | mŭs′ tər | *n.* **1.** A gathering, especially of troops, for inspection, roll call, etc.

nim·ble | nĭm′ bəl | *adj.* **1.** Moving or able to move quickly, lightly, and easily; agile.

no·tion | nō′ shən | *n.* **1.** A general idea, belief, opinion, etc.

o·blig·ing | ə blī′ jĭng | *adj.* Ready to do favors or to help others. **o·blig′ ·ing·ly** *adv.*

ob·long | ŏb′ lông′ | or | -lŏng′ | *adj.* Shaped like or resembling a rectangle or ellipse.

oc·u·list | ŏk′ yə lĭst | *n.* **1.** A specialist who examines eyes.

op·po·nent | ə pō′ nənt | *n.* A person or group that opposes another in a battle or contest.

or·deal | ôr dēl′ | *n.* A very difficult or painful experience, especially one that tests a person's character or strength.

o·ver·rule | ō′ vər rool′ | *v.* **-ruled, -rul·ing** **1.** To rule against (in a trial).

pan·try | păn′ trē | *n.* A small room or closet, usually next to a kitchen, where food, china, silver, linens, etc., are stored.

parch·ment | pärch′ mənt | *n.* **1.** The skin of a sheep or goat, prepared as a material to write on. **2.** A piece of writing on a sheet or roll of parchment.

par·lor | pär′ lər | *n.* **1.** A room for entertaining visitors.

pat·ter | păt′ ər | *v.* **2.** To walk or move softly and quickly.

pe·cu·liar | pĭ kyool′ yər | *adj.* **1.** Unusual or eccentric; strange.

406

peer | pîr | v. **1.** To look carefully, searchingly, or with difficulty.

per·pen·dic·u·lar | pûr′ pən dĭk′ yə ler | adj. **1.** Intersecting at or forming a right angle or right angles.

pierc·ing | pîr′ sing | adj. Sharp; penetrating.

pin·a·fore | pĭn′ ə fôr′ | or | -fōr′ | n. A sleeveless garment like an apron, especially one worn over a little girl's dress.

plank | plăngk | n. **1.** A thick, wide, long piece of lumber.

plunge | plŭnj | v. **plunged, plung·ing 5.** To rush or move forward into or towards something quickly and rapidly.

por·ce·lain | pôr′ sə lĭn | or | pōr′- | n. **1.** A hard, white, translucent material made by baking a fine clay at a high temperature and glazing it with one of several variously colored materials.

por·ridge | pôr′ ij | or | pŏr′- | n. Oatmeal or other meal boiled in water or milk until thick.

prance | prăns | v. **pranced, pranc·ing 3.** To move in a proud, bold, self-important way; strut.

prin·ci·pal | prĭn′ sə pəl | adj. First or foremost in rank, degree, and importance.

pro·found | prə found′ | adj. **1.** Very deep, strong, or important.

prong | prông | or | prŏng | n. One of the sharply pointed ends of a fork or other such tool.

pros·pect | prŏs′ pĕkt′ | n. **2.** Something expected or foreseen; an expectation: *Hurried home with the prospect of a good dinner.*

pur·sue | pər soo′ | v. **5.** To follow (a course of action).

quail | kwāl | n. Any of several rather small, plump, short-tailed birds with brownish feathers.

quar·ry | kwôr′ ē | or | kwŏr′- | n. An open excavation from which stone is obtained by digging, cutting, or blasting.

quar·ter | kwôr′ tər | v. **2.** To furnish with a place to stay or lodgings.

quo·rum | kwôr′ əm | or | kwōr′- | n. The minimum number of members of a committee or organization that must be present to conduct business.

raft·er | răf′ tər | or | răf′- | n. One of the beams that support a roof.

ram·shack·le | răm′ shăk′ əl | adj. Close to falling apart; broken-down; shaky.

rapt | răpt | adj. **2.** Deeply absorbed; giving one's complete attention to.

raw·hide | rô′ hīd′ | n. **1.** The hide of cattle before it has been tanned. **2.** A whip or rope made of such hide.

re·bound | rĭ bound′ | v. **1.** To spring back or bounce away, often after hitting an object.

reck·on | rĕk′ ən | v. **3.** *Informal.* To think, guess, or assume.

reed | rēd | n. **1.** Any of several tall, hollow stemmed grasses or similar plants that grow in wet places.

ref·use | rĕf′ yoos | n. Worthless matter; waste.

re·lent·less | rĭ lĕnt′ lis | adj. **1.** Not stopping, without pity.

re·proach·ful | rĭ prōch′ fəl | adj. Expressing blame.

rep·u·ta·tion | rĕp′ yə tā′ shən | n. **1.** The general esteem in which a person is held by others or by the general public. **3.** A particular characteristic for which someone or something is noted.

ring·dove | ring dəv | n. **1.** A common European pigeon with a whitish patch on each side of the neck and wings edged with white.

roam | rōm | v. To travel over or through (an area) without a fixed goal; wander.

round·house | raund′ haus′ | n. A cabin or apartment on the stern of a quarterdeck (of a ship).

route | root | or | rout | n. **1.** A road or course for traveling from one place to another.

rum·mage | **rŭm′** ĭj | *v.* **1.** To search thoroughly by turning over or disarranging things.

sat·in·y | **săt′** n ē | *adj.* Having the look or feel of satin; smooth and glossy.

saun·ter | **sôn′** tər | *v.* To walk in a slow, relaxed way.

scroll | skrōl | *n.* **1.** A roll of parchment, paper, etc., used especially for writing a document.

seal | sēl | *n.* **2.b.** A small circle of wax, lead, or paper bearing such a mark used to show that a document or statement is genuine or true or to fasten an envelope.

sen·ti·nel | **sĕn′** tə nəl | *n.* **1.** A sentry. **2.** Something that serves to guard or give warning of approaching danger.

sen·try | **sĕn′** trē | *n., pl.* **sen·tries.** A guard.

sex·ton | **sĕks′** tən | *n.* A man hired to take care of a church.

shaft | shăft | or shäft | *n.* A long, narrow passage: *An elevator shaft.*

shin·ny | **shĭn′** ē | *v.* **shin·nied, shin·ny·ing, shin·nies.** To climb by gripping and pulling with the hands and legs.

shuck | shŭk | *v.* **1.** To remove the husk or shell from: *shuck corn; shuck oysters.*

si·mul·ta·ne·ous | sī′ məl **tā′** nē əs | or | **sĭm′** əl- | *adj.* Happening, existing, or done at the same time.

soar | sôr | or | sōr | *v.* **1.** To rise, fly, or glide high in the air.

sol·emn | **sŏl′** əm | *adj.* **1.** Serious.

sol·i·tude | **sŏl′** ĭ tood′ | or | -tyood′ | *n.* **2.** A lonely or private place.

span·gle | **spăng′** gəl | *n.* **1.** A small disk of shiny metal or plastic that may be sewn on cloth, clothes, etc., for decoration; a sequin.

spar | spär | *n.* A pole, used as a mast, boom, yard, or bowsprit on a sailing vessel.

spec·ta·cles | **spĕk′** tə kəls | *n.* **4.** A pair of eyeglasses.

spec·tral | **spĕk′** trəl | *adj.* **1.** Of or resembling a specter (ghost).

spire | spīr | *n.* **1.** The top part or point of something that tapers upward. **2.** The pointed top of a steeple.

spout | spout | *n.* A tube, mouth, or pipe through which liquid is released or discharged.

spur | spûr | *n.* **2.** Something that urges one to action in pursuit of a goal, or the goal itself; an incentive.

stealth·y | **stĕl′** thē | *adj.* Quiet so as to avoid notice.

steth·o·scope | **stĕth′** ə skōp′ | *n.* An instrument used to listen to sounds made within the body, such as a person's heartbeat.

stout | stout | *adj.* **3.** Fat, overweight, or big.

stren·u·ous | **strĕn′** yoo əs | *adj.* **2.** Very active; energetic.

strew | stroo | *v.* **strewed, strewn** | stroon | **1.** To spread here and there; scatter. **2.** To cover (a surface) with scattered or sprinkled things.

sup | sŭp | *v.* **supped, sup·ping.** To eat supper.

sur·feit | **sûr′** fĭt | *n.* **1.** Too much of something.

surge | sûrj | *v.* **surged, surg·ing. 1.** To move with a gathering force and fullness, as rolling waves do. **2.** To move or rush forcefully.

tack·le | **tăk′** əl | *n.* **2.b.** A system of ropes and pulleys used on a ship to hoist, pull, or apply tension.

tat·tered | **tăt′** ərd | *adj.* **1.** Torn or worn to shreds; ragged. **2.** Dressed in ragged clothes.

taunt | tônt | *v.* To insult or tease.

tran·quil | **trăng′** kwĭl′ | or | **trăn′**- | *adj.* Calm; peaceful.

tread | trĕd | *v.* **1.b.** *n.* Footstep or footsteps. **2.** To walk or step.

tu·ber·cu·lar | too **bûr′** kyə lər | or | tyoo- | *adj.* Of or affected with tuberculosis (a contagious disease of human beings and animals that affects the lungs and other body tissues.)

turf | tûrf | *n.* **1.** A surface layer of earth containing a thick growth of grass and roots.

un·be·knownst | ŭn′ bĭ nōnst′ | *adv.* *unbeknownst to.* Without the knowledge of.

vague | vāg | *adj.* **3.** Indistinctly or poorly understood or recalled.

vast | văst | or | väst | *adj.* Very great in area or size.

ven·ture | věn′ chər | *n.* **4.** To dare or show the courage to go.

ve·ran·da | və răn′ də | *n.* A roofed porch or balcony.

vig·il | vĭj′ əl | *n.* **1.** A period of watchfulness.

vig·or·ous | vĭg′ ər əs| *adj.* **1.** Full of or done with vigor; lively.

vi·tal·i·ty | vī tăl′ ət ē | *n.* Lively character, energy.

vow | vou | *n.* A serious promise.

wail | wāl | *n.* A long, high-pitched, sad cry or sound.

wea·ry | wîr′ ē | *adj.* **1.** Tired, as after work or effort.

weath·er | wĕth′ ər | *v.* **1.** To expose to the action of the weather, as for drying, seasoning, or coloring: weathered wood. **2.** To change through exposure to wind and rain.

whim | hwĭm | or | wĭm | *n.* A sudden wish, desire, or idea.

with·er | wĭth′ ər | *v.* **1.** To dry up or cause to dry up from lack of moisture. **2.** To become or cause to become wasted, worn out, etc., as if by drying out.

wiz·ard·ry | wĭz′ ər drē | *n.,pl.* **wiz·zard·r ies** The practice of magic.

wor·sted | woos′ tĭd | or | wûr′ stĭd | *n.* **1.** Smooth, firmly twisted yarn made from long strands of wool.

Handbook

of Literature, Reading, Vocabulary, and Research Skills and Terms

act A part of a play. Acts may be divided into *scenes*.

almanac A book containing many facts. Almanacs are published every year so that the facts will be up to date. The subjects almanacs cover include government leaders of the world, sports records, weather records, awards like the Nobel Prize, and the size and population of different countries. The facts may be given in the form of lists and charts.

When to use an almanac. Almanacs give facts, but they do not discuss or explain them. Use an almanac when you are looking for a particular name or date, especially if the information is too recent to be in an encyclopedia. For example, if you wanted to find out who won the Nobel Prize for literature in 1986, an almanac would be the best place to find the information.

How to use an almanac. To find the topic you want in an almanac, look it up in the index. The *index* is a section at the back of the book that lists topics alphabetically. If you were looking for Nobel Prize winners, you would look under *n* for *Nobel*. The index would tell you what page or pages the information is on.

Use the newest almanac you can get to be sure of finding the most recent information.

alphabetical order The order of the letters in the alphabet. To put words in alphabetical order, look at the first letter of each word first. If the first letters are the same, look at the second letters, and so on.

Many research materials are arranged in alphabetical order, including *card catalogs, dictionaries, encyclopedias*, and *indexes*.

Remember, if you are looking for a person's name in alphabetical order, look for the last name first. If you are looking for a book title, ignore the articles *a, an,* and *the.*

antonyms Words that have opposite meanings. *Up* and *down* are antonyms.   [Section 4]

412

article A short, nonfiction work; not a made-up story. Articles appear in newspapers, magazines, and books. (See also news story.)

atlas A book of maps. Some atlases also give other geographical information, such as the products of various regions, countries, or states.

When to use an atlas. Use an atlas when you need information on a map, including directions, locations of particular places, and distances between places. For example, if you wanted to know how far Miami, Florida, is from Gainesville, Florida, you would use an atlas.

How to use an atlas. Most atlases have an *index*, a section at the back of the book where the places shown on the maps are arranged in alphabetical order. The indexes will usually tell you both the number of the map you need and the particular section of the map that shows the place you are looking for.

For example, if you look up *Gainesville, Florida*, in the index, you might see a notation like this after it: "42 E 4." You would turn to map number 42 in the atlas. You would see that the map is divided into squares. You would look along the top of the page until you found the square marked *E*. Then you would look along the side of the page for the square marked *4*. Where the two

squares meet, in square E 4, you would find Gainesville.

author The writer of an article, a story, a play, a poem, or a book. If you know who wrote a book, you can find the book in the library by looking at the *author card* in the *card catalog*.

author card A card in the library's *card catalog* that has the author's name at the top. Author cards are arranged alphabetically by the author's last name.

(For more information about author cards, see catalog cards.)

author's purpose The author's goal in writing. Authors may wish to *entertain* readers by making them laugh as in "Stuart and Snowbell" (page 34), or by scaring them as in "The Boy Who Drew Cats" (page 27). Or an author may want to give readers a serious message about life as in "All the Cats in the World" (page 20), explain something to readers, or give them information as in "Kites" (page 204).   [Sections 1, 6]

autobiography Someone's true account of his or her own life. An autobiography is usually written from the *first-person point of view*, using the pronouns *I* and *me*. It tells important events from the author's life and says how the author feels about those events. "You Are Somebody Special" (page 54) is an example of an autobiography.   [Sections 2, 3]

bibliography   A list of writings. Many books contain lists of other books and articles on the same subject. Here is part of a bibliography from a book about zoos. Notice that the entries are arranged alphabetically by the authors' last names. After each author's name comes the title of the book, the place where it was published, the publisher, and the date:

> Crandall, Lee S. *Management of Wild Mammals in Captivity*. Chicago: University of Chicago Press, 1964.

> Elgin, Robert. *The Tiger Is My Brother*. New York: Morrow, 1980.

Bibliographies are usually at the end of a book, although sometimes short bibliographies are given at the end of each chapter.

By looking at a bibliography, you can find the authors and titles of other books that may give you more information about the subject you are interested in.

For a list of bibliographies, look up your subject in *The Bibliographic Index*. It will tell you which publications contain bibliographies on the subject.

biographical dictionary   A special dictionary that gives information about famous people. Some biographical dictionaries are *Webster's Biographical Dictionary*, which includes information about people from many nations; the *Dictionary of American Biography*; and *Who's Who in America*, which is revised every second year and includes only people living at the time of publication.

When to use a biographical dictionary. Use a biographical dictionary when you need brief, factual information about a famous person. Biographical dictionaries usually give information such as birth (and death) dates, birthplaces, and important accomplishments. Many biographical dictionaries do not include details about a person's life. You may be able to find more details in an *encyclopedia*. If there is a *biography*, or book about the person's life, it would contain the most information of all.

How to use a biographical dictionary. If the person you are looking up became famous recently, make sure the biographical dictionary you are using is new enough to list him or her. Check to see whether the dictionary includes people from your person's country.

In most biographical dictionaries, people are listed in alphabetical order by their last names. If you wanted information about George Washington, you would look for *Washington, George*. However, if you wanted information about Queen Victoria, you would look for *Victoria*; people are not listed by their titles.

biography   A true story about a person's life written by another person. A booklength biography will give you a lot of information about a person. "Janette's Winter" (page 62) is a short biography.   [Section 2]

To find out whether your library has any biographies about the person you are interested in, look for the person's name in the *subject cards* in the *card catalog*. The person would be listed there in alphabetical order, last name first. On library shelves, biographies are arranged together, alphabetically by subject's names.

Books in Print   A list of books that are available for purchase from publishers doing business in this country. *Books in Print* is published every year in three sets. One set lists books alphabetically by author; another set lists books alphabetically by title; and a third set, *The Subject Guide to Books in Print*, lists books alphabetically by subject.

Books in Print is excellent for finding out what books are available at regular bookstores. Remember, though, that there are millions of books that are no longer "in print" but can still be found in libraries and second-hand bookstores.

call number   The *Dewey Decimal Classification* number. A number written on library books and at the upper- left hand corner of *catalog cards* to show where the books are placed on the library shelves.

635.91F

Daniels, Anthony

635.9F

Fort, Victoria Pearl
A Complete Guide to
Flower Arranging
New York: Viking Press, 1962.
Ill. 226 pp.

635.9F

card catalog   A large cabinet in the library whose drawers, called trays, contain filing cards listing all the books in the library. There are three types of *catalog cards*: author, title, and subject. All are usually combined in the cabinet in alphabetical order. Letters on the front of each drawer, or tray, show which section of the alphabet it contains. The trays

themselves are placed in the cabinet in alphabetical order, from top to bottom.

The illustration above shows what the card catalog looks like.

When to use the card catalog. Use the card catalog when you want to find out whether your library has a book whose title you know, or when you want to see what books your library has by a particular author or on a particular subject.

How to use the card catalog. See the next section, catalog card, for information on how to use the card catalog.

catalog card There are at least three cards in the *card catalog* for every nonfiction book in the library: an author card, a title card, and a subject card. Here is an example of an author card:

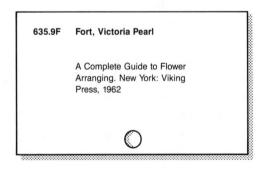

635.9F   **Fort, Victoria Pearl**

A Complete Guide to Flower Arranging. New York: Viking Press, 1962

The top of this card tells you the author's name. Her name is Victoria Pearl Fort, but last names are listed first on catalog cards. Below the author's name are the title of the book, the place where it was published, the publisher's name, and the date of publication. At the top of the card is the call number that you should look for on the shelf in order to find the book: 635.9F. This card is called the *author card* because it has the author's name at the top.

The other two catalog cards contain the same information in a different order. Here is an example of a title card for the same book:

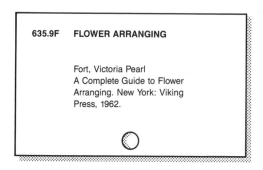

This is called a *title card* because it has the title at the top. Otherwise, the information is the same as on the author card.

Here is an example of a subject card:

635.9F   **FLOWER ARRANGING**

Fort, Victoria Pearl
A Complete Guide to Flower
Arranging. New York: Viking
Press, 1962.

This is the *subject card* because it has the subject of the book at the top. If a book covers several subjects, it will have a separate subject card for each subject. Fiction books usually do not have subject cards.

When to use catalog cards. Use catalog cards to find out what books your library has and where they are located on the shelves.

How to use catalog cards. If you know the title of a book, you can look in the card catalog for the title card. Remember, all the cards are arranged in alphabetical order. If you were looking for *A Complete Guide to Flower Arranging*, you would look in the catalog drawer containing the letter *c* (for *Complete*), because the articles *a*, *an*, and *the* are ignored in alphabetizing titles. If you find the card, your library has the book. Note the call number given in the upper left-hand corner of the card. It will help you find the book on the shelves.

If you are looking for books by a particular author, look for author cards with that author's name. In this case, you would look in the *f* drawer *Fort, Victoria Pearl*. There will be a separate card for each book the library has by that author. Make notes of the titles and call numbers.

If you are looking for books on a particular subject, look for subject cards. If you were interested in flower arranging, for example, you would look in the *f* drawer for cards with this heading. There will be a card for each book the library has on the subject. Note the titles, authors, and call numbers.

Now you can find the books on the library shelves. Look at the call numbers you wrote down. For the book we have been discussing, it is *635.9F.* This book would probably be on a shelf marked *635.* It would come after books with the call number *635.8.* (In a library, call numbers are marked on the side of the books, or *spines.*) The *F* in the call number is the initial of the author's name.

There are some exceptions to the rule. *Fiction* books are arranged on the shelves not by call number but alphabetically by the author's last name. *Biographies* are shelved together alphebetically by the subject's name. *Reference books*, including *dictionaries* and *encyclopedias*, are kept on special shelves.

cause Something that makes something else happen. (See also cause and effect.)

cause and effect In some stories and some sentences, there is a cause-and-effect relationship. The *cause* is something that makes another thing happen. What happens is called the *effect.*

In "All the Cats in the World" (page 20), when the old man asks Mikila why she feeds the cats, she finally answers, "BECAUSE THEY ARE HUNGRY!" That Mikila knows the cats are hungry is the cause. That Mikila feeds them is the effect.

Effects may have more than one cause. Mikila may also be feeding the cats because she is lonely and because she is a good person. Similarly, causes may have more than one effect.

Think about cause-and-effect relationships as you read. Noticing clue words and phrases such as *because, since, so, so that, as a result of,* and *for this reason* will help you. [Section 7]

character A person or an animal in a story. (See also flat character and round character.) [Section 1]

characterization The way an author informs readers about characters. *Direct characterization* is when the author describes the character directly. For example, in "All the Cats in the World" (page 20), the author states that Nella and Mikila "were still quite nimble and strong." *Indirect characterization* is when the author lets readers find out about a character through the character's own thoughts, speech, or actions. For example, we can tell that Nella and Mikila were nimble and strong because of their actions: "They would clamber down among the rocks...."

Pay attention to the characters' thoughts, words, and actions when you read a story. They may be related to the message or *theme* that the author wants you to discover. [Sections 1, 4, 6, 7, 10]

chart An orderly list of facts. Here is an example of a chart:

Noun	Adjective
Danger	Dangerous
Beauty	Beautiful
Remark	Remarkable

You can read this chart down or across. If you read down each column, you see a list of nouns and a list of adjectives. If you read across, you see which nouns and adjectives are similar.

climax The highest point of action in a story. The climax is the same as the *turning point*. [Sections 5, 10]

cloze exercise A reading test in which words are left out of a selection and the reader is asked to fill in the blanks. [Section 10]

compare To say how two or more people or things are alike. (See also comparison and contrast.)

comparison and contrast Comparison involves identifying how two people or things are alike. Contrast involves finding out how they are different.

If you say that "The Boy Who Drew Cats" (page 27), and "The Naming of Cats" (page 32), are both about cats, you are making a comparison. If you say that "The Boy Who Drew Cats" is a story but "The Naming of Cats" is a poem, you are making a contrast.

In your writing, you will often be asked to compare and contrast two people or things; to say both how they are alike and how they differ. [Section 8]

comparison of unlike things See figurative language.

composition See writing.

compound word A word made up of two or more smaller words. *Cowboy* is an example of a compound word. It is made up of the words *cow* and *boy*. Notice that the meaning of the compound word is different from the meaning of each word alone. [Section 7]

conclusion 1. The end of an article, a story, a play, a poem, or a book. 2. An opinion or judgement. To find out how to form opinions about stories and characters, see drawing conclusions.

conflict A struggle or fight. Many selections contain conflict, because conflict helps make a story interesting. Readers want to find out who or what will win the struggle.

There are several types of conflict: (1) *Conflict of a person against another person or group.* For example, in "All the Cats in the World" (page 20), Mikila and the old man have a conflict. (2) *Conflict of a person against nature.* This type of conflict is found in "Janette's Winter" (page 62). (3) *Inner conflict.* A person struggles with his or her own different feelings. Bently in "The Bookman" (page 250) has this type of conflict. [Section 8]

contents See table of contents.

context The selection or part of a selection that contains a particular word or group of words. The context can affect the meaning of words or sentences. If you just read the sentence "Laura was hurt," you might think that Laura had been injured. However, if the sentence was in a story about someone refusing a

present Laura had bought, you would know it meant she was insulted. [Section 6]

context clues Other words in a sentence, a paragraph, or lines of poetry that help you figure out the meaning of a word you do not know. Here is an example: "The teacher's *lucid* explanation helped the students understand." The explanation helped the students understand, so it must have been clear. [Sections 5, 10]

contrast To say how two or more people or things are different. (See also comparison and contrast.)

copyright date The date a book was published. The date is usually printed like this: © 1987. If you need up-to-date information, be sure the book was published recently.

critical reading Making judgments about what you read. To read critically, you must try to find the author's message and understand how the characters think and feel. You must read the author's descriptions and the characters' words and actions.

Here are some of the questions you might think about as you read critically:

What is the *author's purpose*, and how well does he or she accomplish it?

In a story, does the *plot* make the message clear?

If *facts* are presented, are they correct?

Are the characters in a story believeable?   [Section 9]

decoding Figuring out unfamiliar words from the sounds of the letters they contain. Knowing the sounds that different letters and groups of letters may make is important in decoding. Here are some examples that are given in this book:

a The letter *a* usually stands for the short *a* sound when it is followed by two consonants, as in *batter,* or by one consonant and no vowel, as in *tag. A* usually stands for the long *a* sound when it is followed by i, y, or a consonant and a vowel, as in *daily, day,* and *race.*   [Section 1]

ch When the letters *ch* come together in a word, they may stand for the sounds at the beginning of *child.* That is the sound they always make when a *t* comes before the *ch,* as in *patch.* At other times, though, the letters *ch* together make a sound like *k,* as in *character.* If you are not sure which sound *ch* stands for, try saying the word both ways. See which way sounds like a word you know.   [Section 2]

ea When the vowels *ea* come together, they usually stand for the long *e* sound, as in *teach.* However, sometimes they stand for the short *e* sound *thread,* the long *a* sound *great,* the vowel sound in *her, heard,* or the vowel sound in *here, beard.* If you are not sure which sound *ea* makes in a word you are reading, try pronouncing the word different ways until one pronunciation sounds like a word you know.   [Section 8]

-ed Many words end with the suffix *-ed.* Sometimes the suffix is pronounced like a *t,* as in *skipped.* Sometimes it sounds like a *d,* as in *demand.* At other times it stands for the *ed* sound, as in *batted.* If you know the base word, you can figure out which sound *-ed* has.   [Section 5]

g The letter *g* usually stands for the sound at the beginning of *go.* However, when *g* is followed by an *e, i,* or *y,* it may make a *j* sound, as in *badge, giant,* or *gym.* Often when a *g* and a *h* come together, they are both silent, as in *night.*   [Section 10]

i The letter *i* usually stands for the long *i* sound when it is followed by a consonant and then a vowel, as in *kite.* It usually stands for the short *i* sound when it is followed by two consonants, as in *kitten,* or by one consonant and no vowel, as in *him*. When *i* is followed by the letters *gh*, the *i* usually stands for the long *i* sound, as in *night*.   [Section 8]

-ly Some words end with the suffix -*ly*. When the letters -*ly* come together at the end of a word, they make the sounds *lee*, as in *slowly*. [Section 4]

-ous When the letters -*ous* come together at the end of a word, the suffix is usually pronounced like the word *us*. *Dangerous* is an example.   [Section 6]

-tion Some words end with the suffix -*tion*. The letters -*tion* almost always make the sound *shun*, which rhymes with *run*. *Perfection* is an example.   [Section 7]

y When the letter *y* comes at the beginning of the word, it usually stands for the sound you hear at the beginning of *yes*. When *y* comes at the end or in the middle of a word, it may stand for a vowel sound, as in *my, flying*, or *city*. When *y* comes after a vowel, it usually helps the vowel make a vowel sound, as in *say, joy*, or *saying*.   [Section 3]

definition   The meaning of a word or term. Definitions are given in *dictionaries*.

description   A word picture of what someone or something is like. Authors include details about the person, place, or thing being described to help the readers form pictures in their minds.   [Section 1]

detail   A small piece of information. In a paragraph, the *main idea* tells what the paragraph is about, and the details give information to support or explain the main idea.

In a *mystery* story, some of the details may be important clues that help solve the mystery. In "Sarah Tops" (page 324), the dying man's last words turn out to be the most important detail.

Sometimes important details are called *significant details*. *Significant* means "important" or "meaningful."   [Sections 2, 9]

Dewey Decimal Classification System A system of arranging books according to their subject matter that was invented by Melvil Dewey. The subjects are divided into nine main classes and many sub-classes. The *call number* that is written on library books and *catalog cards* is the number the book is given in this system.

diagram   A drawing that shows the parts of something or shows how something works. There is a diagram of a microscope on the next page.

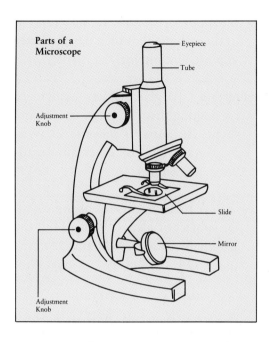

Parts of a Microscope

- Eyepiece
- Tube
- Adjustment Knob
- Slide
- Mirror
- Adjustment Knob

dialogue The conversation in a story or a play. The exact words the characters say. In a story, quotation marks point out the dialogue.

dictionary A book that lists words in alphabetical order and gives their meanings, pronunciations, and other information.

When to use a dictionary. Use a dictionary to find out any of the following things: the meaning of a word; how a word is spelled; how it is pronounced; where it is divided into syllables; where it comes from; synonyms (words that mean the same) and antonyms (opposites) for a word; the meanings of prefixes (word parts added to the beginning of a word) and the meanings of suf-

fixes (word parts added to the ending of a word).

How to use a dictionary. Look up your word in alphabetical order. Guide words at the top of each dictionary page will tell you the first and last words contained on that page. Following a word are letters and symbols that tell you how to pronounce it. If you are not sure what the symbols stand for; turn to the pronunciaton key at the beginning of the dictionary. That explains the meanings of the symbols.

direct characterization An author's direct description of a person or an animal in the story. Readers do not have to form an opinion about the character from his or her thoughts, speech, or actions, because the author says what the character is like. An example is in "The Boy Who Drew Cats" (page 27), when the author says that the boy's brother "was strong enough when only 14 years old to help his father." [Section 7]

drawing conclusions Making your own decisions about a story and its characters. The happenings and details in a story help you draw conclusions. For example, in "All the Cats in the World" (page 20), when the old man feeds the cats, you can safely conclude that he has changed his mind about Mikila being foolish to feed them. [Section 8]

editorial An item in a newspaper or magazine that expresses the opinions or beliefs, of the editors.

effect Something that happens as a result of a cause. (See also cause and effect.) [Section 7]

elements of plot The plot is the sequence, or order, of important events in a story or a play. The plot usually has four elements, or parts: (1) the *problem* that the characters face; (2) the *rising action* as the characters try to solve the problem; (3) the *turning point*, the highest point of the action, as the characters find a solution; and (4) the *resolution*, when readers learn how the solution affects the characters. (See also plot.) [Sections 5, 10]

encyclopedia A book or set of books containing information about many topics.

When to use an encyclopedia. Use an encyclopedia when you need a lot of information about a subject. For example, if you wanted to find out the history of libraries, the names of some famous modern libraries, and how libraries arrange their books, it would be a good idea to look up *library* in an encyclopedia.

How to use an encyclopedia. The articles in encyclopedias are arranged in alphabetical order. If the encyclopedia you are using is in more than one book or *volume*, be sure to look in the volume that includes the letter you are looking for.

entertain To give readers enjoyment by making them laugh or by scaring them. An *author's purpose* in writing may be to entertain readers. [Sections 1, 4]

essay A brief discussion of a particular subject or idea. "What About the Midnight Ride of William Dawes?" (page 174) is an essay. [Section 5]

explain To state how or why something happens. An *author's purpose* may be to explain. [Section 1]

explanation An account of how or why something happens. When you write an explanation, help your readers understand by stating the events clearly and in the correct order. [Section 9]

expression A word or a group of words with a specific meaning; an idiom. For example, *hanging around* is an expression that means "waiting." [Section 2]

fact Something that can be proved or observed. For example, in "Kites" (page 204), the author says that Polynesia "includes New Zealand and Micronesia, as well as the Hawaiian Islands." This is a fact that can be proved. You can look up Polynesia in a dictionary or an encyclopedia and see if the author's definiton is correct. The author also says that kites are made of "sticks and cloth and vines and paper." This is a fact that can be observed. You can examine kites to see what they are made of. When you read, think about which statements are facts and which are *opinions* (ideas, beliefs, or feelings that cannot be proved.) [Section 3]

fiction   Made up stories. Many of the stories in this book are fiction. Fiction that contains imaginary characters and events that are very much like people and happenings in real life is called *realistic fiction*. "Take Care of Dexter" (page 97) is an example of realistic fiction. "The Boy Who Drew Cats" (page 27) is an example of fiction that is not realistic because some of the events could not happen in real life. "Stuart and Snowbell" (page 34) is not realistic fiction because it contains a character that could not exist in real life.   [Section 3]

figurative language   Words used in a fresh, new way to appeal to the imagination. The words take on more than their usual meanings. Figurative language often compares two things that are not usually thought of as alike. Here are some examples:

The man's hair was as smooth as velvet. (The man's hair is compared to velvet.)
His voice was thunder. (His voice is compared to thunder.)
The clouds frowned at the earth. (The clouds' appearance is compared to a person's frown.) (See also *simile, metaphor,* and *personification*.) [Section 6]

first-person point of view   Telling a story by using the pronouns *I* and *me*. Some stories told from the first-person point of view are *autobiographies*, or true accounts of a person's life. "A Grain of Wheat" (page 92) is an example. Other stories told in this way are *fiction*, or made-up stories, but the author pretends to be a character in the story and writes as if the events had happened to him or her.   [Section 2]

finding facts   First decide what kind of fact you are looking for. For facts about words, you would look in a *dictionary*. For facts about places, you might use an *atlas*, an *encyclopedia*, or an *almanac*. For facts about people, you might use a *biography*, an *autobiography*, a *biographical dictionary*, an *encyclopedia*, or a *newspaper*. Sometimes you will want to read a *nonfiction* book to find facts. The *catalog cards* in the library's *card catalog* will tell you what books the library has and where to find them on the shelves.

flat character   A person in a story who is described only briefly. The author does not provide much information about the character. Sometimes that is because the character does not have a big part in the story. Other characters are more important. At other times, even the main characters in a story are flat, because the author wants readers to concentrate on other things. Flat characters are often found in folktales such as "The Most Marvelous Thing" (page 264) because the lesson or message of the folktales may be more important than the characters.   [Section 9]

folktale   A story that has been handed down from generation to generation. Originally, folktales were spoken rather than written. Many folktales contain these elements:

They happened long ago and far away.

They contain unusual characters.

There is a *moral*, or lesson, to be arned from the story. "The Most Marvelous Thing" (page 264) is an example of a folktale.   [Section 6]

foreshadowing   Clues in a story that hint at what is to happen at the end. "The Phantom Cyclist" (page 342) is an example of a story that contains foreshadowing. All through the story, there are clues to Sigrid's true

nature, although the girls do not discover it until the end.   [Section 9]

form   The particular way in which an author chooses to write a story, an article, or a poem. For example, an author may choose to write a modern story as though it were an old folktale. Or an author may choose to write an article by stating the main idea and then giving examples that support it.   [Section 6]

glossary   A list of important or hard words in a book, with their meanings. A glossary is usually at the end of a book. Not every book has a glossary.

graph   A drawing that shows how two kinds of information are related. There are several kinds of graphs. Here is a bar graph that shows average summer temperatures in Juneau, Alaska. The two kinds of informa-

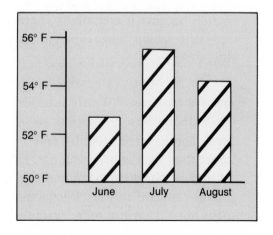

tion that are related on this graph are the months, shown at the bottom of the graph, and the temperatures, shown at the left.

Here is a line graph that shows the same things:

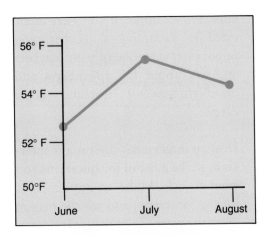

guide words   Words printed at the top of dictionary and encyclopedia pages to let you know the first and last words or topics on that page.

humor   The quality of being funny. An *author's purpose* or goal may be to entertain readers by making them laugh. In other cases, the author's main purpose may be to teach readers a message about life, but he or she uses humor to keep readers interested.

Authors can create humor in several ways. They may use funny events or situations. They may use funny characters. They may use *word play*, such as nonsense words and words with double meanings.

"Precious Jade" (page 140) contains humorous events, humorous characters, and word play.   [Sections 4, 6]

imagery   Words that appeal to the senses of sight, hearing, taste, touch, or smell. "The saw screeched through the wood," for example, is an image that appeals to the sense of hearing. Imagery is used in all forms of writing, but it is most common in poetry.   [Section 1]

index   A section at the back of a nonfiction book that lists the topics in the book in alphabetical order and tells what pages they are on. Use an index to see if facts you need are in the book.

Indexes in atlases usually give map numbers and sections instead of page numbers; see *atlas* to find out how to use this type of index. Indexes in newspapers are usually printed on the first page. They list sections and pages of regular features in the newspaper, such as the crossword puzzle.

indirect characterization   Instead of describing a character directly, the author tells about the character's thoughts, speech, and actions and leaves it up to the reader to decide what the person is like.

For example, in indirect characterization, an author would not say, "Ken was helpful." He or she might say, "When Ken had finished eating, he immediately cleared the table."

Readers should be able to see for themselves that Ken was helpful. [Section 7]

inference A conclusion or guess based on the information presented. When you make an inference, you recognize clues the author gives as well as information he or she presents directly.

For example, in "Precious Jade" (page 140) you read that in China, Plum Blossom and Peony "married two brothers of the Cheng family and left their village to live with their husbands' family." From this you can infer that in China at that time it was the custom for women to live with their husbands' families. From the following quotation, "There they grew homesick and would often beg their father-in-law to let them visit their mother," you could infer that the father-in-law was the head of the family and that the younger people had to ask his permission for many things. [Section 4]

inform To give readers information about some topic. An *author's purpose* may be to inform, as in "Kites" (page 204). [Section 6]

inner conflict A person's struggle with his or her own different feelings. If you love pizza but you are on a diet, you may have an inner conflict when you are offered a slice of pizza. (See also conflict.) [Section 8]

interview A meeting in order to get information from a person.

When to use an interview. Interviews are a good way of getting first-hand information from somebody with special experience or knowledge. For example, if you were interested in becoming a teacher, you might interview one of your teachers and ask about the advantages and disadvantages of teaching as a career.

How to interview. Before the interview, make a list of the questions you want to ask. Make an appointment for the interview, and tell the person what the purpose of the interview is. Ask permission to take notes. Notes will help you remember what the person said. If you have a recorder, you can use that instead of taking notes, but again you will need the person's permission. Ask permission to use the person's name if you are going to write about the interview or speak.

joint author A book with more than one author is said to have joint authors. There is an author card for each author in the *card catalog*.

journal 1. A diary. 2. A magazine, newspaper, or other work that is published every day, every week, or at other intervals.

legend A story handed down from earlier times that tries to explain how or why something in nature came to be. Every country and group of people has legends. "Kites" (page 204) tells about some Polynesian and Eastern legends.   [Section 6]

librarian A person who works in a library.

library 1. A collection of books and/or other materials. 2. The place where such a collection is kept. For information on finding books in a library, see catalog card.

library card A card that allows a person to borrow books from a library.

Library of Congress system A way of classifying and arranging books that is used in the National Library in Washington, D.C., and some other large libraries. The system is different from the *Dewey Decimal Classification System*, which is used in most school libraries.

magazine A publication that contains stories, articles, pictures, and/or other features written by different authors. Magazines are published weekly, monthly, or at other intervals.

map A drawing or diagram of a place. Here is a map of California.

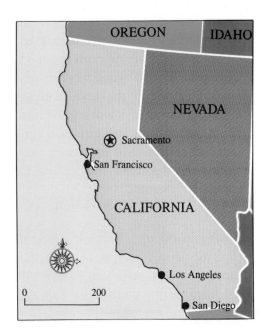

On the map, a special symbol stands for the capital city. You can tell that the capital of California is Sacramento.

Most maps contain a *compass rose* that shows directions. You can tell that San Diego is southeast of Sacramento.

The above map is called a *political map*. Political maps show divisions such as countries, states, and boundaries. There are other kinds of maps as well. For example, *physical maps* show physical features of the earth's surface, such as mountains and valleys.

For information about books of maps, see atlas.

main idea The most important idea in a paragraph; the sentence that tells what the paragraph is about. The main idea may be at the beginning, the middle, or the end of a paragraph. In this paragraph from "A Grain of Wheat" (page 92) the main idea is given in the first sentence: "There was always work to be done on a farm. Boys and girls had their special chores. My first ones were filling the woodbox and feeding the animals." [Section 2]

meaning in poetry Because poets often use words in special ways that appeal to your senses and allow you to form mental pictures, it is important to read the whole poem and examine all the words and ideas carefully so that you can understand the full meaning of the poem. [Section 4]

message An important idea about life that the author wants to tell readers. An author's purpose in writing may be to give readers such a message. (See also theme.) [Section 1]

metaphor A comparison of two things that are not usually thought of as alike. Metaphors do not contain words such as like or as. Here is an example of a metaphor: "The football player's legs were tree trunks." The author does not mean the legs were really tree trunks. He or she is just comparing them to tree trunks.

Metaphors are a type of *figurative language*.

mood The strongest feeling or emotion in a work of literature. Plots, descriptions, conversations, and actions contribute to the mood. Examples of mood are *humor* and *suspense*.

moral A message or lesson about right and wrong. In some works, the moral is stated directly. In other works, readers can figure it out for themselves from the plot and the actions, thoughts, and speeches of the characters. Not every work has a moral.

multiple meaning of words Some words have more than one meaning. From the context clues, or the way a word is used in a sentence, you can decide which meaning is correct. For example, *bat* can mean "a flying mammal" or "a stick." In the sentence "Joanne stepped up to the mound and lifted her bat," you can tell that *bat* means "a stick." [Section 3]

mystery A story or a play that contains a puzzle that the characters—and the readers—try to solve. [Section 9]

myth A story told by people in ancient times to explain life and nature. Many myths, including the Greek myths, are about gods and goddesses. "Kites" (page 204) tells about some Polynesian and Eastern myths.

narration Writing or speaking that tells a story.

narrative essay See personal narrative essay.

narrative poem A poem that tells a story. Like a story, a narrative poem has characters and a *plot* (a sequence of important events). The events occur in a particular order, or *sequence*. The poem has a beginning, a middle, and an end. "The Midnight Ride of Paul Revere" (page 169) is an example of a narrative poem.   [Section 5]

narrator A person who tells a story. Some stories, poems, and plays have a narrator who is a character in the work. For example, in "The Miracle Worker" (page 364), there is a narrator who helps explain the action. On the stage, an actor or actress would play the part of the narrator.   [Section 10]

newspaper A paper that contains news, editorials, (writings giving the editors' opinions), features, and that usually is published every day or every week.

When to use a newspaper. Use a newspaper to find out about important recent happenings and about sports and entertainment events. Use newspaper advertisements to find out products for sale and jobs that are available.

How to use a newspaper. Most newspapers have indexes on the front page that tell the sections and the pages of regular features, such as movie listings.

Libraries usually have old copies of newspapers. Sometimes they have been reduced in size and copied on film called *microfilm*. Libraries have special machines for viewing these films.

news story A nonfiction story that appears in a newspaper or news magazine; an article. A news story should answer these questions: *Who? What? When? Where? Why? How?* [Section 9]

nonfiction Writing about real people and real events. Articles, essays, biographies, and autobiographies are examples of nonfiction. Some nonfiction works such as encyclopedias and dictionaries, give information used for reference. Among the nonfiction selections in this book are "You Are Somebody Special" (page 54) and "What About the Midnight Ride of William Dawes?" (page 174)   [Section 3]

notes When you are doing research, it helps to take notes on what you read so that you will remember it. Write down the important information and the title, author, and page number of the book where you got it.

novel A book-length piece of writing that tells a story. Novels are *fiction*; that is, they are made-up stories.

numbers In alphabetical order, numbers appear as though they were spelled out. For example, if you were looking for a catalog card for a book title that started with *12*, you would look under *t* for *twelve*.

opinion A statement about a person's ideas, beliefs, or feelings. Opinions cannot be proved true or false. Another person may have a different opinion. For example, in "A Grain of Wheat," (page 92) the author says, "Ripe gooseberries were good. . . . Wild blackberries were even better. Wild raspberries were best of all." Each of these statements is an opinion. You may agree or disagree.

Authors often support their opinions with *facts* (statements that can be proved) that they hope will convince readers to share their beliefs.
[Section 3]

out-of-print book A book that is no longer available for sale from the publisher or regular bookstores. You can often find out-of-print books in libraries or second-hand bookshops.

parts of a book The front cover of a book gives the title and author and perhaps the person who did the pictures. The *spine* of the book is the side that shows on the library shelves. The spine also gives the title and author. In libraries, the call number of the book is marked on the spine so that you can find the book on the shelf. Here is a picture of a book's spine:

Inside the book, one of the first pages is the *title page*, which again gives the title and author. Next to it is the *copyright page*, which tells when the book was published. If you need up-to-date facts, be sure the book was published recently.

Two parts of a book help you find out what topics are covered in the book. The *table of contents*, which is in the front of many books, lists all the chapters in the book. The index, which is at the back of many nonfiction books, is an alphabetical list of the topics in the book and the pages they are on. Use the table of contents to find out what broad subjects are covered in the book. Use the index to see whether facts you need are in the book.

periodical A publication that comes out daily, weekly, monthly, or at other intervals. Magazines are periodicals.

personal narrative essay A brief, non-fiction work in which an author expresses his or her own beliefs about a particular subject or idea. "What About the Midnight Ride of William Dawes?" (page 174) is a personal narrative essay. [Section 5]

personification Writing about a non-human thing as if it were human. For example, an author might say, "The wind grabbed at my coat." Personification really compares a nonhuman thing to a human being. In the example, the wind is compared to a person, who can grab a coat. Personification is a type of *figurative language*. [Section 6]

persuasion Convincing people to share your beliefs.

persuasive writing Writing that tries to convince people to share the author's beliefs. The author usually states his or her opinions, or beliefs, and then supports them with facts, or true statements, and examples that may convince readers. [Section 4]

places You can find information about places in *atlases, encyclopedias,* and *almanacs.*

play Something written to be performed before an audience. A play may be divided into parts called *acts.* The acts are often divided into smaller parts called *scenes. Stage directions* tell the director or actors how the stage should look and how the characters should act, move, and speak.

Like stories, plays have plots, characterization, and settings. The *plot* is the sequence, or order, of important events. *Characterization* is the way an author informs the reader or the audience about the characters. In a play, you can learn about the characters through their speech and actions or through a narrator's descriptions. *Setting* is the time when and the place where the events of the story happen. The characters' speeches, the narrator's descriptions, and the stage directions all may give information about the setting.

The plays in this book are "The Vision of Lucila Godoy" (page 126), "Skeeter" (page 245), "The Bottle Imp" (page 298), "The Redheaded League" (page 329), and "The Miracle Worker" (page 364). [Sections 4, 7, 9, 10]

plot The sequence, or order, of important events in a story, a narrative poem, or a play. The plot has a beginning, a middle, and an end. The events are planned to get the reader interested and to show what the *theme*, or most important idea in the selection, is.

Usually the events that make up the plot can be divided into four elements, or parts:

1. At the beginning of the story, readers learn about a *problem* that the characters have. For example, in "The Phantom Cyclist" (page 342), the problem is, "Who is Sigrid?"

2. *Rising Action* is the part of the plot where the story becomes more exciting and complicated as the characters try to solve the problem. In "The Phantom Cyclist," Sigrid reappears several times, and the other girls make several attempts to find out who she is.

3. The *turning point* is the highest point of the action. The characters find a way to solve the problem. In "The Phantom Cyclist" the girls get a good idea of who Sigrid is. Now all they need is proof.

4. The *resolution* is the last part of the plot. The problem is solved, and readers learn how the characters react. In "The Phantom Cyclist," the girls get their proof. They know that they will not see Sigrid again, and will miss her.

poem A written or spoken work with language chosen for its sound, beauty, and power to express feelings. (See also poetry.)

poet The author of a poem.

poetry Poems. Poetry looks and sounds different from other forms of writing. It looks different because poets arrange their words in lines instead of sentences and group these lines into stanzas instead of paragraphs. It sounds different because poets often use rhythm, rhyme, imagery, and figurative language.

Rhythm is the arrangement of the syllables in a line to make a particular sound pattern, or beat, as in music. You can hear the rhythm of a line of poetry best when you read it aloud. The punctuation and capitalization in a poem will help you decide when to pause and what to stress in order to hear the rhythm.

Rhyme is an element that many poems have. Two words rhyme when they end with the same sound: *cat, fat*. Two lines rhyme when they end with rhyming words. Here are rhyming lines from "Paula the Cat" (page 26):

"Paula the cat
not thin not fat"

Imagery is language that appeals to the senses of sight, hearing, taste, touch, or smell. These words from "The Stray Cat" (page 44) appeal to the sense of touch: "a silky satiny coat."

Figurative language means words that are used in a new way to appeal to the imagination. Two things that do not seem alike may be compared. In "The Stray Cat," for example, the cat is compared to a "little bag of old bones."

There are other elements poets may use: for instance, humor. The words and elements a poet chooses are part of the poet's *style*. [Sections 1, 2, 4, 6]

point of view The position from which a story is told. In the *first-person point of view*, an author tells a true story about his or her own life; or, in a made-up story, the author pretends to be one of the characters. The first-person point of view uses the pronouns *I* and *me* in telling the story. In the *third-person point of view*, the story-teller is not a character in the story. The author uses the pronouns *he, she*, and *they* to tell the story. "You Are Somebody Special" (page 54) is an example of a true story told from the first-person point of view. "Janette's Winter" (page 62) is an example of a story told from the third-person point of view. [Section 2]

predicting outcomes Guessing what will happen next in a story. You have a better chance of being right if you keep in mind what has already happened and what the characters are like. [Section 4]

prefix A word part added to the be-ginning of a word. Each prefix has

its own meaning. For example, the prefix *un-* means "not." If you add a prefix to a word, you change the meaning of the word. For example, *done* means finished. Add the prefix *un-* and you get *undone*, meaning "not finished." If you do not know a meaning of each part can help you figure out the word.

The meaning of these prefixes are given in this book: *un-*, "not;" *re-*, "again;" and *pre-*, "before." [Section 8]

problem A difficult situation that the characters in a story have to solve. The problem is the first part of the *plot*. In "The Redheaded League" (page 329), for example, the prob-lem is to find out what the mysteri-ous league is and what it wants from Mr. Wilson. [Sections 5, 10]

prose Written work that is not poetry.

pun A humorous play on words, usu-ally using a word or phrase with a double meaning. The names of the animals in "Oh How Beastly" (page 200) are puns. [Section 4]

publisher A person or company that prints and sells books, newspapers, magazines, and/or other written materials.

realistic fiction Stories that contain made-up characters and events that are similar to people and happenings in real life. "Ribsy's Return" (page 228) is an example of realistic fiction. [Section 7]

Readers' Guide to Periodical Literature A guide that comes out once or twice a month and lists recent magazine articles by their subjects. If you wanted to see what magazine articles had been written recently about whales, you would take a recent copy of the *Readers' Guide* and look under *w* for *whales*. If you wanted to read one of the listed articles, you might be able to borrow the magazine from the library. Large libraries have copies of many old and new magazines.

reference books Books that are not meant to be read from cover to cover like a story but instead are used to look up particular facts. *Dictionaries, encyclopedias, atlases, almanacs,* and *biographical dictionaries* are important types of reference books. Reference books are kept on special shelves in the library.

research Investigation to find facts.

resolution The last part of the *plot*, when the problem is solved, and you learn how the solution affects the characters. In "The Redheaded League" (page 329), the resolution comes when Sherlock Holmes has the thieves arrested. [Sections 5, 10]

rhyme An element found in many, though not all, poems. Words rhyme when they end with the same sound. Lines rhyme when they end with rhyming words. The following lines from "The Microscope" (page 78) rhyme because of the italicized words: Anton Leeuwenhoek was *Dutch*, He sold pincushions, cloth, and *such*." [Section 4]

rhythm The arrangement of the syllables in a line of poetry so that they make a particular sound pattern, or beat, as in music. When you read poetry aloud, listen for the rhythm. The punctuation and capitalization in a poem will help you decide when to pause and what words to stress to make the rhythm clear. [Section 4]

rising action The second part of a *plot*. The story becomes more exciting and complicated as the characters try to solve the problem. In "The Redheaded League" (page 329), Sherlock Holmes visits the pawnshop, meets with the men from Scotland Yard, and goes to the bank in this part of the play. [Section 5, 10]

root word A word from which other words can be made. By adding a *prefix* to the beginning of a root word or a *suffix* to the end, you can change the word's meaning. For example, if you add the prefix *re-* to the root word *play*, you form the word replay, which means "play again." If you add the suffix *-ful* to the end of the root word, you get *playful*, which means "full of play" or "fun-loving." [Section 8]

round character A character that is described fully. The author includes details that help you understand how the character thinks, acts, looks, and feels. Abe Lincoln in "Peculiarsome Abe" (page 71) is a round character. [Section 7]

scene Part of a play. Plays are often divided into parts called *acts*, which, in turn, may be divided into smaller parts, the scenes.

sensory imagery Words that appeal to the senses of sight, hearing, taste, touch, or smell. [Sections 4, 10]

sequence of events The order in which events occur in a story or play. The events are put in a particular order, or sequence, so that the reader will understand what the story is about. The order of important events in a story makes up the *plot*. [Sections 4, 5, 10]

setting The time when and the place where the events of the story happen. You can tell what the setting is by looking for words or phrases that tell when and where.

Pay attention to time and place words throughout the selection, be-cause the setting may change as the story or play goes on. For example, in "The Miracle Worker" (page 364), the setting shifts from the Kellers' home to Annie's school and back again. It also goes to a time five years later. [Sections 1, 10]

short story A brief work of *fiction* (made-up story).

significant detail A small but important bit of information. (See also detail.) [Section 9]

simile A comparison. Usually similes contain the word *like* or the word *as*. Examples of similes are "Her hands were like ice" and "Her hands were as cold as ice."

speaking and listening See decoding.

speech A formal talk given in public before an audience. Speeches may present facts or opinions or both.

spine The *part of a book* that shows when the book is on the library shelf. The spine tells the book's title and author and, in a library, is marked with the book's *call number*.

stanza A division of a poem that is longer than a line. Lines in poetry are grouped into stanzas in much the same way that sentences in other works are grouped into paragraphs.

The following stanza is part of the poem "Harriet Tubman" (page 76):

"Harriet Tubman didn't take no stuff

Wasn't scared of nothing neither

Didn't come in this world to be no slave

And wasn't going to stay one either" [Section 2]

stage directions Directions in a play that tell the director or actors how the stage should look and how the characters are to act, move, and speak. Stage directions are not meant to be spoken out loud to the audience.

style The words an author uses and the type of sentences he or she writes. For example, some authors use more *imagery*, or words that appeal to the senses, than other authors. Some authors write in short sentences, while others prefer to use long sentences. An author may change his or her style for different types of writing. In poetry, for instance, the author might use more imagery. than when he or she was writing a nonfiction article. [Section 6]

suffix A word part added to the ending of a word. Each suffix has its own meaning. For example, the suffix *-less* means "without." If you add a suffix to a word, you change the meaning of the word. For example,

care means "concern." Add the suffix *-less* and you get *careless*, which means "without concern." If you do not know a word, look at the word parts. The meaning of each part can help you figure out the word.

The meaning of these suffixes are given in this book: *-less*, "without;" *-ful*, "filled with;" and *-able*, "able." [Section 9]

subject card A card in the library's *card catalog* that has the subject at the top. The subject tells what the book is about. Subject cards are arranged alphabetically in the card catalog. *Fiction* books do not have subject cards. (For more information about subject cards, see catalog cards.)

summary A brief retelling of a story. A summary tells the main events. In order for people who have not read the story to understand it, the events should be in the correct order, or *sequence*. [Section 7]

surprise ending an ending that is different from what readers have been led to believe would happen. In most stories, the ending follows logically from the rest of the plot, or sequence of events. However, in stories with a surprise ending, the story takes an unexpected twist at the end. In "Janey by Moonlight" (page 162), the ending comes as a surprise both to the readers and to the characters in the story. [Section 5]

suspense A quality that produces feelings of curiosity and tension in the reader, because the reader is not sure what will happen next. The suspense keeps you reading the story.

Mystery writers carefully present details in the plot that make you curious and build suspense. An example is Mr. Wilson's strange job in "The Redheaded League" (page 329). The author wants you to wonder why anyone would hire a person to copy an encyclopedia. [Section 9]

synonyms Synonyms are words that have the same or almost the same meaning. *Try* and *attempt* are synonyms. [Section 1]

symbol Something that stands for something else. For example, a heart may be a symbol of love. In "A Grain of Wheat" (page 92), the prize the author wins in the newspaper contest is, to him, a symbol of success as a writer.

table of contents A section at the front of many books that lists all the chapters in the order in which they appear in the book. The table of contents tells you what broad subjects are covered in the book.

telephone directory A list of names, addressess, and telephone numbers.

theme The author's message; the most important idea in a written work.

The *plot*, or sequence of important events in a story, helps to show what the theme is. So does the *characterization*, or what the author lets readers know or discover about the characters. Even if the author does not state the theme directly, you can figure out the message by thinking about the events in the story and the characters' thoughts, words and actions.

In "The Vision of Lucila Godoy" (page 126), the theme is that beauty is in the eye of the beholder. Each event in the story leads the reader (and Lucila's classmates) to this understanding.

In "The Wrestling Match" (page 132), the theme is that the key to success is believing in yourself and doing what is right. The characters' thoughts and actions show that this is the theme.

In some stories readers learn a lesson about life while laughing at the characters or the situations. The author uses humor to develop the theme. "Precious Jade" (page 140) is an example of this. The theme of the story is "Cleverness can solve any problem." Amusing incidents teach readers the value of being clever. [Sections 3, 4]

third-person point of view Telling a story by using pronouns *he, she,* and *they*. Most *biographies*, or true accounts of another person's life, are written from the third-person point of view. "Janette's Winter" (page 62) is an example. Most (though not all) made-up stories are also written in a third-person point of view. (See also first-person point of view.) [Section 2]

title card A card in the library's *card catalog* that has the book's title at the top. Title cards are arranged alphabetically in the card catalog. The articles *a, an,* and *the* are ignored in alphabetizing the cards. (For more information about title cards, see catalog cards.)

title page A page at the beginning of a book that gives the book's title and author.

turning point The highest point of the action in a story. At the turning point, the characters finally find a way to solve the problem they have been facing. In "The Redheaded League" (page 329), the turning point comes when Sherlock Holmes confronts Clay. (See also plot.) [Sections 5, 10]

volume 1. A book. 2. One book in a set of books. 3. A group of issues of a magazine or other periodical.

word origin Where a word comes from. Most dictionaries include this information.

word parts Root words, prefixes, and suffixes. A *root word* is a word from which other words can be made. A *prefix* is a word part added to the beginning of a word. A *suffix* is a word part added to the ending of a word. If you know the meaning of each word part, you can figure out the word.

For example, in the word *prepayable*, the prefix *pre-* means "before;" the root word *pay* means "to give money;" and the suffix *-able* means "able to be." By putting all these meanings together, you can see that *prepayable* means "paid for in advance." [Sections 8, 9]

word play A humorous use of words. In order to be funny, authors sometimes use nonsense words and *puns*, or words with double meanings. The poems in "Oh How Beastly" (page 200) contain many examples of word play. [Section 6]

writing These four steps will help you in your writing:

Step 1: Set Your Goal
Choose the topic that you will write about.

Step 2: Make a Plan
Plan what you are going to say. Often this involves making a list.

Step 3: Write the First Draft
Use your plan to write a first draft.

Step 4: Revise
Read what you have written. Make sure that it says what you want to say in a clear way. Correct any errors in spelling, grammar and punctuation. Make a final, neat copy.

Here are the main writing assignments given in this book:

comparison and contrast of two characters Saying how two characters in a selection are alike and how they are different. For step 2, your plan, you make one list of examples from the story that shows how the characters are alike, and another list that shows how they are different. [Section 8]

description of an animal Telling what a particular animal is like. For step 2, your plan, you list details that describe the animal. [Section 9]

explanation Stating step by step how or why something happened. For step 2, your plan, you list important events that support your explanation in the order in which they occurred. [Section 9]

first-person account An account that is written as though it happened to the author. Use the pronouns I and me. For step 2, your plan, you list actions that took place and your feelings about those actions. [Section 2]

new ending Using what happens at the beginning and in the middle of a story to write a new ending for it. For step 2, your plan, you identify the main idea of the story and list actions that your character might perform at the end. [Section 5]

opinion A person's belief, idea, or feeling about something. For step 2, your plan, you list facts (true statements) and examples that support your opinion and that may convince your readers that you are right. [Section 3]

persuasive letter A letter to convince other people to share an opinion (belief) that you have. For step 2, your plan, you list facts (true statements) and examples that support your opinion. [Section 4]

poem A written work with special sounds and words. For step 2, your plan, you list words and phrases you will use to paint a word picture of an imaginary animal. [Section 6]

speech A formal talk, in public, to an audience. For step 2, your plan, you list facts (true statements) and opinions (beliefs) that support the topic you have chosen to speak about. [Section 10]

summary A brief retelling of a story. For step 2, your plan, you list the important events in the original story. [Section 7]

AUTHOR AND TITLE

ACKNOWLEDGMENTS

(continued from page 6)

Howard Goldsmith for Lafcadio Hearn's "The Boy Who Drew Cats" from SPINE CHILLERS, edited by Roger Elwood and Howard Smith. Copyright © 1978 by Roger Elwood and Howard Smith.

Harcourt Brace Jovanovich, Inc. and Faber and Faber, Ltd. for "The Naming of Cats" from OLD POSSUM'S BOOK OF PRACTICAL CATS by T. S. Eliot; renewed 1967 by Esme Valerie Eliot.

Harper & Row, Publishers, Inc. for Chapters I-V and 6 illustrations from STUART LITTLE by E. B. White, illustrated by Garth Williams. Copyright 1945, 1973 by E. B. White. Illustrations copyright renewed 1973 by Garth Williams

Marian Reiner for "The Stray Cat" from JAMBOREE *Rhymes For All Times* by Eve Merriam. Copyright © 1962, 1964, 1966, 1973, 1984 by Eve Merriam.

McGraw-Hill Book Company for adaptation of "You Are Somebody Special" by Bill Cosby from YOU ARE SOMEBODY SPECIAL, edited by Charlie W. Sheed. Copyright © 1978 by Quest, Inc.

Barbara Bloom for Parts 1 and 2 of "Janette's Winter." Copyright © 1985 by Barbara Bloom.

Harcourt Brace Jovanovich, Inc. for excerpt from ABE LINCOLN GROWS UP by Carl Sandburg, Copyright 1926, 1928 by Harcourt Brace Jovanovich, Inc.; renewed 1954, 1956 by Carl Sandburg.

Harper & Row, Publishers, Inc. for "Harriet Tubman" from HONEY, I LOVE AND OTHER POEMS. Copyright © 1978 by Eloise Greenfield.

Curtis Brown, Ltd. for "The Microscope" by Maxine W. Kumin, which originally appeared in The Atlantic Monthly. Copyright © 1963 by Maxine W. Kumin.

Farrar, Straus and Giroux, Inc. for "Louise Nevelson" from LIVES OF THE ARTIST by M. B. Goffstein. Copyright © 1981 by M. B. Goffstein.

David R. Godine, Publisher, Inc. for excerpt from Clyde Robert Bulla's A GRAIN OF WHEAT: A WRITER BEGINS. Copyright © 1985 by Clyde Robert Bulla.

Harper & Row, Publishers, Inc. for adaptation of DEXTER by Clyde Robert Bulla. Copyright © 1973 by Clyde Robert Bulla.

Harriet Wasserman Literary Agency, Inc. for "The Vision of Lucila Godoy" by Walter Dean Myers. Copyright © 1982 by Scholastic Inc.

Alfred A. Knopf, Inc. for adapted selection from IN BIKOLE: EIGHT MODERN STORIES ABOUT LIFE IN A WEST AFRICAN VILLAGE by Thomas Gilroy. Copyright © 1978 by Thomas Gilroy.

Delacorte Press for "Precious Jade," "excerpted from THE SKULL IN THE SNOW AND OTHER FOLKTALES by Toni McCarty. Copyright © 1981 by Toni McCarty.

Alfred A. Knopf, Inc. for "Aunt Sue's Stories" from SELECTED POEMS OF LANGSTON HUGHES. Copyright 1926 by Alfred A. Knopf, Inc. and renewed 1954 by Langston Hughes.

Joseph Bruchac for "Birdfoot's Grandpa" from ENTERING ONONDAGA by Joseph Bruchac. Copyright © by Joseph Bruchac.

Eleanor Cameron for "Janey by Moonlight." Copyright © 1983, Open Court Publishing.

Doubleday & Company, Inc. for "The Bat" from THE COLLECTED POEMS OF THEODORE ROETHKE. Copyright 1938 by Theodore Roethke.

Doubleday and Company, Inc. for "What About the Midnight Ride of William Dawes?" from THE PEOPLE'S ALMANAC by David Wallechinsky and Irving Wallace. Copyright © 1975 by David Wallace and Irving Wallace.

Helen Thurber for MANY MOONS by James Thurber. Copyright © 1943 by James Thurber. Copyright © 1971 by Helen Thurber.

Philomel Books for poems by Jane Yolen from HOW BEASTLY! by Jane Yolen. Copyright © 1980 by Jane Yolen.

Philomel Books for "A Contract of Glory" by Jane Yolen from WORLD ON A STRING: THE STORY OF KITES by Jane Yolen. Copyright © 1968 by Jane Yolen.

Curtis Brown, Ltd. for "The Seventh Mandarin" by Jane Yolen. Copyright © 1970 by Jane Yolen.

William Morrow & Company for abridgment of from Chapters 6 and 7 of RIBSY by Beverly Cleary. Copyright © 1964 by Beverly Cleary.

Michael Bonner for "Skeeter." Copyright © 1984 by Scholastic Inc.

Sterling Lord Agency, Inc. for "The Bookman" by Howard Fast. Copyright © 1936, 1938, 1939, 1941, 1942, 1943, 1944, 1945 by Howard Fast.

Ricardo E. Alegría for "The Three Brothers and the Marvelous Things" from THE THREE WISHES: A COLLECTION OF PUERTO RICAN FOLKTALES. Copyright © 1969 by Ricardo E. Alegría.

(Acknowledgments continue on page 446)

Art Direction: Michaelis/Carpelis Design Associates

Illustrations: pp. 32–33, 148–149, 342–343, 345, 347, 350, 352–353, Donna Ayers; pp. 174, 247, 248, 329, 331, 332, 335, 337, David Celsi; p. 17, Paul Davis; pp. 127, 129, 130, 325, 327, Julie Evans; p. 161, Lynne Foster; pp. 169, 170–171, 172, Paul Frame; pp. 141, 142–143, 144, Geyer and Geyer; pp. 26, 200, 201, 202, Jackie Geyer; p. 197, Hokusai; pp. 125, 199, Armen Kojoyian; pp. 299, 302, 304–305, 306–307, 308, Will Kefauver; pp. 251, 254, 256, 258, 260, 262, 281, 312–313, Keith Kohler; pp. 78–79, 227, 323, Narda Lebo; p. 53, Cynthia Lechan; pp. 17, 97, 98–99, 100–101, 103, 107, 108, 111, 112–113, 115, 150–151, 363, Bryce Lee; pp. 177, 427, Joseph Le Monnier; p. 123, Henri Matisse; pp. 44, 51, James McMullen; p. 363, Alfred Munsel; pp. 181, 182–183, 185, 186–187, 189, Jürg Obrist; p. 159, Georgia O'Keefe; pp. 147, 163, 165, 166, 168, Roseanne Percivalle; p. 359, Lisa Purcell; pp. 63, 65, 66, 67, 69, 76–77, Anna Rich; pp. 21, 24, 132, 134, 136–137, 138, Roger Roth; p. 280, John Singer Sargent; pp. 204–205, 206–207, 208–209, Marti Shohet; pp. 228, 231, 232–233, 235, 236–237, 240–241, 243, 413–415, Rose Mary Slader; pp. 211, 213, 214–215, 216–217, Leslie Stall; pp. 265, 267, 268, 269, 271, Judith Sutton; pp. 28, 30, Steve Takanaga; pp. 340–341, Ellen Thompson; p. 227, Vincent Van Gogh; pp. 34, 36, 38, 40, 41, 42, Garth Williams; pp. 89, 91, Grant Wood; pp. 279, 283, 285, 287, 288, 293, 294, 296, N. C. Wyeth.

Photography: pp. 364, 368, 371, 373, 379, 382, 385, 387, 391, 393, 395, American Foundation for the Blind; p. 362, Carole Allen; pp. 55, 57, 58, 60, Courtesy of Temple University Office of Public Information; pp. 89, 91, CRMA/CRSDC for Grant Wood "Fall Plowing," Grant Wood "Young Corn;" pp. 72–73, 74, 376, Library of Congress; pp. 80, 81, Pace Gallery for Louise Nevelson, and Louise Nevelson "Night Presence IV;" p. 123, Spencer Collection for Henri Matisse "Le Coeur;" pp. 159, 361, Malcolm Varon for Georgia O'Keefe "Ladder to the Moon," for Alfred Munsel "Helen Keller at 14;" p. 198, Jason Stemple; p. 197, New York Public Library for Hokusai "Additional Views of Mt. Fuji;" pp. 227, 323, Museum of Modern Art, New York for Vincent Van Gogh "Hospital at Saint Rêmy" Edward Hopper "House by the Railroad;" p. 280, Taft Museum, Cincinnati, Ohio for John Singer Sargent "Robert Louis Stevenson."